# NATIONAL TRANSPORTATION POLICY

# THE BROOKINGS INSTITUTION

The Brookings Institution—Devoted to Public Service through Research and Training in the Social Sciences—was incorporated on December 8, 1927. Broadly stated, the Institution has two primary purposes: the first is to aid constructively in the development of sound national policies; and the second is to offer training of a supergraduate character to students of the social sciences.

The responsibility for the final determination of the Institution's policies and its program of work for the administration of its endowment is vested in a self-perpetuating board of trustees. It is the function of the trustees to make possible the conduct of scientific research under the most favorable conditions, and to safeguard the independence of the research staff in the pursuit of their studies and in the publication of the results of such studies. It is not a part of their function to determine, control, or influence the conduct of particular investigations or the conclusions reached, but only to approve the principal fields of investigation to which the available funds are to be allocated, and to satisfy themselves with reference to the intellectual competence and scientific integrity of the staff. Major responsibility for "formulating general policies and coordinating the activities of the Institution" is vested in the president. The by-laws provide also that "there shall be an advisory council selected by the president from among the scientific staff of the Institution."

Authors of studies published by the Institution have had the advice, criticism, and assistance both of an administrative officer and of a cooperating committee selected from the staff. In manuscript accepted for publication, the author has freedom to present his final interpretations and conclusions, although they may not necessarily be concurred in by some or all of those who cooperate with him or by other members of the staff. The Institution in publishing the work assumes the responsibility that it meets reasonable tests of scholarship and presents data and conclusion worthy of public consideration.

---

# National Transportation Policy

By

CHARLES L. DEARING

and

WILFRED OWEN

GREENWOOD PRESS, PUBLISHERS
WESTPORT, CONNECTICUT

**Library of Congress Cataloging in Publication Data**

Dearing, Charles Lee, 1903-
    National transportation policy.

    Reprint of the ed. published by Brookings Institu-
tion, Washington.
    Includes index.
    1.  Transportation and state--United States.
I.  Owen, Wilfred, joint author.   II.   Title.
HE206.D4  1980        380.5'0973        79-28670
ISBN 0-313-22301-7 lib. bdg.

Reprinted in 1980 by Greenwood Press,
a division of Congressional Information Service, Inc.
51 Riverside Avenue, Westport, Connecticut 06880

Printed in the United States of America

10 9 8 7 6 5 4 3 2 1

# FOREWORD

The national government dominates American transportation policy. It determines when, where, and under what conditions interstate transportation enterprises may be established, expanded, or abandoned, and at what rates the service may be offered to the public. It provides large sums of money for the construction and maintenance of transportation facilities and for the support of transport operations.

National regulatory and promotional efforts are supposedly dedicated to the maintenance of a financially sound and physically adequate national transportation system based on fair competitive standards and impartial regulation. In practice, however, these programs are working at cross purposes. Governmental assistance is distributed unevenly among the several transportation agencies; promotional programs conflict not only with each other but with the attainment of regulatory objectives; and mounting friction between government control and the functions of private management makes it difficult if not impossible to fix responsibility for transportation efficiency and progress.

This book is based in part on a study of federal transportation activities which the authors undertook at the request of the Hoover Commission on government reorganization. The analysis proceeds on the theory that national policy must be clarified and made consistent before an acceptable prescription can be made for the organization and administration of transportation programs. Emphasis is therefore placed on basic issues of public policy rather than on details of administration. The resulting proposals call for fundamental revisions in national transportation policy as the first step. These in turn have led to recommendations for extensive overhaul of current administrative organization.

The study was prepared with the assistance of Margaret J. Myers, Jean Brownlee, and Louise Bebb of the Institution's staff. Dr. Marvin L. Fair and Dr. Frederick F. Blachly served as consultants on various phases of the study.

v

We wish to acknowledge the co-operation of the Commission on Organization of the Executive Branch of the Government, and to thank the federal agencies which generously supplied basic information.

The co-operating committee of the Institution included Cleona Lewis, Harold Metz, and myself.

HAROLD G. MOULTON
*President*

# CONTENTS

|  | PAGE |
|---|---|
| FOREWORD | v |
| INTRODUCTION | 1 |
| The Transportation System | 1 |
| The Federal Role | 4 |

## PART I. PROMOTION OF TRANSPORTATION FACILITIES AND SERVICES

CHAPTER

| | |
|---|---|
| I. BACKGROUND OF THE PROBLEM | 9 |
| Scope and Results of Federal Action | 11 |
| Nature of the Problem | 13 |
| II. AIRWAYS AND AIRPORTS | 17 |
| The Federal Airways | 19 |
| The airways system | 19 |
| Future airway requirements | 22 |
| User charges for airways | 25 |
| Present and future cost responsibility | 27 |
| Conclusion | 28 |
| Federal Airport Policy | 29 |
| Airports in the United States | 29 |
| Trend in federal airport activity | 30 |
| The 1946 Federal Airport Act | 33 |
| The National Airport Plan | 33 |
| The current airport program | 35 |
| User payments for airports | 35 |
| Conclusion | 43 |
| III. AIR-MAIL PAYMENTS | 44 |
| Description of Air-Mail Payments | 44 |
| Development of Air-Mail Service | 46 |
| Current Trends | 48 |
| The Subsidy Question | 51 |
| The Problem Raised | 55 |
| Conclusion | 57 |
| IV. AVIATION SAFETY | 59 |
| Nature of the Safety Problem | 60 |
| Federal Safety Activity | 63 |
| Congressional Testimony on Safety Organization | 65 |
| Special Studies on Safety Organization | 67 |
| Testimony on Recently Proposed Legislation | 72 |
| Federal Delegation of Responsibility | 75 |
| Conclusion | 76 |
| V. WATER TRANSPORTATION | 81 |

                                                              PAGE
Rivers and Harbors .............................      81
    Facilities and traffic ..........................      83
    Authorization procedure ......................      84
    Current waterway program ....................      85
    Financing waterways ..........................      86
Government Barge Lines ........................      89
    Conclusion ...................................      92
The Merchant Marine ...........................      94
    Development of merchant marine policy ..........      96
    Current status of merchant marine activity ........      99
    National defense problem .....................     100
    Conclusion ..................................     104
VI. HIGHWAY TRANSPORTATION .......................     105
    Development of Federal Highway Activity ..........     105
    Financial trends ............................     108
    The 1944 act ...............................     110
    Other federal road activity .....................     112
    The Future Federal Role .......................     114
    The highway problem .........................     115
    Federal interest and responsibility ..............     117
VII. ISSUES RAISED BY FEDERAL PROMOTION ..............     121
    The Federal Role ............................     121
    Principles of Finance .........................     125
    The possibility of financial revision ..............     129
    Federal Policy and Methods .....................     131
    Relation of Promotion to Regulation ..............     134
VIII. PROBLEMS OF NATIONAL SECURITY ..................     138
    Federal Action and World War II ................     139
    Civil Aviation and War Requirements.............     142
    Recent war experience ........................     143
    Future role of the airlines .....................     144
    Aircraft manufacturing industry .................     149
    Railroads and National Defense .................     150
    Highway Transportation in Wartime ..............     155
    The Role of Water Transportation ...............     157
    Conclusions on Defense ........................     161

PART II. REGULATION OF TRANSPORT ENTERPRISES

INTRODUCTION ...........................................     167

CHAPTER
    IX. THE OBJECTIVES OF TRANSPORT CONTROL ............     171

PAGE

Problems of Public Control ..................... 171
The Interstate Commerce Act: Objective and Scope .. 175
The Civil Aeronautics Act, 1938 .................. 178
Merchant Marine Policy ......................... 181
Summary ....................................... 182
X. THE RIGHT TO OPERATE TRANSPORT ENTERPRISES .... 185
The Interstate Commerce Act .................... 186
Railroad construction and abandonment ......... 187
Highway and water transportation .............. 187
Civil Aeronautics Act of 1938 ................... 196
Declaration of policy and CAB interpretation .... 197
Comparison of objectives ...................... 198
Overexpansion of Trunk-line Air Routes ............ 200
The illogical route pattern ..................... 202
The financial consequences of overexpansion ...... 203
Evaluation of program ......................... 207
Defective control system ...................... 211
Corroding effects of subsidies ................. 212
Feeder Routes—Extension into Areas of Least Relative
Advantage ................................... 218
Summary ....................................... 225
XI. RATE REGULATION AND DISCRIMINATION ............. 229
The Concept of Nondiscriminatory Treatment ....... 230
Statutory requirements apply to all transport agen-
cies ......................................... 231
Interterritorial discrimination ................... 233
Conflict between Nondiscriminatory Standards and
Promotional Action .......................... 236
Use of railroads as vehicle for distributing water
subsidies ................................. 237
Public interest in differential rail-barge rate .... 239
Justification for differentials .................. 240
XII. RATE REGULATION AND FAIR COMPETITION .......... 246
Interstate Commerce Commission Administration of
Competitive Rates ........................... 246
Technical problems of cost-finding ............. 248
Rail-barge competition and the subsidy issue ...... 250
Dissipation of carrier revenue .................. 255
Rate control and inherent advantage ............. 256
Rail-coastal water competition and national security
issues ....................................... 259
Rate Regulation Under the Civil Aeronautics Act ......265

PAGE

Contrast between ICC and CAB rate regulation .. 265
Air cargo and minimum rate control ............ 266
Summary ...................................... 270
XIII. RATE REGULATION AND RAILROAD EARNINGS ......... 272
The Commission Assumes Functions of Management . 273
Significance of Divided Authority Over Business De-
cisions ...................................... 278
Procedural delays and immediate financial conse-
quences ..................................... 278
1946 Increased Freight Rates (*Ex Parte 162*) .. 279
1947 Increased Freight Rates (*Ex Parte 166*) .. 281
Procedural delays and long-term financial implica-
tions ....................................... 286
Is There Need for Continuing ICC Control Over the
General Level of Rates? ...................... 293
XIV. CO-ORDINATION AND INTEGRATION ................... 305
Combination of Like Carriers ................... 306
Combination of Dissimilar Carriers .............. 308
The ICC interpretation ...................... 308
The CAB interpretation ...................... 309
Experience of steamship companies ........... 309
Railroad experience ......................... 311
XV. THE PROBLEM OF RAILROAD CONSOLIDATION ......... 316
Background of the Problem ..................... 316
Consolidation and Recapture Under the 1920 Act .... 318
Defects of the program ...................... 318
Failure of the consolidation program ........... 319
Shift of emphasis to transport co-ordination, 1933 .. 320
Present Status of Consolidation Program ........... 321
The Need for Consolidation ..................... 324
Relation to railroad efficiency ................... 324
Rate regulation and the weak and strong problem . 325
Commission experiment with pooling of revenue .. 327
Fifteen Percent Case of 1931 ............... 327
The 1937 pooling experiment ................ 328
Unifications have not solved weak and strong road
problems .................................... 331
Improved capital structure has not solved the prob-
lem ........................................ 334
The Need for Revision of Consolidation Policy and
Reassignment of Administrative Responsibility ... 339
Failure of voluntary program and need for a general
plan of consolidation ....................... 339

                                                               PAGE
Responsibility for formulating general consolidation
    plan ..................................... 344
    Hostile administrative setting ................. 344
    Relation between the consolidation plan and pro-
        motional programs ...................... 345

PART III. REVISION OF NATIONAL POLICY

XVI. CRITICAL DEFECTS OF NATIONAL TRANSPORTATION
    POLICY ...................................... 351
    Defects in Programing and Public Expenditure Poli-
        cies ...................................... 353
    Conflict Between Promotional Action and Regulatory
        Program .................................. 362
    Intrusion of Regulation into Functions of Management 371
    Railroad Consolidation and the Role of the National
        Government .............................. 375
    Summary ................................... 377
XVII. REORGANIZATION OF FEDERAL TRANSPORTATION AGEN-
    CIES ....................................... 379
    Past Reorganizations and Proposals ............. 379
    A Department of Transportation ................. 387
    Powers, duties, and internal organization of the
        Transportation Department ................. 390
        Office of Water Transportation ............. 391
        Office of Civil Aviation .................... 394
        Office of Highway Transportation .......... 397
        Office of Railroad Transportation .......... 399
    Office of the Secretary of Transportation ........ 402
    Summary of departmental organization ......... 404
    A Transport Regulatory Commission ............. 405

APPENDIXES

A. STATISTICAL DATA ............................. 413
B. FEDERAL AGENCIES PERFORMING ANCILLARY SERVICES FOR
    AIR AND WATER TRANSPORTATION ............... 432
C. PROPOSALS FOR REORGANIZING NATIONAL TRANSPORTATION
    ACTIVITIES ................................. 440
INDEX ......................................... 449

# LIST OF TABLES

PAGE

Federal Transportation Expenditures, 1948 .............. 9
Federal Airways System ................................ 20
Federal Airways in the United States, 1925-48 .............. 21
Civil Airports in the United States, December 1, 1948 ........ 30
Capital Expenditures for Civil Airports in the United States .. 31
State Apportionments of Federal Funds for Airports, Appropri-
ated for the Fiscal Year, 1948 ...................... 32
The 1949 Airport Plan and Estimated Cost ................ 34
Federal-Aid Airport Program as of December 31, 1948 ...... 36
Air-Mail Payments to Air Carriers, 1926-49 .............. 45
Source of Domestic Air Carrier Revenues, 1938-48 ......... 49
Mail Pay as Percentage of Total Operating Revenues—Sched-
uled Domestic Carriers ............................ 50
Mail Pay as Percentage of Total Operating Revenues—Feeder
Lines ............................................ 50
Revenues and Expenses of Post Office Department for Do-
mestic Air-Mail Service, 1930-48 ..................... 52
Domestic Air-Mail Subsidies, 1931-41 ................... 53
Accidents on Scheduled Domestic and International Flights
and in Non-Air-Carrier Flying, 1938-48 ............... 61
Federal Expenditures for Rivers and Harbors, Through Fiscal
1948 ............................................ 82
Ton-Miles of Freight Carried on Inland Waterways, 1940 .. 83
Planned Construction Program for Waterways ............. 86
Federal Expenditures for Merchant Marine ............... 95
Federal Funds for Highway Construction Exclusive of Relief
Programs, 1917-48 ................................ 107
Cost of Improving Designated Federal-Aid Road Systems ... 116
Status of Applications for Operating Rights Filed by Motor
Carriers with the Interstate Commerce Commission to
October 31, 1947 ................................. 190
Water Carrier Applications Filed Since Part III of Interstate
Commerce Act Became Effective until October 31, 1946 .. 193
Disposition by the ICC of Applications Filed by Water Car-
riers for Operating Rights ......................... 194
Changes in Certificated Air Route Miles, Domestic and Inter-
national 1938-48 ................................. 203
Revenue per Passenger Mile 1940-48 ..................... 206
Revenue Passenger Miles, Class I Railroads 1940-48 ......... 207
Operating Revenues and Net Profit and Operating Ratios for
Domestic Air Carriers, 1948 ....................... 208

xii

PAGE

Rate of Return—Net Income After Taxes as Per Cent of Average Invested Capital "Big Five" Air Carriers ...... 217

Passenger Load, Mail Pay per Passenger, and Average Passenger Ticket, All Feeder Lines, 1947 ................. 222

Percentage Change in Physical Quantities Produced or Exchanged and in Their Aggregate Values, 1939-47 ...... 288

Gross Expenditures for Additions and Betterments to Railway Property, Class I Railways, 1923-47 ................. 292

United States Transportation Facilities ................... 413

Distribution of Intercity Transportation in the United States, 1947 ........................................... 414

Passenger Transportation by Intercity Public Carriers, 1937-48 ......................................... 414

Transportation Expenditures by Shippers and Travelers, 1947 415

Current Appropriations and Personnel, Federal Transportation Agencies ......................................... 416

Federal Expenditures for Transportation, 1940-50 .......... 417

Mail Pay Yield per Mail Ton-Mile, 1948 .................. 417

Federal Expenditures for Rivers and Harbors, 1922-48 ....... 418

Federal Funds Authorized for Highways, 1917-48 ........... 419

Federal Support for Highways, 1921-48 .................. 420

Apportionment of Federal Highway Authorizations Among the States, Fiscal Year Ending June 30, 1948 ............. 421

Traffic, Mileage, and Financial Data for Domestic Trunk Line Carriers, 1938-48 .................................. 422

Chronology of Increased Railway Rates, Fares, and Charges, 1946 ........................................... 423

Rate of Return, Expenditures for Additions and Betterments, National Income, Traffic Units, Class I Railroads, 1920-48 424

Chronology of Increased Railroad Freight Rates, 1947 ...... 425

Chronology of Nonoperating Organizations' 1948 Wage and Hour Demand ...................................... 426

Chronology of 1948 Increased Railway Rates and Charges ... 427

Average Rate on Dividend Yielding Stock, Percentage of Stock Not Yielding Dividends and Net Income as Percentage of Stockholders' Equity, Class I Railroads, 1920-47 ...... 428

Operating Results of 131 Class I Railroads, 1939-41 Average 429

Operating Results of Missouri Pacific System and Atlantic Coast Line System, 1939-41 Average ................ 430

Operating Results of 127 Class I Railroads (Representing 131 Carriers), 1947 ..................................... 431

# LIST OF CHARTS

PAGE

Federal Expenditures for Transportation, 1940-49 .......... 10

Federal Expenditures for Rivers and Harbors, 1922-48 ...... 82

Federal Funds as Percentage of Total Revenues for Highways, 1921-48 ........................................ 109

Selected Mileage and Financial Data for Domestic Air Carriers, 1938-48 ........................................ 205

Rate of Return, National Income, Traffic Volume and Capital Expenditures, 1920-48 ............................. 282

Average Rate on Dividend-Yielding Stock, Percentage of Stock Not Yielding Dividends, and Net Income as Percentage of Stockholders' Equity, 1920-47 .............. 289

Operating Results of 131 Class I Railroads Classified by Rate of Return, 1939-41 Average ......................... 333

Operating Results of 19 Systems (Comprising 66 Carriers) Classified by Rate of Return, 1939-41 Average ........ 335

Operating Results of 127 Class I Railroads (Representing 131 Carriers) Classified by Rate of Return, 1947 .......... 337

Operating Results of 19 Systems (Comprising 60 Railroads) Classified by Rate of Return, 1947 ................... 338

Organization, Civilian Transportation Agencies, July 1, 1949 .. 386

Proposed Organization, Civilian Transportation Agencies .... 391

# INTRODUCTION

Dependence of a progressive society on adequate transportation is demonstrated by the extraordinary development and use of transport facilities in the American economy. The United States owns one third of the railroad mileage and nearly half of the merchant marine of the world. On its highways, which make up a third of the surfaced road mileage of all countries combined, more that 70 per cent of the world's motor vehicles operate. Thousands of miles of inland water routes, pipelines, and airways provide additional passenger and cargo services. In no other nation does the volume of transportation approximate the levels reached in the United States.

Recent war experience has added striking evidence of the essential role of transportation. It was the tremendous capabilities of the transportation system which enabled us to maintain the domestic economy during hostilities and at the same time to satisfy the logistic requirements of worldwide military operations. Economic activity since the war has placed further heavy demands on the transportation system, and today traffic volumes are in many cases well above the peaks of the war economy. Morever, the absence of settled international relations means that potentially vast additional requirements may have to be met. Under these conditions the future of the transportation system and of federal policy upon which transport development and control are so dependent have assumed extraordinary importance.

## I. THE TRANSPORTATION SYSTEM

The nation's transportation system, composed of railroad, highway, pipeline, water, and air facilities, is the product of a unique joint undertaking. Private enterprise has supplied much of the inventive genius, the production technology, and the managerial drive that have given direction and impetus to the development of the newer forms of transportation. And, until recently, the private investor has furnished the bulk of the capi-

1

tal required to finance experimentation, the launching of new enterprises, and their subsequent expansion. Public enterprise, on the other hand, has supplied a substantial part of the basic facilities over which private equipment has operated, and has participated in a number of other ways in the transport revolution.

The result of this volume and variety of services has been an abundance of freight and passenger transportation at rates which have encouraged widespread use of all forms of transport and a high degree of dependence on them. This in turn has contributed in no small degree to the enrichment of social life and the efficiency of economic processes. But the fundamental differences among the several methods of transportation and the joint responsibilities of government and private industry have likewise created a highly complex and difficult system to manage.[1]

Trends during the past three decades have drastically altered the nature of the transportation system and its problems. Since 1920 significant changes have taken place: a million miles of highways have been surfaced, and the number of motor vehicles in operation has increased by 30 millions. The mileage of the pipeline transportation system has more than doubled. Air transportation constitutes the newest element in the transportation system, and the number of passengers carried per year on domestic airlines has increased to a thousand times the 1927 figure. Expenditures for waterway facilities during this period have exceeded the total of all previous outlays for this purpose, and extraordinary provisions have been made to develop the most extensive merchant marine in the world. In contrast to these trends, the physical expansion of the railroads, in the sense of extending lines into new territory, was completed by 1920. Since then, adjustments have come mainly in the form of abandoning obsolete trackage.

The development of our transportation plant has continued to the point where effective and almost universal competition has supplanted monopoly. Passengers may travel on the highway

[1] United States transportation facilities and equipment are enumerated in App. A, Table 1.

by bus or by automobile, and in most communities of any size they are offered the additional choice of rail or air service. Similarly, the movement of freight is possible on the highway in private, contract, or common carrier truck, as well as by rail or water; and more recently, air cargo has introduced a new and rapidly expanding service. For special purposes, the pipeline network offers cheap and efficient transport. In international commerce there is now the choice of ship or plane.

Although passenger transportation is furnished by a variety of carriers, the private automobile accounts for between three and four times as much passenger movement as all other forms of transportation combined. Considering public carriers alone, however, the railroads in 1947 were still carrying well over half of total passenger traffic: 46 billion passenger-miles compared to 23 billions by intercity bus and 6 billions by airline. The volume of both rail and bus traffic in 1947 was approximately double what it had been ten years before, while airline travel during the same period had multiplied to a volume half as great as all first-class rail travel.[2]

With regard to the carriage of freight, the railroads continue to be the major transportation medium in terms of volume. During the war, when total freight movement reached an unprecedented trillion ton-miles, the railroads carried 70 per cent of the total; and today they continue to account for nearly this proportion of intercity common carrier operations. The second highest tonnage of freight movement is by carriers operating on inland waterways, approximately 80 per cent of which is accounted for by the Great Lakes. These carriers moved 15 per cent of intercity freight traffic in 1947, more than half of which was petroleum and coal.

During 1947 the amount paid by travelers and shippers for all freight and passenger transportation, intercity and local, amounted to approximately 38 billion dollars.[3] Approximately

[2] See App. A, Tables 2 and 3.

[3] An additional sum of approximately 2.5 billion dollars was spent by federal, state, and local governments for transportation facilities and services not paid for by the users, so that the grand total spent for transportation, both by users and in the form of public aid, was in the neighborhood of 40.5 billions of dollars.

46 per cent was paid for private automobile transportation, including the cost of vehicles, gasoline, and other operating outlays, plus the amounts contributed in special taxes to defray the cost of highways. Total highway transportation services, including truck, bus, and automobile, accounted for well over half of all transportation expenditures; and approximately one fourth of the total was for railroad transportation.[4]

## II. THE FEDERAL ROLE

The full significance of national policy is measured not simply by federal action itself, but by the influence of federal action on the grand total of transportation expenditures. The policies which govern federal activity in the promotion and regulation of transportation are major factors in determining the size of the transportation bill, and how it is incurred. They influence to an important degree the price and quality of transportation service, the allocation of traffic, and the pattern of transportation investments. And since transportation is one of the principal means by which the resources of the nation are developed and the products of the economic system utilized, it is clear that the impacts of federal transportation policy extend to almost every phase of the nation's economic life.

The federal government has gradually assumed major and controlling responsibility both for the regulation of transport agencies and for the programing and financing of airports, airways, waterways, highways, and ocean shipping. In fact, the federal role has grown in scope and magnitude to a point where national policy exerts a dominant influence on the transportation future.

Federal action in some cases involves the granting of financial assistance to the states and local units of government, while in other cases it consists of actual construction, maintenance, and operation of facilities. Federal activities also embrace research activities, the granting of construction and operating subsidies to ship and aircraft operators, and the provision of

[4] See App. A, Table 4.

various services to transportation, including such aids as communications, lighthouses, channel markers, search and rescue facilities, weather information, maps and charts.

With respect to the control of carriers, federal action involves comprehensive powers over every important phase of rail operation and management, including the price, quality, quantity, and safety of the service. This control is exercised through the granting of operating rights, the determination of route extensions and abandonments, the prescribing of rates, the review of financial methods, and the establishment of safety rules and their enforcement. The federal government determines who may operate air transport services, and exercises close supervision over the operations of the carriers. This control includes not only matters of finance and economics, but encompasses safety standards governing aircraft design, maintenance, and operation. The right to carry persons or goods on the highways in interstate commerce also requires a federal certificate, and both rate regulation and the prescribing of safety standards are federal responsibilities. Extensive federal control is also exercised over ocean shipping services, including the selection of carriers eligible for federal subsidy and the routes to be operated in foreign trade.

A large number of government agencies participate in federal promotional and regulatory functions. For the fiscal year 1949 these activities involved a billion dollars in federal appropriations; and 93,000 persons were employed in carrying out the work. Some of these agencies are concerned exclusively with transportation matters, generally with one particular form of transportation, while others may perform services which are utilized in significant degree by the transportation industries.[5]

The extensive range and complex character of government action in the field of transport promotion and regulation are set forth in Parts I and II of this study. Part I describes the types of transportation facilities that are constructed, maintained, and financed by the national government; how the government is organized for this purpose; and how transport

[5] See App. A, Table 5.

programs are financed. Consideration is likewise given to the special problems of national defense. Part II is devoted to analysis of the government's regulatory functions. The varying objectives of regulatory action and the administrative devices used in the attempt to achieve these goals are described; and the major issues of public policy are identified.

Part III is a general summary. It includes an evaluation of national transportation policy and specific recommendations for revision of policy and administrative organization.

# PART I
# PROMOTION OF TRANSPORTATION FACILITIES AND SERVICES

# CHAPTER I

# BACKGROUND OF THE PROBLEM

During the fiscal year 1948, federal expenditures for transportation reached nearly a billion dollars. The largest single item was federal aid for highways, which accounted for 37 per cent of total federal expenditures. The provision of waterway facilities and navigation aids accounted for 24 per cent, and merchant marine expenditures for 19 per cent, bringing the total for water transportation to 43 per cent. Expenditures for aviation were 14 per cent of all federal transportation outlays, and the balance of funds was absorbed by regulatory functions and miscellaneous transport services. (See table below.)

FEDERAL TRANSPORTATION EXPENDITURES, 1948[a]

| Purpose of Expenditure | Total | Per cent |
| --- | --- | --- |
| Provision of highways | $356,178,721 | 37.3 |
| River and harbor improvement and navigation aids | 231,334,453 | 24.2 |
| Promotion of the merchant marine | 182,709,336 | 19.1 |
| Promotion of aviation | 136,175,017 | 14.3 |
| Other services | 33,558,975 | 3.5 |
| Regulation of transportation | 14,831,849 | 1.6 |
| Total | $954,788,351 | 100.0 |

[a] *The Budget of the United States Government for Fiscal Year 1950*, p. A-32.

Federal transportation expenditures, as estimated for 1949, amount to approximately two and one half times the expenditure rate of the immediate prewar years. Comparison of 1949 expenditures with 1940, shown in the chart on page 10, reveals that nearly half a billion dollars of the increased outlay is accounted for by water navigation aids and highway programs. The largest rate of increase, however, is to be found in aviation expenditures which were estimated to be 8 times higher in 1949 than in 1940.

Spectacular expansion of federal action occurred as a result of the tremendous increase in transportation requirements in

9

wartime. In 1944, when transportation expenditures of the federal government reached an all-time peak, 4.3 billion dollars were expended. Merchant marine outlays constituted the greatest part of the total, while aviation expenditures were second in importance. This ascendancy of national security

FEDERAL EXPENDITURES FOR TRANSPORTATION, 1940-49[a]

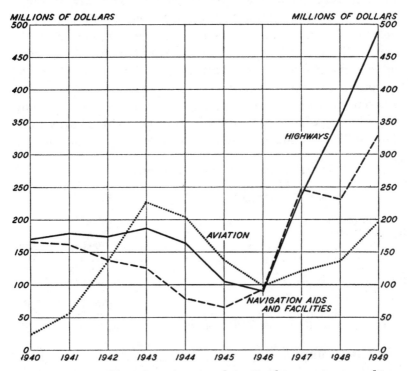

[a] See App. A, Table 6 for supporting data. Merchant marine expenditures are not shown in the chart.

objectives in the federal transportation program continues to be reflected in current federal transportation activities.

The outlook for federal action is indicated by the current high level of economic activity and the consequent heavy demands on the nation's transportation system. Thus far, federal activity in transportation since the war has been directed primarily to meeting the deferred maintenance requirements which accumulated during the war, and little has been done in the way of effecting long-range improvements. However, plans are being formulated for extensive additions and improvements to existing facilities. Establishment of a billion-dollar all-weather airways system is one of these projects. The program will include installation of landing aids and the modernization of air navigation facilities to promote the safety and regularity of air transportation. In addition, expansion of federal aviation activities has resulted from the new seven-year program of federal aid for airport facilities. Extensive modernization of the highway system is also under way, and expenditures under the present federal-aid program will continue roadbuilding operations at the rate of nearly half a billion dollars annually through 1951. New federally subsidized ship construction is planned to provide a more balanced fleet for national security requirements; and demand for further river and harbor development involves uncompleted projects totaling over 3 billion dollars.

## I. SCOPE AND RESULTS OF FEDERAL ACTION

Federal activity in the provision of transportation facilities and services represents long-established policy. Beginning in the early 1800's, federal grants of land and right of ways, as well as direct congressional appropriations, aided the development of canals and the improvement of waterways. After 1850, to aid the development of railroad transportation, the federal government made land grants equal to nearly 10 per cent of the total area of the United States; and altogether federal aid to the railroads amounted to 1.4 billion dollars.

Federal aid for the development of highways, including regular federal aid, emergency funds, and relief expenditures, has amounted to approximately 10 billions of dollars, and since 1916 net expenditures of 15 billions have been made for the merchant marine. Since the beginning of river and harbor work, some 3 billion dollars have been spent for this purpose. In more recent years civil air transport development has involved expenditures of more than a billion dollars.

The reasons for federal participation in transport development have been varied. In the case of the railroads, the desirability of opening up new lands and reducing the cost of transportation in the absence of private capital prompted federal action. Highway development was federally sponsored on the general grounds of promoting commerce and the postal service, together with considerations of national defense. Federal action was designed to meet the needs created by rapidly growing use of the motor vehicle through the achievement of uniform standards and practices in highway construction, and through steps designed to encourage a concentration of highway development in accordance with priority needs. The bulk of federal expenditures for the merchant marine has been made in time of war for specific military objectives; but congressional policy stresses, in addition to security objectives, the need for providing necessary facilities for foreign trade. Air transportation has been promoted partly on national defense grounds, and partly for the improvement of the postal service and the fostering of a new transport industry.

Federal action in the promotion of transportation has been rewarded by spectacular accomplishments, not only in terms of physical facilities and transportation services, but in the furtherance of broad national objectives made possible by transportation developments. Railroad promotion permitted the early realization of reduced transportation costs and the development of new lands and resources, the importance of which was attested by the growth of industry and population in previously undeveloped areas accessible only by boat or wagon. In most instances the aided railroads would have been built in time without public support, but the public would have paid the bill in the form of retarded national development. Federal highway activity has hastened the realization of a national system of roads, and has promoted the acceptance of planned highway development. The states and localities would undoubtedly have provided highway facilities without federal aid, but the influence of the federal program on the speed and quality of highway development, and on the concentration of effort on a limited system of roads has been unmistakable.

The efforts of the federal government in the building of a merchant marine capable of meeting the requirements of war have been equally fruitful. The policies initiated under the Merchant Marine Act provided for the establishment of a nucleus shipbuilding and shipping industry which permitted spectacular expansion when emergency requirements developed. Similarly, through early federal pioneering with air-mail service, commercial airlines were brought into being, and the cost of air travel was reduced to furnish a new medium of transportation. More recently, federal promotion of air transportation provided the nucleus of personnel and facilities which enabled us, after war had been declared, to achieve the almost incredible expansion of air power necessary for successful military operations.

## II. NATURE OF THE PROBLEM

Review of the activities of the federal government in the provision of transportation facilities and services establishes the fact that federal initiative has been responsible for a substantial part of the development of the American transportation system. The capacity and quality of our transport facilities far surpass those of any other nation, and much of this development can be attributed to the expenditure programs of the federal government.

It is not enough simply to have the best transportation system in the world, however; the objective must be to achieve the best possible system at the lowest possible cost. The results of federal promotional activity, examined from this point of view, provide evidence that despite its accomplishments federal policy has not been designed to achieve the goal of maximum service and economy.

Mistakes have been made, and are being repeated, which seriously detract from the full potentials of our transportation system. Historically, public aids led to an overbuilding of railroad lines, the effects of which are still felt today. Federal assistance contributed to corruption and ill-advised methods of finance and promotion, and the exploitation of these aids by those who received them. In the case of water transportation, benefits have to a large degree been confined to special interests and localities, and large shippers have generally been in the best position to take advantage of free facilities provided by the general taxpayer. In recent years highway development has expanded beyond the original purpose of aiding the states in the improvement of a limited system of main highways, and now embraces work on extensive mileages of local routes, giving rise to fundamental questions as to the most effective federal role. Current promotion of air transportation, too, appears destined to lead to ultimate difficulties for the industry and the user, as in the case of earlier aid to railroads. The adverse effects of operating subsidies on managerial efficiency, and the wastes of ill-advised expansion, may prove a lasting detriment.

In the discussion of promotional policy which follows, several basic problems will be apparent. First, federal promotion of the several agencies is based on no consistent policy, but each program is conceived, justified, and administered without reference to the other. At no point in the process of formulation and approval of federal promotional programs are the expenditures or economic implications entailed in each separate proposal evaluated in terms of (1) the total amount of the national budget which is being devoted to the promotion of transportation facilities; (2) the relative merits of promotional proposals for the different media; that is, the desirability of spending a particular sum for highways or waterways compared to airways; (3) the possible effect which the added facilities will have upon the operation of those already available; and (4) the possible physical co-ordination of facilities.

Second, with respect to finance, the nation's railroads and pipe-lines are operated by private management without government aid, whereas other forms of transportation rely to varying degree on general tax support. Highways are to a major degree financed by users, but receive heavy additional support from general tax funds. Users pay little or nothing for the improvement and maintenance of waterways and aids to water navigation. The federal government also furnishes the airways without charge; and airport expenses are defrayed only in part by the user. This situation raises the question whether, because of the general and widespread benefits which transportation confers on the community and nation, it is desirable to include transportation facilities in the same category as general government services, as is the case today; or whether it would be more desirable for transportation to be financed by the user, as in the case of other goods and services, since transportation constitutes an integral part of the cost of production and distribution.

There are many legitimate reasons to support the financing of transportation facilities out of general tax funds. These have, in fact, been sufficiently persuasive to cause the federal government to finance such facilities without requiring those who use them to pay the bill. But as long as general tax funds are applied to the provision of transport facilities, and in varying amounts determined by legislative fiat, the difficulties of determining how much money should be spent, and for what purposes, are inevitably increased. And this method of finance leads to unfair competitive conditions and to an uneconomic division of traffic among the several transport agencies.

However desirable it may be from an economic standpoint to finance transportation facilities through charges imposed on the user, such a goal is in practice beset by many difficulties. First, it does not follow that user payments designed to meet the total cost of transport facilities would necessarily achieve the kind of transport system we need. Certainly this would not have been the case had we insisted that motorists in the 1920's pay their fair share of the total highway bill. Similarly, in the 1930's, when air-mail subsidies were creating a new transportation system by air, a policy of requiring full costs to be covered by transportation rates would have meant that the development of aviation in the United States would have lagged far behind the rest of the world. And the conduct of our merchant marine policy on the basis of economic criteria might have meant national catastrophe. There are, in fact, a number of considerations other than economics which must be recognized in determining financial policy. Among these are such objectives as the promotion of new industries, the development of regions and resources, the provision of useful public works projects to combat depression, the development of uniform standards, and provision for the national defense.

The problem, therefore, is one of weighing the arguments for the use of general funds with those favoring user charges, and of determining, in the light of federal objectives, the extent to which general fund support may be necessary. The current trend toward greatly increased federal expenditures in this field calls for close examination of this question in an effort to achieve as nearly as possible a considered program of transportation development.

The following chapters will review for each of the agencies of transport the various types of activities in which the federal government now engages, with a view to defining what the scope and responsibility of federal action should be, what problems are encountered in each field of promotion, and what revisions in federal policy and method are necessary to correct present deficiencies.

# CHAPTER II

# AIRWAYS AND AIRPORTS

The principal federal activities directed to the development of civil aviation are performed by the Civil Aeronautics Administration in the Department of Commerce. These functions include responsibility for airways, airports, and safety. Important promotional work is also performed by the Civil Aeronautics Board, which, despite its primary responsibility for economic regulation, is also charged with assisting aviation development.[1]

As the principal federal agency in this field, the Civil Aeronautics Administration fosters the development of civil aeronautics and air commerce by the establishment, maintenance, and operation of the federal airways and the various air navigation aids and facilities which they comprise; by the planning of a national airport system and the administration of the federal-aid airport program; by provision for the control and protection of air traffic; by technical development work in the field of aeronautics; by the conduct of various activities related to aviation safety; and by maintaining and operating the Washington National Airport. The Administration spends approximately 100 million dollars annually and maintains a staff of approximately 17,000 employees.

In the field of safety regulation, the CAA enforces the civil air regulations and in connection with this responsibility investigates all aircraft accidents. Its functions also include the examination and rating of airmen, the testing of aircraft, testing of equipment and facilities, the issuance of safety certificates, and the registration of aircraft.

The other organization having basic responsibilities in this field, the independent five-member Civil Aeronautics Board, is concerned primarily with the economic regulation of public air carriers, including the determination of air routes, certification

---

[1] The Civil Aeronautics Administration and the Civil Aeronautics Board had their origins in the Civil Aeronautics Act of 1938, 52 Stat. 973.

of carriers to operate over them, and the regulation of rates to be charged for air services. The Board also has the responsibility of promulgating civil air regulations and investigating accidents. In addition, the CAB is charged with promoting air transport development by setting rates for carriage of the mail at levels which will assure to the carriers a sound financial condition. This promotional aspect of air-mail payments may be applied not only to established carriers but to the promotion of new aviation ventures, such as the current experiment with feeder-line and helicopter mail service. Control over international air carriers by the Board is likewise basically promotional in nature. Decisions in this sphere are made with the advice and assistance of the secretary of state and are subject to the approval of the president.

In addition to the work of these two agencies, several other organizations are actively engaged in the conduct of services to air transportation. The National Advisory Committee for Aeronautics conducts basic aviation research. The Post Office Department is responsible for providing the air-mail payments, including subsidies, determined by the CAB. Responsibility for certain navigation aids and the conduct of miscellaneous aviation matters are vested in the Coast Guard, the Weather Bureau, and the Coast and Geodetic Survey. In matters involving international aviation, the State Department is an active participant; and United States' membership in the International Civil Aviation Organization provides the machinery for an orderly development of international air transportation. Finally, the Air Coordinating Committee provides a formal liaison among the several civil and military agencies of the government dealing with both domestic and international aviation.

In this chapter, the airway and airport activities of the CAA are discussed. The chapters following are concerned with the air-mail policies carried out by the CAB and the joint responsibilities of the CAA and CAB with respect to the promotion of aviation safety.[2] The several federal agencies performing

---

[2] Discussion of the principal functions of the CAB in the field of economic regulations is included in Pt. 2.

ancillary services in the interests of aviation are described in Appendix B.

## I. THE FEDERAL AIRWAYS

Except for the early period of aviation development, airway facilities and services in the United States have been constructed, maintained, and operated by the federal government through the Civil Aeronautics Administration and its predecessors and with the assistance of the Weather Bureau. Prior to the establishment of this responsibility, however, facilities were provided by the airlines, the Post Office Department, the Army and Navy, and some of the states.[3]

The evolution toward federal control has been the result of several factors. Basically, the range and speed of the airplane and the medium through which it passes, cause this method of transportation to have minimum respect for political boundaries. The necessity for uniform navigation aids on a national scale is obvious. An additional impetus to federal action during the early development period was the difficulty encountered in obtaining contractors for transcontinental air mail when individual carriers were left to provide their own navigation aids. And since the navigation problems of the airlines were comparable to those of military aircraft, the joint-use characteristics of airway facilities likewise pointed to the desirability of federal action. For these reasons, and because of the public interest in achieving greater safety in air transport, a centralized and uniform system of federal airways was adopted.[4]

*The airways system.* For a number of years the airways consisted primarily of lighted beacons and intermediate landing fields. Route mileage expanded from approximately 2,000 miles prior to 1926 to 22,000 miles in 1935. In that year, a committee of Congress invited airline operators to recommend a desirable

[3] Up to 1938 the air lines had spent several million dollars for aids to navigation. *To Create a Civil Aeronautics Authority,* Hearings before the House Committee on Interstate and Foreign Commerce, 75 Cong. 2 sess (1938), p. 348.

[4] Board of Investigation and Research, *Public Aids to Domestic Transportation,* H. Doc. 159, 79 Cong. 1 sess., (1944), p. 466. The Board was established by the Transportation Act of 1940, 54 Stat. 952.

program for expanding and improving the airways system.[5] The result was a plan for the establishment of full-power radio ranges and broadcasting stations and weather teletype circuits; and beginning in 1937 an improvement program was inaugurated which has since been carried out through the Civil Aeronautics Administration.

FEDERAL AIRWAYS SYSTEM[a]

(As of December 31, 1948)

| Facilities | Continental United States and Territories |
|---|---|
| Implemented airways, mileage | 57,368[b] |
| Intermediate fields | 189 |
| Beacon lights | 1,812 |
| Approach light lanes | 93 |
| Radio ranges | 709 |
| Radio markers | 508 |
| Instrument landing systems | 79 |
| Communications stations | 452 |
| Airport traffic control towers | 150 |
| Airways traffic control centers | 30 |
| Weather reporting circuits (mileage) | 65,747 |
| Teletype drops, weather | 862 |
| Traffic control circuits (mileage) | 68,031 |
| Teletype and interphone drops (traffic control) | 3,044 |

[a] "Facilities Maintained and Operated by the Office of Federal Airways," CAA, Program Engineering Section, Jan. 14, 1949, (mimeo.)

[b] In addition, there were at this date 5,561 miles of unimplemented airways and 21,423 miles of ocean routes.

By 1949 there were approximately 57,000 miles of implemented airways in the United States and its territories, all federally owned and operated. (See table above) These consisted of radio beams delineating the routes between important centers of population, together with equipment to guide the flight of aircraft and to promote safe and regular operations. Included in the airways system were: (1) aids to navigation, including radio ranges, markers, beacon lights, and other

[5] *Safety in the Air*, Senate Committee on Commerce, S. Rept. 185, 74 Cong. 1 sess. (1937). This report was the outcome of S. Res. 146 to investigate certain aircraft accidents.

FEDERAL AIRWAYS IN THE UNITED STATES, 1925-48[a]

Mileage and Expenditures

| Fiscal Year | CAA Implemented Mileage[b] | Cost of Establishment[c] | Cost of Maintenance and Operation | Total Cost[c] |
|---|---|---|---|---|
| 1925 ............ | | $ 514,406 | $ 295,212 | $ 809,618 |
| 1926 ............ | 2,041 | 27,703 | 307,255 | 334,958 |
| 1927 ............ | 4,468 | 269,533 | 357,248 | 626,781 |
| 1928 ............ | 6,988 | 1,481,610 | 1,468,600 | 2,950,210 |
| 1929 ............ | 12,448 | 1,740,000 | 2,630,013 | 4,370,013 |
| 1930 ............ | 15,258 | 1,521,000 | 3,659,738 | 5,180,738 |
| 1931 ............ | 17,152 | 2,121,600 | 5,382,155 | 7,503,755 |
| 1932 ............ | 19,500 | 1,471,500 | 6,684,647 | 8,156,147 |
| 1933 ............ | 18,655 | 75,210 | 5,562,180 | 5,637,390 |
| 1934 ............ | 19,081 | 279,917 | 4,185,001 | 4,464,918 |
| 1935 ............ | 22,012 | 2,181,258 | 4,413,255 | 6,594,513 |
| 1936 ............ | 22,245 | 294,199 | 4,709,971 | 5,004,170 |
| 1937 ............ | 22,319 | 791,545 | 4,722,896 | 5,514,441 |
| 1938 ............ | 23,723 | 2,654,606 | 6,197,391 | 8,851,997 |
| 1939 ............ | 27,074 | 4,543,189 | 6,957,465 | 11,500,654 |
| 1940 ............ | 32,100 | 5,595,352 | 9,027,716 | 14,623,068 |
| 1941 ............ | 36,062 | 5,694,927 | 11,006,701 | 16,701,628 |
| 1942 ............ | 38,498 | 6,872,879[d] | 16,665,234 | 23,538,113 |
| 1943 ............ | 41,506 | 12,619,174[d] | 21,007,827 | 33,627,001 |
| 1944 ............ | 42,549 | 7,058,151[d] | 20,009,477 | 27,667,628 |
| 1945 ............ | 43,285 | 4,067,860 | 24,559,163 | 28,627,023 |
| 1946 ............ | 43,403 | 13,212,000 | 30,042,127 | 43,254,127 |
| 1947 ............ | 45,393 | 19,622,200 | 38,626,118 | 58,248,318 |
| 1948 ............ | 51,321 | 11,149,066 | 55,513,369 | 66,662,435 |
| 1949 (est.) ....... | 54,000 | 22,440,499 | 65,075,391 | 87,515,890 |
| Total expenditures | | $128,899,384 | $349,066,150 | $477,965,534 |

[a] Mileage data for 1926-47 from CAA Statistical Handbook of Civil Aviation (1948), p. 19. Cost data for 1925-44 from CAA, Charging for Federal Airways Services, Dec. 31, 1946, Pt. 2, p. 17. Other data from Office of Federal Airways, CAA.

[b] Data for 1940-48 include mileage in Hawaii and Alaska.

[c] Data for 1945-48 represent only appropriations and do not include expenses.

[d] Includes Army and Navy funds transferred to CAA.

facilities; (2) aids to landing, including instrument landing systems, approach light lanes, markers, etc.; (3) airways traffic control, including traffic control centers, teletype traffic control circuits, and interphone circuits; (4) airway weather reporting service, including teletype weather reporting circuits; (5) communications stations; (6) intermediate landing fields for emergencies; and (7) traffic control towers at terminal airports.

The responsibilities of the Civil Aeronautics Administration in this field include aerial and ground surveys for new routes; selection of sites for the necessary installations; preparation of plans and specifications for facilities; supervision of construction; negotiation of power and communication contracts; purchase and installation of radio range and communication equipment; operation of the airways traffic control system; maintenance and operation of air navigation facilities; operation of airport control towers; and the conduct of research for the development of air navigation aids.

The cumulative expenditures for federal airways from fiscal 1925 through 1949 amount to 478 million dollars, of which approximately one third has been spent for establishing the system and two thirds for its maintenance and operation. The total annual requirements for construction, maintenance, and operation of the airways had by 1949 reached approximately $87,500,000. (See table p. 21.)

*Future airway requirements.* Despite these outlays, the present system of federal airways constitutes a serious bottleneck in air transportation. The inability of existing airway facilities to accommodate traffic, particularly under adverse weather conditions, is well known. The tools now available depend on manual operation by traffic controllers and estimates of positions reported by aircraft pilots. These methods may be in error due to inadequacies of instruments, delays in communications, or mistakes of personnel. In many areas saturation of communication channels has already been reached.

The possibilities of improved methods of air navigation aids have a direct bearing on the achievement of self-support in the air transportation industry. When the airlines are able to operate without cancellations and with a high degree of safety and dependability, their financial position is certain to improve. United States airlines in 1947 lost 22 million dollars, yet estimates of the amount of loss attributed to inadequate navigation facilities, including congestion at airports, far exceed this figure.[6] The United States in 1948 had an estimated total of 6 billion dollars invested in civil airports, but this investment was useless approximately 15 per cent of the time due to weather.

In view of the growing inadequacies of the airways system, and the implications from the standpoint of military requirements, the Joint Research and Development Board early in 1947 conducted an over-all study of problems in the field of navigation.[7] The military problems of detection, identification, and control of space occupancy, and the problems of traffic control and navigation encountered in civil aviation are closely interrelated; and the study committee was specifically charged with determining the extent to which requirements for military and civil air navigation, as well as an air warning network, could be integrated.

Conclusion was reached that military effectiveness demands the maximum standardization and common use of navigation facilities for all types of transportation, including air navigation, marine navigation both under and on the surface of the water, and tactical land vehicles.[8] Because air-transport facilities have introduced operational requirements far in advance of available navigation aids, however, this phase of navigation was given major consideration. The report concluded that for most purposes a common system of air navigation would adequately serve both military and civilian aviation, but that certain additional facilities would be needed to meet the tactical requirements of the military. According to the committee:

There appears to be no major difference between the requirements for civil transport and *nontactical* military transport operations.

[6] Radio Technical Commission for Aeronautics, *Air Traffic Control*, Special Committee 31, May 12, 1948, p. 5.

[7] The Joint Research and Development Board was created by the secretaries of War and Navy in 1946 to co-ordinate all research and development work of joint interest to the War and Navy Departments. The JRDB has since been replaced by the Research and Development Board in the National Military Establishment. 61 Stat. 495, July 26, 1947.

[8] The National Military Establishment, Research and Development Board, *Navigation and National Security* (1948).

However, equipment limitations, necessity for detailed ground command and direction of air combat units, and other factors, create special requirements for *tactical* military operations which cannot be met fully by any efficient Common System. . . ."[9]

It was recommended that in time of peace, the common air navigation system, except for certain installations at military bases, should be installed, operated, and maintained by the Civil Aeronautics Administration. In time of national emergency, the Military Establishment should assume control of the system and effect the required integration with existing air-warning and intercept systems.

The first step toward the ultimate realization of an efficient all-weather airways system is a five-year interim program of installing presently available electronic aids. The "target" program, to be carried out over a fifteen-year period, will be based on radar, although the exact nature of the aids has not as yet been determined. The program has been drawn up on the assumption that approximately 100,000 equipped aircraft will be in operation by 1960.

The interim program will cost approximately 375 million dollars. It will be based primarily on improved very high frequency and micro-wave equipment, but will also include certain nonelectronic aids. Most of the installations for the interim program will be used in the target program, with some improvement and simplification. The entire program will involve a minimum expenditure of 1,113 million dollars.[10]

The air navigation facilities which will replace the existing system introduce an entirely new concept of air navigation. The use of omnidirectional ranges will permit the abandonment of the existing "airways," which are, in effect, highways in the air, delineated by radio beams. The new ranges will provide instead for navigation aids blanketing the entire country, permitting navigation between any points in continental United States. These facilities will operate on very high frequencies,

[9] The same, p. 10.
[10] Radio Technical Commission for Aeronautics, *Air Traffic Control*, Special Committee 31, May 12, 1948, Tables, pp. 34-35.

in contrast to the present low-frequency ranges, providing static-free communications and other advantages.[11]

The CAA estimates that maintenance and operation of these navigation aids will require approximately 100 million dollars a year, and that the interim program will add about 75 million dollars for equipment installation over the next five years. In other words, compared to expenditures of 67 million dollars in 1948, air navigation facilities will require some 175 million dollars per year in future years, or more than 2.5 times the present rate of expenditure.[12]

*User charges for airways.* The large capital requirements involved in the establishment of an all-weather airways system and the rapid increase in airway maintenance and operating costs which have occurred during the past few years indicate that the provision of these facilities in the future will require substantially larger sums of money. The question arises, therefore, as to whether these funds are to be obtained through general appropriations, or whether payment is to be divided among those who use the facilities, including the military and the several classes of civilian users.

In the study of public aids to transportation made by the Board of Investigation and Research, an attempt was made to determine the annual cost of the federal airways and to allocate this cost among the several users on the basis of airplane miles.[13] Although these figures do not reflect current costs of airway use, they indicate the policy questions to be considered, the nature of the cost allocation problem, and the size of the financial requirements which would have been involved in any plan to recoup those costs from the users at that time.

Total annual costs were computed at nearly 14 million dol-

[11] Until the new installation is completed, the CAA will continue to maintain the existing low-frequency radio ranges.
[12] Data from Office of Assistant Administrator for Federal Airways, CAA. The Air Navigation Development Board set up by the secretaries of commerce and defense has the responsibility for research and development work in connection with the new air navigation system. The Board comprises three members representing the Air Force, the Navy, and the CAA and is contained in the Department of Commerce for housekeeping purposes.
[13] H. Doc. 159, 79 Cong. 1 sess.

lars for 1940.[14] It was determined that approximately 34 per cent of this cost should be borne by the scheduled air carriers, approximately 39 per cent by nonscheduled operators, and the remaining 27 per cent by government operators. Thus in fiscal 1940 the cost assigned to scheduled air carriers was 4.7 million dollars and to nonscheduled civil aviation 5.4 million dollars, with the balance of 3.9 millions charged to the federal government.

It was concluded by the Board that:

. . . unless it is held to be desirable as a matter of national policy to foster the further development of aviation by continuing to furnish airway aid to commercial and other civilian users at public expense, consideration might well be given to the means by which these direct beneficiaries might pay for such part of the costs as may properly be attributed to them.[15]

It was stated that if a user charge were to be imposed, a specific tax on fuel used in aircraft would be feasible for this purpose.

Further study of the problem of paying for civil airways was made in 1946 by the Civil Aeronautics Administration, at the request of the appropriations subcommittees of the United States House of Representatives and Senate.[16] The CAA report stated that: "Contributions by the Federal Government to the Federal Airways system without eventual recovery from airways users can be justified only if the interest of national defense requires the promotion and expansion of civil aviation beyond its normal economic level."[17] However, it was felt that there was justification in delaying full recovery of costs during the development period of aviation; that only partial recovery should be sought until such time as the full potential use of the airways has been realized.

With respect to methods of collecting airways charges, it was pointed out that among the possible methods of recovery, a federal aviation gasoline tax and an aircraft registration fee

[14] The same, Table 85, p. 479.
[15] The same, p. 481.
[16] Frederick B. Lee, *Charging for Federal Airways Services,* U. S. Department of Commerce, CAA (1946).
[17] The same, p. V-6-7.

might be most feasible. The study took the position that the amount of fuel consumed by an aircraft is roughly proportional to its capacity, and gasoline consumption represents a fair approximation of the relative use of navigation facilities. With regard to the registration fee, the belief was expressed that all users should pay a stand-by charge regardless of the extent of use which they make of the system. Presumably, the fee would be graduated along the lines of the present differentiation in motor vehicle taxes between private automobiles and trucks and buses.

It was concluded that a few of the large airline companies, at the time of the study, could have paid a nominal charge for the use of the airways without hardship. For the great number of small companies, such charges could not be paid either then or under traffic conditions expected over the next 2 to 4 years, except by paying these amounts out of capital or obtaining increased mail subsidies. The issue, therefore, was considered to be whether the development of the smaller companies, and in particular the nonscheduled and contract carriers, was of sufficient national importance to warrant the temporary withholding of federal charges for airways.

*Present and future cost responsibility.* Although the financing of air navigation facilities through user payments is a desirable objective, a number of difficult questions must be answered as to a feasible level of charges. In view of the large capital improvements which will be necessary in the immediate future, an attempt to recoup total annual expenditures would place an undue burden on airway users during the initial development period. Obviously, too, user charges based on current traffic volumes would fail to take into account the potential levels of traffic made possible by the new facilities.

A second difficulty lies in allocating total costs to reflect the relative use of air navigation facilities by the several classes of users. Available statistics indicate a steady growth in commercial airline use of these facilities; but these statistics pertain principally to the use of the airways under instrument conditions, and fail to measure airway use under visual flight conditions. The most reliable index of the relative use of airways under instrument flight plans, however, namely, the number of fix postings, shows that during 1946 between 75 and 80 per cent were accounted for by scheduled air carriers. By the end of the year, approximately 15 per cent of all fix postings were for military aircraft and 8 per cent for civilian aircraft other than scheduled air carriers. The preponderance of service to the airlines on instrument flights is likewise indicated by the fact that during a recent month more than 16,000 out of 20,000 instrument approaches were accounted for by these carriers. Approximately 75 per cent of airport traffic control tower operations in 1947, on the other hand, involved noncommercial civil aircraft, with approximately 16 per cent of total operations accounted for by commercial carriers and the remaining 9 per cent by military aircraft.

To what extent this division of responsibility for costs will be altered in the future as a result of stepped-up military aviation and the availability of instrument equipment to private aircraft is a matter of conjecture. At present, most private planes are not equipped for instrument flight. But it has been estimated that more than half the planes to be accommodated by the "target" program for air navigation facilities will be in this light plane category.

*Conclusion.* The provision of air navigation facilities is clearly a function in which the federal government has primary interest and capacity. The inadequacies of the navigation techniques employed to date have demonstrated that achievement of safety and regularity in air transportation depends on a complete revision of the federal airways system. Such a program will require annually about ten times the expenditure incurred for navigation facilities before the war.

Assuming that the recommended joint military-civilian all-weather navigation system is the most desirable method of eliminating present traffic hazards and congestion, the question of how this program should be financed remains. If air transportation is to develop on a sound basis, it must ultimately be able to pay its way. This means avoiding the difficulties which are bound to arise if the maintenance and improvement of essential facilities are to be dependent upon general fund appropriations reflecting political factors rather than transportation needs. Because the desirability and feasibility of this goal are governed in part by considerations relating to other phases of air transport development and to federal transportation policy in general, further discussion is reserved for Chapter VII.

## II. FEDERAL AIRPORT POLICY

A second activity of the federal government in the promotion of aviation has been the financing and construction of airport facilities. Current federal airport policy was established by the Federal Airport Act of 1946, which authorized the expenditure of 520 million dollars of federal funds for this purpose over a seven-year period, with annual appropriations not to exceed 100 million dollars.[18] These funds are distributed among the states in accordance with a prescribed formula and must be matched by the state or local sponsors. The program makes available for the first time substantial amounts of grant-in-aid money on a continuing and nonemergency basis, thus marking a new approach to federally sponsored airport development.

*Airports in the United States.* By the end of 1948 there were approximately 6,000 civil airports in the United States. Half of the total were commercial facilities and one third were owned by municipal governments. With respect to size, over 60 per cent of all airports were either in the smallest classification (Class I) or were too small to qualify even in this class. Five hundred sixty-eight airports were the larger facilities in Class IV or above.

The expansion of the airport network has been very rapid during the past several years, and there are now more than twice as many ports as there were before the war. The use of these facilities, measured by the number of landings and take-offs, has likewise shown substantial increase. At the principal airports throughout the country, total landing and take-off

[18] 60 Stat. 170, approved May 13, 1946.

operations in 1947 numbered 17.7 millions, compared to 12.7 millions in 1946.[19]

*Trend in federal airport activity.* Until 1933 civil airport construction activity was confined for the most part to local government sponsorship and private investment. Capital expenditures prior to that date were supplied 50 per cent from commercial and private sources and nearly 48 per cent by municipal governments. Federal financing was less than 1 per cent of the total. Under the Air Commerce Act of 1926, provision

CIVIL AIRPORTS IN THE UNITED STATES, DECEMBER 1, 1948[a]

| By Class of Airport[b] | Number | By Type of Ownership | Number |
|---|---|---|---|
| I and under | 4,007 | Commercial | 3,000 |
| II | 967 | Municipal | 2,044 |
| III | 467 | CAA Intermediate | 162 |
| IV and over | 568 | All Other, except military[c] | 803 |
| Total | 6,009 | Total | 6,009 |

[a] CAA Release 319, Dec. 29, 1948, p. 3.
[b] Class I airports are those having a usable landing strip length of 1,800 feet to 2,700 feet (unpaved); Class II, 2,700 feet to 3,700 feet; Class III, 3,700 feet to 4,700 feet (unpaved); Class IV, 4,500 feet to 5,500 feet (paved); Class V, 5,500 feet to 6,500 feet; and Class VI, over 6,500 feet. All figures at sea level.
[c] There were 396 military airports as of Feb. 1, 1949.

was made for federal establishment of civil airways and air navigation facilities, but airports were specifically excluded.

The rapid development of aviation in the thirties, however, combined with the financial difficulties of local governments, changed this picture abruptly. Federal participation in airport development increased rapidly as part of the work relief program, and from 1933 through 1940 over 70 per cent of all airport capital outlays were made through the Civil Works Administration, the Federal Emergency Relief Administration, and the Work Projects Administration. (See table p. 31.)

In the Civil Aeronautics Act of 1938, important changes were made in federal policy. Temporary work relief projects on airports were replaced by a specific program of federal aid. The

[19] Air Transport Association release dated Feb. 17, 1948.

act gave the Administrator of Civil Aeronautics power to plan airports and to acquire, construct, maintain, and operate them. An additional provision of the act was that further relief expenditure for this purpose would require the approval of the Administrator of Civil Aeronautics.[20]

Although the Civil Aeronautics Act of 1938 permitted the federal government to construct and maintain a national system

CAPITAL EXPENDITURES FOR CIVIL AIRPORTS IN THE UNITED STATES[a]

(Amounts in millions of dollars)

| Sources of Funds | Prior to 1933 | | 1933-40 | | 1941-44 | | Total | |
|---|---|---|---|---|---|---|---|---|
| | Amount | Per cent | Amount | Per cent | Amount | Per cent | Amount | Per cent |
| Federal | 1.1 | .7 | 194.8 | 71.4 | 544.8 | 89.6 | 740.7 | 72.1 |
| State | 2.9 | 2.0 | 4.1 | 1.5 | 3.1 | .5 | 10.2 | 1.0 |
| Municipal | 69.7 | 47.6 | 65.7 | 24.1 | 57.6 | 9.5 | 193.0 | 18.8 |
| Commercial and private | 72.6 | 49.7 | 8.2 | 3.0 | 2.5 | .4 | 83.3 | 8.1 |
| | 146.3 | 100.0 | 272.8 | 100.0 | 608.0 | 100.0 | 1,027.2 | 100.0 |

[a] L. L. Bollinger and Arthur H. Tully, Jr., *Personal Aircraft Business at Airports*, Division of Research, Harvard Gaduate School of Business Administration (1948), p. 225.

of airports, the act omitted any authorization for this purpose, and instead stipulated that a study of airport requirements be made. It was concluded in the *Airport Survey* which carried out this provision of the act that airports are a matter of national concern and a proper object of federal expenditure. The report recommended that a definite proportion of relief expenditures be made available for airports, that such projects be limited to work of exceptional national interest, and that the federal government should not contribute to the cost of maintenance except in the case of airports owned by the federal government for special purposes.[21]

The program recommended by this survey of the Civil Aeronautics Authority was acted upon by Congress in 1940, when it appropriated 40 million dollars for the construction, improvement, and repair of not to exceed 250 public airports. The projects were to be selected by the administrator with the approval of the secretaries of War, Navy, and Commerce, in accordance with national defense requirements. Thereafter,

[20] Secs. 302 and 303 of the act.
[21] *Airport Survey*, H. Doc. 245, 76 Cong. 1 sess.

with the outbreak of war, airport activity was almost exclusively under federal jurisdiction, and the airport program was expanded very rapidly to provide new and improved airports for military purposes. Part of this activity was carried out

STATE APPORTIONMENTS OF FEDERAL FUNDS FOR AIRPORTS
APPROPRIATED FOR THE FISCAL YEAR 1948[a]

| State | Appropriation | State | Appropriation |
|---|---|---|---|
| Texas | $ 1,468,673 | Massachusetts | $ 388,897 |
| New York | 1,302,752 | Nebraska | 379,916 |
| California | 1,128,036 | Kentucky | 376,887 |
| Pennsylvania | 979,468 | New Jersey | 372,468 |
| Illinois | 855,680 | Virginia | 369,804 |
| Michigan | 774,024 | Louisiana | 369,209 |
| Ohio | 727,424 | Florida | 368,454 |
| Montana | 562,919 | Wyoming | 364,559 |
| Missouri | 557,265 | Mississippi | 349,886 |
| Minnesota | 533,619 | Arkansas | 347,487 |
| Wisconsin | 491,667 | Utah | 343,655 |
| North Carolina | 480,103 | Idaho | 336,782 |
| New Mexico | 471,184 | South Dakota | 323,674 |
| Georgia | 464,925 | North Dakota | 301,177 |
| Colorado | 458,866 | South Carolina | 266,453 |
| Arizona | 441,255 | West Virginia | 242,008 |
| Oklahoma | 438,512 | Maryland | 193,627 |
| Kansas | 437,685 | Maine | 190,488 |
| Oregon | 430,742 | Connecticut | 160,774 |
| Alabama | 417,188 | New Hampshire | 73,270 |
| Indiana | 411,358 | Vermont | 63,414 |
| Iowa | 407,285 | Rhode Island | 63,230 |
| Nevada | 397,294 | District of Columbia | 55,009 |
| Washington | 391,288 | Delaware | 30,464 |
| Tennessee | 389,186 | | |
| | | Total | $21,750,000 |

[a] CAA, *3rd Annual Report of the Federal Airport Act* (1948), App. A, p. 1.

directly by the War and Navy Departments, and part by the CAA under the "Development of Landing Areas for National Defense" program. This program provided 400 million dollars to be spent by CAA specifically for Army-Navy requirements.[22]

[22] It has been estimated that altogether 3.2 billion dollars was spent for air-

*The 1946 Federal Airport Act.* The present program for airport development, established by the Federal Airport Act of 1946, authorizes the expenditure of 500 million dollars of federal money for airport development in the United States.[23] After deduction of administrative expenditures, 75 per cent of the remainder is divided among the states on the basis of population and area. (See table p. 32.) The other 25 per cent is placed in a discretionary fund which can be used without regard to any allocation formula. The federal share of construction costs, exclusive of land acquisition, is 50 per cent for the smaller airports (Class III and under); but in states where 5 per cent or more of the total area is federal land, the federal share may be as high as 75 per cent. With respect to the larger airports, federal matching is 50 per cent for the first 5 million dollars of construction cost, but declines to 20 per cent for that portion of the total cost which exceeds 11 million dollars.[24] Any public agency, or two or more agencies jointly, may submit a request or application for federal aid except that when the law of the state prohibits local agencies from making such requests direct to the federal government, the state may act on behalf of the sponsor.

*The National Airport Plan.* Federal aid airport activity prior to the passage of the Federal Airport Act of 1946 developed haphazardly as a result of the size and urgency of work-relief programs and the emergency requirements of the military. These airport activities, as well as local airport programs, led to a considerable degree of planless development. Facilities were so located and of such size and design that much of the investment was ultimately lost. According to one CAA witness testifying before a congressional committee: "We found that

---

ports during the war, and that approximately 700 of these ports have since been released to civilian use or abandoned. Stanley L. Colbert, "Airports as Base of Air Power," *Aviation Week*, Feb. 23, 1948.

[23] An additional 20 million dollars was authorized for Alaska, Hawaii, and Puerto Rico.

[24] Department of Commerce, CAA, *Regulations for Administering Federal Airport Act*, July 1, 1948, p. 11. Federal share in the cost of land acquisition is limited to 25 per cent for all classes of airports.

about 60 per cent of the new airports under the Civil Works Administration went back to hay or cotton."[25]

This situation is guarded against under the Federal Airport Act. An airport project, to be eligible for federal aid, must now be included in the current National Airport Plan. The Civil Aeronautics Administrator is responsible for the preparation and annual revision of this national plan for the development of public airports in the United States and its territories. The

THE 1949 AIRPORT PLAN AND ESTIMATED COST[a]

(Dollar figures are in millions)

| Class of Airports | Number of Airports | Millions of Dollars | | |
| --- | --- | --- | --- | --- |
| | | Federal Share | Sponsor Share | Total Cost |
| Class I .............. | 2,358 | $ 76.8 | $ 85.6 | $ 162.4 |
| Class II ............. | 1,048 | 81.0 | 85.4 | 166.4 |
| Class III ........... | 608 | 105.7 | 107.0 | 212.7 |
| Class IV and up ..... | 567 | 239.6 | 320.7 | 560.3 |
| Seaplane Bases ...... | 331 | 6.6 | 5.0 | 11.6 |
| Heliports ........... | 65 | .9 | 1.0 | 1.9 |
| Total ........... | 4,977 | $510.6 | $604.7 | $1,115.3 |

[a] Department of Commerce, CAA, National Airport Plan for 1949, p. 4.

purpose is to provide a comprehensive guide to the development of new airports and the improvement of existing airports, based on study of the country's aeronautical needs as estimated for the following three years.[26] Changes in the plan from year to year reflect current appraisal of the adequacy of the airports serving the nation and the changing requirements for safe and efficient air transportation.

The 1949 plan includes 4,977 airports. Of this number, 2,794 are new airports or locations where the choice of developing a new airport or improving an existing facility is pending, and

[25] Federal Aid for Public Airports, Hearings on S. 2 and S. 34 before a Subcommittee of the Senate Committee on Commerce, 79 Cong. 1 sess., March 1945, p. 59.

[26] Only public airports are included in the plan, but in determining the needs of a community the existence of an adequate nonpublic airport precludes designation of a public airport for that locality.

2,183 are existing airports which require improvement. Estimated cost of the program is $1,115,300,000 of which approximately 45 per cent would be provided by the federal government and 55 per cent by the sponsors.

Types of facilities making up the plan include 567 Class IV or larger airports; 4,014 smaller airports (Classes I, II, III); 331 seaplane bases; and 65 heliports. Approximately 50 per cent of the total estimated cost is for the large airports, 49 per cent is for smaller airports, and the remaining 1 per cent for seaplane bases and heliports. (See table p. 34.)

*The current airport program.* Using the airport plan as a basis, the actual program of airport development is determined annually according to the availability of federal appropriations. Appropriations of $77,500,000 were made for the fiscal year 1947-48, and $40,000,000 for 1949. The list of airport projects making up the program for a given year is determined in consultation with state and local officials; and congressional authority is required before projects on Class IV or larger airports are eligible for federal funds.[27]

The airport program, as of the end of 1948, called for the construction or improvement of 1,021 airports in the United States.[28] The estimated cost to the federal government was 104 million dollars, while state and local sponsors were to provide an additional 112 million dollars. Of the total program expenditure of 216 million dollars, 12 per cent was for land, 13 per cent for buildings, and 75 per cent for airport construction.[29] Projects in the continental United States included 769 small airports and 252 airports of Class IV and larger, but approximately three fifths of federal expenditure was allocated to the smaller number of larger airports. (See table p. 36.)

*User payments for airports.* The number of airports has more than doubled since prewar years, and the demand for facilities

---

[27] A list of such projects must be submitted yearly to the Congress for approval. See *Development and Improvement of Certain Airports,* S. Doc. 151, 80 Cong. 2 sess.

[28] An additional 13 airports in the program were in United States territorial possessions.

[29] Department of Commerce, CAA, *National Airport Plan for 1949,* p. 10.

has continued to increase in terms of planes and volume of traffic. During the expansion there has been a pronounced trend toward public ownership. Private and commercial facilities still outnumber those which are government owned, but the major expenditures involve public airports of the large terminal type designed primarily to meet the needs of commercial airlines.

It has been noted that the 1948 airport program, reflecting the foreseeable needs of only three years, includes a billion

FEDERAL-AID AIRPORT PROGRAM AS OF DECEMBER 31, 1948[a]

| Class of Airports | Number of Airports | Amount |
|---|---|---|
| Class I | 319 | $ 7,358,149 |
| Class II | 235 | 11,079,138 |
| Class III | 215 | 23,604,687 |
| Class IV and larger | 252 | 61,496,130 |
| Total | 1,021 | $103,538,104 |

[a] Department of Commerce, CAA, *National Airport Plan for 1949*, p. 10. This table includes domestic airports only.

dollars of airport construction. The question of how these funds are to be obtained is of urgent and growing importance. A sound financial basis for airport development will permit adequate facilities yet forestall imprudent expansion and ultimate burdens on air transportation. Some indication is needed, therefore, as to the degree to which government, and the federal government in particular, should provide general tax support for this purpose. Or, conversely, it must be determined whether, or to what extent, the users of the airports should be expected to pay the bill.

Before the war the Board of Investigation and Research estimated the annual cost of all publicly owned airports at 21.6 million dollars. Based on the relative use made of the facilities, 22 per cent of airport costs, or 4.7 million dollars, was assigned to scheduled air carriers. Subtracting from this allocated cost $893,000 paid by the scheduled carriers in landing fees and other airport charges, the difference between the contributions of the air carriers and the costs assigned to them was estimated at 3.8 million dollars for the year.[30] The Board allocated 12.5 million dollars of annual airport costs to non-scheduled flying, reflecting the much greater frequency of landings and take-offs by this class of user. Annual cost assigned to government, principally for military use of the airports, was 4.5 million dollars.

At the time of the Board's study a trend toward greater self-support with respect to airport facilities was already indicated. In 1938 the ratio of income to maintenance and operating expenses for all publicly owned airports was 54 per cent, and this ratio had increased to 77 per cent by 1940.[31] The Board of Investigation and Research took the position that users should, insofar as possible, pay the cost of airports other than those specifically required for national defense. At the same time it was maintained that as long as commercial carriers are dependent on public aid through air-mail payments, it would be doubtful public policy to charge them the full cost of airport facilities. This would merely shift the burden of financing airports to the postal service. It was concluded, however, that the gradual adoption of user charges would contribute to the sound development of air transportation, and the suggestion was made that taxes on aviation fuel might ultimately become an important source of revenue for financing an integrated airway and airport system.

Conditions with respect to airport costs and use have changed appreciably since 1940, and therefore the conclusions drawn by the Board of Investigation and Research require reconsideration. In a more recent study by the Harvard Business School the annual cost of terminal airports in 1946 was estimated at 58 million dollars; and since the total investment in these facilities was expected to pass the two-billion dollar mark "within a comparatively few years," this indicated a rise in annual cost to 200 millions.[32]

[30] H. Doc. 159, 79 Cong. 1 sess., p. 505.
[31] These ratios do not include capital costs.
[32] L. L. Bollinger, Alan Passen, R. E. McElfresh, *Terminal Airport Financing and Management* (1946), p. 3.

It was concluded, however, that despite these figures "the majority of terminal type airports can be made self-supporting within a comparatively few years without an undue burden on aviation, provided that a sound financial plan is established and all revenue sources, including terminal building concessions, are aggressively developed."[33] At the time of this study, however, such a goal appeared unattainable without radical change in management policies. Criticism was leveled not simply at government administration, but at the failure of private interests and the airlines to assume adequate responsibility for accomplishing the desired objective of establishing and maintaining a self-supporting airport system paid for by users in proportion to their requirements.

It was recommended by the Harvard study that after deductions from total airport costs in the form of hangar and terminal building rentals, payments by the several classes of users should meet the balance of costs. For commercial carriers the number of landings, adjusted for weight of aircraft, has been found to be a satisfactory index for allocating airport costs to transport aircraft. Private flying would pay through a percentage-of-gross charge on the aircraft service operator; and reimbursement for military use would be made to the airport enterprise out of the military budget.[34]

Examination of 30 terminal type airports having adequate financial records revealed only one which was covering total costs, including interest and depreciation. Sixteen airports, however, were covering all out-of-pocket expenses despite wartime restrictions on traffic. It was concluded that with good management and a fair rate structure practically all terminal airports could have been covering out-of-pocket expenses, and that by the early 1950's the majority should be covering capital costs as well.

In view of the fact that most public airports are under state

[33] The same, p. 4. See also Department of Commerce, CAA, *Non-aviation Revenue Producing Functions for Airports*, November 1947.

[34] Bollinger, Passen, McElfresh, *Terminal Airport Financing and Management*, pp. 8-9.

or municipal ownership, it appears that federal promotion of this desirable trend toward self-sufficiency could be accomplished in only two ways: either by eliminating the federal-aid program altogether, or by using this device to stimulate state and local action in the adoption of revenue-producing measures. The choice between these alternatives rests on whether or not there are convincing reasons for federal participation in the development of airports.

One argument frequently cited in support of a federal-aid program for airport development is that the federal government has spent and is spending large sums of money for other forms of transportation. For example, an assistant secretary of commerce, testifying in favor of federal aid for airports, pointed out that: "Since 1822 the Government has aided in the improvement of rivers and harbors—Federal expenditures in this field now totaling some $3,000,000,000."[35] In view of the precarious grounds on which some federal expenditure programs rest, however, justification on this basis is both unconvincing and hazardous.

Other reasons given for the airport program have been equally questionable. It has been stated that ". . . Federal-aid highway development adopted by the Congress at the close of the last World War laid the foundation for the development of our great automobile industry,"[36] and therefore that an airport program would have similar effect on the market for aircraft. Actually, however, automobiles created the demand for roads, and at the time of the passage of the first federal-aid act for highways there were already 3.5 million motor vehicles in operation. The further contention that widespread acceptance of the airplane by the private flyer "cannot be accomplished without a great improvement in our national system of airports"[37] is also open to question, for the future of the private plane is more likely to lie in its emancipation from airport facilities than

[35] *Federal Aid For Public Airports*, Hearings before Subcommittee on Aviation of the Senate Committee on Commerce on S. 2 and S. 34, 79 Cong. 1 sess., March 1945, p. 44.
[36] The same, p. 31.
[37] The same, p. 32.

its dependence on them. At least it can well be argued that increased airport development could hardly compensate for the current shortcomings of light plane design.

Nevertheless, the desirability of federal participation in airport development at this time is not difficult to establish, and the attempt to draw analogies with other transport media to establish such justification seems beside the point. The basic objective of the federal airport program is to bring about, through a grant-in-aid program, "the establishment of an integrated Nation-wide system of public airports adequate to anticipate and meet the needs of civil aeronautics. . . ."[38] Safety alone requires that a central agency establish minimum requirements and uniform standards for the country as a whole, and that airports be properly planned as to size and location, runway length, approaches, lighting, and radio facilities. Moreover, the airport plan must be co-ordinated with the federal airways. The achievement of greater utility for air transportation also calls for a nationwide development of facilities, since a community which has no airport deprives not only itself but other communities desiring access to it. No matter how adequately a city might meet its airport requirements, its own facilities would be of little use were there no other comparably adequate airports in other cities. Finally, the joint use of airport facilities by civil and military aircraft and the stand-by value of the larger airports for military purposes make clear the interest of the federal government in developing a national system.

The question seems not to be whether the federal government has a legitimate role to perform in the development of airports, but rather what that role should be and to what ultimate goal federal action should be directed. The present federal-aid program, involving an average of approximately 70 million dollars annually, is a relatively inexpensive program if it can achieve such desirable national goals as a planned development of facilities and the adoption of uniform standards. The encourage-

[38] *Federal-Aid Airport Act, and Amendments Relating to Air-Navigation Facilities*, H. Rept. 844, 79 Cong. 1 sess. (1945), p. 2.

ment of state planning in this field and the extension of user support are likewise desirable objectives which might be achieved through federal participation.

Neglect of the airport problem has been characteristic of most state administrations, and much improvement is necessary if the states are to assume their proper role in aviation development. The national airport program was originally developed without adequate consultation between federal and state governments, and in many cases state aviation authorities were in substantial disagreement with the CAA.[39] Yet this situation can be explained by the fact that when the airport plan was requested by the Congress, a majority of states had no airport plans or aeronautical agencies in a position to prepare them. This situation in turn was the result of the rapid transition from predominantly local and private airport construction to federal emergency undertakings, which caused state governments to be almost completely by-passed with respect to airport work.

At the present time, however, the states are "catching up" with their responsibilities in this field. All but two states now have an aeronautics body of some type; and in 33 states these organizations have the authority to construct, operate, and maintain airports. State approval of projects included in the federal-aid airport program is required in 23 states, although state supervision of construction is mandatory in only seven states.[40] With regard to the method of channeling federal funds, it has been previously noted that the federal law provides for direct federal contact with local governments when this is not prohibited by state law. This provision creates large numbers of contacts with the federal government rather than limiting negotiations to the 48 states.[41] By mid-1948, however,

[39] Letters received from state aeronautics authorities addressed to the Council of State Governments in 1945 were almost unanimous in their contention that the so-called National Airport Plan was sketchy and hastily contrived, as well as unrealistic and lacking in basic supporting data. Department of Commerce, CAA, *Legislative History of the Federal Airport Act* (1948), Vol. 1, pp. 533-37.

[40] State supervision may be provided on a voluntary basis in 9 other states; and 29 states offer technical assistance to local governments.

[41] Sec. 9 (b) of the Federal Airport Act states that: "Nothing in this Act shall

21 states required that projects be channeled through state agencies, and such arrangements were voluntary in 17 states.[42] It may be concluded, therefore, that the trend is now in the direction of the states assuming responsibility for airport planning, in conformity with federal standards, similar to the pattern followed in the case of federal aid for highways.

A further question relates to the types of airport facilities which should properly be included in a federal-aid program. The desirability of concentrating federal financial aid on a designated system of facilities seems indicated in the case of airports, as it has been proved in the case of highways. Federal action should be specifically limited to those facilities serving predominantly national interests, such as interstate commerce and national defense. In these terms it is doubtful that small airports of Class I and under warrant federal planning and finance; and the inclusion of these facilities in the federal-aid program hinders the objective of completing the most urgent national requirements first. For example, many airline routes now certificated by the federal government for commercial service are not in operation because adequate airport facilities are lacking. The need for supplying these requirements is sufficiently compelling to warrant a concentration of federal attention.

The importance of concentrating federal aid on a limited system of airports will be highlighted when the new omnidirectional ranges are in operation, since these facilities will place every community on the "airway" system. Realization of air services will then depend, insofar as basic physical facilities are concerned, only on the provision of airports. Under these circumstances the demand for airports will undoubtedly increase to the point where greater selectivity, based on the most

authorize the submission of a project application by any municipality or other public agency which is subject to the law of any State if the submission of such project application . . . is prohibited by the law of such State."

[42] The preceding state statistics were compiled by the Civil Aeronautics Administration, Office of the General Counsel, *Tabulation of State Legislation Pertaining to the Regulation and Enforcement of Civil Aviation*, June 1, 1948.

important national interests, will be an urgent need in formulating the national airport plan.

*Conclusion.* Federal aid should be limited to an eligible system of airports designated as of primary national interest, so that airport plans may be co-ordinated insofar as possible with the route pattern prescribed by federal authority for commercial carriers, and in order that the most urgent airport needs may be met first. Because of the uncertainty of personal aircraft design in the future, it appears doubtful that the federal government should concern itself with the financing of small airports used by private planes. If federal policy should indicate the desirability of promoting private flying, much more productive investment might be found in personal plane research, with the objective of hastening the introduction of changes in aircraft design which may reduce airport requirements for private flying. Finally, in view of the economic desirability of airport self-support through landing fees, rentals, and nonaviation enterprises, the trend in that direction should be encouraged by the federal government to the extent possible; and the ultimate goal must be the withdrawal of general tax support, except to the extent that military aircraft operations or other national defense requirements dictate.

# CHAPTER III

## AIR-MAIL PAYMENTS

One of the most important federal aids to aviation development has been the payments made for carrying the mail. In the early years of aviation these payments were the principal method of subsidizing air carrier operations, and the amounts involved represented a substantial part of the total revenues realized by the carriers. More recently, with rapid growth of passenger and other nonmail traffic, the relative importance of air-mail payments to the principal airlines has decreased sharply. For feeder-lines and most international trunk-line carriers, however, these payments continue to be a major source of revenue; and they still constitute a very important factor in the earning position of the domestic airlines.[1]

### I. DESCRIPTION OF AIR-MAIL PAYMENTS

Insofar as air-mail payments supply funds to the carriers in excess of the cost of providing the service, these payments are similar in nature to other federal promotional activities such as the provision of airways and airports. At the present time there are no adequate data identifying the precise amount of air-mail payments which are in the nature of a subsidy. However, the significant fact is that the federal government at present is dedicated to a subsidy policy, as prescribed by the Civil Aeronautics Act of 1938. The act specifies that mail payments shall provide whatever may be needed, together with revenues from other sources, to enable the carriers to maintain and develop adequate service. Under the act, air-mail carriers are compensated either on the basis of ton-miles or pound-miles of service rendered (these are the so-called "service rate" carriers), or they are paid on the basis of plane-miles operated, without reference to volume of service rendered. The latter are

[1] Air-mail payments are further discussed from the standpoint of air carrier regulation in Pt. 2.

44

the so-called "need" carriers. The distinction made is that "a compensatory or service rate should be paid those carriers normally in a sound condition, as payment for service rendered," whereas in the case of undeveloped traffic routes where self-support is impossible, "a need rate is awarded by the

AIR-MAIL PAYMENTS TO AIR CARRIERS, 1926-49[a]

(In thousands of dollars)

| Fiscal Year Ending June 30 | Domestic Carriers | International Carriers | Total |
|---|---|---|---|
| 1926 .................. | 90 | [b] | 90 |
| 1927 .................. | 1,363 | [b] | 1,363 |
| 1928 .................. | 4,043 | 148 | 4,191 |
| 1929 .................. | 11,169 | 1,151 | 12,320 |
| 1930 .................. | 14,618 | 4,300 | 18,918 |
| 1931 .................. | 16,944 | 6,565 | 23,509 |
| 1932 .................. | 19,938 | 6,963 | 26,901 |
| 1933 .................. | 19,400 | 6,984 | 26,384 |
| 1934 .................. | 11,738 | 6,942 | 18,680 |
| 1935 .................. | 8,838 | 6,829 | 15,667 |
| 1936 .................. | 12,179 | 6,620 | 18,799 |
| 1937 .................. | 13,165 | 7,878 | 21,043 |
| 1938 .................. | 14,740 | 8,582 | 23,322 |
| 1939 .................. | 17,020 | 9,327 | 26,347 |
| 1940 .................. | 19,426 | 12,432 | 31,858 |
| 1941 .................. | 20,687 | 15,629 | 36,316 |
| 1942 .................. | 23,473 | 14,298 | 37,771 |
| 1943 .................. | 23,308 | 5,563 | 28,871 |
| 1944 .................. | 28,401 | 3,231 | 31,632 |
| 1945 .................. | 35,536 | 6,022 | 41,558 |
| 1946 .................. | 26,788 | 10,025[c] | 36,813 |
| 1947 .................. | 21,736 | 27,262[c] | 48,998 |
| 1948[d] .................. | 47,000 | 40,500 | 87,500 |
| 1949[d] .................. | 47,401 | 29,925 | 77,326 |
| Total .............. | 459,001 | 237,176 | 696,177 |

[a] Data for 1926-31 from "Air Transport Facts and Figures," *Air Transport*, February 1948, p. 12; 1932-48 from "Air Transport Fact and Figures," *Aviation Week*, Mar. 21, 1949; 1949 from Air Payments Section, Post Office Department.
[b] Not available.
[c] Reflects United States mail compensation for all carriers, in certain instances based on temporary mail rates prescribed by the Civil Aeronautics Board which were applicable at the time of preparation of this statement.
[d] Preliminary.

Civil Aeronautics Board to aid in bridging the financial gap between the compensatory rate and sufficient funds for operating at a reasonable profit. . . ."[2]

Payments thus far made to domestic and international air carriers for the transportation of mail amount to an estimated 700 million dollars. (See table p. 45.) Payments to domestic carriers have accounted for two thirds of this total. Annual payments have increased from an average of approximately 15 million dollars in the period from 1930 to 1940, to an estimated 47 million dollars in 1949. Payments for mail transportation on international routes averaged approximately 7 million dollars per year in the period 1930-40, but 40 millions were appropriated in 1948.

## II. DEVELOPMENT OF AIR-MAIL SERVICE

Transportation of mail by air was at first conducted directly by the Post Office Department. These operations, which continued from 1918 to 1927, were replaced by a policy of contracting with private operators for the carrying of air mail.[3] The period since that time has been one of frequent changes in air-mail compensation, postage rates, and methods of operation.[4] For example, the method of compensating the airlines was changed from the allocation of a fixed proportion of postal revenues to payment in accordance with the weight of the mail carried; and the Post Office Department established a flat air-mail postage rate in place of the complex route and zone system previously in effect. A further amendment of the Air Mail Act provided for the issuance by the Postmaster General of route certificates instead of contracts to those air-mail carriers who had satisfactorily operated their routes for a minimum of two years.

As both the government and the operators experienced

[2] "Public Aid to Air Transportation," *National Transportation Inquiry*, H. Rept. 1612, 80 Cong. 2 sess. (1948), p. 4.
[3] The first Air Mail Act, known as the Kelly Act, provided for the contract system under the jurisdiction of the Postmaster General. 43 Stat. 805.
[4] Board of Investigation and Research, *Public Aids to Domestic Transportation*, H. Doc. 159, 79 Cong. 1 sess. (1944), pp. 428-37.

losses from air-mail service during the first five years of contract operations, the Watres Act, passed in 1930, amended the Air Mail Act of 1925 to provide that the Postmaster General contract with the lowest responsible bidder at rates determined on a space-mile basis, regardless of whether or not any mail was actually carried.[5] All air-mail carriers were required to provide combination passenger and mail services, so that under the space-mile method of payment, a substantial part of the added expenses of passenger service was covered by air-mail compensation.

Following the cancellation of domestic air-mail contracts in 1934 on grounds of "fraud and collusion," and after three months of Army air-mail operations, a new air-mail act was passed which provided that contracts be issued by the Postmaster General for an initial period of not more than one year, with rates prescribed on a plane-mile basis.[6] A uniform postage rate was fixed by Congress and discretion in this matter was withdrawn from the Postmaster General. The Postmaster General, however, retained his authority to designate routes, award contracts, and enforce mail regulations. Regulation of air-mail rates of compensation was placed under the Interstate Commerce Commission. and certain duties pertaining mainly to matters of safety were delegated to the Secretary of Commerce.

This division of authority among the Post Office Department, Department of Commerce, and Interstate Commerce Commission led to difficulties which created a demand for new legislation. The result was the Civil Aeronautics Act of 1938. The Civil Aeronautics Board was given the authority to determine and prescribe the rates of compensation to be paid the carriers. In setting the rates the Board was directed to take into consideration:

. . . the need of each such air carrier for compensation for the transportation of mail sufficient to insure the performance of such service, and, together with all other revenue of the air carrier, to

[5] 46 Stat. 259.
[6] 48 Stat. 933.

enable such air carrier under honest, economical, and efficient management, to maintain and continue the development of air transportation to the extent and of the character and quality required for the commerce of the United States, the Postal Service, and the national defense.[7]

Contract operation of air-mail service was abolished, and any carrier authorized by its certificate to carry mail is now required to do so whenever directed by the Postmaster General. The Post Office Department also promulgates orders for the safe and expeditious transportation of the mail, requires changes in schedules, and requests issuance of certificates to provide additional service. The Post Office Department has supervision of all domestic and foreign air-mail routes flying the American flag, and is responsible for research and analysis with respect to proposed new air services, and for the maintenance, development, improvement, and expansion of transportation by air mail.

### III. CURRENT TRENDS

Recent increases in mail payments, previously noted, reflect for the most part the sharp increase in mail carried, and have occurred despite a substantial decline in the rates of payment to the carriers over a period of years. Between 1936 and 1948, ton-miles of mail carried by domestic airlines increased from 5.7 millions to 37.5 millions. Payments to the carriers for this service dropped from a rate of $1.09 per plane-mile in 1929 to an estimated 14 cents in 1948. International air mail quadrupled in volume between 1945 and 1947; and the change in rates paid to international carriers is indicated by the reduction in mail pay from $1.90 per plane-mile in 1941 to 17 cents in 1944 and 44 cents in 1948.

The importance of air-mail payments to the airlines has declined rapidly as passenger traffic has developed. In 1938 air-mail payments to all domestic carriers were 37 per cent of total revenues. In 1948 mail payments were 11.6 per cent of the total. (See table p. 49.) Five of the 16 trunk carriers received less than 15 per cent of their revenues from air-mail payments dur-

[7] *Civil Aeronautics Act of 1938*, 52 Stat. 998, sec. 406 (b).

ing 1948. (See table p. 50.) Several carriers, however, were much more dependent on air-mail payments. Mail payments to international carriers during 1948 amounted to approximately 24 per cent of total revenues. The international carriers were therefore more than twice as dependent on air-mail payments as were the domestic carriers. And among the feeder lines, the percentage of revenue derived from air mail represented more than half the total, with the exception of one carrier. (See table and footnote p. 50.)

SOURCE OF DOMESTIC AIR CARRIER REVENUES, 1938-48[a]

| Year | Total Revenues (In millions of dollars) | Per cent of Total Provided By | | |
|------|------|------|------|------|
| | | Passenger | Mail | Express and Freight |
| 1938 ........ 42.9 | | 57.9 | 37.0 | 3.0 |
| 1939 ........ 55.9 | | 62.3 | 33.0 | 2.9 |
| 1940 ........ 76.9 | | 69.4 | 26.1 | 2.7 |
| 1941 ........ 97.3 | | 71.7 | 23.3 | 3.0 |
| 1942 ........108.2 | | 69.1 | 21.7 | 6.4 |
| 1943 ........123.1 | | 71.0 | 19.7 | 6.8 |
| 1944 ........160.9 | | 72.3 | 20.7 | 5.2 |
| 1945 ........214.7 | | 77.5 | 15.7 | 5.0 |
| 1946 ........316.2 | | 87.2 | 6.6 | 4.3 |
| 1947 ........364.8 | | 84.6 | 8.1 | 5.3 |
| 1948 (est.) ....416.5 | | 80.8 | 11.6 | 5.8 |

[a] "Air Transport Facts and Figures," *Aviation Week*, Mar. 21, 1949. The percentages do not total 100 due to omission from table of certain miscellaneous revenues.

The yield to the carriers from air-mail payments per ton-mile of mail carried also indicates the varying importance of this source of revenue to the several airlines. During 1948, for example, American received 57 cents per ton-mile and Eastern 68 cents, while $12.90 per ton-mile was paid to Colonial, and $16.97 to Northeast. Among the feeder lines, payments ranged from $83.88 for Florida to $13.09 for Los Angeles. In international operations mail pay yield per ton-mile of mail carried ranged from a low of 67 cents for Eastern to $172.21 for Chicago and Southern.[8]

[8] See App. A, Table 7.

MAIL PAY AS PERCENTAGE OF TOTAL OPERATING REVENUES
SCHEDULED DOMESTIC CARRIERS[a]

| Trunk Lines | 1938 | 1948 |
|---|---|---|
| American | 29.6 | 5.4 |
| Braniff | 49.8 | 15.4 |
| Chicago and Southern | 54.8 | 22.4 |
| Colonial | 60.7 | 29.4 |
| Continental | 78.5 | 27.9 |
| Delta | 50.3 | 22.7 |
| Eastern | 26.7 | 4.5 |
| Inland | 79.0 | 28.7 |
| Mid-Continent | 72.1 | 17.5 |
| National | 70.9 | 19.6 |
| Northeast | 60.3 | 27.4 |
| Northwest | 57.8 | 14.7 |
| PCA (now Capital) | 32.7 | 21.0 |
| Transcontinental & Western | 36.0 | 12.6 |
| United | 36.6 | 11.5 |
| Western | 59.3 | 18.1 |

[a] 1938 data from *Report on Air Mail Subsidy*, H. Rept. 1958, 80 Cong. 2 sess., May 13, 1948, p. 41. 1948 data from CAB *Recurrent Report of Financial Data*, 4th quarter, 1948.

MAIL PAY AS PERCENTAGE OF TOTAL OPERATING REVENUES
FEEDER LINES[a]

| Carrier | 1948 |
|---|---|
| All American | 98.6 |
| Challenger | 73.0 |
| Empire | 81.9 |
| Florida | 86.4 |
| Los Angeles | 100.0 |
| Monarch | 72.3 |
| Pioneer | 51.9 |
| Southwest | 59.3 |
| Trans-Texas | 82.5 |
| West Coast | 51.0 |

[a] CAB *Recurrent Report of Financial Data*, 4th quarter, 1948. Ratios for more recently inaugurated feeder services for which less than 12 months' experience is available: Wisconsin Central, 82.7; Piedmont, 62.0; Robinson, 49.7.

#### IV. THE SUBSIDY QUESTION

Several questions arise concerning the present program of air-mail compensation. First, to what extent is the Post Office Department incurring deficits because of the financial requirements of air-mail service? Second, to what extent are the air carriers being paid for mail service in excess of what a strict allocation of airline costs warrant? And third, is it necessary or desirable for the government to provide operating subsidies for the airlines?

Regarding the first question as to the impact of air-mail payments on the Post Office Department, the air-mail profit or loss position of the Department is determined by balancing the revenues from air-mail postage against the total cost of providing the service. Total cost includes payments to the air lines, direct costs incurred by the Department in handling air mail, plus a fair allocation of general Department overhead. During the period 1930 through 1942, deficits on domestic air-mail carriage were incurred each year by the Post Office, ranging from nearly 18 million dollars in 1932 to 3 millions in 1942. (See table p. 52.) This period was followed by four years of substantial surplus revenues, after which there was a resumption of annual losses. The total deficit for the nineteen-year period 1930-48 was just over 67 million dollars, and there were record losses of 19 million dollars in 1947, and over 27 millions in 1948.[9] The 1949 appropriation bill for the Post Office Department contained $58,583,000 for payment of air-mail costs and subsidy to commercial airlines; and, according to the Senate Committee on Appropriations: "The subsidy represents the major portion of this amount, and has no direct relationship to the cost of air-mail transportation. Increasing competitive air transportation will unquestionably result in further increasing this subsidy payment."[10]

The air-mail deficits of the Post Office Department can be the result either of payments to the airlines in excess of the

[9] H. Rept. 1612, 80 Cong. 2 sess., p. 5.
[10] *Treasury and Post Office Departments Appropriation Bill, Fiscal Year 1949,* S. Rept. 1389, 80 Cong. 2 sess., p. 5.

cost of carrying the mail, of postal rates too low to cover total costs, or of both. With regard to the relation of air carrier costs and air-mail payments, it was concluded both by the Federal Coordinator of Transportation and by the Board of Investi-

REVENUES AND EXPENSES OF POST OFFICE DEPARTMENT
FOR DOMESTIC AIR-MAIL SERVICE, 1930-48[a]
(In millions of dollars)

| Fiscal Year | Payments to Airlines | Total Air-Mail Expenditures[b] | Air-Mail Revenue | Post Office Air-Mail Deficit |
|---|---|---|---|---|
| 1930 | 14.6 | 15.2 | 5.3 | 9.9 |
| 1931 | 16.9 | 17.6 | 6.2 | 11.4 |
| 1932 | 19.9 | 23.8 | 6.0 | 17.8 |
| 1933 | 19.4 | 23.0 | 6.1 | 16.9 |
| 1934 | 11.7 | 15.3 | 5.7 | 9.6 |
| 1935 | 8.8 | 12.6 | 6.6 | 6.0 |
| 1936 | 12.2 | 16.9 | 9.7 | 7.2 |
| 1937 | 13.2 | 19.2 | 12.4 | 6.7 |
| 1938 | 14.7 | 21.8 | 15.3 | 6.5 |
| 1939 | 17.0 | 25.1 | 16.3 | 8.7 |
| 1940 | 19.4 | 28.0 | 19.1 | 8.9 |
| 1941 | 20.7 | 30.9 | 23.9 | 7.0 |
| 1942 | 23.5 | 36.5 | 33.4 | 3.1 |
| 1943 | 23.3 | 44.5 | 62.8 | 18.4[c] |
| 1944 | 28.4 | 49.9 | 79.4 | 29.5[c] |
| 1945 | 35.5 | 49.9 | 81.2 | 31.3[c] |
| 1946 | 26.8 | 49.0 | 68.4 | 19.4[c] |
| 1947 | 21.7 | 73.3 | 54.4 | 19.0 |
| 1948 | 47.0 | 80.7 | 53.6 | 27.1 |
| Total | 394.7 | 633.1 | 565.9 | 67.2 |

[a] "Public Aid to Air Transportation," National Transportation Inquiry, H. Rept. 1612, 80 Cong. 2 sess. (1948), p. 5. 1947-48 data from "Air Transport Facts and Figures," Aviation Week, Mar. 21, 1949.

[b] Includes Post Office costs as estimated in annual Post Office Department Cost and Ascertainment Reports.

[c] Profit.

gation and Research, that substantial subsidies were involved during the period 1931-41. Total aid, in excess of payments for service rendered, was estimated at 106 million dollars during that eleven-year period for domestic air-mail transportation.[11]

[11] H. Doc. 159, 79 Cong. 1 sess., p. 452. Also Federal Coordinator of Transportation, Public Aids to Transportation (1940), Vol. 1, pp. 141, 146.

In these studies it was indicated that for the entire period under investigation approximately 62 per cent of air-mail payments to domestic carriers had been in the nature of a subsidy. This percentage ranged between 65 and 75 per cent in the immediate prewar period. (See table below.)

DOMESTIC AIR-MAIL SUBSIDIES, 1931-41[a]

(Dollar figures are in millions)

| Fiscal Year | Excess of Air-Mail Payments Over Allocated Costs and Allowance for Return | |
|---|---|---|
| | Amount | Per cent |
| 1931 | $  5.2 | 30.8 |
| 1932 | 10.8 | 54.3 |
| 1933 | 13.6 | 70.1 |
| 1934 | 6.0 | 60.0 |
| 1935 | 3.6 | 42.9 |
| 1936 | 8.2 | 66.7 |
| 1937 | 8.2 | 64.1 |
| 1938 | 9.7 | 66.0 |
| 1939 | 11.9 | 69.6 |
| 1940 | 14.5 | 74.4 |
| 1941 | 14.2 | 70.0 |
| Total | $106.1 | 62.0 |

[a] Board of Investigation and Research, *Public Aids to Domestic Transportation*, H. Doc. 159, 79 Cong. 1 sess. (1944), Table 75, p. 449, and Table 76, p. 452.

It was indicated in the testimony before the Air Policy Commission, by both the Post Office Department and CAB representatives, that no data are available to indicate the specific amount of subsidy which is included in present air-mail payments to the carriers. The Post Office Department, however, has made a rough estimate of the subsidy, using readily available data. During 1947 the average cost to the government, or the average revenue to the airlines, was $1.02 per ton-mile of mail carried. Passenger travel, the most costly type of traffic to accommodate, yielded 50 cents per ton-mile, or less than half the 1947 ton-mile cost of transporting the mail. Using this rough comparison, about half of the amount paid to the airlines by the Post Office Department was considered to represent subsidy.[12] It was pointed out by the House Committee on Post Office and Civil Service that "in all fairness to the so-called service rate carriers which carried more than 80 per cent of all air mail at rates of 45 cents per ton-mile, as well as those in the 60 cents a ton-mile group, it is obvious that very little of the deficit can be properly chargeable to them."[13]

The situation underwent considerable change in 1948, however, due in part to the increasing costs of the carriers, and in part to changes in air-mail payments. The CAB in 1948 increased air-mail payments to the nation's five major trunk lines. American, Eastern, TWA, and United had received 45 cents per ton-mile since January 1, 1945, at which time the rate had been cut from the previous 60 cents a ton-mile. Under the 1948 scale of payments, the total amount of mail pay received by the five carriers was estimated at 27.2 million dollars annually, compared to an annual rate of less than half this amount prior to the increases. The Civil Aeronautics Board, in issuing its order, stated that these rates were service rates; that is, rates which reflected the cost to the carriers of providing the service, as distinguished from "need" rates involving subsidy.[14]

The Post Office Department, however, took exception to the Board's contention that these rates of air-mail payment were, in fact, "service" rates devoid of any element of subsidy; and it charged that the rates were "not based upon a procedure designed to determine the true cost of the mail service."[15] It was concluded by the Postmaster General that "until an adequate cost study has been made, there is no competent evidence to support the Tentative Findings and Conclusions of the Board."[16] It was requested accordingly that the Board institute

[12] *Report on Air Mail Subsidy*, H. Rept. 1958, 80 Cong. 2 sess (1948), App. 1, p. 9.
[13] The same.
[14] CAB Docket Nos. 3309, 3021, 3211, 2849, and 3014, *Statement of Tentative Findings and Conclusions*, adopted Mar. 29, 1948 (mimeo.), p. 64.
[15] *Answer of the Postmaster General Pursuant to Section 285.13 of the Economic Regulations of the Board* (mimeo.), p. 3.
[16] The same, p. 4.

a cost study of operations of each carrier involved, to be conducted jointly by the Board, the carriers, and the Post Office Department.

In its most recent action with respect to mail pay rates, the CAB has pointed out that special mail rate provisions should be made to compensate the carriers for losses incurred as a result of the grounding of aircraft incident to design modifications.[17] To carry out this policy, the Board increased temporary mail rates to cover amortization of capitalized costs related to the grounding of DC-6 and Constellation aircraft.[18]

### V. THE PROBLEM RAISED

It is obvious from this situation that the problems involving air-mail payments will not be clarified, let alone brought to satisfactory solution, until generally acceptable findings have been made available as to the cost of carrying the mail. Current policy provides that the Post Office Department must pay out of its own budget whatever the Civil Aeronautics Board determines is necessary to achieve the desired development of aviation. The Department is accordingly in the position of having no control over its expenditures for air-mail service, and of being obliged to provide the funds necessary to assure profitable airline operations in amounts which are not distinguishable from reasonable charges for the service.

The Post Office Department wrestling with the problem of a 325 million dollar deficit, points out that it is being called upon "to finance inefficient management, parties, hotel suites, entertainment, excessive public relations costs, and to finance competition between existing scheduled carriers."[19] In addition the Department charges that it has been placed in the position of financing a rate war between the scheduled and nonscheduled carriers. "Many of the scheduled carriers have

[17] *Civil Aeronautics Board Economic Program for 1949, Statement of Policy,* Feb. 21, 1949 (mimeo.).
[18] *Summary of Orders Issued to Implement Civil Aeronautics Board Statement of Policy,* Feb. 25, 1949 (mimeo.).
[19] *Survey and Study of the Postal Service,* H. Rept. 1242, 80 Cong. 2 sess., p. 6.

reduced air-freight rates in the commodities and at the shipping points available to the air-freight carriers, while at the same time they have applied for increased air-mail pay."[20] Thus the Department is in the position of injecting itself into areas of responsibility reserved for the Board; and the Board, through its decisions, interferes with the budgetary position of the Department.

These conflicts in interest between the two federal agencies are burdensome to each, and present a clear case for separating payment for air-mail service from the provision of operating subsidies. The separation is essential if the agencies are to meet their individual responsibilities. A thorough study of airline costs and the determination of a fair allocation of these costs to air-mail carriage is the first step.

It is generally conceded that "separation of the amount of subsidy paid domestic airlines from purely compensatory payments for carrying air mail will correct many evils in the existing situation."[21] However, the report of the House Interstate and Foreign Commerce Committee on "Public Aid to Air Transportation" takes a cautious view. This report acknowledges "some merit" in the contention that the present system of air-mail payments "does not constitute an incentive to low cost and economy of operation," and, in addition, "confuses the Post Office budget." It nevertheless rejects the proposal that service payments and subsidies be separated because such a step "would necessitate elaborate cost studies."[22]

On this subject, the Secretary of Commerce has taken a different view:

The practical difficulty of breaking down the cost of the total service of an air carrier into its constituent parts to determine to what extent existing rates are an accurate reflection of the proportional cost of each category of service is readily appreciated.

[20] The same.
[21] The same.
[22] H. Rept. 1612, 80 Cong. 2 sess., p. 5. This report nevertheless proceeds to the statement that: "Costs under economical and efficient management constitute the yardstick, under the Civil Aeronautics Act of 1938, by which reasonable rates are measured." p. 6.

We nevertheless believe that some method of cost determination can be established which will reward efficient management and prevent inefficiency from perpetuating itself.[23]

Accepting the latter view that the problem of cost determination is not insurmountable,[24] the question arises as to what steps should be taken once the service cost and subsidy elements have been separated. To what extent and for what purposes should operating subsidies be granted to air transport companies? The availability of government aid to compensate for airline deficits has frequently been viewed as placing a premium on inefficiency and perpetuating ineffective management. The House Committee on Post Office and Civil Service has concluded that the practice of granting retroactive mail pay as "a means of underwriting any losses whatever" is, in effect, "a situation similar to 'cost plus' contracts." And it quoted the Secretary of Comerce as follows:

I believe that we should critically examine the habit and method of subsidizing air carriers. We should evaluate the situation to see if there is not a dulling of incentive resulting from the method of fixing of payments. I fully recognize the current need for a sympathetic—even more generous—attitude toward the need of the air carriers, but we must not get into cost-plus habits in industry. When increased costs do not affect profits, it seems reasonable to presume that some of the incentive toward efficiency and progress will be lost.[25]

### VI. CONCLUSION

The question of whether operating subsidies should continue to be granted to the airlines, in addition to the aid which has been granted in the provision of airways and airports, depends in part on the nature and purpose of these operating aids.[26] In international air transportation, the subsidy problem must be viewed in the light of subsidized foreign competition affecting

---

[23] *Statement of the Department of Commerce on the Reports of the President's Air Policy Commission and the Congressional Aviation Policy Board,* May 22, 1948 (mimeo.), pp. 21-22.

[24] The problem of cost-finding in connection with minimum rate regulation by the Interstate Commerce Commission is discussed in Pt. 2.

[25] H. Rept. 1958, 80 Cong. 2 sess., p. 3.

[26] See Chap. 6 for discussion of air transport subsidies for national defense.

the operation of American flag carriers. To the extent that foreign carriers can maintain an advantage over American carriers through government aid, it will be necessary to provide compensating government support. A firmer foundation for international air transportation must await the establishment of internationally acceptable standards through the International Civil Aviation Organization.

In domestic air transportation there is no similar justification for operating subsidies; and the charge cannot be ignored that "high salaries, stock warrants and options to officers, together with losses resulting from poor management and overexpansion are cost factors in establishing 'need' upon which mail pay is based."[27] The air transportation industry, despite its financial difficulties, has failed in many instances to adopt measures capable of achieving a reasonable degree of economy; and the financial protection afforded by the Civil Aeronautics Act has undoubtedly played an important part in removing incentive to economy and efficiency. Under present air-mail policies, the disadvantages of federal paternalism will not be easily remedied. The fact should not be overlooked that overexpansion and the ultimate financial evils which result from it continue to plague the railroads many years after their initial promotion.

It appears that, wholly aside from the desirability of operating subsidies, disassociating air-mail payments from any subsidy element is a prerequisite to intelligent government policy. The contention that arriving at an acceptable allocation of costs would prove difficult does not alter the fact that the task must be undertaken. To the extent that it is considered essential to provide operating subsidies, the problem should be handled by the promotional agency rather than by the regulatory body in connection with rate making. The promotional agency should likewise assume the responsibility of appearing before the Congress to justify the necessary appropriations.

[27] H. Rept. 1958, 80 Cong. 1 sess., p. 2.

# CHAPTER IV

## AVIATION SAFETY

A large part of the activities of the federal government in the field of aviation relates to the achievement of safety. The promotion of safety is a primary reason for the provision of navigation facilities, landing aids, and weather service. It also involves the granting of certificates for aircraft, equipment, and facilities, and for pilots and other personnel; the prescribing of traffic rules and other operating regulations; the administration and enforcement of standards and regulations; and the investigation of accidents.

At the present time the responsibility for aviation safety is divided between the CAA and the CAB. The CAB has the responsibility for promulgating the civil air regulations, investigating accidents, and conducting hearings with regard to the competence of certificate holders. The CAA is concerned primarily with interpretation, administration, and enforcement of the CAB regulations, but it also performs over 90 per cent of the accident investigation work through delegation of this function from the CAB. This division of responsibility, and the way it has worked out in practice, are matters which have given rise to considerable criticism, focused on the questions of whether the CAA and CAB can both operate effectively in this field, and whether the setup permits impartial investigation of accidents. Recently there have been a number of conflicting viewpoints and recommendations emanating from witnesses representing CAA and CAB before congressional committees, and from such groups as the President's Air Policy Commission, the Congressional Aviation Policy Board, and the President's Special Board of Inquiry on Air Safety.

The high priority of importance which attaches to safety in the field of air transportation, and the considerable differences of opinion which have arisen with respect to the organization of government necessary to assure maximum safety, require that the issues be described and considered in some detail.

## I. NATURE OF THE SAFETY PROBLEM

During 1948 there were over 8,000 aircraft accidents in the United States, and over 1,200 fatalities. (See table p. 61.) Most of these involved private aircraft; but the 6 fatal accidents which occurred in domestic and international certificated airline service killed 128 passengers and crew members. These accidents on public carriers were of particular severity and of particular public concern. Moreover, they were highly significant from the standpoint of the economic position of the carriers. Accidents cost the airlines many millions of dollars, in part from the grounding and modification of defective aircraft and in part from the general reduction in traffic following an air crash. For example, some 50,000 fewer passengers were carried in June 1947 than during the month before, and this contraseasonal traffic decline was attributed almost wholly to three fatal accidents which occurred during May and June.[1] (And the grounding of the DC-6 cost the airlines an estimated 10 to 12 million dollars.)

Although the priority of importance attaching to air carrier accidents is apparent, the large number of accidents involving other types of aircraft is likewise a primary obstacle to the development of air transportation. A principal deterrent to private flying lies in the absence of safety, for without reasonably safe operation the airplane has neither utility nor economy. One out of every eight private aircraft has been involved in an accident every year, and aviation insurance coverage constitutes a heavy proportion of total costs.

The safety problem, however, is not described by the accident situation alone. Accidents themselves are only an index of the extent of failure to achieve safety. Accident data provide invaluable aid in the prevention of similar occurrences, but far more important are the measures taken daily to prevent the mishaps in the first instance.

This point is emphasized because much of the discussion concerning federal administration of aviation safety activities

---

[1] "Airline Traffic Trends Show Growth Depends on Safety," *Aviation Week*, Feb. 23, 1948.

ACCIDENTS ON SCHEDULED DOMESTIC AND INTERNATIONAL FLIGHTS
AND IN NON-AIR-CARRIER FLYING, 1938-48[a]

### I. SCHEDULED DOMESTIC OPERATIONS

| Year | Total Accidents | Fatal Accidents | Total Fatalities | Passenger Fatalities per 100 Million Passenger Miles |
|------|------|------|------|------|
| 1938 | 23 | 5 | 35 | 4.5 |
| 1939 | 28 | 2 | 12 | 1.2 |
| 1940 | 30 | 3 | 45 | 3.0 |
| 1941 | 27 | 4 | 44 | 2.3 |
| 1942 | 23 | 5 | 71 | 3.7 |
| 1943 | 23 | 2 | 30 | 1.3 |
| 1944 | 30 | 5 | 58 | 2.2 |
| 1945 | 40 | 8 | 88 | 2.2 |
| 1946 | 33 | 9 | 97 | 1.2 |
| 1947 | 43 | 8 | 222 | 3.2 |
| 1948 | 51 | 5 | 98 | 1.4 |

### II. SCHEDULED INTERNATIONAL OPERATIONS

| Year | Total Accidents | Fatal Accidents | Total Fatalities | Passenger Fatalities per 100 Million Passenger Miles |
|------|------|------|------|------|
| 1938 | 9 | 3 | 26 | 13.2 |
| 1939 | 6 | 1 | 14 | 12.8 |
| 1940 | 6 | 0 | 0 | 0 |
| 1941 | 5 | 1 | 2 | 1.2 |
| 1942 | 2 | 0 | 0 | 0 |
| 1943 | 2 | 1 | 14 | 3.9 |
| 1944 | 7 | 1 | 17 | 5.3 |
| 1945 | 5 | 2 | 27 | 3.7 |
| 1946 | 14 | 2 | 52 | 3.6 |
| 1947 | 9 | 3 | 33 | 1.1 |
| 1948 | 11 | 1 | 30 | 1.1 |

### III. NON-AIR-CARRIER OPERATIONS

| Year | Total Accidents | Fatal Accidents | Total Fatalities |
|------|------|------|------|
| 1938 | 1,861 | 176 | 274 |
| 1939 | 2,222 | 203 | 315 |
| 1940 | 3,471 | 232 | 359 |
| 1941 | 4,252 | 217 | 312 |
| 1942 | 3,324 | 143 | 220 |
| 1943 | 3,871 | 167 | 257 |
| 1944 | 3,343 | 169 | 257 |
| 1945 | 4,652 | 322 | 508 |
| 1946 | 7,618 | 690 | 1,009 |
| 1947 | 9,253 | 882 | 1,352 |
| 1948 | 8,000 | 750 | 1,100 |

[a] 1938-47 data from *CAA Statistical Handbook of Civil Aviation* (1948), pp. 93, 99, 105; 1948 data are estimates from CAB Accident Analysis Division.

has been predicated on the assumption, at least implied, that the principal task in the field of aviation safety is to investigate and analyze accidents, and to take remedial action. Although the importance of this function must not be underestimated, the fact remains that the degree of safety which has been achieved in aviation is the product of many other factors: safe aircraft design, air crew and ground crew proficiency, adequate regulations, communications, airport facilities, and the like. When the whole safety function is considered in its broader aspects, the nature of federal responsibility and of the organization to achieve aviation safety can be more readily determined.

## II. FEDERAL SAFETY ACTIVITY

The Civil Aeronautics Act of 1938, which created the Civil Aeronautics Authority, divided federal aviation activity into three catagories:

1. The Authority, a five-member board, performed functions largely regulatory in character, and its operations included, in addition to responsibility for economic regulations, the function of safety regulation. This included the issuance of all types of safety certificates (pilot, mechanic, air-carrier operating, type, production, airworthiness, etc.). In addition, it was responsible for the promulgation of safety standards, rules, and regulations, and their enforcement by such means as the suspension and revocation of safety certificates and the initiation of proceedings to impose civil penalties.

2. The administrator was responsible for the establishment, maintenance, and operation of the civil airways, and of air navigation facilities, as well as other promotional and administrative activities.

3. The Air Safety Board was responsible for investigating accidents and reporting to the Authority the causes of such accidents. The Board also made recommendations as to measures designed to prevent recurrence of accidents.

Reorganization Plan No. III, included in the Reorganization Act of 1939, became effective on June 30, 1940. This plan transferred from the Authority to the present Civil Aeronautics Administration the functions of safety regulation described in Titles V and VI of the Civil Aeronautics Act of 1938, except functions of prescribing safety standards, rules, and regulations and of suspending and revoking certificates after hearing.[2]

Reorganization Plan No. IV transferred the functions of the Office of Administrator of Civil Aeronautics to the Department of Commerce, abolished the Air Safety Board and consolidated the functions of the Air Safety Board with those of the Civil Aeronautics Authority (now the Civil Aeronautics Board).

Many of the functions of the Authority with respect to safety regulation were transferred to the present CAA under terms of Reorganization Plan No. III. The CAA took over the entire field staff engaged in safety regulation, including aeronautical and engineering inspectors and airworthiness engineers. It became the duty of CAA to provide for the flight testing and examination of applicants for airman certificates, the examination and flight testing of aircraft, the examination of aircraft manufacturing facilities, maintenance facilities, flying and mechanic schools, and the continuing supervision over the holders of these various certificates. It is also the duty of the administrator, through his inspection staff, to investigate violators of the safety provisions of the act and of the safety standards, rules, and regulations, and to take such enforcement measures as appear necessary. The CAA carries out this enforcement responsibility through reprimands and civil penalties, and certificate suspension, revocation, or denial of renewal.

In performing functions relating to air safety, therefore, the CAA is bound by the safety standards, rules, and regulations prescribed by the Board. The CAA may recommend to the Board the issuance and amendment of such rules and regulations as appear to be necessary. On the other hand, the Board may take the initiative in prescribing new or amended safety standards, rules, and regulations where such action appears desirable.

---

[2] Title V related to registration of aircraft engines, propellers, and appliances; Title VI related to rules and regulations setting minimum standards for aircraft design, construction, maintenance, operations, and airmen's certificates.

The CAA, in summary, exercises the functions of:

1. Recommending changes in safety rules and regulations in cases where it appears desirable from experience in the field that changes be adopted.

2. Interpreting safety standards, rules, and regulations in connection with their administration and enforcement.

3. Making the necessary inspections and flight tests and conducting the necessary examinations preceding issuance of the various types of certificates.

4. Recommending punitive and corrective actions to the Board, including recommendations for the issuance of orders requiring holders of certificates to show cause why such certificates should not be suspended or revoked.

5. Effecting emergency suspension of certificates.

6. Requesting the Board for a formal investigation of safety matters when such action appears necessary.

7. Acceptance of offers in compromise of civil penalties and transmission to the attorney general of uncompromised civil penalty cases.

The safety work of the CAB involves exercise of the functions of:

1. Preparing and prescribing safety standards, rules, and regulations in such detail as appears proper, including those proposed by the CAA as well as those proposed on its own initiative.

2. Interpreting safety standards, rules, and regulations and applicable statutes in connection with suspension and revocation safety proceedings.

3. Receiving petitions for reconsideration of a denial of an application for an airman's certificate.

4. On the recommendation of the CAA or on its own initiative, issuing orders to show cause, directed to holders of safety certificates.

5. Receiving and considering all formal complaints with respect to safety matters and holding hearings.

6. In co-operation with the Department of Justice, handling

all appeals to the courts from its orders relating to safety matters.[3]

### III. CONGRESSIONAL TESTIMONY ON SAFETY ORGANIZATION

Since the reorganization of aviation functions in 1940, there has been widespread criticism of federal safety activities. This criticism has centered around the question of overlap and confusion between CAA and CAB responsibilities, and the matter of independent accident investigation.

The desirability of reconstituting the independent Air Safety Board has been the most widely debated of these issues. When the Civil Aeronautics Act of 1938 was under consideration it was believed that (contrary to the provisions of the Air Commerce Act of 1926) an agency could not reasonably be expected, in investigating an accident and determining its probable cause, to criticize its own judgment or efficiency in performing its regulatory duties or in installing, operating, or maintaining air navigation facilities. Accordingly, under the terms of the Civil Aeronautics Act of 1938, the function of investigating accidents was made the responsibility of an independent agency.

Abolition of this independent investigating body under Reorganization Plan No. IV created considerable opposition, particularly among flying personnel. The Air Line Pilots Association has been particularly opposed to the reorganization, and has consistently taken the position that the answer to the accident problem is "to reactivate . . . with as little delay as possible, the former independent Air Safety Board."[4]

In 1943 further support for an independent Air Safety Board was lent by the House of Representatives Select Committee to Investigate Air Accidents. This Committee concluded that the abolition of an independent safety agency was "a serious error, and that the Air Safety Board should be reconstituted."[5]

[3] Foregoing summaries from *Annual Report of Civil Aeronautics Board 1941.*

[4] Testimony of David L. Behncke, President of the Air Line Pilots Association, *Safety in Air Navigation,* Hearings before House Committee on Interstate and Foreign Commerce, 80 Cong. 1 sess., Pt. 1, p. 472.

[5] *Air Accidents,* H. Rept. 1, Report of the House Select Committee to Investigate Air Accidents, 78 Cong. 1 sess., p. 8.

Opposition to this view was expressed in 1940 by the director of the budget. He testified before a Senate committee that since the jurisdiction of the Air Safety Board was confined to the investigation of accidents, it could take no positive steps toward the prevention of the recurrence of such accidents. It is true that the Board was expected to submit recommendations for the consideration of the Authority, and to issue public reports intended to force the Authority into action. But these advantages were said to be more than offset by the misunderstandings bound to result from the activities of an agency which could on the one hand be extremely critical and on the other hand claim credit for any progress achieved without taking any responsibility.[6]

Further, it was claimed, the Air Safety Board actually had very little independence, either in matters of expenditure, procedures under which it received notification and report of accidents, or even with respect to the custody of its own records. According to the budget director, it was not the Air Safety Board, but rather the Bureau of Safety Regulation under the direction of the administrator which was responsible for the adoption of improved safety regulations and their actual enforcement. It was concluded from these observations that the Air Safety Board was not indispensable to air safety.[7]

More recently, the chairman of the Civil Aeronautics Board has testified on this subject as follows:

. . . I wish that I could come in here and say "Recreate the Air Safety Board." I wish that were the answer. I do not have any feelings one way or the other about the Air Safety Board, but I have tried to line up the arguments that I think are in favor of it and the arguments that are against it, and judgment on my part does not lead me to believe that the recreation of the Air Safety Board of itself will be a sort of panacea to all of these evils. I have studied rather carefully the record of the Air Safety Board. It is a good record, but I think as good a record has been made since.[8]

[6] The Civil Aeronautics Authority took no action on 75 per cent of the Safety Board's recommendations.

[7] Statement of Harold D. Smith, Director of the Bureau of the Budget, *Fourth Plan on Government Reorganization,* Hearings before Senate Select Committee on Government Organization, 76 Cong. 3 sess. (1940), p. 4.

[8] Testimony of James M. Landis on *Safety in Air Navigation, Hearings,* p. 152.

Mr. Landis concludes that "from examining the history of the Air Safety Board . . . I could not make, in all good conscience, a recommendation to this committee to say that that is the answer."[9]

The administrator of the Civil Aeronautics Administration has also expressed little enthusiasm for independent accident investigation:

. . . We feel that the Board should have authority to delegate the accident investigations function to the Administrator with the responsibility for gathering facts in connection with aircraft accidents. We have been working on a rather fuzzy basis there inasmuch as the Board has the whole responsibility, but by force of necessity we have been doing . . . about 90 percent of the actual investigation. We feel that the act should be clear-cut and that it should permit the Board to delegate that authority to the Administration.[10]

It was further stated, however, that if the shortcomings of the former Air Safety Board were rectified and "if the Congress feels that the general philosophy of government is better served by having an independent Board, so that you get this check and balance of which our Government is made, I have no quarrel with that at all." On the other hand, the administrator affirmed his belief in the honesty of CAA officials:

. . . I do not think we are whitewashing CAA people when they are involved. I think the Congress has got to rely on the integrity of its administrative people and not set up so cumbersome an organization, administratively, that it will defeat its own purpose. Mind you, no matter what you do, I do not believe you will ever be able to get the field staff for an independent board that can do a 100 per cent investigation job. . . .[11]

### IV. SPECIAL STUDIES ON SAFETY ORGANIZATION

Several significant but conflicting studies were made during 1947 and 1948 which shed further light on the nature of the issues involved in establishing a desirable administrative setup

[9] The same, pp. 152-53.
[10] Testimony of T. P. Wright. The same, p. 240.
[11] The same, p. 255. Note that under the old Safety Board, there were only 16 men in the field. Only a small percentage of total accidents were investigated.

for aviation safety. These studies include the President's Air Policy Commission, the Joint Congressional Aviation Policy Board, and the President's Special Board of Inquiry on Air Safety.

The President's Air Policy Commission recommended that aviation promotional activities, including all aviation safety activities with the exception of accident investigation, should be included in the functions of an executive agency (a Department of Civil Aviation in the Department of Commerce). This transfer of safety activity from the CAB was predicated on the basis of relieving the CAB of time-consuming work which interferes with the Board's principal objective of economic regulation. The Board "should be as free as possible for the performance of its economic functions."[12]

With respect to investigation of accidents, the Air Policy Commission stated that while it was aware of the difficulties encountered by the earlier Air Safety Board, "the logic of the situation compels the establishment of such a Board."[13] According to the Commission, the function of accident investigation and analysis should not be in the Department of Civil Aviation "for such an arrangement would not provide the desired independence of the investigators."[14] The proposed Air Safety Board would consist of three members appointed by the president and subject to confirmation by the Senate. Its duties would be to investigate and analyze air accidents and to submit reports to the secretary of civil aviation to be made public by him. The Board would be established within the Department of Civil Aviation for housekeeping purposes only, but the secretary of commerce would be responsible for determining that no unnecessary duplication or overlapping occurred between the Air Safety Board and the Department of Civil Aviation.[15]

[12] Report of the President's Air Policy Commission, *Survival in the Air Age* (1948), p. 139.

[13] The same.

[14] The same.

[15] Because of the very extensive duplications inherent in the situation, this provision raises a serious question with respect to the ability of the proposed Board to achieve independence.

The Joint Congressional Aviation Policy Board raised the question of whether the present division of safety responsibility between the CAA and the CAB permits the federal government to promote aviation safety to the extent desirable and necessary.[16] To correct the situation, it recommended a number of changes in organization:

1. The administration and enforcement functions of the CAA relating to aircraft and airmen should be transferred to the CAB.

2. The CAB should promulgate, administer, and enforce regulations relating to the competency of airmen, certification and airworthiness of aircraft, air carrier operations, and other regulations relating to the economics of operations. The Federal Airways Service should promulgate and administer regulations relating to the movement of aircraft in flight and at airports. The CAB should hear and determine appeals from the Federal Airways Service in cases involving violations of regulations.[17]

The above recommendations are based on the Policy Board's belief that the same agency which promulgates particular civil air regulations should also interpret and administer them. It is not necessary, however, according to the Board, for the same agency to promulgate and administer both air traffic rules, and rules relating to equipment and competency. The distinction is one between rules and procedures to be administered in the course of operating the airways and airport traffic control facilities ("rules of the road") and all other rules governing the operation of aircraft and air services. Thus the CAB would be made responsible for promulgation, administration, and enforcement of regulations relating to aircraft and airman certificates, which concern the safe and economic operation of air carriers and aircraft generally. To discharge these duties the personnel of CAA now administering and enforcing the safety regulations would be transferred to the CAB. This field staff would be administered by an executive director.

[16] *National Aviation Policy,* S. Rept. 949, 80 Cong. 2 sess., Mar. 1, 1948.
[17] According to F. B. Lee, Acting Administrator of Civil Aeronautics, this recommended separation of closely related CAA functions "came to the Administration as quite a shock." Supplementary statement on H. R. 6144, May 1948 (mimeo.), p. 6.

3. The CAB should continue as an independent agency charged with the administration of economic responsibilities, including the civil air regulations having a direct bearing on the economics of air operations.[18]

4. An independent director of air safety investigation should be appointed by the president and confirmed by the Senate. He would be responsible for investigation and analysis of civil air accidents and for submitting reports and recommendations to the Air Coordinating Committee. The ACC would be required to make such reports public and to transmit them to the Congress, CAB, and the Office of Civil Aviation in the Department of Commerce. The director of air safety investigation would be responsible for safety education programs and for "instilling a consciousness of the importance of safe operation in all echelons of air operations."[19] It is pointed out that accident investigation and analysis are fundamentally operating functions, and because of their importance to the development of civil aviation, they should be handled by an independent agency. A single director was considered preferable to a board in order to handle this work expeditiously.

In December 1947 a report on air safety was submitted to the president in response to his request that a special board review the problems of aviation safety and submit recommendations to him. With respect to administrative problems, the special board stated that because of its membership it considered itself an inappropriate agency to recommend governmental reorganization.[20] It pointed out, however, that the CAB with its present staff is unable to conduct a formal investigation of every serious accident and that this is unnecessary since all accidents are informally investigated by the administrator to determine whether a violation has occurred. Moreover, it was contended that only a limited number of accidents in private

[18] S. Rept. 949, 80 Cong. 2 sess., p. 51. The registration and recordation of aircraft would be handled by the Board, since it is charged with the certification of civil aircraft.

[19] The same, p. 53.

[20] Among the 5 Board members there were included the chairman of the CAB and the administrator of CAA.

flying involve structural defects or methods of flying that can be corrected. Most of them involve human errors, including recklessness and carelessness. Airline accidents, on the other hand, are generally the result of causes which, when thoroughly understood, suggest ways of preventing future accidents. For this reason the special board found no fault with the scope of CAB accident investigation, which is limited to major airline accidents or noncarrier accidents which appear to have a significance from the standpoint of the general cause of flying safety.

The special board did not wish to take a stand on the subject of recreating the "independent" Air Safety Board. Its members were reported to hold different ideas concerning the validity of the contention that where the investigating agency is concerned with the efficiency of its own regulations "it may incline against a too thorough self-criticism and tend to look elsewhere for such fault as may exist."[21] But the special board did express the opinion that the investigating function is of great importance and if properly exercised can do much to further the cause of safety. In this regard it recommended that investigators turn their attention from the determination of the blame for an accident to an understanding of the chain of events leading up to an accident, with a view to ensuring against recurrence of these events. This type of approach would call for more than mere investigation. It would demand constant scrutiny of the entire field of aviation and the planning of remedies in the light of the situation found to exist. The CAB, it was contended, has not always been able to study the results of accident investigation in such a way as to reap the full benefits of accident information. Since the main objective has been the economic regulation of air transport, the Board has devoted its prime energies to this task, despite the fact that analysis of accidents should receive an equally comprehensive and continuing attention.

The president's board stated its belief that the aviation in-

[21] Report to the President of the United States by the Special Board of Inquiry on Air Safety, Dec. 29, 1947, p. 104, mimeo.

dustry is now more conscious than ever of the necessity for safe operation. Accordingly, the government can in the future delegate more and more of its detailed responsibilities to the industry. The government should be able to content itself with specifying broad regulations and leave to the industry the manner in which such standards will be met.

With respect to safety regulations, the board points out that the effectiveness of regulations lies in the way they operate. Consequently, the agency that has the authority to issue regulations should be in close touch with operations and have a practical appreciation of the needs and problems of the industry.

### V. TESTIMONY ON RECENTLY PROPOSED LEGISLATION

As a result of the Congressional Aviation Policy Board's recommendations, legislation was introduced in the Eightieth Congress to carry out the objectives outlined in the congressional study. Testimony by the CAA and CAB sharpened the differences and similarities of opinion with respect to safety organization.

The chairman of the CAB stated that provisions relating to transfer of certain safety administration and enforcement functions from the Civil Aeronautics Administration to the Civil Aeronautics Board met with the approval of the Board. "In the Board's opinion, it is highly desirable to unify all aspects of the safety regulations, the formulation, promulgation, and interpretation of rules and standards, certification pursuant to such rules and standards, and enforcement thereof, under common supervision and direction."[22] It was stated that such unified handling of the safety problem would contribute to an integrated safety program and aid in avoiding the difficulties encountered as a result of the existing division of responsibilities. Specifically, it would aid in eliminating problems caused by the CAA interpreting regulations contrary to the Board's intention.

[22] Statement of Joseph J. O'Connell, Chairman of the CAB, *Independent Office of Air Safety*, Hearings before the House Committee on Interstate and Foreign Commerce on H. R. 6144, 80 Cong. 2 sess., p. 77.

It was stated that the Board regarded it as essential that the responsibility for rule-making in the field of safety remain vested in the Board, because of the close relationship between economic and safety regulations. According to the Board chairman: ". . . it is our opinion that the present split between the legislative power and the administration and enforcement functions is disruptive of sound administration, tends to promote confusion, and prevents a co-ordinated, integrated regulatory program."[23]

With respect to the creation of an Independent Office of Air Safety, the CAB did not oppose such a transfer of its accident investigation functions, but considered such transfer unnecessary.

Testifying on the same subject the undersecretary of commerce likewise took the position that "The consolidation of the promulgating functions with the inspection and enforcement function in one agency undoubtedly would obviate certain operating difficulties between the Civil Aeronautics Administration and the Civil Aeronautics Board."[24] It was pointed out that a major source of present difficulties is the necessity for the CAA to interpret the civil air regulations issued by the CAB. The solution which was suggested by the Department of Commerce, however, was not to consolidate the safety function in the CAB but rather to place greater responsibility for safety in the CAA.

The function of prescribing safety regulations since it deals primarily in the techniques to be employed in the manufacture and operation of aircraft, is essentially administrative and operational in character. The agency which provides the facilities necessarily used by the aircraft in their operations is the agency which should perform this function. Attempted separation of the two could result in serious consequences. . . .[25]

In developing this point it was stated that transfer from the Board to the Administration of the responsibilities for promul-

---

[23] The same.
[24] Statement of William C. Foster, the same, p. 38.
[25] The same, pp. 39-40.

gation of air safety standards would be desirable in view of the fact that these regulations are so technical in an engineering sense that judgments could better be made, after appropriate hearing, by an organization comprised of technical personnel. It was pointed out that such an arrangement is well established in the case of the Coast Guard which, in addition to operating aids to navigation, promulgates safety regulations, inspects vessels, licenses crews, and carries out enforcement activities.

With respect to the reconstitution of the Air Safety Board, the undersecretary of commerce stated the belief that establishment of an independent agency to check on the proper performance of functions by other agencies having safety responsibilities is, in effect, "an expression of a lack of faith in the officials charged with these responsibilities."[26] It was stated that a statute requiring public hearing with respect to air accidents would be sufficient to assure the public of full and fair disclosure of all the facts. By handling the problem this way, the power of the accident investigating body to recommend is not divorced from the power to act, and unnecessary duplication of personnel engaged in the same activity is avoided. It was pointed out that while the excellent safety record in aviation established during the existence of the Air Safety Board is often attributed to the work of the Board, this claim is without foundation.

It was concluded in the testimony of the under secretary that many of the objectives of proposed changes in this field could be achieved by the passage of legislation which would authorize the CAB to delegate certain functions to the administrator of civil aeronautics.[27] Under this authorization, the prescribing of safety regulations and the investigation of accidents could be transferred to the CAA, under such terms as the Board might specify, and the Board would retain the power to modify, suspend, or terminate such delegation of authority. The Board would continue to be a high court which

[26] The same p. 42.
[27] Public Law 872, 80 Cong. 2 sess., permits this objective to be accomplished.

would hear any person aggrieved by the regulations of the administrator; and it would also continue to determine the causes of accidents from the facts made available by the administrator.

In a statement by the assistant administrator of the CAA in charge of aviation safety, further expression of the CAA position has been presented. It was pointed out that the CAB has been in the difficult position of trying to issue regulations in a rapidly changing field without any close contact with the engineering phases of aviation, and that "the Civil Air Regulations are in their present unwieldy condition because the duty of issuing such regulations has been separated from the duty of administering and enforcing them."[28]

## VI. FEDERAL DELEGATION OF RESPONSIBILITY

The rapidly increasing work load on the CAA as a result of expanding aviation activities has led to increasing delegation of CAA responsibilities in the field of safety. The designee program, which has been in operation for several years, provides for the designation of qualified volunteer personnel in the aviation industry, who perform safety regulation work under CAA supervision. Such designees are appointed to give airman examinations and to carry out inspection work for aircraft and component manufacturing, scheduled and non-scheduled airline operations, aviation schools, and medical examination. By mid-1947 there were approximately 8,000 such designees in the field.[29]

The question of further delegating federal responsibilities, or of transferring certain activities from federal jurisdiction to state control, has arisen in a number of additional areas. For example, although the desirability of nationwide uniformity of safety regulations is recognized, the need for individual state participation in enforcing such regulations is equally apparent.

[28] Quotation attributed to A. S. Koch in an address by Ben Stern, CAA Assistant Administrator for Aviation Information at the Parks College of Aeronautical Technology, June 11, 1948, p. 11.
[29] *Thirty-fifth Annual Report of the Secretary of Commerce, 1947*, p. 68.

To this end the CAA has been working with state authorities to arrive at mutually agreeable policies with respect to the enforcement of air traffic rules. Legislation to achieve local enforcement was introduced in the Eightieth Congress to provide for state suspension of airman certificates.[30] Hearings on this legislation brought out the fact that both the CAA and CAB "are stacked high with hundreds of cases," and that "we have not been able to obtain prompt enforcement through the Federal agency . . . because the agency would hesitate to ask for the amount of money necessary for the force that it would take for a complete coverage. . . ."[31] It was further pointed out that such a federal force would be unnecessary in view of the fact that the states are much better equipped to carry out enforcement responsibilities than is the federal government.

At present the states are assuming many responsibilities previously carried out by the CAA. State licenses are required for aircraft and airmen in approximately half the states, and about the same number have laws relating to reckless flying. Thirty-one states conduct aircraft accident investigation or co-operate with the federal government in this work. It is increasingly apparent that these activities, together with registration of aircraft and licensing of operators, must eventually be taken over by the states for all but interstate commercial aviation. The trend in this direction places important responsibility on the federal government to achieve uniform standards and satisfactory federal-state relations.

### VII. CONCLUSION

The basic objections to the present method of handling aviation safety problems in the federal government appear to be two: (1) The CAA, which administers and enforces safety

[30] H.R. 6147, *A Bill to Amend the Civil Aeronautics Act of 1938, as Amended, With Respect to Local Enforcement of Safety Regulations of Civil Aviation, and for Other Purposes,* 80 Cong. 2 sess.

[31] Statement of Merrill Armour, CAB, *Local Enforcement of Safety Regulations,* Hearings on H.R. 6147 before the House Committee on Interstate and Foreign Commerce, 80 Cong. 2 sess., May 1948, p. 47.

regulations, is in an awkward position created by the separation of these responsibilities from the promulgation of the regulations. This is true partly because of the difficulty of interpreting CAB regulations properly, and partly because the CAB, being concerned principally with economic regulation, does not have the adequate technical personnel and the close day-to-day operating contacts with the industry which are essential to prescribing proper regulations. (2) The CAB, which promulgates safety regulations and investigates important accidents, is said to be in a position of acting as a judge of its own regulations when it determines accident causes.

There is general agreement that the prescribing, administering, and enforcing of safety regulations should be lodged in one agency. The CAA and CAB have both taken this position. The difference between the two agencies lies in the opinion as to where this unified safety activity should be located. The CAB regards it essential that this responsibility in general remain vested in the Board because of the necessary relation between economic and safety regulations. The CAA, on the other hand, considers itself to be the logical agency for this unified safety function in view of its large technical force, its extensive field staff, and the fact that its principal operations lie in the field of promoting safety.

The arguments of both the Administration and the Board are admissible; but the contentions of the Administration, viewed in the light of over-all problems of federal aviation organization, come closest to a theoretically sound as well as practically feasible solution. Responsibility for safety, including the prescribing of regulations, their administration and enforcement, and the investigation of accidents, must with one exception (discussed below) be vested in a single agency. Ambiguity and divided responsibility must be avoided. The fact that the operations of the CAA are to a major degree directed to the goal of safe aircraft operation points to this agency as the logical focus of safety activities. The fact that its present functions require engineering and technical personnel and an extensive field staff add a further practical basis for vesting this responsibility in the promotional agency. The Board, on the other hand, is concerned not with technical matters but with economic and legal problems. For the Board to carry out these responsibilities, together with those which relate to the very different problems of aviation safety, would mean a diverting of energy and attention from the main responsibilities of economic regulation. To suggest that the Board attempt to maintain a technical staff duplicating CAA, both in Washington and the field, would be not only wasteful but productive of the kind of confusion which compels a reorganization of these activities.

The contention that safety regulation is closely allied to economic regulation is accepted; but it cannot be concluded from this fact that the promotional agency charged with fostering the development of aviation is in a position to ignore the economic implications of its safety regulations. On the contrary, the CAA has a greater direct responsibility than CAB for an economic development of aviation in all its phases.

Concerning accident investigation, there is no disagreement with the principle that this function must be free of bias. All agree that accident investigation must be impartial. The question raised, however, is whether an independent agency is essential to impartiality, or whether, in fact, it provides it. This question is important because of the very substantial practical difficulties involved in the creation of an independent investigating agency. One of these is the problem of staff. The federal government cannot justify duplicating the present CAA field staff, which, in addition to its inspection and other duties, already is investigating all accidents to determine violations. Moreover, if most of this work continued to be delegated to CAA, as at present, the independent investigating body would be limited, as it was in the past, to investigating very few accidents, and would be unoccupied a large part of the time. A second practical problem arises from the attempt to place the responsibility for accident investigation in a vacuum, isolated from the authority or responsibility for taking the necessary corrective action, and divorced from the day-to-day operations which make safety possible. It is conceded that the possibility of achieving greater independence of judgment in the investigation of certain aircraft accidents by a special board might offer a potential advantage, but this potential could hardly compensate for the weaknesses in safety promotion which are bound to result from a continuation of divided responsibility in this field.

The contention that accident investigation must be performed by an independent body logically calls for similar independent investigation of other aviation matters involving the federal government. The efficient operation of the radio ranges, for example, is highly important to safety. If the federal organization operating these facilities cannot provide honest investigation of accidents, it can hardly be considered capable of maintaining the navigation facilities upon which safety depends.

The case made for independent accident investigation is based, in part, on the erroneous contention that an opportunity exists to conceal facts. Actually, the manner in which accident investigation is carried out, the different interests represented at the scene, and the holding of public hearings, make the possibility remote that known facts can be withheld. The basic fallacy, however, is the implied assumption that safety depends on accident investigation; that accident investigation is the most important phase of safety work, and therefore that a super agency is required to meet this particular need. In reality, accident investigation, while a highly useful tool in the promotion of safety, is only part of the total effort. It is the final resort which marks the failure of positive provisions to achieve safety.

The fact remains, however, that in the case of airline accidents, which command extensive public attention, and which offer exceptionally difficult problems of accident determination, some special machinery may be desirable to assure that the aviation promotional agency, however conscientious, will not be in a position of determining accident causes when these involve intricate questions as to the effectiveness of its own rules and operations. Accordingly, the reorganization plan presented later in this study provides special machinery to accomplish an independent determination of accident cause in the case of major airline accidents.[32]

Finally, it is apparent that the problems of administering and enforcing the rules and regulations pertaining to 100,000 aircraft and 450,000 pilots present a difficult task for the federal government. With the further development of private flying, the volume of these activities will eventually be such as to make it impractical for the federal government to handle the problem. The progressive shifting of these operating responsibilities from federal to state jurisdictions, and from government to designated industry representatives is, therefore, essential to the effective functioning of the federal government in its policy-making role.

[32] See p. 395.

# CHAPTER V

# WATER TRANSPORTATION

The fostering of transportation by water is a traditional interest of the federal government, which has been the chief source of financial support in this field during the past century. Federal expenditures have provided harbors and channels, an extensive inland waterway system, lighthouses, markers, and other navigation aids. In addition, federal barge line service is furnished on the inland waterways. Extensive financial support is likewise provided for the development of the merchant marine, including ship construction and operating subsidies, and a variety of services to marine operations.

## I. RIVERS AND HARBORS

The federal government has thus far spent more than three billion dollars for river and harbor work. This sum has been used for the improvement, maintenance, and operation of harbors on the seacoasts and Great Lakes, and for the development of the Mississippi River system, the intracoastal canals, and other waterways. The two largest items have been the cost of improving the Mississippi River system and the improvement of seacoast harbors and channels, each involving 1.2 billion dollars of federal expenditure. (See table p. 82.)

In recent years the magnitude of the federal program for river and harbor development has been increasing rapidly. (See chart p. 82.) Peak expenditures were reached in the period 1934 to 1940, when over 900 million dollars were spent. This was approximately three times the sum spent over a comparable length of time in the previous decade. There has been no attempt on the part of the federal government to charge the users for the special facilities provided for them.

81

FEDERAL EXPENDITURES FOR RIVERS AND HARBORS, 1922-48[a]

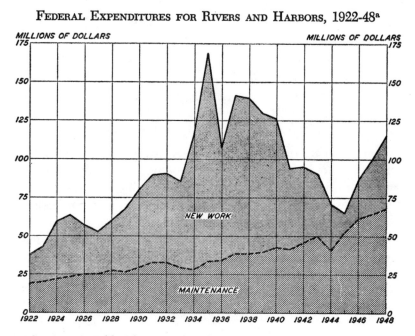

MILLIONS OF DOLLARS

NEW WORK

MAINTENANCE

[a] See App. A, Table 8 for supporting data.

FEDERAL EXPENDITURES FOR RIVERS AND HARBORS
THROUGH FISCAL 1948[a]

(In Millions of Dollars)

| Purpose | New Work | Maintenance | Total Expenditures[b] |
|---|---|---|---|
| Seacoast harbors and channels ........... | 789.3 | 420.4 | 1,207.4 |
| Intracoastal canals and other waterways .... | 197.5 | 115.2 | 311.3 |
| Mississippi River System ............... | 881.9 | 367.4 | 1,248.1 |
| Lake harbors and channels .............. | 222.9 | 115.0 | 336.6 |
| Examinations, surveys, contingencies ...... | 9.0 | 76.8 | 85.7 |
| Removing sunken vessels ............... | — | 11.0 | 11.0 |
| Plant: river and harbor ................. | — | — | 52.4 |
| Total ..........................| 2,100.6 | 1,105.8 | 3,252.5 |

[a] *Annual Report of the Chief of Engineers, U. S. Army, 1948,* Pt. 1, Vol. 1, p. 22.
[b] Totals in this column differ from the sum of construction and maintenance expenditures due to the omission from this table of accounts payable and receivable, and value of plant, stocks, and undistributed items.

*Facilities and traffic.* Exclusive of the Great Lakes, there are 27,300 miles of improved navigable inland waterways in the United States. The majority of these have authorized project depths of less than 6 feet, but 4,400 miles have been improved or are authorized to be improved to a depth of 12 feet or more. The mileage of the improved navigable inland waterways in the United States is as follows.[1]

| Group or System | Miles |
|---|---|
| Atlantic Coast Rivers Group | 5,800 |
| Mississippi River System | 12,000 |
| Gulf Coast Group | 4,000 |
| Pacific Coast Rivers Group | 1,440 |
| Atlantic Intracoastal Waterway | 2,000 |
| Gulf Intracoastal Waterway | 1,100 |
| Total | 27,300 |

The Mississippi River and some 30 tributaries make up the most extensive system of waterways, affording more than 12,000 miles of navigable channels and accommodating some

TON-MILES OF FREIGHT CARRIED ON INLAND WATERWAYS, 1940[a]

| System | Billions of Ton-Miles | Per cent |
|---|---|---|
| Atlantic Coast rivers | 1.9 | 1.6 |
| Gulf Coast rivers | .6 | .5 |
| Pacific Coast rivers | 1.2 | 1.0 |
| Mississippi River System | 13.9 | 11.8 |
| Canals and connecting channels | 4.8 | 4.1 |
| Great Lakes System[b] | 95.6 | 81.0 |
| Total | 118.0 | 100.0 |

[a] Office of Defense Transportation, *Civilian War Transport,* July 1948, p. 308. Data are exclusive of coastal and intercoastal traffic, and exclude 9.5 million ton-miles carried on "other waterways."
[b] Excludes traffic between foreign ports.

1,500 self-propelled and 6,000 non-self-propelled units.[2] This system in 1940 was carrying about 14 billion ton-miles of traffic compared to approximately 8.5 billion ton-miles on all other waterways combined (excluding the Great Lakes). The

[1] The American Waterways Operators, Inc., *Inland Waterway Transportation in America,* February 1948, pp. 2-3.
[2] The same.

Great Lakes normally account for approximately 80 per cent of all inland waterway traffic. (See table p. 83.)

*Authorization procedure.* Since 1819 the Corps of Engineers has been responsible for investigating proposed river and harbor improvements, and most of the work authorized by the Congress has been carried out by this agency.[3] Authorization of a river and harbor project involves a complicated procedure. Local interests, either individuals or groups, request their representatives in Congress to include a desired project in a river and harbor bill, which will authorize the Corps of Engineers to determine the feasibility and economic soundness of such a project. The chief of engineers then orders a preliminary investigation by the district engineer for the area in which the project is located, and an open public hearing is held. A preliminary investigation report is then forwarded through the chief of engineers to the Board of Engineers for Rivers and Harbors for study and recommendation. The purpose is to determine whether sufficient merit exists in the project to warrant a more detailed survey.[4]

If the project is not deemed feasible, an unfavorable report is sent to Congress with the recommendation that no further action be taken. The nature of large numbers of these proposals is indicated by the fact that preliminary investigation results in the rejection of half the projects submitted.

If the preliminary investigation indicates that further study is warranted, a detailed survey is made to determine a practical engineering solution and the estimated cost. The results of the detailed surveys are referred to the Board of Engineers for Rivers and Harbors, which makes the final recommendation to the chief of engineers.

At this stage, the chief of engineers sends the report, together with his proposed recommendations, to the governors of the states involved, and the formal views of other federal agencies are also obtained, together with a statement from

[3] For a description of the origins of federal activity in this field, see Board of Investigation and Research, *Public Aids to Domestic Transportation,* H. Doc. 159, 79 Cong. 1 sess., pp. 325-29.

[4] Preliminary surveys are based on existing information rather than field studies, and most of them involve an expenditure of less than $1,000.

the Bureau of the Budget as to the relationship of the project to the program of the president.[5] At no point in this process is there an objective consideration of the relation of the proposed undertaking to over-all transportation requirements. The Budget Bureau can at best do no more than attempt to exclude the least desirable proposals.

Finally, the report is submitted to Congress to be considered by the appropriate committees. The report is then included in an omnibus river and harbor bill and is subsequently enacted into law. Funds for executing the project are later included in budget estimates for the civil functions of the Department of the Army. After consideration and possible revision by the Bureau of the Budget, these estimates are submitted to the appropriations committee of the Congress.[6]

*Current waterway program.* The present program for federal improvement of rivers and harbors for navigation and allied purposes as authorized by Congress includes projects located in the continental United States, Puerto Rico, Alaska, and the Hawaiian Islands. There are now approximately 1,100 active projects. The total estimated cost of completing all authorized river and harbor work considered necessary in the interest of navigation is about $1,966,000,000. Surveys which have been completed on projects as yet unauthorized involve an estimated additional cost of more than $1,983,000,000. There is thus a backlog of authorized and recommended river and harbor projects in excess of $3,949,000,000.[7] The Army Civil Functions Appropriation Act for 1949, which makes available $166,989,100 for rivers and harbors, includes construction and planning funds of $90,412,100 to be applied to the authorized program.

[5] The Corps of Engineers is required, in accordance with the nature of the project, to obtain the views of the Bureau of Reclamation, Federal Power Commission, and the Fish and Wildlife Service. Also, through the Interagency River Basin Committee, the Departments of Agriculture and Commerce may express their views. It will be observed that no check is required with any transportation agency.

[6] Statement of Lt. General R. A. Wheeler, *River and Harbor Legislation*, Hearings before the Subcommittee on Rivers and Harbors, House Committee on Public Works, 80 Cong. 1 sess., Feb. 28, 1947, pp. 4-5.

[7] *Annual Report of the Chief of Engineers, U. S. Army*, 1948, Pt. 1, Vol. 1, p. 2.

Maintenance, operation, and other nonconstruction expenditures account for the remaining $76,577,000.[8]

The extent to which the federal government has been committed to carrying out further work of this nature in the future is indicated by the six-year construction program maintained by the Corps. The program assumes a sharp rise in annual construction outlays from the 1949 level, reflecting the backlog of authorized projects on which no construction has as yet been started. The 1950 level of construction in the six-year plan calls for expenditures twice as great as the 1949 appropriations of 90 millions; and by 1952 the level of construction activity planned would be three times the 1949 figure. (See table below.)

PLANNED CONSTRUCTION PROGRAM FOR WATERWAYS[a]

| Year | Amount |
|------|--------|
| 1949 | $ 90,412,100 |
| 1950 | 186,449,190 |
| 1951 | 231,659,670 |
| 1952 | 269,308,480 |
| 1953 | 259,391,700 |
| 1954 | 230,581,150 |
| After 1954 | 546,487,150 |

[a] Figures, except for 1949, are from *Civil Functions, Department of the Army, Appropriations Bill for 1949*, Hearings before the Subcommittee of the House Committee on Appropriations, January 1948, p. 279.

*Financing waterways.* The large sums of general tax funds spent in recent years for inland waterway facilities, and the financial requirements for the completion of projects already started, indicate that greater consideration needs to be given to the economic justification and appropriate financing of these facilities. This question has been raised many times in the past, and the desirability of establishing future waterway policy on an economic basis has been frequently stated. To date, however, the obstacles in the way of achieving this goal have proved greater than the conviction that remedial steps need to be taken.

[8] Public Law 782, 80 Cong. 2 sess.

Some indications of the waste of general tax funds resulting from the overenthusiastic development of waterways is provided by the public aid studies of the Board of Investigation and Research. In these studies comparison was made of the annual cost per ton-mile of carrying traffic on the various sections of the waterway system. For ports, rivers, and short connecting channels, the amount of federal aid required per ton of traffic is available for 289 active projects. The cost to the federal government of the improvements made on these facilities ranged from less than half a cent per ton of traffic moved to more than five dollars a ton.[9] For another group of 326 active projects covering longer rivers and canals, records of ton-miles of traffic reveal that average annual waterway costs ranged from one fifth of a cent to $1.90 per ton-mile.

These variations in unit cost of providing waterway transportation are the result of a combination of factors. Some projects are relatively new and have not had an opportunity to develop traffic. Others have extremely high cost due to losses of traffic resulting from industrial relocation or the development of more economical means of transportation. In other cases projects were ill-conceived from the outset.

When one form of transportation is subsidized by public expenditures for basic facilities, traffic may be attracted to the subsidized agency, because rates do not have to cover total economic costs. In the case of water transportation, rates reflect only the cost of owning and operating the equipment, and not the cost of providing the waterways. The user of the subsidized water carrier pays only the "transportation cost," and the remaining cost is borne by the general taxpayer. Savings accrue to the shipper, but from a national viewpoint the economy of water transport is illusory since the balance of total cost is met by non-shippers.

The report of the federal coordinator pointed out that there are two possible approaches to the question of placing water transportation on an economic basis.[10] One relates to the question of charging tolls and the other to the possibility of local

[9] H. Doc. 159, 79 Cong. 1 sess., p. 586.
[10] Federal Coordinator of Transportation, *Public Aids to Transportation*, Vol. 3 (1939).

matching of federal expenditures. One of the objections to the imposition of tolls is the fear that such a reversal of long-standing federal policy would cause serious economic disturbances to carriers, shippers, and specific localities. Secondly, it is contended that such a reversal of policy would destroy the value of the government's investment by reducing the use of the waterways. And third, the position is taken that such a policy would be unfair inasmuch as government applies general funds to other forms of transportation.

It is true that charging tolls would result in dislocations, yet the absence of tolls means hardships on those carriers, shippers, and sections of the country which do not have the advantage of cheap transportation on toll-free facilities, but which must nevertheless help defray their cost.[11] The contention that establishment of tolls would seriously impair the use of existing water investments is more to the point, but the wide variation in the cost of providing waterway transportation, previously noted, indicates that it might be more economic to abandon some of these projects altogether than to attempt to maintain them for the light traffic now being carried.

Although it may be impossible or undesirable to levy tolls on facilities already provided, the coordinator's report suggested that it might be possible to avoid further mistakes by insisting that future projects be made to pay their way. Discrimination would result, however, if tolls were levied only on new projects, with existing waterway facilities left free. As to abandoning waterways already built, a few projects might be terminated without protest, but "the presence of permanent structures having a long life and the intermingling of navigation with flood control, power, and other nonnavigation objectives . . . all indicate that abandonment of any sizable project is purely an academic question."[12]

Consideration of the problem of providing a more economic basis for water transport development points also to the need

[11] Rate discrimination stemming from subsidies is analyzed in Chap. 11.
[12] Federal Coordinator of Transportation, *Public Aids to Transportation*, Vol. 3, p. 127.

for revising the method of evaluating waterway projects. The Board of Investigation and Research recommended a strict test of ability to earn full annual cost in the case of all future proposals for new construction. Any proposal unable to meet this test would not be undertaken. The Board also recommended the adoption of more precise cost allocation on multiple-purpose projects where flood control, reclamation, power, and navigation objectives are involved; and it proposed more exacting standards to determine the amount of traffic which could reasonably be expected on proposed waterways.[13]

With regard to the question of charging tolls, it is apparent that an economic allocation of traffic would be furthered if costs were reflected in rates. The Board of Investigation and Research pointed out, however, that abrupt termination of water subsidies would create extensive economic disruption in affected areas and industries. It was recommended, therefore, that tolls should reflect total costs only on waterways where full traffic potentialities had been developed, or where it could be demonstrated that abrupt application of user charges would not cause undue disruption of activities which had grown up around subsidized water transportation. A transitional policy of gradually imposing tolls would be warranted in the case of facilities on which traffic potentials had not yet been developed. Any project which would not bear user charges sufficient to cover at least current maintenance should be abandoned; but since waterway investments, however uneconomic, represent "sunk" costs which cannot be recovered, they should be available to users willing to pay current maintenance.

## II. GOVERNMENT BARGE LINES

The Inland Waterways Corporation, created by act of Congress in 1924,[14] operates a government barge service on the inland waterways. The Corporation finances its operations by means of a revolving fund rather than through annual appropriations from the Congress. The authorized capital stock

[13] H. Doc. 159, 79 Cong. 1 sess., pp. 393-99.
[14] 43 Stat. 360, June 3, 1924.

is 15 million dollars, of which 12 millions had been appropriated through 1948.[15] An additional 2 million dollars was appropriated in 1949 to enable the Corporation to obtain new capital equipment.

Prior to 1930 the operations of the Corporation resulted in annual losses except in two years. From 1930 to 1939, with the exception of 1934, operations were reported to be profitable, resulting in an earned surplus of 2.7 million dollars. The operations from 1939 to date have resulted in continued and increasing annual losses, reaching a peak of 2.5 million dollars in 1946. Losses in 1947 were 1.9 millions.[16]

The objective of the Inland Waterways Corporation is to demonstrate the feasibility of water transportation on the inland rivers and to extend the benefits of this service. The Corporation operates common carrier service by barge on the Mississippi, Illinois, Missouri, and Warrior Rivers, subject to regulation by the Interstate Commerce Commission. All types of freight except livestock and perishables are handled, and operations are conducted over a system of 3,300 miles of inland rivers. Equipment includes 22 boats and 273 barges. Cargo is handled through numerous private terminals, as well as through general merchandise facilities.

In accordance with the declared policy of the Congress,[17] the Inland Waterways Corporation is to be continued until (1) the rivers on which the Corporation operates are adequate for dependable transportation service; (2) terminal facilities are provided adequate to meet the needs of transportation; (3) joint service with rail carriers has been established on reasonable terms; and (4) private industry is ready and willing to engage in common carrier service on the waterways served by the Corporation. Under this declaration of policy it is unlikely that the Inland Waterways Corporation will ever be terminated.

[15] *Annual Report of the Inland Waterways Corporation, Calendar Year 1946 and Fiscal Year Ending June 30, 1947*, p. 51.
[16] Statement of A. C. Ingersoll, President of the Inland Waterways Corporation, *Government Corporations Appropriation Bill for 1949*, Hearings before the House Committee on Appropriations, 80 Cong. 2 sess., p. 367.
[17] 43 Stat. 360.

As long as the capital costs of the waterways are met by general fund appropriations, the subsidized service provides no demonstration of the economic desirability of operating such service. Further, it is doubtful that any private agency would undertake to achieve the objectives stated by Congress, since the standards of adequacy set by the government would be difficult to meet if the carriers were to operate at a profit. For example, the Corporation now has under way a rehabilitation program which will require substantial investment. It is stated that: "Whoever has the responsibility of carrying on these common carrier services must, if he is to fulfill this responsibility, carry the rehabilitation program through to its completion."[18] Private enterprise is assured, however, that this provision "should not be a hindrance to negotiations for the sale of the property, since obsolescence of the present equipment is largely responsible for the poor financial showing of the Corporation."[19] Yet elsewhere, according to the statement of A. C. Ingersoll, President of the Inland Waterways Corporation: "Rehabilitation has been handicapped by a shortage of funds, as operating losses have eaten into the capital needed for new equipment. . . ."[20]

With respect to the provision of joint rail-water rates, although savings may accrue to particular shippers by reason of rail-rate reductions designed to meet water competition, the railroads must compensate for these rate reductions by raising their rates on other traffic. Thus there is merely a shift of benefits among groups of users, and from a national viewpoint the argument is unconvincing.[21]

Opposition to the continuance and proposed expansion of the activities of the Inland Waterways Corporation has been expressed by the operators of privately owned inland water transport services. The American Waterways Operators, representing private enterprise in the field, have taken the position that while the Inland Waterways Corporation served a useful

[18] Statement of William C. Foster, *Government Corporations Appropriation Bill for 1949*, Hearings, p. 364.
[19] The same.
[20] The same, p. 373.
[21] This phase of the problem is analyzed further in Pt. 2.

purpose in reviving water transportation when it was at its lowest ebb, the project should now be discontinued.[22] The act creating the government corporation specifically provides that it shall be sold and discontinued when private enterprise is ready and willing to take over its activities. This time, according to the Waterways Operators, has come.

That the Federal Barge Line's mission . . . has been successful is attested by the fact that there are now several hundred privately-owned barge lines operating in competition to it . . . and the service on such routes is completely adequate to handle all traffic that can possibly be economically attracted to water transportation.

Instead of making plans to give way to private enterprise, as the law creating it definitely contemplates, the Federal Barge Line has embarked upon a program of expansion and rehabilitation designed solely to enable it to more effectively and successfully compete with private enterprise.[23]

Private carriers on the inland waterways are therefore urging Congress to order the Federal Barge Line to discontinue its activities on all routes now being served by privately owned barge lines.[24]

*Conclusion.* In appraising the Inland Waterways Corporation, it is clear not only from the standpoint of the financial record, but from the present condition of the equipment being used, that the barge line is no longer justified. For example, in 1946 it was determined by the Corporation that of the 26 towboats and 273 barges in the fleet, only 5 towboats and 99 barges had any useful life left.[25] Further, in the first quarter of 1948, "108 barges have had to go to the shipyards for patching; 22 barges are now in such bad condition that their use is restricted to deck loads only, and 7 are out of service entirely awaiting repairs. This condition will become much worse in the coming months."[26] The fact that the Corporation

[22] Chester C. Thompson, president, The American Waterways Operators, Inc., in an address at the annual convention of the Ohio River Improvement Association, Cincinnati, Ohio, Apr. 28, 1947.

[23] The same, pp. 11-12.

[24] The same, p. 13.

[25] *Government Corporations Appropriation Bill for 1949,* Hearings, p. 387.

[26] The same, p. 369. The president of the Federal Barge Line stated before

has failed to meet its costs or maintain its equipment, despite the use of free waterways and the provision of capital from the federal treasury, demonstrates that the service has proved economically infeasible.

In conclusion, the Congress, in setting up the Inland Waterways Corporation, made clear what the limitations of its experiment were to be:

. . . If this bill becomes a law the Government can and will within the next 5 years demonstrate not only the practicability of water transportation, but the great advantage and the economy to shippers, and the profitable results that will reward private capital invested in transportation facilities on our rivers. And when that time comes, it is the judgment of the committee that the Government can dispose of its properties to private capital to an advantage, and withdraw entirely from such activities.

After the enactment of this bill the Secretary of War can operate the barge lines in accordance with the same business principles that would be followed by a private transportation company. And it is the opinion of the committee that if they cannot then operate it successfully and at a fair profit private capital could not do so; that further expenditure of Government funds for the improvement of our inland waterways would be useless and should be stopped.[27]

Today, nearly a quarter of a century after this statement by the House Committee on Interstate and Foreign Commerce, the operations of the Inland Waterways Corporation continue on the grounds that they constitute an experiment which must yet be given time to prove itself; and the Interstate Commerce Commission in 1948 lends support to this position by quoting what it said 25 years ago to justify its stand today:

In our first report dealing with relations between Federal and the railroads 25 years ago (77 I.C.C. 317,353) we said:

The Mississippi-Warrior service is owned and operated by the Government, as we understand the situation, not necessarily as a

---

a Subcommittee of the House Committee on Appropriations in 1947 that "many barge operators, private, contract and common carriers have better, more efficient fleets and provide faster and more dependable service than the Federal Barge Line." *Rail and Barge Joint Rates,* 270 I.C.C. 591, 606, July 7, 1948.

[27] Report of the Committee on Interstate and Foreign Commerce on creation of the Inland Waterways Corporation, H. Rept. 375, 68 Cong. 1 sess., Mar. 26, 1924.

permanent governmental undertaking, but to test the possibilities of transportation by barge upon these great inland waterways. . . . Clearly everything that can be done ought to be done to give this experiment a fair opportunity to demonstrate its worth, and in this endeavor the project should be viewed in the light of the service which can reasonably be anticipated and without permitting vision to be obscured by the difficulties and embarrassments which surround every new enterprise and particularly one which has been compelled to start life with a heritage of worn-out and inadequate facilities. On the other hand, it is equally clear that the experiment will not be fairly conducted if the barge line is permitted to tap the resources of the rail lines by depriving them in any way of just compensation for the services which they perform in connection with its operation.[28]

According to the Commission, this statement is "worth recalling" because the Federal Barge Line "once more is struggling with worn-out and inadequate facilities."[29] According to this reasoning, the difficulties and embarrassments resulting from failure of the enterprise can be looked upon as identical with the problems of starting anew with a heritage of worthless equipment. The life cycle of the experiment starts anew.

### III. THE MERCHANT MARINE

During the period from 1916 to 1947, the federal government spent over 16.5 billion dollars for the development of its merchant marine. These expenditures have related primarily to the requirements of the first and second world wars. Shipbuilding programs have accounted for 14.4 of the 16.5 billions spent, while construction and operating differential subsidies have amounted to 359 million dollars. (See table p. 95.)

Current federal action in the promotion of United States shipping is governed by the provisions of the Merchant Marine Act of 1936 and certain subsequent legislation.[30] This act

[28] 270 I.C.C. 591, 612.
[29] The same.
[30] 49 Stat. 1985. The Merchant Marine Act established the U. S. Maritime Commission to assume the functions previously performed by the U. S. Shipping Board and altered by the Bureau of Shipping of the Department of Commerce, and to perform other duties imposed by the act. The Commission is an independent body, the members of which are appointed by the president by and with the consent of the Senate.

inaugurated a new basis for government support of the merchant marine, replacing the policy of indirect subsidy through mail contracts by a policy of direct subsidy. The latter was based upon differentials which might exist between the cost of

FEDERAL EXPENDITURES FOR MERCHANT MARINE[a]

| Expenditures by Government | Millions of Dollars |
| --- | --- |
| Loans—to June 30, 1946 | **483.6**[b] |
| Mail contracts | 206.1 |
| Building programs to government accounts to April 30, 1947 | 14,433.0 |
| Construction—differential subsidies to April 30, 1947 | 307.7 |
| Operating—differential subsidies to December 31, 1946 | 51.3 |
| Expenditures on shipbuilding facilities to April 30, 1947 | 599.2 |
| Administrative expenses to December 31, 1946 | 371.1 |
| Total Expenditures | 16,452.0 |

[a] *Report of the President's Advisory Committee on the Merchant Marine,* November 1947, p. 64.
[b] Includes funds amounting to $313,890,691.70 advanced by the Federal Reserve Bank on loans which were guaranteed by the Maritime Commission.

constructing vessels in United States and foreign shipyards, and between principal expenses of ship operation by American flag and foreign operators. This change of policy was designed to provide a more certain and adequate basis for American flag lines to maintain fleet and services. It committed the federal government to paying whatever amounts are necessary to maintain a merchant marine adequate for the purposes enumerated in the act, and specifically to maintain adequate service on the routes which the Commission held to be essential.

Administration of merchant marine policy on the scope attempted since 1916 constitutes one of the most difficult tasks of the federal government. The maritime agency is called upon to exercise extensive controls and supervision over every phase of a complex and unique industry. There are two industries to be fostered: shipbuilding and ship operation. The conduct of a program which will assure a merchant marine capable of meeting the requirements of commerce and defense must include the maintenance of a minimum scale of shipbuilding capacity as well as a minimum of vessels available for emergency. The carrying out of the promotional program requires that the agency first determine what the size and pattern of the ship construction industry shall be, and of the fleet, both operating and reserve. It must then provide for carrying out the program established. For example, under the present direct subsidy program the agency must determine the essential routes to be served and the amount of service required under the American flag on each route. It must administer the construction and operating subsidy contracts with private operators; construct vessels in connection with the construction subsidy program; sell government-built vessels; charter and operate vessels pending disposal to private owners or to the reserve fleet; and, finally, maintain vessels, active and reserve, owned by the government. The administration of the accounting, finance, research, and claims incident to these activities is very extensive.

*Development of merchant marine policy.* Recent merchant marine policy may be said to have had its beginning in the enactment of the Shipping Act of 1916.[31] This act established the United States Shipping Board, with powers to purchase, construct, equip, lease, charter, maintain, and operate merchant vessels in the commerce of the United States, with a view to developing a merchant marine to promote the national defense and commerce of the United States. This marks the beginning of a determination on the part of Congress that, through the development of a shipbuilding industry and the operation of vessels in commerce, the United States would have a merchant marine of considerable size and importance.

The Shipping Act authorized the Board to establish whatever corporations it considered necessary to carry out its responsibilities. Accordingly, in 1917, there was created the United States Shipping Board Emergency Fleet Corporation, to which was delegated the ship construction program.

In general, the objectives of policy with respect to promotion of the merchant marine have been basically consistent through

---

[31] 39 Stat. 728, approved Sept. 7, 1916.

the various amendments to the Shipping Act and the later merchant marine acts and their amendments. As stated in the Merchant Marine Act, 1936, and repeated in the Merchant Ship Sales Act of 1946,[32] the merchant marine should be sufficient to carry the domestic water-borne commerce and a substantial portion of the foreign trade of the United States, and to provide service on all routes essential for maintaining the flow of domestic and foreign water-borne commerce.[33] The merchant fleet should be capable of serving as a naval and military auxiliary in time of war, and should be composed of the best-equipped service and most suitable types of vessels, constructed in the United States and manned with a trained citizen personnel.

A substantial shift in emphasis from regulation to promotion is to be found in the various acts. While it was contemplated that regulation would take comparable rank with promotion when the act of 1916 passed, the early entry of the United States into World War I precipitated a broad program of construction, requisition, and operation, which relegated regulation to the background. After the war the principal task of the Shipping Board was that of ship disposal. The Merchant Marine Acts of 1920[34] and 1928[35] were devoted to the objective of promotion. The act of 1928 provided for direct operating subsidy through mail contracts. Previously, aid to shipping had been confined to construction loans and sale of government ships at prices far below actual cost.

In the Intercoastal Shipping Act of 1933[36] the United States Shipping Board was given more extensive authority in the regulation of common and contract carriers in domestic commerce through the Panama Canal. This authority was extended to all deep-sea common carriers in interstate commerce in the

---

[32] 60 Stat. 41.

[33] Operating-differential subsidies, suspended in 1942 when ships were requisitioned, were resumed on Jan. 1, 1947, for the 12 lines holding suspended contracts. By the end of 1947, six new applications had been approved.

[34] 41 Stat. 988, approved June 5, 1920.

[35] 45 Stat. 689, approved May 22, 1928.

[36] 47 Stat. 1425, approved March 3, 1933.

amendment of 1938.[37] However, in the Transportation Act of 1940,[38] the regulation of all interstate water carrier operations, except those applying to shipping in the noncontiguous trades, was placed under the Interstate Commerce Commission. Since the noncontiguous trades are limited in number and do not involve competition with other domestic carriers, the problem of regulation is a comparatively simple one. Extensive jurisdiction over discriminatory rates and service of lines engaged in foreign shipping was assured by the government under the act of 1916 and has been continuing to the present. However, neither the original Shipping Board nor the United States Maritime Commission has given great attention to regulation. These agencies have generally relied upon complaints of gross discrimination, although in a few instances investigations have been instituted on their own motion.

The program for long-range shipbuilding provided for in the act of 1936 was accelerated by the war and supplemented by the emergency ship construction program, causing further emphasis in federal policy on problems of promotion and development. This emergency program was carried out by the War Shipping Administration.[39]

In summary, then, the Maritime Commission carries out the following promotional functions:

1. Applies the provisions relating to construction-differential and operating-differential subsidies.

2. When necessary, supplements private ship construction and operation, subsidized and nonsubsidized, by construction and operation of vessels.

3. Administers sale of war-built tonnage as provided by the Merchant Ship Sales Act of 1946.

4. Provides for the establishment of the National Defense Reserve Fleet.

---

[37] 52 Stat. 964.

[38] 54 Stat. 898.

[39] The War Shipping Administration was established within the Office of Emergency Management on Feb. 7, 1942 by Executive Order 9054, issued under the First War Powers Act (55 Stat. 838). It was absorbed by the Maritime Commission in 1946.

5. Performs services and functions in support of the merchant marine operation as a whole, including the training of personnel and the acquisition of vessels by purchase or charter.

6. Charters vessels owned by the government.

7. Conducts investigations in regard to the condition of the merchant marine and recommends policies for its improvement.

*Current status of merchant marine activity.* Restoration of the merchant marine to private ownership or operation has been almost fully accomplished, and the disposal of a large proportion of war-built vessels, under the Merchant Ship Sales Act of 1946, has been completed. Practically all of the 900 requisitioned vessels in government service on VJ-day had been redelivered to their owners by mid-1947, and in the same period, private operators had chartered 1,510 vessels from the government on a bare boat basis. Most of these vessels were engaged in carrying relief cargoes abroad. Of some 400 vessels transferred to foreign governments under lend-lease or other provisions, and operated since the war on charter, arrangements had been made for the sale or return of all except those lend-leased to Russia. By mid-1948 nearly half of the 4,000 large vessels available under the Merchant Ship Sales Act of 1946 had been sold for about 1.7 billion dollars. In addition, nearly all of approximately 11,000 small vessels available for sale had been disposed of for 66 million dollars.[40] By the end of the fiscal year 1948, 1,675 surplus ships not sold or chartered had been placed in 10 reserve fleets.

In 1947 the United States built only about 4 per cent of all ships under construction in the world's shipyards. Total United States construction in the fiscal year 1948 was 33 ships.[41] The Maritime Commission's long-range dry cargo shipbuilding program calls for 1,044 vessels, of which about 900 vessels presently in use are considered suitable, leaving some 144 vessels to be built in the next 10 years. To prevent the fleet from becoming obsolete at one time, the Commission has suggested a twenty-

---

[40] *United States Maritime Commission Report to Congress for the Fiscal Year ended June 30, 1948,* pp. 40-42.

[41] The same, p. 71.

five-year long-range program which would provide for building about 25 ships a year for the first ten years and 64 ships a year for the succeeding 15 years. The principal activity in American shipyards in recent months has been the reconstruction and conversion of war-built vessels being prepared for peacetime service.

*The national defense problem.* The Advisory Committee on the Merchant Marine was appointed by the president in March 1947 to study the problems of the American merchant marine and of the American shipbuilding industry. The Committee pointed to the fact that a modern, efficient merchant fleet, and an effective and progressive shipbuilding industry are "indispensable to national security and would have to be maintained even should there be no other benefits accruing."[42] At the outset of World War I and again at the beginning of World War II, the United States undertook an emergency shipbuilding program of tremendous proportions, but on both occasions the country was granted a period of warning and time after the declaration of war in which to prepare. However, a realistic view of any future war requires acceptance of the position that we will not again have the advantage of a preparation period.

The recommendations of the President's Committee on the Merchant Marine were offered with a view to avoiding a repetition of the periodic breakdowns which have occurred from 1865 up to the passage of the 1936 act in attempts to maintain an adequate merchant marine. The fact that more than two and one-half billion dollars were spent for emergency merchant ship construction in World War I, and 12 billions for the same purpose in World War II, is evidence of the need, under the threat of a sudden war, for maintaining shipbuilding and ship operation in time of peace. The preservation of shipbuilding skills and the know-how of ship operation is essential to national security. The difficulty of preserving these national assets lies in the fact that even "under the most favorable condi-

---

[42] *Report of the President's Advisory Committee on the Merchant Marine,* November 1947. p. 2.

tions and regardless of the amount of aid furnished by the government, it will be impossible for the economy of this country to support in time of peace an active merchant marine and an active shipbuilding industry of the size which will be required in the event of a future major war."[43]

Although it is not possible to state in precise terms what the size of the active peacetime merchant fleet should be in order to meet future emergencies, estimates have been made by various government departments. All the estimates fall within a lower limit of 860 ships of 8.9 million deadweight tons and an upper limit of 1,325 ships of 13.4 million deadweight tons. The mean of these estimates is about 1,000 ships of between 11 million and 12 million deadweight tons, which the President's Committee considered to be a "reasonable minimum size of an active seagoing merchant fleet to meet the country's security requirements."[44] As of June 30, 1948, our active fleet more than met this minimum requirement. The Maritime Commission reported 477 vessels in the domestic trade with a deadweight of approximately 6 million tons; and in overseas trade there were 1,246 vessels with a deadweight of 13.8 million tons. The number of vessels in domestic and foreign trade was 1,723 aggregating 20 million tons.[45]

In addition to this large active fleet, there is also an extensive reserve of laid-up vessels; and the military services are maintaining fleets of merchant vessels, both active and inactive. The active and laid-up fleet comprises 3,565 vessels of 1,000 gross tons or over, with a total gross tonnage of 37 million deadweight tons. With respect to military fleets, the Navy now has 128 active vessels and 61 in reserve, making 189 vessels exclusive of oilers. This fleet includes tankers, dry cargo, reefers, and troop vessels. The Army's fleet comprises 168 vessels totaling

[43] The same, p. 49.

[44] The same, p. 52. Since the reserve fleet is to be maintained solely for wartime and emergency use, the Committee recommended that it be placed under the administration of the Secretary of Defense, and that its size and composition be determined by the Joint Chiefs of Staff.

[45] *United States Maritime Commission Report to Congress for the Fiscal Year Ended June 30, 1948*, p. 68.

over one million tons.[46] This fleet will for the next decade assure us of an unprecedented supply of vessels available for emergency.

Despite the adequacy of merchant fleet facilities at the present time, it must be recognized that the active fleet today is being maintained by a volume of traffic created by abnormal conditions growing out of the war. In addition, although the aggregate tonnage is high, there is a serious unbalance in the present fleet, the most important aspect of which is the shortage of passenger vessels which might be required as troop transports in case of war. A further shortage is said to exist in the category of high-speed tankers. This lack of balance is indicated in the recent communication to the president from the chairman of the Maritime Commission and the secretary of defense.[47] In this letter it was stated that a program of ship construction which might be economically justified at the present time would include 18 modern passenger and combination passenger-cargo vessels, and 20 modern high-speed tankers.

The major question, however, is whether it will be possible over a period of years to maintain an adequate fleet when traffic requirements have returned to a more normal level, and whether it will be possible to replace and modernize the fleet in an orderly program which will permit the maintenance of minimum shipbuilding capacity. The present high volume of foreign shipping can be expected to continue only as long as military occupation and the Economic Recovery Program require. Further, up to this time there has been no serious competition from foreign merchant fleets; but these are now being rebuilt to their prewar levels, and in some cases beyond. The principal maritime nations of Europe are actively engaged in the construction of modern vessels in contrast to the low-level activity in American shipyards; and even the limited American shipbuilding operations at the present time are in large measure for foreign accounts.

[46] Water Transport Service Division, Office of Chief of Transportation, Department of the Army.
[47] Letter dated July 1, 1948.

In the case of domestic shipping, too, the situation continues unfavorable. Most of the present tonnage is operating under charter, and the majority of operations to date have been unprofitable. The requisition of vessels for war purposes has meant a heavy loss of patronage by coastal and intercoastal shipping, most of which will be difficult to retrieve. This difficulty is accentuated by the fact that vessels in use were for the most part built in the emergency war construction program and are, therefore, inadequately designed for economical transportation. Moreover, the present high cost of cargo handling at ports has placed marine transportation at a further disadvantage.[48]

Finally, since the life cycle of ships is approximately 20 years, a large proportion of the present American-flag fleet will be old and obsolete within a matter of 10 to 15 years unless it is possible to develop adequate means of replacement. Numbers of ships alone do not constitute a merchant marine, for the fleet must be of modern, efficient design. The President's Advisory Committee on the Merchant Marine estimated that to maintain an active and modern United States merchant fleet of approximately 1,000 vessels would require the construction of approximately 50 ships or about 500,000 deadweight tons a year. Such a program would give employment to approximately 75,000 men in the shipbuilding industry. Based on various Maritime Commission estimates for similar ships, at present price levels the approximate gross initial money outlay for such a program would average about 150 million dollars a year. "Of this amount, due to industry participation through the purchase of the vessels, the Government's net expenditures should aggregate somewhat less than half."[49]

Because of the importance of our merchant fleet for national defense, it is necessary that any ships built be suitable for wartime auxiliary naval service. Should some modification in the design of a proposed vessel be found necessary in order to equip it better for wartime service, there is provision in existing law for

---

[48] The regulatory aspects of rail-water competition are discussed in Chap. 12.
[49] *Report of the President's Advisory Committee on the Merchant Marine,* November 1947, p. 59.

the cost of such modifications, which may be classed as national defense features, to be met by the expenditure of government funds.

*Conclusion.* The test of the merchant marine program from the standpoint of maintaining an adequate fleet for national security will not be faced until the return of more normal patterns of trade, until other maritime nations have had an opportunity to rebuild their fleets, and until it has been determined whether a restoration of domestic merchant shipping can be achieved through modernization of equipment and other necessary measures. Ultimately, however, the federal government will be faced with highly important problems if it is to preserve the merchant fleet and shipbuilding facilities necessary for national defense. As a result of World War II, the United States now ranks first among the nations with respect to merchant marine facilities. It must be remembered, however, that between the first and second world wars a substantial decline took place in the active dry-cargo tonnage under the American flag, and that efforts to stop this decline were unsuccessful. Our ability in the past to compensate during wartime for inadequate peacetime policies has been based on the fact that time was available to build up an emergency fleet without enemy interference. It is apparent that merchant marine policy cannot be predicated on the assumption that similarly favorable conditions will obtain in the future.[50]

[50] Agencies performing other services for water transportation are described in App. B. These include the Coast Guard, Panama Canal, Coast and Geodetic Survey, and the Office of Transport and Communications in the State Department.

# CHAPTER VI

# HIGHWAY TRANSPORTATION

For more than thirty years the federal government has participated in highway development work in the states through a recurring grant-in-aid program. The federal-aid program, which currently involves the expenditure of 450 million dollars of federal funds annually, is administered by the Public Roads Administration. Funds are matched by the states and distributed among them in accordance with formulas prescribed in the statute. Federal funds are limited to construction and must be spent on designated systems of roads which the states have established in conformity with federal legislation. The federal government acts in an administrative and policy-making capacity; actual planning and construction work is performed by the states.

Although the Public Roads Administration is the principal agency concerned with federal highway activities, the National Park Service in the Department of the Interior and the Forest Service in the Department of Agriculture carry out additional road functions in co-operation with Public Roads.

The present chapter describes the role of the federal government in highway development, the origins and trends of federal activity, and the relation of federal finance to the over-all problem of providing highways in the United States. With this view of current and developing federal policy, discussion is directed to the highway problems ahead and the alternatives to federal participation in their solution.

## I. DEVELOPMENT OF FEDERAL HIGHWAY ACTIVITY

In contrast to the predominant role of the federal government in the provision of air and water transport facilities and services, federal action in highway development has traditionally been centered in local and state governments. Prior to the advent of the motor vehicle, almost all highway construction

105

and maintenance was the responsibility of local governments, including the county, township, and municipality. At approximately the turn of the century, the states began to assume responsibility for limited mileages of highways having state-wide importance; and later, partly because the state became the collector of highway user revenues, state influence extended in varying degrees to greater segments of the highway system. This was accomplished through the assumption of local road and street mileage or through state highway grants-in-aid to local units of government.

The beginnings of federal action on a nation-wide basis occurred with the passage of the Federal-Aid Road Act of 1916, which authorized and appropriated 75 million dollars over a period of 5 years for the construction of rural post roads. The share of federal participation was not to exceed 50 per cent of total construction costs.[1] The original act was amended in 1921 to require that each state designate a system of interstate and intercounty highways eligible for federal aid, such system not to exceed 7 per cent of total highway mileage in each state.[2]

The 1921 act, which appropriated 75 million dollars for the fiscal year 1922, was the last instance in which the authorization and appropriation of regular federal-aid funds were combined. In 1923 Congress adopted the policy of authorizing appropriations of federal funds, leaving the actual appropriation to be made when needed. The authorized appropriations are contractual obligations on the part of the federal government to pay the states their allotted share of the total when projects approved under the program have been completed.[3] This method provides the states with advance notification of federal-aid policy, permitting them time to plan their work accordingly. At present, for example, the federal government

[1] 39 Stat. 355. Annual appropriations were increased from 5 million dollars for the first year to 25 millions for the fifth year.

[2] 42 Stat. 212.

[3] Payments of federal funds are made as the work progresses, with the states making claims for reimbursement to cover the federal share of the work performed. Advances of funds are permitted for states having insufficient funds to carry on their programs. *The Public Roads Administration and Its Work*, (1946) pp. 13 and 16.

is committed to a 450 million dollar aid program for each of the fiscal years ending June 30, 1950 and 1951. This authorization was approved June 29, 1948.[4] Altogether a total of some 4.5 billion dollars was authorized from the beginning of the program in 1917 through fiscal 1948. Other special appropriations made available during the depression of the 1930's have also been spent under the general supervision of the Public Roads Administration, bringing the total of the Public Roads program to nearly 6 billions.[5] (See table below.) In addition, nearly 4 billion dollars

FEDERAL FUNDS FOR HIGHWAY CONSTRUCTION EXCLUSIVE
OF RELIEF PROGRAMS 1917-48[a]
(In millions of dollars)

| Type of Federal Program | Total Authorized |
|---|---|
| Regular federal aid | 4,010 |
| Special authorizations[b] | 1,550 |
| Forest highways | 253 |
| National parks and parkways | 149 |
| Public lands | 26 |
| Total | 5,988 |

[a] Includes only those programs supervised by the Public Roads Administration. For detailed data see App. A, Table 9.
[b] Includes National Recovery funds, Emergency Relief appropriations, and Defense Highway Act funds.

have been spent for highways in connection with work relief programs, most of it under the jurisdiction of the Works Projects Administration.[6] Thus, over a period of 30 years, the federal government has contributed 10 billion dollars for roads and streets, or approximately 20 per cent of the total spent by all levels of government for this purpose.

[4] Public Law 834, 80 Cong. 2 sess.
[5] From 1930 to 1935, an outright grant of $1,200,000,000 was made available to the Public Roads Administration for the purpose of stimulating business recovery.
[6] Beginning in 1935 and continuing for several years, the Work Projects Administration spent 3.7 billion dollars on highway projects to furnish employment. The work involved some 600,000 miles of road, largely under county control.

Notwithstanding the large temporary relief program for highways, the Public Roads Administration in the Federal Works Agency is the principal road building agency of the federal government.[7] It is engaged principally in administering annual authorizations to aid the states in road construction, and operates on a percentage of the total funds authorized in the federal-aid acts.[8] It also co-operates with the Department of Agriculture and the Department of the Interior in the construction of roads in federal areas, conducts research, and participates in the development of highways in foreign countries.

In the co-operative work with the states, the federal role is one of financial and engineering management, involving approval of state plans and specifications, supervision of construction, and inspection of projects. Annual authorizations are apportioned to the states on the basis of population, area, and road mileage. The law places with the states the responsibility for initiation of projects, preparation of plans, and the completion of the work, subject to federal approval. It is the responsibility of the Public Roads Administration to see that all steps are taken in conformity with federal law and in a manner that will best accomplish the established objectives.

*Financial trends.* Relating federal outlays to the amount spent by all units of government for highways indicates the full significance of the increasing role of federal finance. In the United States during the past quarter of a century close to 50 billion dollars has been spent for highways. The bill has been paid in part through state levies on highway users—including motor vehicle registration fees and gasoline taxes—and partly through local property taxes and general tax funds made available by federal, state, and local governments. Over a period

[7] The federal road agency had its beginning as the Office of Road Inquiry, created by the Secretary of Agriculture in 1893. It has since functioned under various names. Under the reorganization effected July 1, 1939, all functions of the Secretary of Agriculture relating to the administration of the Bureau of Public Roads were transferred to the Federal Works Administrator. Today the Public Roads Administration employs 614 people in its Washington office and 2,515 in the field.

[8] Not to exceed three and three quarters per cent of all moneys appropriated or authorized. (Public Law 834, 80 Cong. 2 sess., sec. 6.)

of years the contribution of user charges to the total funds available for highways has increased steadily, and the 1.8 billion dollars raised from these special taxes in 1947 was approximately 60 per cent of all highway revenues.

Along with this trend toward a higher proportion of user-

FEDERAL FUNDS AS PERCENTAGE OF TOTAL
REVENUES FOR HIGHWAYS, 1921-48[a]

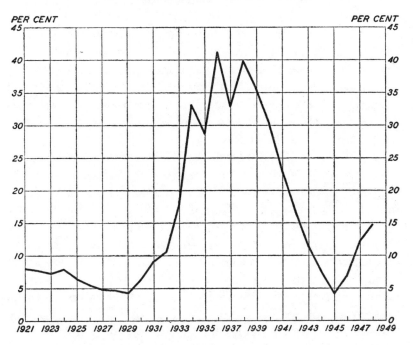

[a] See App. A, Table 10 for supporting data.

tax revenues has been a sharp decline in property tax and state and local general fund support for highways. At the same time the participation of the federal government has expanded, both as regards the scope of federal activity and the percentage of the bill accounted for by federal money. During this period of expanding federal activity, the proportion of federal financing to total highway revenues increased from 9 per cent in 1931 to 41 per cent in 1936. By 1941 federal funds had decreased in importance, but they still accounted for 23 per cent of all funds available for highway purposes. (See chart p. 109.)

The primary federal-aid system now totals 232,000 miles. This includes 7 per cent of the rural road mileage in each state plus additions to the system permitted as the original network has attained a high degree of improvement.[9] Federal activity was confined to improvements on this primary system of rural federal-aid roads until 1933 when, as part of the emergency program to provide employment, federal participation was broadened to include grants for extensions of the federal-aid system through cities, and for secondary roads. Two years later the first specific appropriation was made for railroad grade-crossing elimination. These revisions in federal action later became established policy, with federal-aid authorizations for 1941 including an item for grade crossings and one for secondary feeder roads.

*The 1944 act.* The Federal-Aid Highway Act of 1944 introduced the principal change of emphasis in the federal highway program. In addition to making available the unusually large sum of 1.5 billion dollars over a three-year period, the 1944 act supplemented the basic 1921 act by providing funds for exclusive use of the federal-aid system within municipalities and urban places of over 5,000 population. This provision was made in recognition of the acute problems of providing adequate facilities in congested urban areas. The 1944 act also permits the expenditure of federal funds for right of way and property damage costs, and provides for the co-operation of local road officials in the selection of roads to be included in the rural secondary and feeder road system. It also provides for designating an interstate system of the most important routes, not to exceed 40,000 miles in length.[10] Thus the scope of federal action was extended from the 48 states and territories included in the

[9] An additional 1 per cent of total highway mileage within a state may be incorporated in the primary federal-aid system when 90 per cent of the existing designated system has been improved.
[10] 58 Stat. 838.

previous legislation to embrace the 3,071 counties and 2,070 cities of over 5,000 population.[11]

The act of 1944 authorized appropriations of $500,000,000 a year for each of three successive postwar fiscal years. The sum authorized for each year was divided among the following programs: (1) $225,000,000 for projects on the Federal-Aid Highway System; (2) $150,000,000 for projects on a selected system of the principal secondary and feeder roads in each state, including farm-to-market roads, rural free delivery mail and public school bus routes either in rural areas or municipalities of less than 5,000 population; (3) $125,000,000 for projects on the Federal-Aid Highway System in urban areas.

Apportionment of federal funds for the federal-aid system is determined on the basis of area, population, and mileage of rural mail routes. Secondary road money is similarly apportioned, except that rural population is used instead of total population; and in the case of funds for urban highways, the population index is based on the population in municipalities and other urban places of 5,000 or more.[12]

The federal share on projects provided for by this act generally cannot exceed 50 per cent of total construction costs other than right of way, and cannot exceed one third of the cost of right of way. However, the federal share is increased in states containing public lands. In addition, the entire cost of projects for the elimination of hazards at railway-highway crossings may be paid from federal funds, except land and property damage costs, of which not more than 50 per cent may be paid from federal funds.[13]

In providing for the designation within continental United States of a national system of interstate highways, the 1944 act

[11] Statement of Thomas H. MacDonald, Commissioner of Public Roads, *Independent Offices Appropriation Bill for 1949*, Hearings before the Subcommittee of the House Committee on Appropriations, 80 Cong. 2 sess., p. 697.

[12] See App. A, Table 11 for actual apportionments among the states for 1948.

[13] Not more than 10 per cent of the amount apportioned to a state may be used for railway-highway projects.

stipulated that these be so located as to connect the principal metropolitan areas, cities, and industrial centers, to serve the national defense, and to connect at suitable border points with routes of continental importance in the Dominion of Canada and the Republic of Mexico. All routes included in this network, if not already part of the Federal-Aid Highway System, are added to the system.

*Other federal road activity.* Another class of federal activity involves road construction in national forests, national parks, public lands, and Indian reservations. Since the forest program was initiated in 1917, nearly a quarter of a billion dollars has been spent for the improvement of a forest highway system designed primarily for the development and better use of resources. A smaller system of roads in national parks has been improved with federal funds since 1924. All these appropriations are spent by federal agencies co-operating with the Public Roads Administration.

Authorizations included in the 1944 act provide for these roads as follows: $25,000,000 per year for forest highways; $12,500,000 for forest development roads and trails; $4,250,000 a year for the construction, reconstruction, improvement, and maintenance of roads, trails, and bridges in areas administered by the National Park Service; $10,000,000 a year for the construction and maintenance of parkways over United States land; $6,000,000 a year for the construction, improvement, and maintenance of Indian reservation roads and bridges under the general supervision of the Public Roads Administration.

Ten per cent of all money received from the national forests during each fiscal year is appropriated for the construction and maintenance of roads and trails within the national forests. Money so appropriated becomes available to the Secretary of Agriculture and remains available until expended.[14] This fund is apportioned by the Secretary of Agriculture among the states, according to the area and value of the land within the national forests, and expended through the Public Roads Administra-

[14] 37 Stat. 843.

tion. The Federal-Aid Highway Act of 1944 also authorizes $25,000,000 for each of the three postwar fiscal years for forest highways.

Forest highways include Class 1 routes on the federal-aid system and Class 2 routes on state highway systems, as well as Class 3 routes on the secondary or feeder system. The approved Forest Highway System amounts to some 23,500 miles, about 80 per cent of which is on either the federal aid or state system. Forest highways are located in 36 states, Alaska, and Puerto Rico, but about 86 per cent of all this work is located in the 11 Pacific Coast and Rocky Mountain states and Alaska.

The selection of routes to be included in the system are made jointly by representatives of the Public Roads Administration, the Forest Service, and the various state highway departments concerned. All surveys and preparation of plans, specifications, and estimates for forest highways are made by the Public Roads Administration and are submitted to the state highway departments and the Forest Service for their concurrence before construction is started. Practically all construction work is performed by contract. Maintenance of forest highways is generally performed by Public Roads for a period of two years after completion of construction work, after which the obligation is ordinarily assumed by the state and maintenance is performed by the same forces which maintain the federal-aid projects with which forest projects ordinarily connect.[15]

Federal funds authorized for the construction of national park roads and parkways are under the control of the National Park Service until allotments are made to Public Roads for specific projects. Surveys and preparation of plans are made by the Public Roads Administration and are submitted to the state highway departments and the National Park Service for their concurrence. Maintenance is generally performed by the Park Service, but in some cases is performed by Public Roads

[15] Public Roads Administration, *The Public Roads Administration and Its Work*, November 1946, pp. 29-30.
[16] The same, pp. 31-33.

under formal agreement with the Park Service.[16] Public Roads also supervises the construction of main roads through public lands and in some cases through Indian reservations.

The federal government is also concerned with the promotion of foreign highway facilities to further cultural relations and for defense purposes. A 3,267 mile highway link between this country and the Panama Canal Zone is now more than half completed with all-weather surfacing, an accomplishment which has been furthered by United States co-operative action with the countries to the south. Effort on behalf of this Inter-American Highway was authorized by Congress in 1928, and funds were appropriated in 1930 for a reconnaissance survey to establish the route. This work, undertaken by the Public Roads Administration at the request of the State Department, was carried out from 1930 through 1933. In the past 12 years congressional authorizations of several millions have been made, and, under co-operative agreements with several Central American republics, materials, machinery, and technical direction have been provided. Financial arrangements have also been made through the Export-Import Bank of the United States, which has made loans to Panama, Nicaragua, and Costa Rica.[17]

The Public Roads Administration has recently been called upon to do further work outside continental United States. This has included rehabilitation of highways in the Philippines and supervision of work in Bolivia and Ecuador for the Export-Import Bank. Work has also been done in Alaska, Hawaii, Puerto Rico, and the Virgin Islands, and at the request of the State Department, work has been performed in Turkey under the Greek-Turkish Relief Program.[18]

## II. THE FUTURE FEDERAL ROLE

The scope and magnitude of federal highway aid have increased markedly during the past two decades. Federal activity, previously limited to the improvement of the primary

[17] National Resources Planning Board, *Transportation and National Policy*, H. Doc. 883, 77 Cong. 2 sess., May 1942, pp. 252-53.
[18] *Independent Offices Appropriation Bill, 1949*, Hearings, p. 705.

federal-aid system, has now expanded to include large mileages of secondary roads and city streets. Along with this expanded scope of operations, there has been an increase in regular federal-aid contributions to a new peacetime high of half a billion dollars a year.

We have proceeded to the extent, at this time, of selecting a 370,000-mile system of secondary roads, of which 230,000 are county or local roads and 140,000 are on the State highway systems. The progress in the urban system extends to about 14,000 miles, so that we have at the moment a total Federal-aid primary, secondary, and urban system approximating about 600,000 miles, which indicates something of the undertaking for the future.[19]

The question to be answered is the extent to which the federal government should attempt to share in this undertaking in the future.

*The highway problem.* The Commissioner of Public Roads at the hearings of the House Subcommittee of the Committee on Appropriations in a recent session of Congress (considering appropriations for fiscal 1949) pointed out the magnitude of the highway construction problem ahead:

The compelling reasons for an expanded program of construction are the depreciation and accumulated obsolescence of our highways during the war years. Our studies and inspections this last year have shown that we have about 30,000 miles of our major Federal-aid system in urgent need of rebuilding.[20]

This condition has been accentuated by the increase in total highway traffic from 333 billion vehicle-miles in 1941 to 400 billions in 1948, a rise of over 20 per cent. During the same period, registrations increased from 34 to 40 millions, or 17.6 per cent. But the major increase has been in the number of trucks and buses which rose from 4,900,000 in 1941 to 7,700,000 in 1948, an increase of 57 per cent.

A further reason cited for an expanded highway program is the greatly increased cost of maintenance. Prewar maintenance cost was 725 millions per year. In 1948 it was about 1,132 mil-

---

[19] Statement of T. H. MacDonald, *Federal-Aid Highway Act of 1948*, Hearings, p. 194.

[20] *Independent Offices Appropriation Bill for 1949*, Hearings, p. 702.

lions, an increase of 56 per cent. "This indicates why it is so impossible to do away with the reconstruction and construction program and postpone it for some other day."[21]

In his special message to the Congress on February 9, 1948, concerning new highway legislation requirements, the President of the United States pointed out that in recent years highway construction has not kept pace with the growth in traffic. And he expressed the opinion that "future demands will in-

COST OF IMPROVING DESIGNATED FEDERAL-AID ROAD SYSTEMS[a]
(Dollar figures are in millions)

| Highway System | Total Miles in System | Total Miles Needing Improvement | Total Cost of Needed Improvement |
|---|---|---|---|
| Federal-aid primary ...... | 191,936 | 123,042 | $ 9,818 |
| Federal-aid secondary ..... | 299,595 | 202,128 | 4,635 |
| Federal-aid urban ........ | 13,349 | 8,547 | 5,694 |
| Total ................ | 504,880 | 333,717 | $20,147 |

[a] These data were compiled by the American Association of State Highway Officials from a survey dated Dec. 31, 1947. Data include information from 43 states and the District of Columbia.

evitably be greater as business traffic continues to expand, as our population grows, and as we build roads to reach needed resources now relatively inaccessible. Furthermore, we must reconstruct important stretches of road which were not built to carry heavy traffic safely and at reasonable speed."[22] Taking these factors into account, it was recommended that the Congress enact legislation continuing the federal-aid highway program for the fiscal years 1950 and 1951 at an annual rate of 500 million dollars. According to the President:

The program I am recommending now is a conservative one, necessary to maintain prudently our investment in highways. When conditions permit in the future, we should plan to accelerate our progress toward a highway system adequate to carry our expanding agricultural and business traffic, to accommodate with safety and

[21] The same, p. 703.
[22] Congressional Record, Vol. 94, Pt. 1, 80 Cong. 2 sess., p. 1228.

speed the personal travel of our people, and to meet the needs of our national security.[23]

The size of the program which would be involved in bringing to adequate standards all roads and streets eligible for federal aid has been indicated by a survey conducted by the state highway departments. It was indicated that for the approximately 500,000 miles of roads and streets included in the 43 states surveyed, more than 20 billion dollars of construction work would be required. (See table p. 116.)

*Federal interest and responsibility.* To what extent, then, should the federal government assist in the modernization of this extensive system of roads and streets? It has been pointed out previously that as a matter of principle federal-aid activity should be limited to the development of facilities having national significance, or to projects on which federal participation is necessary as an aid in the establishment of uniform standards and minimum quality of service. The recent extension of federal aid from a limited system of main highways to a much larger mileage of roads and streets having a predominantly local function makes this question of particular importance at the present time. The problem faced by the federal government is whether it shall proceed with the new pattern laid down by the Federal-Aid Highway Act of 1944, or whether it should return to the more limited scope of activity originally conceived as the federal role.

It could very well be argued that the federal government has an interest not only in providing uniformly adequate standards on the primary system of highways serving interstate traffic, but also in providing minimum standards for the development of local roads to assist agriculture, promote rural mail service, and further the development of rural education. Despite the possible justification of federal aid for either or both of these programs, determination of what the federal government should do is based not simply on the merits of the program itself, but on the advantages of accomplishing the program

[23] The same.

through federal rather than state or local action. The development of highways is an activity in which the states have achieved considerable success. This is due in part to the generally strong administrative bodies charged with this responsibility at the state level, and to the healthy financial position of the states made possible by state-collected gasoline taxes and registration fees. In part, too, the states as geographic and political entities have generally proved logical agencies for the conduct of road work.

Historically, the automobile brought about a shift in the nature of the road problem from one of purely local concern to one of state-wide characteristics. Later the growing interstate nature of highway travel introduced nationwide considerations calling for greater federal participation. Today the interstate character of highway use on our principal arteries is more pronounced than at any previous period. On secondary roads, however, even where their use may have developed beyond a strictly local radius, there is no clearly federal interest. The extension of state aid to these roads has been a logical development; but the participation of the federal government is difficult to justify in terms of the basic concepts of federal responsibility.

There is, on the other hand, what appears to be a highly appropriate federal role relating to the interstate traffic which has grown rapidly with the availability of good roads and better vehicles. The fact that these facilities are often of widely varying degrees of adequacy, and that little uniformity exists among the states with respect to regulations governing their use, offers a challenging federal role. The federal government can assist in bringing about the adequacy and uniformity essential to a truly interstate highway transportation system.

Evidence that the most important federal highway program is the development of a national system of interstate highways is contained in a recent statement by the Commissioner of Public Roads:

> . . . the conception of an interstate system of highways is a logical outgrowth of the concentration of traffic on a limited mileage of major roads. This is a National rather than a local characteristic.

It was acutely apparent during the war. It is factually confirmed during peace times. So the idea of an interregional, or legally an interstate, system of roads, was a logical conclusion when through the State-wide planning surveys the fact was established that a National system of about one percent of our public road mileage could be selected having a potential service totaling 20 percent of our rural highway traffic.[24]

With regard to national defense requirements, according to the chairman of the National Security Resources Board the priority plan for highways is the projected national system of interstate highways. The importance of this system was recognized in the 1949 legislation extending federal aid for highways, which called for study by the Public Roads Administration of the problems associated with the development of this system, and a review of the findings by the National Security Resources Board.[25]

Further testimony on this point is furnished by the Commissioner of Public Roads, who has stated that the interstate system is, in effect, a refinement of the 78,000 mile strategic network established in conjunction with the War Department in 1922. "It seems apparent that the system of highways of greatest importance to the national defense, having its genesis in the routes of the 1922 Pershing Map, . . . has now culminated in the national system of interstate highways."[26]

Despite the attention which has been directed to the planning of this system, however, and the primary national importance involved in its construction, no change in federal policy has thus far been made to implement the program. Federal funds are specifically designated for application to primary federal-aid roads, urban streets, and secondary rural roads; but no specific provisions have been made to further the development of what is generally conceded to be the most important national responsibility.

[24] Thomas H. MacDonald, "Interstate or Super Highways," an address before the 29th Annual Meeting of the North Carolina Society of Engineers, Raleigh, North Carolina, Jan. 24, 1947, p. 2 (mimeo.).
[25] Public Law 834, 80 Cong. 2 sess., sec. 2.
[26] Statement of T. H. MacDonald, *Federal-Aid Highway Act of 1948*, Hearings, p. 188.

The desirability of concentrating federal attention on the interstate system, where national interest and the benefits of national participation are most apparent, seems clear. But the very broad scope of federal activity established in the 1944 act goes far beyond the area in which the role of the federal government is to be preferred over state and local action. There is danger in such a federal program that varying local needs cannot be properly reflected, and that eventually the problem of maintaining federal projects will in some areas prove unsolvable for local governments. Federal highway legislation requires that all roads on which federal-aid money has been spent must be inspected by the Public Roads Administration and that notice will be served upon the state highway department if proper maintenance is not provided. In the case of the present secondary road program, however, many of the state highway departments do not have authority to spend funds on secondary roads so that there is a danger of local units failing to apply proper maintenance without any recourse on the part of the federal government.

One of the principal assets of the federal-aid highway program in the past has been the encouragement of a policy of concentrating road-building efforts on a limited system of roads to accomplish the most important things first. Although it is recognized that secondary and local roads are no less important to those who use them than are the principal interstate highways, it does not follow that the federal government rather than the states and localities immediately concerned should assume the responsibility for local highway projects. Moreover, even on roads of national importance the extent of federal action should be tailored to what is essential to carrying out necessary federal objectives, since the expenditure of general tax funds by the federal government defeats the goal of achieving a self-supporting highway system.

# CHAPTER VII

## ISSUES RAISED BY FEDERAL PROMOTION

Federal responsibility for the provision of transportation facilities and their financing has been increasing in recent years with respect to both the extent of activity and the amounts of money involved. In no previous peacetime period has the scope and magnitude of federal participation in transportation development reached the proportions of the current program. Moreover, present indications suggest still further expansion of federal influence in this field. The extent of these growing obligations makes an appraisal of federal policy especially fitting. The principal questions to be answered are whether the federal government is playing an appropriate role in transportation development; whether means of financing are conducive to the provision of maximum service and economy; whether the methods used to carry out the development program are designed to achieve the desired results; and whether promotional activity is properly correlated with regulation.

### I. THE FEDERAL ROLE

It has been seen in the previous chapters that the federal government plays a dominant role in the provision of transport facilities. In the case of water transportation it constructs, maintains, and operates the inland waterways and provides the necessary channels and other harbor work on the Great Lakes and along the coasts. Lighthouses, radio aids, and all other navigation facilities are likewise furnished by the federal government. In addition, the government owns and operates barge service on the inland waterways and dominates the field of ocean shipping through subsidies to promote American ship construction and to aid American-flag operations.

The trend in federal promotion of water transportation indicates an accelerated program for the future. It has been pointed out that a program of shipbuilding and of maintaining the

American merchant marine at levels adequate for emergency requirements may involve the construction of some 500,000 tons of new vessels annually, and the maintenance of a fleet comprising some 11 to 12 million gross tons. Such a program, far in excess of any previous peacetime objective, will require substantial federal funds to finance reserve fleets and to permit American shipbuilders and operators to survive in the face of lower cost or subsidized foreign competition. Present plans for inland water transportation likewise involve heavy expenditures by the federal government. Construction projects now planned or under way will require some 3 billion dollars to complete; and the cost of maintaining and operating existing waterway improvements continues to mount as the extent of the improved system increases.

In the highway field, which to date has involved federal expenditures of 10 billion dollars, a new and expanded federal role was introduced in the 1944 Federal-Aid Highway Act. At a result of this legislation, regular federal aid has been extended to the improvement of a designated system of secondary roads and city streets. There has now been selected in excess of 600,000 miles of roads and streets which are eligible for federal expenditures. That the 1944 act has established the pattern for a continuing federal-aid program is indicated by the recent authorization of annual grants totaling 450 million dollars to be applied to the expanded system in each of the fiscal years 1950 and 1951.

The promotion of aviation presents a similar picture of rapidly increasing activity. A half-billion dollar federal-aid program for airport development, effective over a seven-year period, replaces the previous emergency character of federal airport work. Plans for an all-weather electronic airways system have introduced the largest peacetime project yet undertaken for civil aviation, involving a billion dollars of new equipment to be installed over a fifteen-year period. These aids to aviation, together with operating subsidies for both domestic and foreign operators, constitute a program of aviation promotion many times the cost of prewar activities.

Current federal action focuses attention on the question of how and to what extent the federal government should participate in the provision of transportation facilities. As a nation we are interested in the development of interstate commerce and the provision of adequate standards for interstate facilities. An example of federal activity designed to achieve this goal is the attempt to aid the states in building a system of highways for interstate commerce which will furnish an adequate nationwide system. Federal assistance provides a means by which the several states may participate in a national plan; and it furnishes financial aid to lessen the variations in financial capacity among the states. The interstate character of waterways and of aids to ocean navigation similarly calls for federal action because of the need for uniformity and for the provision of facilities which frequently involve two or more states. And the provision of airways is perhaps the most obvious example of the need for national planning, nationwide uniform standards, and centralized operation.

A further basis for federal action lies in the promotion of certain national objectives which are beyond the interest of individual states. Among these are the conduct of basic research in aerodynamics, or the development of electronic aids to navigation; the provision of merchant marine facilities for national security; and the maintenance of national park or forest roads for the development and protection of our natural resources. In a word, federal action is warranted when national interest is involved, and when the work required can be accomplished only by federal participation, or better by the federal government than by the states, local governments, or private industry.

In reviewing the present program of the federal government, it has been apparent in several areas that the degree of national interest in some promotional programs is not impressive; or at least that the choice of federal activity is not always the most fruitful from the standpoint of national interest. Doubts have been raised, for example, concerning current highway aids. One question is whether the national interest in secondary roads is of sufficient relative importance in the highway system to warrant expenditure of federal funds. Granted that the availability of good roads throughout the country is a national asset, the assumption that local units of government, assisted by state aid, are not capable of carrying out local road programs is difficult to accept. Or, from another viewpoint, the assumption that the federal government is in a better position to formulate or finance a local road program than are the state or local governments immediately concerned is equally doubtful. But current federal road policy is also open to question by reason of the fact that it makes no specific provision for federal participation in what appears to be the most important system of roads from a national viewpoint.

Again, the question arises as to whether the current role of the federal government in the development of airports reflects a proper emphasis on facilities of national interest. The development of small airports for private flying, which for the most part serve local users, is one aspect of this question. Considerable emphasis was at one time placed on the private flier as a national defense asset; but the expanding gulf between private flying and military aviation casts considerable doubt on this assumption now. Furthermore, the large reserve of World War II pilots has usurped the private flier's position as the nation's potential military reserve.

Granting, however, that national interest may be served by encouraging this new form of transportation, the development of airport facilities as a means of achieving such an objective appears to be a relatively ineffectual approach. The principal obstacle to the expansion of light plane ownership and use lies not in the lack of airports but in the inadequacy of the airplane, including its dependence on airports. Should federal interest demand the promotion of personal flying, it is probable that research directed to the development of aircraft design would more readily accomplish the desired goal. Under any circumstances, it would appear that the first responsibility of the federal government lies in assuring that the airport program is integrated with the granting of federal certificates for airline routes. Otherwise, approved air transportation services may be held up indefinitely due to lack of airport facilities.

Other areas have been cited in which current federal activity appears dubious. Among these are many river and harbor development programs and the barge line experiment of the Inland Waterways Corporation. The present air-mail subsidy policy for domestic air carriers is likewise open to question as an effective device for promoting aviation. And many of the activities carried on in connection with aviation safety suggest state and local rather than federal action.

## II. PRINCIPLES OF FINANCE

In addition to the question of what functions properly belong in the category of federal action, there is the further question of how these functions should be paid for—by the direct beneficiaries or out of general tax funds. For example, although it is clear that the federal government should be responsible for the provision of airway facilities, there is still the question of whether these facilities should be paid for by the several classes of users through specific charges for the service, or whether, as at present, they should be supplied through general taxes.

It has been noted in previous chapters that the development of transportation facilities on an economic basis requires that those who use them pay the bill. In this way the desirability of transportation projects can be judged in the light of the costs involved and the ability or willingness of users to defray these costs. Such an approach in turn requires careful estimates of probable traffic, of benefits to be derived, and of the levels of user charges feasible. Willingness to pay for improvements provides a rough indication of the desirability of undertaking them. Moreover, raising the necessary funds from users assures a predictable source of revenue with which to maintain and improve the facilities, and shifts the financial burden from the general taxpayer to those who specifically benefit. Finally, to the extent that the rates charged by public carriers reflect the full cost of supplying the service, there is provided a basis for allocating traffic among the several competing forms of transportation in accordance with cost and service considerations. The distortions of traffic distribution and resource allocations created by unequal government aid are thus avoided.

There are many advantages, therefore, to the imposition of user charges as a means of financing transportation facilities. In the first place, these charges are a useful financial expedient in lieu of less dependable general tax sources, as the productivity of the gasoline tax and vehicle registration fee for highway purposes has demonstrated. User charges impose restraints on wasteful or unnecessary undertakings because those who advocate such projects know they must pay the bill. They introduce the concept of balancing costs against benefits, and of measuring traffic potentials, and they therefore serve as a rough guide in the difficult problem of determining appropriate levels of expenditure and project priorities. They are useful, accordingly, in achieving a productive allocation of resources.

It would be a mistake to conclude, however, that the user charge has no weaknesses, or that the goals which it permits in theory will always accomplish the expected practical results. Actually there are numerous exceptions where it is either impractical or undesirable to levy charges on the user of public facilities, or where the imposition of such charges would have no measurable effect either on the allocation of traffic or on the determination of desirable investments. Several considerations may stand in the way of achieving an organization of the transportation system based on costs:

1. The federal government has the right and the obligation to finance minimum standards for transport facilities of national interest through grants of aid from general funds. It has been noted that stricter economic tests need to be applied in determining the amounts and purposes of these grant-in-aid programs; but it has also been pointed out that there exists a legitimate federal interest which warrants general fund use for these projects. Federal aid is a useful device for providing uniformity and adequacy of transport facilities, and for achieving other objectives such as the development of resources and the promotion of commerce or national security.

2. Fundamental differences exist between privately provided rail facilities and publicly provided highways. Even were it feasible or desirable to collect the total spent for public facilities from the users (that is, eliminate federal aid and other general fund support) there would still be an inequity as between the railroads and other methods of transportation using public facilities. The railroads not only pay the full costs of their basic ways, without federal assistance, but pay taxes on their right of ways, interest charges on funded debt, and dividends to stockholders. A heavy debt structure incurred in the financing of basic railroad facilities is in contrast to the legislative appropriation of capital or even the predominant pay-as-you-go policy for financing highways. Even where debt has been incurred specifically to finance public facilities, interest rates are much lower than can be commanded by private borrowers. Under these circumstances, the railroads are at a disadvantage in comparison to other methods of transport regardless of whether user charges are levied for publicly provided facilities.

3. The joint use characteristics of certain transport facilities create decided advantages for those who use them. In the case of airports, for example, substantial military traffic and private flying reduce the share of the cost to be borne by commercial operators. Similarly, the bus and truck have the advantage of sharing the cost of the highways they use with 30 million privately owned automobiles. Furthermore, highways are paid for by the owners of property served, as well as by vehicle users. If federal charges are levied to meet the cost of airways, commercial users will share the burden with many other civil and military users. There is no similar joint use of rail facilities.

4. In some cases a policy of government subsidy followed over a period of years leaves no practical alternative other than to consider past investment a sunk cost, omitting its consideration in the determination of current rates. For example, the possibility would be remote that waterway tolls could yield an amount sufficient to amortize the outstanding investment in these facilities. To abandon the use of existing facilities on

this account, rather than to obtain whatever benefits are possible from the investment, might merely constitute further waste. This would suggest that tolls for existing waterways should reflect only current maintenance, but that new investments should be subject to the test of earning sufficient income to meet all costs.

5. New facilities must be afforded an opportunity to achieve a level of utilization which will permit them to provide the volume of service for which they were intended. The wisdom of this policy is illustrated by the development and financing of the highway system. In 1921 when there were 9 million vehicles using the highway system, the contribution of these vehicles to the cost of providing the highways amounted to only 12 per cent of the bill. By 1948 there were more than four times this number of vehicles, and vehicle owners and operators were paying over 60 per cent of the bill. Today a somewhat similar situation applies in the case of airways. Electronic navigation aids will result in an increased volume of air traffic by reason of the greater regularity and safety of aircraft operations which these facilities will afford; but the allocation of total costs must await the developing use of these facilities.

6. If it is necessary for defense purposes to maintain an ocean-going fleet in excess of what would be warranted by peacetime traffic volumes, the only practical course may be to achieve a higher level of merchant marine development through necessary subsidies. Aids to air navigation may be required for the same reason.

7. It would not be feasible for the cost of certain government transportation services now provided through general taxes to be allocated to or collected from the direct beneficiaries. Various aids to marine navigation supplied by the Coast Guard and the Coast and Geodetic Survey are significant items which fall in this category.

8. Finally, the application of public works funds to transportation projects as a means of combating depression exerts an important influence on competitive relationships. This is

true not only because of variations in the magnitude of the several programs affecting public facilities, but because the railroads are at present excluded from public works programs.

The contention, therefore, that an economic organization of the transportation system through user charges can be effected becomes questionable when the character of the transportation system and its problems are examined. The most that can be said is that in some areas it would be possible to come much closer to the goal of allocating traffic on an economic basis by eliminating to the extent feasible the influence of free facilities.

*The possibility of financial revision.* Are we, then, to abandon altogether the idea of achieving a self-supporting basis for transport development because of the obstacles which impede the full realization of such a program? A negative answer is indicated by several considerations. User charges, to the extent that their imposition is feasible, would make possible a closer approach to an economic division of traffic among the various publicly and privately financed facilities than is now the case. But even in the absence of such effects, other advantages would be derived. Among these would be the development of criteria to aid in determining desirable amounts and programing of expenditures; the creation of barriers to the most obvious waste of public funds; the promotion of fairness as between general taxpayers and benefited special groups: and the provision of tools to permit financial planning and programing based on more realistic concepts of economic justification.

The desirability of user charges and their capacity to reflect the relative economy of various transport agencies would of course be increased if the same method of financing applied to the railroads. We have seen, for example, that the possibilities of achieving an organization of the transportation system based on the economics of full costs is thwarted by the fundamental differences which exist between privately owned rail and publicly provided water, air, and highway facilities. The different manner in which public and private facilities are furnished leads logically to the conclusion that only by uniform methods of providing all basic transportation facilities would it be possible to achieve the environment necessary to attain comparable competitive relationships. It is obvious, because of the public nature and joint use of highways, waterways, and airways, that the goal of uniformity should not be sought by imposing the railroad financial pattern on these public undertakings. On the contrary, comparability among transport agencies would suggest that the basic facilities of the railroads—terminals, right of ways, roadbed, and track—be publicly provided, with privately owned equipment operating over the public ways. Such an arrangement would create a situation comparable to that in which the airline company, privately owned and operated, makes use of public airways and airports. Railroad companies, like privately owned airlines, steamship lines, or truck and bus lines, would operate on (and pay for) the public ways.

This possibility suggests a more desirable solution than the alternative of ultimately resorting to complete public ownership of the railroads. For it would be difficult to conceive that complete government ownership in this segment of the transportion system would not lead to extensive controls over other forms of transportation as a means of preserving railroad investments. In view of the need for extensive study of the practicability of government ownership of railroad right of ways, however, the question must be left to the consideration of those engaged in planning a consolidation of railroad facilities, as recommended elsewhere.[1]

In addition to this possibility, certain measures affecting publicly provided facilities might tend to offer partial remedies for some of the obvious financial inequalities between private and public facilities. A first step toward reducing the number of uneconomic waterway improvements would be the requirement that state and local governments match federal expenditures, following the precedent established in the case of highway and airport aids. Secondly, the possibility of charging tolls to pay the costs of new waterways and of maintaining and

[1] Discussed in Pt. 2.

operating existing facilities should be considered. By the same token, a federal airway charge should be imposed with the ultimate objective of defraying federal costs allocated to civil aircraft. Such charges would require consideration of the developing use of the airways and recognition of the current financial position of the affected carriers. The important objective now is to establish the principle and to make a start toward ultimate self-support for air transportation.

### III. FEDERAL POLICY AND METHODS

The previous sections have been concerned with the problems of defining the proper areas of federal action and of estabishing comparable methods of financing transportation facilities. The basic reasons for many of the inconsistencies found in these two areas lie in the absence of any governing policy by which the several independent federal agencies may evaluate and govern their activities in accordance with a common objective. The federal government has attempted to lay down certain principles which constitute a national transportation policy, but these principles, stated in the Transportation Act of 1940, deal with the problems of transport regulation and are generally disassociated from the issues confronting transport promotion. Moreover, the policy is quite unworkable as long as each form of transportation is considered in isolation by a separate federal agency.

Among the several transport media being supported with federal funds, neither the amounts of money spent, the purposes of expenditure, nor the methods of expenditure are governed by any common considerations. River and harbor projects are financed wholly through federal funds, without any matching requirements on the part of state or local governments, and with no charges on users in the form of tolls or other special levies. Moreover, the federal government not only constructs but maintains and operates these facilities. Airways, similarly, are financed entirely with general funds from the federal government. The users of the airways make no contribution toward defraying these costs. In the case of highways and airports, however, federal support is limited to construction. No federal funds are used to maintain or operate these facilities, as they are in the case of airway and waterway projects. And in the highway and airport programs, federal policy requires that state and local governments match these aids, although in varying proportions.

Methods of arriving at how much federal money should be spent for transportation facilities and where it should be spent present a comparable picture of divergent policies. Waterway projects are submitted for consideration to Congress by individuals or local interests concerned. These projects are unrelated to any over-all consideration of the transportation problem. Authorization of projects is made, and projects are begun without reference to the possibilities of ultimate federal appropriations for their support. By authorizing and starting numerous projects, the federal government embarks on an extensive program which constitutes a long-range commitment and a continuously mounting pressure for larger appropriations.

Highway funds are made available on an entirely different basis. Federal-aid funds for this purpose are authorized in lump sum by Congress and allocated among the states and for specific highway systems in accordance with formulas prescribed by law. Authorizations of funds are considered contractual obligations of the federal government, and appropriations are subsequently made to pay these amounts in full.

In the case of airport aid, the authorization for this purpose does not constitute a federal obligation, and only the actual amounts appropriated for airports in the Department of Commerce budget are available for distribution (on the basis of a prescribed formula) among the several states. Projects must be included in the National Airport Plan to be eligible for federal aid, and the actual airport program is determined by the federal government. This differs from the highway program, which is determined by the states subject to federal approval. The airport program also differs in that federal funds may be channeled through local as well as state governments. Airway appropriations are based on the estimated cost of maintaining and operating the facilities, plus a feasible construction program, and these financial requirements are submitted as part of the Department of Commerce budget.

Each form of transportation, then, is viewed and promoted separately, since the several federal agencies operating in this field have no responsibility to act otherwise. Under these circumstances, the several promotional programs are based on different concepts of need and economic justification, and on different estimates of future traffic volumes. The amounts of money spent for each program are not determined by consideration of relative urgency or desirability from a transportation viewpoint, and at no time is there an effort to decide, for example, whether the national interest would be better served by spending more on one form of transportation and less on another. Finally, no effort is made to consider the impacts of one federal program on another, and to take the necessary steps to correct or compensate for them.

At present the only opportunity in the executive branch of the government for an over-all view of transportation is in the operation of the Bureau of the Budget, which passes on proposed transportation legislation and reviews all proposals to determine whether they conform to the program of the president. The possibility of accomplishing any real review, however, is extremely limited. The small staff of the Bureau provides little opportunity to review agency proposals from the standpoint of over-all transportation objectives; and even were it physically possible to do so, the individual statutes under which the several transportation agencies operate provide no common basis upon which transportation proposals can be judged. The Bureau does find it possible to question and stop some projects which appear to be least justified from an economic point of view, but the political considerations involved make extensive criticism futile.

A second possibility of obtaining a broader view of the transportation implications of individual agency actions lies in the committee hearings of the Congress. At present there are, however, several committees dealing with transportation matters. In the Senate, the Interstate and Foreign Commerce Committee deals with all transportation matters except highways and rivers and harbors, both of which are considered by the Public Works Committee. In the House, the Interstate and Foreign Commerce Committee deals with all matters pertaining to transportation except merchant marine, roads, and rivers and harbors. Merchant marine problems come under the jurisdiction of the Merchant Marine and Fisheries Committee, and the Public Works Committee has subcommittees on Roads and on Rivers and Harbors. Only in the Appropriations Committee do all these bills receive consideration by the same group; but the primary concern here is with funds rather than functions.

In practice, then, individuals and organizations interested in a particular form of transportation appear before the various committees and present their views. These committees, as they become familiar with the field, often become as engrossed as those who come before them; and the result is a growing difficulty to reach objective decisions as to the relative importance and appropriate roles of federal aid for transportation as a whole. The committees have little help from the executive branch, because each form of transportation has its champion and no agency is by law in a position to offer an over-all viewpoint.

## IV. RELATION OF PROMOTION TO REGULATION

In addition to the failure to relate the various promotional activities of the federal transportation agencies, there are other defects which stand in the way of a rational program of transport development. Among these is the fact that many highly important administrative and planning functions which properly belong in the executive branch of the government have come to be confused with regulatory functions and included among the responsibilities of the independent commissions. The most common example of this confusion is the fact that responsibility for determining the location, capacity, and characteristics of basic physical ways—highways, waterways, and airways—is to be found in the executive agencies, while the determination of how these facilities shall be used is to an important degree a function of the independent commissions. To illustrate, the Civil Aeronautics Administration attempts in its airway and airport programs to plan an air transportation system which will meet the objectives laid down by Congress. But obviously a system of air transportation does not consist merely of the basic physical plant; it includes in addition the services provided by equipment operating over these facilities. Determination of the routes over which public carriers shall operate, and the nature of these operations, however, is under jurisdiction of the Civil Aeronautics Board. We thus have the anomalous situation of one federal agency determining the route pattern for air carriers and another planning the federal program to bring the routes into being. Facilitation of the natural community of interest between these functions has been attempted by a CAA-CAB interagency committee, but the fundamental error of dividing over-all planning and development responsibilities is not removed by this improvisation. In the case of international air-route planning, involving close relationships with foreign policy, the even more obvious inadequacies of having route pattern determination in the CAB are partly overcome by providing for presidential approval of all American-flag international certificates and foreign air-carrier certificates. But here again, a division of responsibility exists which is by no means resolved by this expedient.

Another example of the artificial separation of integral parts of the transportation planning function is the determination of waterway improvement programs by the Corps of Engineers, and the authorization of water carrier operations by the ICC. The need for water transportation services, now determined by the ICC, is obviously related to the need for waterway improvement, as determined by the Corps. Yet there is no federal recognition of the complementary nature of these functions.

Again, we have seen that the Maritime Commission's activities are for the most part promotional and administrative in nature; that the basically regulatory functions performed by the Commission are vestigial. Yet the vastly important functions of planning ocean shipping routes and carrying out a merchant marine policy to meet the needs of our national defense are placed in a regulatory framework. From the standpoint of implementing national policy, the independence and freedom from political influence which is presumably characteristic of commission functioning, becomes in more realistic terms an absence of responsibility.

Confusion of the proper functions of the executive branch of the government and the proper role of the independent commissions has likewise been seen in the untenable division of authority for aviation safety, and in the promotional objectives of air-mail payments which are entrusted to the CAB. This confusion between planning, promotion, and administrative responsibilities on the one hand, and the regulatory activities of the independent commission on the other, not only deprives the executive departments of effectively exercising their responsibilities, but imposes burdens and distractions which interfere with the effective conduct of the regulatory function.

A second defect in federal promotion activities stems from the fact that policy in this segment of the transportation field is instituted with complete disregard for the regulatory objectives elsewhere prescribed by Congress. For example, the objectives of achieving fair and impartial regulation and of developing the inherent advantages of the several means of transportation are regulatory goals which are completely impractical when viewed in the light of promotional policies. A rate structure which would permit the objectives set forth for regulatory policy is not possible as long as the total costs incurred in providing the service are not included. The shipper or traveler makes his selection of the various methods of transportation on the basis of rates or fares. From a national standpoint his choice is economically sound only to the extent that the rates charged reflect the true costs incurred. When the general taxpayer finances all or part of the facilities used, full economic costs are not reflected in the charges imposed for the service.

Finally, a third defect in promotional policy is the fact that there is no positive concern for the condition and development of the railroad system comparable to the federal interest in other forms of transportation. We have seen that the federal government has extensive plans for waterway, airway, and highway development. It not only has no similar program for the rehabilitation of the railroad plant; it recognizes no responsibility or concern over what impacts its promotional programs in other fields may have on the railroad system. Yet the fact remains that an efficient railroad system is necessary for mass movement of traffic at low cost, and that adequate capacity is at the present time a national defense requirement without which military preparedness would be futile. In the following chapter the weaknesses of federal promotional policy from the standpoint of national defense will be reviewed in more detail.

# CHAPTER VIII

## PROBLEMS OF NATIONAL SECURITY

The object of achieving an orderly development of the transportation system through equal government treatment of the several forms of transportation is clear on economic grounds; but this nice adjustment in the transportation system is confronted by the fact that other federal objectives may take precedence over economic considerations. The most important of these is the objective of achieving facilities for national defense in excess of what would otherwise be provided through strictly economic processes.

The national defense problem varies in importance among the various transport agencies. In some cases transportation services developed through economic processes may be sufficient to meet essential needs in time of war. Experience has demonstrated that to date it has been possible to obtain the necessary wartime railroad services without continuing federal financial assistance in peacetime. Similarly, motor vehicle equipment financed by the users was generally adequate to meet the essential needs of highway transportation. Extensive federal subsidies for aviation and merchant shipping prior to the war, on the other hand, proved to be an essential factor in the initial availability of ships and air transports, and in the speed and effectiveness of subsequent aircraft and shipbuilding programs. Again, many projects undertaken on the pretext of their national defense significance proved of no security value.

The question today, therefore, is one of determining specifically what federal subsidies are essential to provide transportation facilities adequate for national security, and what specific requirements over and above normal peacetime facilities need to be furnished for this purpose. To the extent that legitimate national defense requirements are indicated in excess of what would otherwise be supplied, these requirements must be taken into account regardless of the resulting departure from considerations of economics. In the future, however, generalities must be abandoned in favor of determining specific defense needs, in order to reduce waste of public funds, eliminate unnecessary dislocations resulting from subsidies, and avoid the hazard of being ill-prepared. The future step must be taken of weighing the impact of essential subsidy programs in terms of the effects of such policy on the economic condition of the transportation system as a whole. Only through such an over-all appraisal is it possible to reach sound conclusions as to national defense requirements.

## I. FEDERAL ACTION AND WORLD WAR II

The importance of transportation in wartime was clearly demonstrated during the recent world conflict. The high level of war production and the magnitude of military shipments and troop movements established new records for both passenger and freight transportation. Specifically, the volume of freight moved by public carriers totaled over one trillion ton-miles annually in each of the years 1943, 1944, and 1945, which was double the volume of service provided in 1939. This tremendous increase in freight movement was accomplished primarily by the railroads, which carried approximately 70 per cent of the wartime load.

The increase in passenger traffic was relatively small due to wartime restrictions on private automobile operation; yet the impact on public transportation facilities, which were called upon to compensate for the reduction in automobile travel, was tremendous. In 1939 the railroads accounted for 24 billion passenger-miles of travel. In 1944 they carried 98 billions, or four times the prewar load.[1] The number of passengers carried by urban transit vehicles increased from less than 13 billions in 1939 to 23 billions in 1944.

While these figures of expanded wartime operations are particularly impressive, they do not alter the fact that each transportation medium played a vital role in the total transportation operation. The private automobile, despite sharp re-

[1] Annual Reports of the Interstate Commerce Commission for 1941 and 1946.

ductions in its use, continued to be a major factor in war worker transportation. The air lines, while accounting for only a small percentage of total traffic, were able to supply almost overnight the equipment and personnel which initiated our far-flung military air transport services. Private trucks, intercity buses, pipelines, and water transport facilities all contributed to meeting the unprecedented transportation requirements.

Finally, in overseas service our vastly expanded merchant marine was able to meet the almost insatiable demand for supplies throughout the world. American shipping transported 7 million troops overseas, and kept them supplied; and it delivered a tremendous volume of material aid to our allies. At the end of the war our fleet was more than five times the prewar tonnage.

The ability of the transportation system and its supporting industries to meet the requirements of the last war cannot be attributed to foresight and planning on the part of the federal government. It is true that federal transportation objectives, as stated in the various statutes establishing transportation policy, have always given prominence to the needs of national defense. The Transportation Act of 1940 declares the ultimate objective of federal action to be one of "developing, coordinating, and preserving a national transportation system by water, highway, and rail, as well as other means, adequate to meet the needs of the commerce of the United States, of the Postal Service, and of the national defense." The Civil Aeronautics Act of 1938 likewise states as its purpose "the encouragement and development of an air-transportation system properly adapted to the present and future needs of the foreign and domestic commerce of the United States, of the Postal Service, and of the national defense." And in the Merchant Marine Act of 1936 it is stated to be "necessary for the national defense and development of its foreign and domestic commerce that the United States shall have a merchant marine."

Implementation of these and similar expressions of concern over national security is seldom to be found in the actual conduct of federal transportation activity. War Department specifications have had a bearing on the design and development of the federal-aid highway system, and a strategic network of highways of primary interest to the military has been designated. In the case of the merchant marine, the Maritime Commission is directed in the planning and development of the fleet to "co-operate closely" with the Navy Department as to national defense needs and the adaptation of vessels to military purposes.

The interest in national security expressed by federal transport legislation, however, has never developed to the point of establishing peacetime administrative machinery which would ensure the effective operation of transportation facilities in an emergency. Thus it was ten days after Pearl Harbor that an executive order was issued establishing an Office of Defense Transportation to "coordinate the transportation policies and activities of the several Federal agencies and private transportation groups in effecting such adjustments in the domestic transportation of the Nation . . . as the successful prosecution of the war may require."[2]

When war broke out, and the demands of the transportation system proved far greater than previous peacetime requirements, we found ourselves only partially prepared. The merchant fleet was far below requirements; there was an acute shortage of rubber on which highway transportation is dependent; no adequate facilities were available for the movement of petroleum; and there was no organization within the government which could assume responsibility for the maintenance of essential transportation services. We were able to organize a transportation agency, build up our merchant marine and air transport facilities, establish a network of pipelines, and create a synthetic rubber industry principally because we had time and freedom from the disruptions of enemy attack. In addition we had an important advantage in that the limited facilities available were in adequate condition. The railroads had experienced some step-up in capital investments after the mid-thirties, and had drafted plans to promote the expeditious movement of

[2] Executive Order 8989, Dec. 18, 1941.

rail traffic in the event of war. Highway construction during the thirties had resulted in extensive new facilities, and the high level of automotive production achieved during the immediate prewar years had provided the nation with a large-scale renewal of automotive equipment. Looking back at the transportation situation as of 1941, then, it is apparent that we were, by reason of a series of good fortunes, better prepared to wage a prolonged war at that time than we would have been, for example, in the mid-thirties.

The questions which the foregoing considerations raise with respect to the wartime adequacy of transportation in the future are: (1) whether, under existing federal promotional policies, we can expect to have in readiness adequate transportation facilities for war requirements if or when another war should develop; and (2) whether, in the event of war, we are organized at the federal level to assure immediate and continuing effective operation of available transport facilities.

## II. CIVIL AVIATION AND WAR REQUIREMENTS

It has been pointed out that on economic grounds the best long-run interests of the air transportation industry would be served by establishing the principle of self-support and moving as quickly as possible toward this goal. Self-support would be achieved by eliminating direct operating subsidies and by requiring users to contribute their share of the cost of airways and airports. This approach would have the advantages of providing a useful guide to the programing of public expenditures and of assuring adequate funds for air transport facilities on a continuing basis. In addition, self-support through user charges would furnish criteria for determining the rightful place of air transport in the transportation system, because traffic moving by air (as well as by other methods) would be attracted on the basis of relative economy as well as service.

It is apparent, however, that the attainment of these objectives may be in conflict with national defense requirements where these requirements call for expenditures in excess of the amount needed for civilian transportation. To the extent that economic objectives interpose obstacles to the achievement of defense objectives, the case is clear for modification of economic standards. A basic question, then, is the extent to which national security requires the development of civil aviation over and above the rate which would be achieved through normal economic processes.

*Recent war experience.* The national defense significance of civilian air transport in World War II is clear from the record. Within six months after Pearl Harbor, the domestic airlines had sold or leased to the government more than half of the 359 planes in airline operations, and the Army and Navy were making use of some 1,200 airline pilots. These aircraft and personnel operated on contract for the Air Transport Command and the Naval Air Transport Service. In addition, the airlines under direct contract with the military provided extensive passenger and freight movement in domestic service.

The airline fleet constituted a substantial percentage of total military aircraft engaged in strictly transport operations. Although the AAF had more than 10,000 transports in operation by 1944, a large proportion of this fleet was engaged in troop carrier and other tactical operations rather than transport. During that year the airlines in military operation provided 1.4 billion passenger-miles of service compared to 2.4 billions by the Air Transport Command.[3]

A number of other military responsibilities were assumed by the airlines. One of these was the instruction of Army and Navy pilots who had completed basic training but who needed additional experience in operating multiple-engined aircraft and navigating ocean routes. Airline schools also trained mechanics, radio operators, navigators, meteorologists, and other specialists. In addition, during the period 1942 through 1944 nearly 50,000 aircraft were adapted to combat requirements through modifications effected at airline ground facilities.

[3] Aircraft Industries Association, *Aviation Facts and Figures* (1945), p. 62. Passenger-mile figures are for ATC only and are not available for NATS. Some indication of the relative amounts of service performed by ATC and NATS is provided by the fact that during 1944, NATS loaded approximately 40 per cent as many passengers as ATC.

*Future role of the airlines.* There are two principal questions which must be answered with respect to the relation between military and civil air transport today. First, to what extent might the military depend on the civil airlines in case of another war? Second, what would be the implications of such dependence in terms of the civilian transportation system?

In 1948 the Military Air Transport Service started operations with a fleet of approximately 275 transport aircraft. The ultimate purpose of MATS is to provide, in time of war, a personnel and cargo lift to the rear areas of the war theaters. (The Marine Transport Command and the Troop Carrier Command supply service into areas of combat.) The small fleet of transports in active military service today compares with approximately 979 commercial planes in certificated airline service, and 1,170 multiple-engine aircraft in nonscheduled operations.[4] Although the active military fleet is relatively small, a reserve of transport aircraft is available for emergency requirements. The enlarged fleet might be manned by reserve pilots, and sufficient World War II pilots would also be available as instructors, at least over the next ten or fifteen years, to relieve the airlines of this responsibility.[5]

As pointed out by the President's Air Policy Commission, however, the Military Air Transport Service could not handle all the traffic which would have to be moved in event of war. "They plan to take over, as they did in World War II, as much of the civilian lines, domestic and international, as circumstances permit."[6] And it should be added that even a combination of presently available military equipment and requisitioned commercial aircraft would undoubtedly be inadequate at the

---

[4] During the fiscal year 1947, the military services carried about the same amount of freight as all United States certificated carriers combined (18 million ton-miles per month) and about one eighth as much passenger traffic. The President's Air Policy Commission, *Survival in the Air Age* (1948), p. 36.

[5] According to the report of the President's Air Policy Commission: "This 15-year availability of World War II pilots for instructor, patrol, and transport duties ensures personnel for these three important emergency functions which were largely performed by private pilots in the early years of World War II." *Survival in the Air Age*, p. 124.

[6] The same, p. 37.

present time to handle total air-lift demand in an emergency. The conclusion of the Policy Commission was, therefore, that "direct Government financial aid to commercial air lines is fully justified on grounds of national security and economic welfare."[7]

In the field of domestic transportation, this approach raises significant questions. If the military is to take over a major part of airline equipment in time of war, consideration must be given to the effect of such a transfer upon the movement of essential civilian traffic, and the alternative means of transportation which would be available to meet the transportation needs of the civilian economy. Airline equipment, personnel, and ground facilities were readily transferred to military operations in 1941 without disrupting civilian transportation. This was partly because the airlines were carrying a very small proportion of total domestic traffic volume, and therefore any shift of traffic from the air was accommodated by the railroads. The 1.4 billion passenger-miles of travel by airline in 1941 was less than one half of one per cent of total passenger-miles of travel performed by all transport agencies. Cargo moving by airplane amounted to less than .01 of one per cent of total domestic freight movement. To the extent that it was necessary to handle airline passengers by other modes of transportation, therefore, there was little dislocation. Furthermore, despite the fact that the civil airline fleet was cut in half, it was nevertheless able to carry a heavier volume of traffic than before the war by stepping up schedules, eliminating competitive runs, and maintaining high-load factors.[8]

In planning for the future, both the desirability and the possibility of contributing to military requirements to any important degree by requisitioning aircraft from the present domestic airline fleet is questionable. The proposal to subsidize an expanded air fleet to increase the availability of standby equipment raises additional questions. In either case the assumption is made that aircraft could be removed from civilian

---

[7] The same, p. 102.
[8] The passenger load factor increased from 64 per cent in 1941 to 91 per cent in 1944.

service without impairment of the transportation system or of the civilian economy which is geared to it. This assumption is similar to the attitude during the early part of the last war of some officials who contended that the automobile could be dispensed with; that workers "could walk or take the bus." It was soon evident, however, that our economy had become geared to private automobile transportation to an extent that would permit no substitutes; that even to accommodate the strictly essential uses of the automobile would have required an impossible multiplication of alternate transportation methods.

The expansion of air transportation now taking place, whether accelerated by defense subsidies or not, will mean a continuing shift of passenger and cargo transport from existing surface carriers and the creation of further dependence on this new form of transportation. Therefore, the problem arises as to how this traffic would be accommodated in wartime, if the military requisitioned airline equipment. Such a shift from civilian to military use could mean a paralyzing effect on the civilian transportation system, not only because of our increasing dependence on the new service, but because the possibility of shifting traffic back to surface transport will become more remote as time passes. This will be true in part because the airplane in many cases will be providing a service which cannot be furnished by any other means, and in part because even where substitute services are feasible it would be possible to shift traffic from the air only if measures were taken to maintain the necessary stand-by equipment.

The problems arising when an established agency is withdrawn from the transportation system in time of war are demonstrated by the experience with petroleum transport in World War II. The coastwise tanker fleet, which was supplying the East Coast with 95 per cent of its petroleum requirements, was subject to immediate call by the Navy. The outbreak of war meant the diversion of a large part of the fleet to military service, and enemy action off the East Coast immobilized most of the remainder. To meet this crisis there were, fortunately, some 145,000 tank cars still held by the railroads, many of them being used for storage or rusting on sidings. Although there was doubt that this equipment could stand the strain of the intensive operations required of it, the fact that it proved equal to the task was the major factor in maintaining petroleum supplies. From 1941 to 1943 the percentages of East Coast petroleum deliveries by tanker declined from 93 per cent of total deliveries to 13 per cent, while rail tank car deliveries increased from 2 per cent to 61 per cent.[9] But this shift from tanker to tank car was possible because the idle tank cars, which had only recently been abandoned in favor of tankers, were still serviceable.

It is true that a certain part of the domestic airline fleet might be made available through consolidation of schedules, the elimination of nonessential travel, and the achievement of improved load factors. But this opportunity assumes in part that substantial service duplication and excess capacity are maintained in peacetime. Such an assumption is in direct opposition to the goal of strengthening the airlines through the achievement of higher load factors, consolidation of routes, and improvements in operating efficiency. The question is whether we should confuse the requirements of a sound domestic air transportation system for national defense with the further national defense objective of assuring an adequate military air transport service. It is apparent that the attempt to achieve both objectives with the same tools encounters serious difficulties.

The President's Air Policy Commission recognized this problem and suggested that one way to meet military requirements would be to let the services buy the transports they need, the same as they buy combat planes. Another proposal was that a stand-by fleet might be created by subsidizing air-cargo operations. But it was pointed out that this would call for consideration of the effects of such a course on competing forms of transportation, and would raise the question of a subsidy or tax reduction to those forms of transportation to maintain them in war readiness.[10]

[9] Office of Defense Transportation, *Civilian War Transport,* A Record of the Control of Domestic Traffic Operations 1941-46, p. 185.
[10] According to the report, "The problem of building up a pool of military transport planes in commercial use seems to warrant a more coordinated study

An important possibility which has developed since the beginning of World War II, however, and which might offer better opportunity for defense planning, lies in the promotion of international air transportation. Aircraft in international service are in a position analogous to the merchant marine. Because of the disruptive effects of war on overseas commerce, it would be feasible to shift a large proportion of these aircraft to military service without paralyzing civilian services. Development of the overseas air fleet as a military adjunct offers an attractive possibility by reason of the fact that international airlines will presumably require continuing subsidization in any event to sustain them in competition with foreign carriers. The competitive effects of such subsidy, moreover, are confined to ocean shipping, which is likewise subject to government aid, so that federal subsidy policy could be adjusted in a manner which would bring about the desired results for both water and air facilities. In addition, the subsidy program would be removed from direct effect on the domestic transportation system, where subsidization is likely to create more problems than it can solve.

Even this approach to the problem, however, creates difficult problems with respect to international relations. For, whereas government support of an expanded American flag international air fleet would have no adverse effect upon our own domestic transportation system, it would obviously affect the international air operations of other nations. A subsidy program of the extent necessary to add materially to the air reserve would jeopardize foreign aspirations in international air commerce and might introduce factors designed ultimately to weaken rather than strengthen our defense.

It must be concluded that the availability of stand-by equipment in international air service, plus equipment withdrawn from domestic service as a result of rationing or stepped-up

---

of the number of transports needed, the potential commercial cargo traffic, and the possible subsidy cost to the Government." It was recommended by the Commission that the Air Coordinating Committee make such a study. *Survival in the Air Age,* p. 115.

efficiency, would not go far toward meeting the needs of the military. It becomes clear however the problem is approached that military air-lift requirements must in the main be provided by expanding the military air-transport reserve. In view of the importance of military air transport, it would appear to be no less essential for the armed services to procure the transport equipment they need than to supply themselves with bombers or fighters.

*Aircraft manufacturing industry.* Of basic importance to the military is the maintenance of a manufacturing industry capable of expansion in time of war, as well as a continuing research and development program which will assure technological supremacy in the production of new types of aircraft. These objectives are in theory furthered by both military and civilian orders for transport aircraft; but the high cost of developing new transports for the commercial market alone is beyond the capacity of most manufacturers. Without military orders to defray prototype costs, it is questionable whether there would be any extensive new transport development by the aircraft industry. For, although the National Advisory Committee for Aeronautics has produced most of the basic aerodynamic and structural data from which commercial and military aircraft have been developed, the cost of actually creating a new transport aircraft is prohibitive for most manufacturers without government aid. For example, the DC-6, despite its similarity to the Army's C-54, cost the Douglas Aircraft Company over 13 million dollars in development costs. With 80 aircraft sold, the company had spent 42 million dollars more than it had received from the DC-6 sales, and it was estimated that the break-even point would not be reached until the 300th plane was delivered. Vast sums continue to be spent on further improvements in the aircraft, so that actually development costs never cease. If these costs are not spread over a large number of potential sales, the possibility of getting the price down to reasonable levels would be remote.

At present, the expanded military aviation procurement and development programs should provide the necessary technological advance in aircraft design and the volume of orders required to maintain minimum capacity in the aircraft industry. The availability of new cargo and transport planes for civilian use should be assured as a by-product of these government efforts. And to the extent that the civilian air fleet would be drawn upon for military purposes, it would be necessary to assure that this equipment was kept technologically up to date. Nevertheless, it must be recognized that the equipment sponsored by the military is notoriously high cost, and that the savings which would accrue to commercial operators by taking advantage of military prototype development would tend to be dissipated by high operating costs and possibly by lack of sufficient adaptability. A policy of depending on the military for aircraft development, therefore, might well defeat the objective of assuring a financially sound civil air transportation system.

In a recent session of Congress, the so-called "Prototype Bill"[11] authorizing the government to sponsor the design, development, and construction of prototype cargo and transport aircraft for commerical purposes failed to pass. Questions arising in connection with this legislation involved the matter of civilian versus miliary control of the development program, and also the fears that the step might lead to nationalization of the industry. It appears now that although the objective of relieving private industry from the financial burden of prototype development will be achieved as a result of intensified military procurement, this remedy will be satisfactory only to the extent that military and commercial requirements are sufficiently comparable to provide a satisfactory degree of equipment interchangeability.

### III. RAILROADS AND NATIONAL DEFENSE

It has been noted above that the railroads carried the major part of the intercity freight and passenger traffic during the last war. In view of the extensive public funds being invested

---

[11] S. 2644, 80 Cong. 2 sess.

in competing forms of transportation, the effects of subsidized competition on the ability of the railroads to maintain themselves in efficient operating condition is a matter of considerable importance. Since the railroads continue to be the backbone of the transportation system, any program designed to promote air, highway, and water transportation must be viewed in the light of these effects, for only by assuring that all essential transport services are maintained can the ultimate objective of national security be served.

In view of the fact that the physical condition of the railroads depends on earnings and on the ability to attract new capital from private investors, the question of whether adequate financial support will be available to maintain and improve the railroad system presents a basic problem. At the present time, despite record high levels of traffic, many railroads are operating at a loss, and few are in a position to finance the necessary program for assuring the adequacy of ways and structures. This condition is extremely serious when it is considered that in the past the prosperity enjoyed in periods of abnormal business activity has provided the fat on which the railroad system has survived during the lean periods which have followed. The possibility of even moderate reductions in traffic from present levels suggests that the future financial condition of the carriers may revert to a state of insolvency when funds will be insufficient to prevent extensive deterioration of the railroad plant.[12]

There are two types of action which might improve the financial outlook of the railroads and permit them to carry on under private ownership. One of these is effecting economies through revisions in the corporate and operating structure of existing railroad companies, and other measures designed to improve railroad efficiency. A second approach lies in a revision of the financial methods (1) with respect to other transport agencies by requiring self-support, and (2) with respect to the railroads, by government ownership of basic facilities or

---

[12] For an analysis of the railroad financial position, see Pt. 2.

other measures to reduce the impacts of subsidized competition. Where the competitive advantages of public transportation facilities are such that the railroads are unable to compete effectively, it may be found necessary to provide compensatory government aid to meet the financial requirements considered essential to the maintenance of adequate railroad facilities for defense.

Following the end of World War I, until the depression years of the 1930's, there was a period of intensive reconstruction and improvement of the railroad plant. Capital expenditures in the years 1921-30 totaled 7.7 billion dollars. At the end of 1930, a sustained program of replacements and additions to equipment found the railroads with a very high level of car and locomotive ownership. During the following decade, however, the railroads suffered an acute loss of traffic and earnings as a result of the depression, and this situation was aggravated by expanding programs of government-financed facilities to aid competing forms of transportation. "At one point in the depression, more than 770,000 freight cars were idle for want of any demand requiring their use. The disastrous economic condition then obtaining plainly was not such as to warrant, or even suggest, a program for complete replacement of car and locomotive units retired because of age, condition, or obsolescence."[13] Instead, the railroads not only were unable to carry on an adequate replacement program, but deterioration of equipment in idle storage was so rapid that thousands of cars were beyond the point of economical repair when the first upsurge of war traffic occurred.

Contrast between the heavy investment period of the twenties and the deterioration of the thirties is indicated by figures of capital expenditures and equipment purchases. In the period 1926-30, gross capital expenditures of Class I railroads averaged 812 million dollars annually, of which 505 millions were for roadway and structures. The gross capital

[13] Statement of James H. Aydelott, Association of American Railroads before the House Interstate and Foreign Commerce Committee in connection with the *National Transportation Inquiry*, 80 Cong. 2 sess., June 7, 1948, pp. 2 and 3 (mimeo.).

figure fell to 207 millions per year in the period 1931-35, of which 148 millions went for road and structures. In terms of physical equipment, 124,000 freight cars were installed annually from 1921 to 1925, and 123,000 were retired, while during the period 1931-35 an average of less than 10,000 cars were installed per year and nearly 100,000 per year retired.[14]

It was largely the extensive capital investments made during the 1920's, therefore, combined with the technological advances in motive power and equipment made during the depression, which enabled the railroads to meet the tremendous traffic loads of World War II. The railroads handled 74 per cent more freight and 100 per cent more passenger traffic than during the First World War with one quarter fewer cars, one third fewer locomotives, and one quarter fewer men.[15] Despite this excellent record, "had V-E Day and V-J Day been much longer delayed, it would take a bold man to say that our transportation system would have continued to suffice. In terms of transportation— whether wittingly or not—a grave gamble was taken on the duration of hostilities."[16]

The question raised by this recitation of events is whether the federal government in the future is to leave to the financial fortunes of the carriers such a basic national defense consideration as the degree of adequacy of the railroad transportation system. Even after the prolonged period of deferred construction during World War II, we find that investments in road and structures for Class I carriers amounted to only 286 millions in 1947 and an estimated 326 millions in 1948.[17] Today only the purchase of new rolling stock is possible on anything resembling an adequate scale for most railroads, despite the high level of economic activity and the need for railroad rehabilitation.

Taking into account the differences in the value of the dollar,

[14] Statement of J. H. Parmelee, Association of American Railroads, the same, Tables V and X.
[15] The same, p. 7.
[16] Statement of James H. Aydelott, the same, p. 7.
[17] Interstate Commerce Commission, *Monthly Comment on Transportation Statistics*, Sept. 15, 1948, p. 2 (mimeo.).

it is apparent that investment in road and structure is now little better than during the depth of the depression period. This situation is extremely hazardous from the standpoint of immediate security requirements. And from a long-range viewpoint, it is unlikely that future conditions will offer greater earning potential than is offered today. Moreover, as public investment in other forms of transport continues, further shift of traffic to rail competitors will take place, reducing still further the ability of the railroads during less prosperous periods to compensate for deferred maintenance and reconstruction. Still the fact must be faced that much of the traffic lost to the railroads in peacetime may again be forced back during war, due either to the requisition of equipment by the government or to the inability to maintain other agencies in the face of material shortages. This shift will occur simultaneously with wartime expansion of traffic in the categories still moving principally by rail.

It must be concluded that the wartime record of the railroads can be attributed in part to good fortune rather than good planning, and that the current situation is much less apt to work itself out in any future emergency. In view of the underlying assumptions as to the sudden and devastating nature of another war, the condition of the railroad system can hardly be left to fortuitous circumstances with the same degree of confidence assumed in the past. Certainly the need is apparent for the federal government to keep itself informed of the condition of the railroad system and to measure the impacts of its development programs in other transportation fields. And, if necessary, the federal government must take steps to provide a continuing program of capital outlay to maintain railroad plant and equipment at required levels.

It will be necessary, therefore, that the federal government include among the functions of a transportation agency the responsibility for maintaining a current inventory of railroad requirements and for recommending necessary action to achieve and maintain adequate physical standards. In addition, it will be necessary, in conjunction with car service operations, to develop plans for the necessary control of traffic in emergency conditions and the necessary co-ordination of rail and other transport facilities.

### IV. HIGHWAY TRANSPORTATION IN WARTIME

The lack of any permanent organization responsible for railroad preparedness and capable of effecting the necessary emergency operations in wartime, is duplicated in the case of highway transportation. During the last war we attemped an inventory of motor vehicle equipment months after the problems threatening this form of transportation had become acute. For many months there was much confusion and little action on the fuel and rubber requirements to maintain essential automobile transportation. Today we are fostering the same condition of unpreparedness by failing to maintain the necessary information concerning motor transport. In any future emergency the truck, bus, and passenger car may be far more urgently needed because of evacuation problems and the demands for emergency services in areas where other transport facilities may be disrupted.

Motor vehicle registrations have now reached the 40-million mark, and demand for new equipment and replacements continues to support a high level of automotive manufacturing activity. Since the user pays the bill for vehicle purchase, the equipment problem in this field differs from those encountered in the case of air or water transportation. The importance of maintaining the operation of automotive equipment in wartime, through provision of rubber, petroleum products, and repair parts, means that federal responsibility must be taken to assure rubber stockpiling and synthetic capacity, manufacturing and repair facilities, and petroleum supply for essential uses.

In World War II, the lack of an adequate rubber supply, confusion over rubber availability, and opposing official views as to the need for conservation created a situation which was extremely hazardous to the war effort. In no field of endeavor was the lack of advance planning more obvious than in the matter of tire and gasoline rationing and other controls on highway transportation. In the future, federal responsibility must be taken to avoid a comparable situation. Estimates of demand for critical materials will have to be maintained by the transportation agency for all forms of transportation, and these reported to the National Security Resources Board for consolidation and adjustment to the demands of other users, civilian and military.[18]

With respect to the highways themselves, it is generally agreed that a system of roads and streets to meet the needs of peacetime traffic is also adequate for war.[19] In fact the need for limiting unnecessary vehicle operations to conserve equipment and materials often provides a substantial increase in highway capacity for emergency purposes. The national defense interest, therefore, is not something apart from the peacetime goals of providing needed facilities on all parts of the highway system. And it may be granted that the entire highway network is important for defense purposes because a principal advantage of highway transportation is the availability of numerous alternate routes which makes it extremely difficult to disrupt motor vehicle operations by enemy attack or sabotage.

It does not follow, however, because of the defense importance of the highway system, that the federal government must participate in the entire program. There are reasonably distinct and appropriate roles for federal, state, and local road-building efforts. Federal interest should be directed to the most important potential war transportation bottlenecks in our highway system, on the principal intercity arteries and their transcity connections. It is on these roads that the greatest design problems and the highest costs are encountered, and

[18] The NSRB is required to advise the president concerning the "relationship between potential supplies of, and potential requirements for, manpower, resources, and productive facilities in time of war." In addition it is responsible for determining "policies for establishing adequate reserves of strategic and critical material, and for the conservation of these reserves." 61 Stat. 499.

[19] An exception in wartime is the need for access roads to serve new or expanded industrial sites and military establishments.

where the need for federal assistance is greatest. It is the priority of these needs and the interstate character of the traffic served which stress the desirability of concentrating federal action; and the 40,000 miles of interstate highways which connect our principal population centers provide a logical point of concentration. If in another war the highway transportation system is called upon for evacuation purposes, or to absorb traffic in critical areas where rail service is disrupted, a modern main road network designed for uninterrupted traffic movement will be a primary need.

## V. THE ROLE OF WATER TRANSPORTATION

It has been pointed out that the national security importance of the merchant fleet and of the shipbuilding industry is such as to call for federal maintenance of ship construction and operation on a scale to assure essential levels of activity in these fields during times of peace. History has demonstrated, however, that the normal requirements of peacetime commerce have in the past failed to provide the necessary demand to achieve this goal. The experience of two world wars demonstrates that "any peacetime shipping and shipbuilding activity in the United States for the purpose of furnishing a waterborne transportation system . . . will fall far short of the country's national security requirements."[20]

. . . even if private operators in the United States had carried all the foreign water-borne commerce of the United States before the war together with the domestic water-borne commerce, they still would have employed considerably less than half the merchant ships used by the United States in World War II.[21]

Actually, the proportion of our ocean-going foreign trade carried by American flag vessels before the war amounted to only 24 per cent of dry cargo shipments and 31 per cent of

[20] *The Use and Disposition of Ships and Shipyards at the End of World War II*, a report prepared for the United States Navy and the United States Maritime Commission by the Graduate School of Business Administration, Harvard University, June 1945, p. 23.
[21] The same, p. 30.

passenger traffic.[22] It is apparent, therefore, that it would be impossible to maintain the United States fleet tonnage necessary to meet war needs on the basis of the peacetime demand for ocean transportation. Moreover, even to achieve this level of foreign shipping operations requires construction and operating subsidies to meet the competition of foreign carriers.

Despite these efforts to maintain our international fleet, the bulk of the water-borne commerce carried in United States vessels before the war was in the coastal and intercoastal trade, which is not directly benefited by the subsidy provisions of the Merchant Marine Act of 1936. These important coastwise and intercoastal shipping services have thus far been unable to recover their prewar position after the almost complete cessation of activities during the war. If, as in the past, the United States is to depend to a large degree on these domestic shipping services to maintain a nucleus fleet and shipbuilding industry, the only possible method may be through direct subsidization of domestic shipping operations to permit effective competition with land transportation. However, such a program would attract substantial volumes of traffic from truck and rail carriers, hence reduce the capacity provided by these agencies. Then, in an emergency, merchant vessels would be shifted to military operations, and land transport equipment would be inadequate to accommodate this shift. This situation raises the issue of whether subsidies to domestic shipping would compel compensating subsidies for competing forms of transportation.

These questions bring into focus once again the fact that a land transportation system which meets the needs of normal commerce can, with the appropriate exercise of public authority, be quickly geared to war requirements. On the other hand, the volume and type of shipping facilities demanded to accommodate the normal requirements of ocean transportation fall far short of what is needed for war, just as the wartime

[22] U. S. Maritime Commission, *Ocean Shipping: Facts and Figures,* Handbook of the Research Division, p. 79 (mimeo.); data for 1939.

demand for aircraft exceeds the size of fleet which can be supported in peacetime. In time of war emergency, the merchant marine deficiency can be supplied only by (1) an intensive shipbuilding effort involving heavy use of materials and manpower;[23] or (2) the maintenance of a standby fleet under the control of the military establishment.

The solution to this problem, then, as in the case of air transport, is clear but costly. To the extent that the needs of the national defense are estimated by the military to be in excess of what would be supplied for peacetime purposes, the difference will have to be made up either through subsidy policies or through the maintenance of reserves, or both. Two important facts which have been ignored in the past, however, must be recognized. First, we have failed to be specific about national security requirements, and have used the term vaguely as an additional justification for government aid, but never concretely to carry out a definite program in conformity with military plans. In our declarations of merchant marine policy:

National defense and the promotion of foreign trade were both being sought not only at the same time but also as if they were actually of equal importance, when as a matter of fact it has since become apparent that the requirements of security far outstripped those of the promotion of foreign trade so far as ships and shipyards were concerned. All the maritime legislation which was enacted during the twentieth century, and all the men who were President of the United States during that time, recognized the dual functions of the merchant marine; as a transportation system and as a necessity in time of war. In most instances, however, the relative importance of each function was not made clear, and it was commonly accepted that a compromise was necessary in order to reconcile the different requirements of almost contradictory purposes.[24]

In the future, when national defense requirements exceed normal levels of supply, the important task of making up the

---

[23] Between 1935 and 1939 "employment in shipyards of the United States, including Government-owned navy yards, ranged between 63,000 and 102,000. At its wartime peak the industry employed more than 1,700,000 people." *The Use and Disposition of Ships and Shipyards at the End of World War II*, p. 13.

[24] The same, p. 23.

difference cannot be considered a by-product of accomplishing other goals. The military must present their best estimates of war shipping requirements, to be reviewed by a top planning agency (the National Security Resources Board), which can compare these demands with estimates of the size and composition of the fleet which would otherwise be provided. The NSRB would then determine a feasible subsidy or reserve fleet program in the light of over-all economic requirements.

In arriving at a merchant shipping program, consideration will also have to be given to estimates of the impacts of merchant marine promotion on the transportation system. For failure to consider each of the individual parts of the transportation system is to risk a possible breakdown of the whole. In the case of the merchant shipping problem, it would be possible to restore considerable tonnage to the domestic trades through a program of construction and operating subsidies if merchant shipping were the only consideration. The problem, however, is not so easily solved. Even if it were possible by this means to create the size of stand-by fleet required for war purposes, by so doing we might impoverish important segments of the railroad system by the diversion of important long-haul traffic. Until the national government is prepared to recognize and take into account all aspects of war transportation, national defense measures are bound to create as many problems as they seek to solve.

When the final determination has been made as to the necessary merchant shipping program for security purposes, the goal may be approached in part through subsidies to international shipping. To the extent that this fails to accomplish the objective, two possible courses of action are open: (1) subsidies may be paid to domestic shipping, with compensating subsidies made available, where necessary, to competing forms of domestic transportation; or (2) the military could be required to meet its needs through a stand-by fleet in the same way that it maintains battleships and cruisers. The latter solution is obviously the most certain and least disruptive approach to assuring the desired results.

### VI. CONCLUSIONS ON DEFENSE

The transportation problem from the standpoint of national defense appears in essence to be as follows:

1. It must be assumed that all methods of transportation are essential. Accordingly, federal policy must provide for maintaining the entire transportation system in satisfactory condition.

2. Generally speaking, a land transportation system adequate for the peacetime economy would ordinarily meet the basic physical requirements for war. In the case of water and air transportation, however, war requirements far exceed peacetime facilities because these types of equipment are in effect instruments of war. From the standpoint of physical facilities, therefore, the problem of providing a transportation system adequate for national security means under present-day conditions that (1) methods must be devised by which air and water transport capacity can be provided during peacetime at levels exceeding peacetime demand; and (2) necessary steps must be taken to minimize or compensate for the impacts of air and water subsidies on the condition of other essential parts of the transportation system.

3. Thus far, we have depended on vague references to the national defense significance of transportation in federal transportation statutes to assure facilities adequate for wartime needs. There has been no attempt to place the responsibility on the military for presenting firm estimates of military requirements, and no attempt to view the war transportation problem as a whole. The United States has been fortunate that in wartime a physically adequate system of transportation has nevertheless been available, and that time has been afforded to organize the system for effective operation and to remedy the failure to plan during peacetime. There is no guarantee of such good fortune in the future, however. The fortuitous circumstances which permitted us during the last war to create a central transportation agency, a synthetic rubber industry, a shipbuilding industry, a pipeline network, a rationing system, and other facilities cannot be relied upon in another emergency.

4. The transportation activities of the federal government are so disorganized today as to make effective programing in this field impossible. Federal operations are scattered over half a dozen major agencies and many less important bureaus; and no one person or agency has the responsibility to assure that the transportation system as a whole is in adequate condition. Moreover, the federal government is supporting the development of highway, air, and water transportation facilities without consideration for maintaining an adequate railroad system, creating a situation in which it may prove impossible to provide for necessary railroad upkeep and modernization.

5. From the standpoint of organization, a basic step is the establishment of federal machinery to provide a continuing evaluation of the transportation situation; to determine the steps necessary for proper maintenance and development of all needed transport facilities; and to assure the necessary plans for wartime transport operations.

6. The National Security Resources Board must provide the necessary liaison between military and civilian transportation agencies; and wherever national security requirements are found to be in excess of what would otherwise be supplied, such requirements should be specified by the military and financed wherever feasible out of the national defense budget. Equipment such as reserve transport aircraft, merchant ships, and railroad cars would be charged to the military budget, as well as the military share of airway costs and special projects undertaken specifically for national defense purposes. The NSRB must also take steps to require periodic estimates of the materials, equipment, and manufacturing facilities needed to assure transport services to meet emergency requirements.

7. Failure to organize transportation activities in such a way as to assure unequivocal responsibility for an adequate wartime transportation system might well result in deficiencies that would constitute a fatal weakness in the economy.

Up to this point it has been seen that the federal government, through a variety of expenditure programs directed to the provision of transport facilities and services, exerts a powerful influence on the character of the entire transportation system. The physical accomplishments of these programs have been extensive, and federal action can be credited with a very substantial share of the progress which finds us today with the world's greatest transportation plant. At the same time there is no escape from the conclusion that federal expenditure policy has failed to promote maximum efficiency and economy in the transportation system; that the conflicts and inconsistencies in basic policy, as well as the absence of administrative machinery to carry out a national transportation policy, have precluded a realization of the full benefits which federal action might otherwise achieve.

The defects of federal promotional policy, however, cannot be fully described without tracing their impact on the individual shipper or traveler, and on the transportation industries themselves. These effects are found in the quality of transportation services offered, in the rates charged, in the nature of competitive relationships among the carriers, and in the financial position of the transportation industries. In Part II, where consideration is directed to the role of the federal government in its control over transport operations, the shortcomings of national policy will be more apparent. In these chapters the influence of the federal government through control over the quality, quantity, and pricing of transport services will be described; and the results of federal promotional policy will be seen in relation to the final product of transportation cost and service.

# PART II
# REGULATION OF TRANSPORT ENTERPRISES

# INTRODUCTION

The national government has assumed heavy responsibility in a vast and complex undertaking in the field of transportation, both domestic and foreign. It is dedicated to the preservation of a transportation system that will be adequate for the needs of commerce and the national security. Ownership, operation, and the basic functions of management are divided between numerous government agencies on the one hand, and thousands of privately owned transport concerns on the other. Progress and efficiency in the provision of transport services have been entrusted initially to the drive, initiative, and vision of private management. And for major segments of the industry, the ability to earn a satisfactory return on total investment still controls the availability of new capital for expansion and modernization. At the same time, the government exercises final authority over all major decisions that determine the size of the transportation plant and its operating organization; the quality of service rendered; and the price at which the service is offered to the public.

The major problem in the field of government relations to transportation stems from the fact that after more than a half century of intensive experimentation, there has been a signal failure to develop effective public standards and procedures to compensate for the removal of transportation from the forces which motivate a private enterprise system. There has developed gradually and subtly a situation in which neither government nor private enterprise can be held firmly accountable for efficiency and progress in transportation.

This precariously balanced joint undertaking is the product of more than six decades of experimentation and evolution. Federal control of domestic transportation started in 1887 with the assertion of limited and primarily punitive authority over the railroads. From that date until 1920 government efforts were exerted in the main to protect the public against the exercise of monopolistic powers by the railroads. Thus, emphasis was placed on the control of exorbitant and discriminatory charging and on the maintenance of effective railroad competition.

With passage of the Transportation Act, 1920, the interests of the national government in this field took new form and direction. Punitive and restrictive regulation gave way to what was characterized at the time as a constructive and forward-looking approach. All previous devices for controlling rate discrimination and for maintaining satisfactory standards of service were retained, but new and far-reaching powers were added to the regulatory system. The Interstate Commerce Commission was, in effect, directed to manipulate the general level of railroad rates in such a way that the carriers could obtain the net earnings required for the maintenance of a transportation system capable of supplying the nation's needs in time of peace and war.

Congress recognized that such a rate level would produce extreme variations in the earning power of individual railroads. Consequently, the Commission was instructed to promulgate a general plan for the consolidation of the railroads into a number of systems that would have reasonably even earning power. Pending the completion of this complex consolidation task, the law provided for the "recapture" of a portion of the earnings made by any carrier over and above a prescribed reasonable rate of return on the transportation investment.

Under the Transportation Act, 1920, the federal government also asserted for the first time authority over the expansion and abandonment of railroad facilities as well as over the issuance of railroad securities. This control was viewed as a necessary corollary to the underlying theory of the act which emphasized a positive government responsibility for the maintenance of sound financial and operating conditions in the industry.

The junction of depression traffic and competition of new transport agencies made it evident that Congress either would have to relax railroad regulation or impose higher standards of public responsibility and competitive practices on the new agencies. The decision was in favor of the latter course, and the first major step was taken in the form of the Motor Carrier Act of 1935. Responsibility for administering the Motor Carrier Act was vested in the Interstate Commerce Commission along with its already extensive authority over railroads, pipelines, and express companies.

Domestic water transportation was not subjected to comprehensive federal control until the passage of the Transportation Act of 1940. With this enactment, a long step was taken in the direction of administrative unification of transport controls. Jurisdiction over coastal and intercoastal shipping was transferred from the Maritime Commission[1] to the Interstate Commerce Commission, giving the latter agency broad and comparable supervision over what at that time constituted all major forms of domestic transportation.

With the passage of the Civil Aeronautics Act of 1938, the federal government segregated air transportation for specialized promotional and regulatory treatment. It set out to promote domestic and international air transportation under the "infant industry" theory through the provision of airports, airways, and direct financial subsidies in the form of air-mail payments supplemented by a promotional regulatory system. Administration of this program was placed in a separate government agency that has evolved into the present Civil Aeronautics Board and Civil Aeronautics Administration. No provision was made for any policy or administrative co-ordination between the regulation of air transportation on the one hand and the unified control program applying to rail, highway, pipeline, and water agencies on the other. This particularistic approach was defended at the time on the grounds that air transportation involved special and highly technical problems

[1] The policy decision to create and maintain an adequate merchant marine began with the Shipping Act of 1916 (39 Stat. 728) followed by the Merchant Marine acts of 1920 (41 Stat. 988), 1928 (45 Stat. 689), and 1936 (49 Stat. 1985), and minor amendments. Although primarily concerned with the promotion of ocean shipping through the payment of various kinds of subsidies, the maritime acts prior to 1940 provided partial jurisdiction over coastal and intercoastal, as well as noncontiguous, shipping. Merchant marine policy is dealt with in Pt. 1 since it is now primarily concerned with promotional as distinguished from regulatory functions.

and that the industry should be fostered to maturity before being subjected to the unified standards of control that had been imposed on the full-fledged members of the transportation system.

In the development of these various methods of transport control, the federal government has not been guided by any single principle with respect either to policy objectives or administrative organization. Problems affecting each form of transportation have been dealt with as they reached a critical stage and in accordance with the theories of administration and political objectives prevailing at the moment. There have been such revolutionary changes in the character and organization of our transport system in recent years that some degree of improvisation in the development of control policies and programs was undoubtedly necessary. For the individual transport media have developed at varying rates and reached maturity at different times. However, government action has, in major respects, dictated the rate and character of such development. Government must, therefore, assume responsibility for correcting contradictory, discriminatory, or uneconomical elements in our national transportation program.

Part II of this study describes the objectives of transport regulation, analyzes the major areas of regulatory action, and identifies the most important issues of public policy that have emerged from the assertion of comprehensive public control over transportation enterprises.

# CHAPTER IX

# THE OBJECTIVES OF TRANSPORT CONTROL

The fact that the federal government has for many years carried on extensive promotional and regulatory activity affecting all forms of transportation would seem to suggest that Congress has adopted a national transportation policy. As a matter of fact, a legislative committee has recently found that such a view is generally held by interested parties:

There is no doubt that carriers and shippers as well as those of the general public who have any informed opinion on the matter agree that we do have a national transportation policy both sound and reasonably comprehensive. Any assertion that we do not have such a policy is directed to administration rather than legislation. There is, however, a difference of opinion among the carriers on the subject of administration and implementation of the policy.[1]

Actually we have neither a single transportation policy nor a series of policies that are mutually consistent. Moreover, the conflicts and inconsistencies do not stem primarily from the imperfections of administrative application as suggested by the observation noted above. On the contrary, they arise inevitably from two circumstances: (1) Congress has adopted regulatory objectives that lead naturally to uneven treatment of the several forms of transportation; and, (2) the results of promotional action run counter to the declared purposes of the major regulatory program.

## I. PROBLEMS OF PUBLIC CONTROL

The revolution in transport organization and operation that began about 1920 and reached mature form in the early thirties posed for Congress an unprecedented problem of transport control. Between 1920 and 1935, when federal regulatory attention was centered on the railroad problem, a new and

---

[1] *National Transportation Inquiry*, Report of Special Subcommittee on Transportation of the House Committee on Interstate and Foreign Commerce, H. Rept. 2735, 79 Cong. 2 sess. (1946), Pt. 1, Summary, p. ix.

complex pattern of transport organization was emerging. The attendant problems of public control were to bear little resemblance to the traditional issues of railroad regulation which Congress strove to resolve by the Transportation Act of 1920. Where before, the bulk of the nation's transportation work was performed by about 100 large-scale and privately owned enterprises, there now emerged a maze of small-scale common carrier, contract, and private operators, using publicly provided highways. Moreover, the range and intensity of water competition was increasing by virtue of federal promotion of rivers and harbors. And to further complicate the structure of transport organization, it was becoming apparent that air transportation would survive the experimental era and develop into a full-scale addition to the transportation plant.

The necessity for adjusting the theory and method of public control to the realities of the transport revolution was hastened by the onset of depression which intensified competition for a reduced volume of traffic. At this juncture, it became evident that Congress either would have to relax railroad regulation in order to give the carriers more freedom to meet the new competition, or impose higher standards of public responsibility and competitive practices on the new agencies.

During the course of debates on this issue, Congress was urged to make a clear choice between two totally different solutions. On the one hand it was contended that all competing transport agencies, the old along with the new, should be unified under common control and management into transportation companies, each using the particular facility best adapted to its area and type of operation. Under this arrangement, no official effort would have been made to preserve the identity of each separate form of transportation, or to maintain effective interagency competition. The public would depend upon effective regulation in the main to guarantee that these integrated and monopolistic companies would supply adequate service at reasonable rates.

At the other extreme, some interests urged Congress to open up the entire transportation field to the workings of competitive enterprise. It was asserted that the railroads no longer possessed either the monopoly power to charge excessive rates or the financial staying power to drive out competition by price cutting. Adoption of this solution would have entailed substantial relaxation of railroad regulation, giving the carriers more freedom to meet the new competition.

As a basis for making a rational choice between these opposed theories, Congress created the Office of Federal Coordinator of Transportation,[2] and instructed that official, among other things, to investigate and report with respect to methods of improving conditions in the transportation system.[3] At the outset he posed the basic problem in transportation:

The presence and use of these differing forms of transportation raises the question whether destructive competition should be lessened and constructive coordination be increased. Stated more concretely, the question is whether it is sound public policy to encourage duplication of facilities and warfare all along the line, or to find the work which each form of transportation can do best and endeavor accordingly to build up a national transportation system in which the various agencies will function with more regard to correlation and less to competition and with a minimum of waste.[4]

Subsequently, the Coordinator advised Congress that the ultimate objective of transportation policy should be the attainment of:

. . . a system of transportation for the Nation which will supply the most efficient means of transport and furnish service as cheaply as is consistent with fair treatment of labor and with earnings which will support adequate credit and the ability to expand as the need develops, and to take advantage of all improvements in the art. This system of transportation must be in the hands of reliable and responsible operators, whose charges for service will be known, dependable, and reasonable, and free from unjust discrimination.[5]

---

[2] *Emergency Railroad Transportation Act, 1933*, 48 Stat. 211, Title I, sec. 2.

[3] Reports made to Congress dealing with this problem are as follows: *Regulation of Railroads*, S. Doc. 119, 73 Cong. 2 sess. (1934); *Regulation of Transportation Agencies*, S. Doc. 152, 73 Cong. 2 sess. (1934); *Report of the Federal Coordinator of Transportation*, H. Doc. 89, 74 Cong. 1 sess.; *Fourth Report of the Federal Coordinator of Transportation on Transportation Legislation*, H. Doc. 394, 74 Cong. 2 sess. (1936).

[4] S. Doc. 152, 73 Cong. 2 sess., p. 4.

[5] *To Amend the Interstate Commerce Act*, Hearings on S. 1629, S. 1632. and S. 1635, 74 Cong. 1 sess. (1935), Pt. 1, p. 51.

He found that in sharp contrast to this desideratum of national policy the actual situation in the transportation field was characterized by financial disintegration of the carriers, irresponsible and unreliable performance by many operators, and unstable and discriminatory rates. He stated before a congressional committee that:

The present situation is, in my judgment, satisfactory to nobody. Certainly it is not satisfactory to the carriers or to investors; there is strong and continually growing evidence that it is not satisfactory to shippers; and it is not satisfactory to labor.[6]

The third and controlling observation flowing from the Coordinator's studies was that transport competition had become "destructive and wasteful," and was therefore working against attainment of the stated transportation objective.

And finally, he concluded that the development of destructive competition and general instability throughout the transportation system was due chiefly to the failure of the federal government to subject all major forms of transportation to similar standards of public control.[7]

To those who contended that the desired "parity of regulation" could be achieved more readily and equitably by relaxing railroad regulation than by imposing authoritative public control on all transport media, the Coordinator answered:

Past experience with free competition of unregulated railroads proved it would be folly to abandon the system of Federal regulation, built up in response to public demand over a long series of years. It was also clear that the evils which had created this demand for railroad regulation were breeding rapidly in the other forms of transportation, to the alarm of a large proportion of the water and motor carriers as well as of many of the more far-sighted shippers. Study of the situation, reinforced by a growing public sentiment, made it plain that the choice should be in favor of extending the system of regulation impartially over all important forms of transportation.[8]

---

[6] The same, p. 50.
[7] H. Doc. 394, 74 Cong. 2 sess., p. 4.
[8] The same.

It will be observed that three principles supply the integrating force of the Coordinator's program for government action in this field:

1. The national interest requires at all times an adequate supply of transportation facilities provided without discrimination among individuals and communities and priced as low as consistent with financial health of the carriers.

2. Unrestrained competition among transport enterprises tends to become "destructive" leading to instability of transport supply and discrimination with respect to rates and service. Consequently, the government must assume responsibility for maintaining acceptable standards of competition and must apply such rules impartially to all segments of the transportation system.

3. In order to achieve maximum efficiency and economy the several individual forms of transportation must be co-ordinated or integrated with a view to serving the national interest rather than the financial advantage of any one agency.

Although clearly influenced by these governing principles in the formulation of regulatory programs controlling some major forms of transportation, Congress has deviated widely with respect to others. Major inconsistencies are revealed in the declarations of legislative policy attached to the three major bodies of law into which Congress has divided its regulatory program: (1) the Interstate Commerce Act administered by the Interstate Commerce Commission; (2) the Civil Aeronautics Act, 1938, administered by the Civil Aeronautics Board; and (3) the Merchant Marine Act of 1936 applied by the Maritime Commission.

## II. THE INTERSTATE COMMERCE ACT: OBJECTIVE AND SCOPE

The Interstate Commerce Act[9] is the product of more than six decades of refinement, expansion, and deletions in regulatory jurisdiction and procedure. This complex body of transportation law constitutes the authority under which the Inter-

[9] 54 Stat. 899.

state Commerce Commission exercises a high degree of managerial control over railroads,[10] pipelines, motor carriers, and domestic water transportation.[11] In 1940 Congress defined its objectives with reference to these transport agencies as follows:

It is hereby declared to be the national transportation policy of the Congress to provide for fair and impartial regulation of all modes of transportation subject to the provisions of this Act, so administered as to recognize and preserve the inherent advantages of each; to promote safe, adequate, economical, and efficient service and foster sound economic conditions in transportation and among the several carriers; to encourage the establishment and maintenance of reasonable charges for transportation services, without unjust discriminations, undue preferences or advantages, or unfair or destructive competitive practices; to cooperate with the several States and the duly authorized officials thereof; and to encourage fair wages and equitable working conditions;—all to the end of developing, coordinating, and preserving a national transportation system by water, highway, and rail, as well as other means, adequate to meet the needs of the commerce of the United States, of the Postal Service, and of the national defense. All of the provisions of this Act

[10] Together with such ancillary agencies as express and sleeping car companies.
[11] The legislative developments of the main body of law administered by the Interstate Commerce Commission are indicated in the following:
"The 'Act to Regulate Commerce,' approved February 4, 1887, and thereafter amended many times, became the 'Interstate Commerce Act' by a provision in the Transportation Act, 1920, approved February 28, 1920. As thereafter further amended, it was amplified and enlarged by the Motor Carrier Act, 1935, approved August 9, 1935. By a provision in the latter act, the Interstate Commerce Act as it stood became 'part I' of the Interstate Commerce Act, and 'part II' was added. It was provided that part I might continue to be cited as 'Interstate Commerce Act,' and part II might be cited as 'Motor Carrier Act, 1935.' Thus, 'Interstate Commerce Act' might apply to the whole act, embracing parts I and II, or to part I alone.
"The Transportation Act of 1940, approved September 18, 1940, made numerous amendments to parts I and II, and added part III, which relates to carriers by water. In this process of amendment, the designation of part II by the short title 'Motor Carrier Act, 1935' for citation purposes, was amended out. The three parts of the Interstate Commerce Act are, therefore, to be cited as such, but the declaration of 'National Transportation Policy' is outside the parts enumerated. Part IV, relating to freight forwarders, was added by the act of May 16, 1942." *The Interstate Commerce Act together with Text of Certain Supplementary Acts and Related Sections of Various Other Acts*, Revised to Jan. 1, 1946, published by the Interstate Commerce Commission, p. iv.

shall be administered and enforced with a view to carrying out the above declaration of policy.[12]

It will be observed that so far as declaration of policy is concerned Congress has directed the Interstate Commerce Commission to maintain fair standards of competition among rail, highway, waterway, and pipeline agencies; to co-ordinate these agencies with a view to achieving efficiency in transportation; to foster sound economic conditions in transportation; and to protect transport users against rate and service discrimination.[13]

The interest of shippers in the maintenance of adequate service at reasonable rates is recognized by the mandate to the Commission "to encourage the establishment and maintenance of reasonable charges for transportation services, without unjust discrimination, undue preferences or advantages." Furthermore, there is a clear indication that transportation users are expected to pay compensatory rates for the services rendered and are not to anticipate windfalls from price wars between the various transport agencies. For the act is unequivocal in its declaration against "unfair or destructive competitive practices."

Manifestly, Congress did not view this declaration merely as a hortative statement. For it directed a commission of eleven

[12] The Interstate Commerce Act, Declaration of National Transportation Policy, 54 Stat. 899.

[13] On the fundamental question as to the extent to which the maintenance of effective interagency competition is contemplated under the Interstate Commerce Act as amended, the following observation of the court is pertinent: ". . . the altered emphasis in railroad legislation on achieving an adequate, efficient, and economical system of transportation through close supervision of business operations and practices rather than through heavy reliance on the enforcement of free competition in various phases of the business, cf. *New York Central Securities Corp. v. United States,* 287 U.S. 12, has its counterpart in motor carrier policy. The premises of motor carrier regulation posit some curtailment of free and unrestrained competition. [Footnote omitted.] The origins [footnote omitted] and legislative history [footnote omitted] of the Motor Carrier Act adequately disclose that in it Congress recognized there may be occasions when 'competition between carriers may result in harm to the public as well as in benefit; and that when a [carrier] inflicts injury upon its rival, it may be the public which ultimately bears the loss.' Cf. *Texas & Pacific Ry. Co. v. Gulf, C. & S.F. Ry. Co.,* 270 U.S. 266, 277." *McLean Trucking Co. v. U.S.,* 321 U.S. 83.

men staffed with some 2,000 employees[14] to administer and enforce all provisions of the act "with a view to carrying out the above declaration of policy."[15]

Moreover, Congress equipped the Commission with substantive powers deemed adequate to control discrimination; to set the standards of and to preserve effective competition; to determine how facilities and services shall be co-ordinated or integrated; to maintain satisfactory standards of safety and service in transportation; and to set the general level of rates, thereby controlling carrier income.

Broadly stated then, the Interstate Commerce Act, which controls all domestic transport agencies, with the exception of air carriers, is permeated by the ethical concepts of fairness, justness, and reasonableness. The objectives are conceived in terms of the general public interest in a unified national transportation system. And the prescribed standards of public responsibility and competitive performance apply uniformly to carriers by railroad, highway, pipeline, and waterway.

### III. THE CIVIL AERONAUTICS ACT, 1938

By this enactment, Congress simultaneously consolidated its activities in the field of air transportation[16] and divorced the entire program from the main body of transportation policy as embodied in the Interstate Commerce Act. The administration of the newly adopted promotional and regulatory program for air transportation was vested in a novel type of organization —the Civil Aeronautics Authority. This agency, composed of three presumably co-ordinate but actually autonomous divisions, enjoyed only a brief independent existence.[17] Responsi-

[14] The ICC appropriation for fiscal year 1949 authorizes 2,437 positions and provides a budget of $10,894,317.

[15] The Interstate Commerce Act, Declaration of National Transportation Policy, 54 Stat. 899.

[16] Prior to the enactment of the Civil Aeronautics Act, 1938 (52 Stat. 973) primary control over air transportation was vested in the Bureau of Air Commerce, Department of Commerce; the Division of Air Mail, Post Office Department; the Bureau of Air Mail, Interstate Commerce Commission.

[17] The original "Civil Aeronautics Authority" was composed of three divisions the members of which were appointed by the president with the advice and

bility for carrying out the provisions of the act is now divided between a Civil Aeronautics Board and the Civil Aeronautics Administration located in the Department of Commerce.[18]

In carrying out the provisions of the Civil Aeronautics Act, these agencies are directed by Congress to:

. . . consider the following, among other things, as being in the public interest, and in accordance with the public convenience and necessity—

(a) The encouragement and development of an air-transportation system properly adapted to the present and future needs of the foreign and domestic commerce of the United States, of the Postal Service, and of the national defense;

(b) The regulation of air transportation in such manner as to recognize and preserve the inherent advantages of, assure the highest degree of safety in, and foster sound economic conditions in, such transportation, and to improve the relations between, and coordinate transportation by, air carriers;

(c) The promotion of adequate, economical, and efficient service by air carriers at reasonable charges, without unjust discriminations, undue preferences or advantages, or unfair or destructive competitive practices;

(d) Competition to the extent necessary to assure the sound development of an air-transportation system properly adapted to the needs of the foreign and domestic commerce of the United States, of the Postal Service, and of the national defense;

(e) The regulation of air commerce in such manner as to best promote its development and safety; and

(f) The encouragement and development of civil aeronautics.[19]

Clearly this is a deliberately promotional approach to the treatment of air transportation. In effect, Congress has taken the

---

consent of the Senate: (1) the "Authority" itself, composed of five members; (2) a single administrator; and (3) the Air Safety Board composed of three members.

[18] This rearrangement was brought about on June 11, 1940, under the provisions of Reorganization Plan No. IV, issued by the president pursuant to the "Reorganization Act of 1939" (53 Stat. 561). Among other things the plan abolished the Civil Aeronautics Authority as an independent agency and transferred its functions to the Department of Commerce. The work previously performed by the Air Safety Board was combined with the regulatory functions of a newly designated "Civil Aeronautics Board" which, although presumably "independent," is supposed to operate within the framework of the Department of Commerce for "housekeeping" purposes.

[19] Civil Aeronautics Act, 1938, 52 Stat. 980, sec. 2.

position that development of commercial aviation is so vital to the nation's commerce and security that preferential standards of public treatment are required for this new transport medium. For at no point in the system of promotion and control developed for aviation is any official concern expressed regarding the competitive impact of the new medium on other forms of transportation.[20] Moreover, the Civil Aeronautics Act of 1938 provides monetary subsidies to air transportation in the form of air-mail payments, thus setting aside that agency as the only form of domestic transportation whose financial solvency is directly underwritten by the government. And here, as in the case of the Interstate Commerce Commission, Congress has provided the organization, personnel, and public funds deemed necessary to administer the program vigorously.[21]

This particularistic treatment of air transportation was justified at the outset and still is by the "infant industry" argument. It is assumed that subsidization will eventually produce a self-supporting enterprise which at some appropriate time can be covered into the general pattern of transport regulation as a full-fledged member of the national transportation system.

So far as declared policy is concerned, we therefore have a head-on conflict between the Interstate Commerce Act and the Civil Aeronautics Act. One program considers the railroads, highways, domestic waterways, and pipelines as fit subjects for unified treatment. The competitive price and service practices of these agencies are to be made responsive to high standards of performance, encompassing nondiscriminatory treatment of public patrons and economic standards of interagency competition. Moreover, the Interstate Commerce

[20] The only point of co-ordination provided between the Civil Aeronautics Board and the Interstate Commerce Commission is with respect to through service and joint rates. Air carriers are permitted to establish these co-operative arrangements with other common carriers. In dealing with such matters, the Civil Aeronautics Board and the Interstate Commerce Commission are directed to designate joint boards composed of a similar number of members from each. (52 Stat. 1020.) There is no record of any such boards having been established.

[21] Appropriations for fiscal year 1949 provide the CAB with funds in the amount of $3,450,000 and 685 positions. The CAA has an appropriation of $100,370,000 and 17,670 positions.

Act embodies the explicit proposition that these agencies should somehow be welded into an integrated and efficiently functioning national transportation system. In sharp contrast, the other line of government action assumes that the movement of goods and people by air carriers produces economic, social, and national security values which are superior to, or at least different from, the values produced by other forms of transportation in the performance of identical services.

### IV. MERCHANT MARINE POLICY

If the term "regulatory policy" is used in the strict sense as excluding promotional objectives, it may be concluded that no basic conflict now exists between the objectives of control applied to ocean shipping and those applicable to domestic transportation. A fundamental reconciliation was accomplished in this matter under the Transportation Act of 1940 which transferred control of coastal and intercoastal shipping from the Maritime Commission to the Interstate Commerce Commission. However, there remain important areas of conflict between the government's efforts to promote ocean shipping and those relating to the development of international aviation.

Since 1936 Congress has sought to promote an adequate merchant marine primarily through the device of ship construction and operating subsidies. At the same time it has been encouraging the development of international aviation by the payment of air-mail subsidies. There is no statutory or administrative co-ordination between these two lines of action—one administered by the Civil Aeronautics Board and the other by the Maritime Commission. Each program involves the selection of so-called "essential routes"; the selection of the concerns that are to provide service over those routes; and the payment of monetary subsidies sufficient to enable the selected operators to meet foreign competition. Manifestly, surface vessels and airlines compete directly for a limited volume of traffic, particularly in the passenger field. Since the government is subsidizing both agencies, failure to co-ordinate the two programs results inevitably in one branch of government competing with another for the expenditure of the taxpayer's dollar. Moreover, when separate agencies are given responsibility for the promotion of individual forms of transportation, there is a natural tendency to resist physical or service co-ordination between the two enterprises. Such an outcome is directly opposed to the co-ordination and integration objectives of the Interstate Commerce Act.

Another area of potential conflict is developing between the objectives of the merchant marine policy and the jurisdiction of the ICC. The Maritime Commission is responsible for maintaining a merchant marine adequate for the national security. Yet the ICC controls the operating rights and rates of coastal and intercoastal shipping. Acute issues of national policy are shaping up around the administrative efforts to discharge both responsibilities.

The Interstate Commerce Commission is obligated to apply uniform standards in the regulation of rate and service competition between water, rail, and other domestic transport agencies. If, as is now thought likely, the amount of coastal and intercoastal tonnage that can be maintained under regulated competition falls appreciably short of the prewar level, national security objectives will be threatened. For, as a practical matter, failure of coastal shipping to regain prewar levels makes the Maritime Commission task difficult, if not impossible. This follows from the fact that in past emergencies the coastal services have supplied a large portion of the total tonnage that was available for military purposes during the early stages of hostilities.

### V. SUMMARY

It will be observed that the three regulatory enactments under consideration embody only two common concepts. Each is explicitly dedicated to the maintenance of transportation plant and facilities adequate to the needs of commerce and national defense. Each is designed to preserve and utilize to the full the energies of private ownership and management rather than to move in the direction of government ownership.

It may be recalled that the issue of government versus private management in the transportation field was fought out bitterly after World War I, and the legislative decision was unequivocally in favor of constructively regulated private ownership of the railroads. In subsequent extension of government control to other transport agencies, government ownership was not a serious issue. And, as Commissioner Aitchison observed, there exists at the moment no articulate interest in substituting government ownership for the current system of comprehensively regulated private enterprise:

Twenty-five years ago, when we were coming out of the period of Federal possession and control in the first world war, it was seriously considered whether that control should not be extended for a further period, five years or so, to let the experiment of Federal operation of the railways be carried on in normal times, as a guide to adoption of a policy for the future with respect to government ownership or operation. No suggestions as to such ownership or operation are receiving attention now. There now seems to be general agreement that the nation should continue its policy of private ownership and operation of transportation facilities and look primarily to the exercise of private initiative, and not to government ownership or management.[22]

Beyond this point of identity in the purposes of government regulation, there exists little organic coherence and no administrative co-ordination among the three main segments of federal regulation.[23]

The existence of conflicts and inconsistencies in national regulatory policy is generally recognized, but their significance is ordinarily minimized. The most important reason for general indifference regarding this problem is found in the failure to trace the divergent lines of federal action through to their logical consequence. If the conflicts between the main bodies

---

[22] "After the War Is Over—Transportation Problems," address by Hon. Clyde B. Aitchison, Apr. 24, 1944, before Chamber of Commerce, Portland, Oregon. *I.C.C. Practitioners' Journal*, Vol. 11, May 1944, pp. 745-46.

[23] It should be kept in mind that we are here dealing primarily with the purpose and structure of transport regulation. As indicated in detail at a later point, there are equally significant conflicts between the purposes of regulation and the results of promotional action.

of declared policy could be viewed as arising only from the temporary application of different methods to achieve common transportation objectives, there would be less occasion for concern. But when the basic objectives are irreconcilable, as seems to be the case here, fundamental revision of policy offers the only prospect for a permanent solution.

The economic impact of legislative policy is, of course, transmitted to the individual concerns that make up our transportation system through continuing application of regulatory provisions. Consequently, as a basis for constructive revision, it is necessary to know how the several regulatory agencies interpret their statutory responsibility and what obstacles have been encountered in the administrative attempt to attain the varying declared objectives of regulation.

The next six chapters deal in turn with the administrative devices and problems encountered in the government's efforts: (1) to regulate the supply of transport services; (2) to prevent discrimination; (3) to set the standards of competition; (4) to regulate the level of railroad earnings; (5) to co-ordinate and integrate transport agencies; and (6) to improve railroad efficiency by consolidation.

# CHAPTER X

## THE RIGHT TO OPERATE TRANSPORT ENTERPRISES

We have already observed that prior to 1920 the federal government exercised no direct control over the establishment or abandonment of transport enterprises. Nor did it prescribe specialized standards of competitive performance for the transportation industry. Construction and abandonment of railroad lines were, of course, controlled by state regulation. And railroad combinations were subject to the restraints of the antitrust laws. Moreover, carrier agreements to pool traffic and divide revenues were specifically prohibited under the 1887 Act to Regulate Commerce. In addition, the Panama Canal Act of 1912 excluded the railroads from the field of water transportation where substantial interagency competition was involved.

During this period the affirmative role of government was asserted primarily through the control over discrimination. (See Chapter XI.) Within these limits, private enterprise was free to establish, expand, or abandon services and to set standards of competition—all in accordance with the ordinary estimates of risk and profitability.

Since 1920, however, the national government has enormously expanded its role in this field and the latitude for private initiative and decision has been correspondingly narrowed. In final analysis, the federal government is attempting to organize the transportation industry in such a way that it can be made to function on a middle course between regulated monopoly and competition.

The plan, as reflected in current regulatory programs, contemplates the allocation of traffic through the device of rate and service competition. There is manifest a desire to utilize as fully as possible the motivating forces of private enterprise. Thus, proposals for the establishment of new transportation enterprises and the formulation of rate schedules are initiated

185

by private management. Responsibility is also placed on private enterprise to introduce technological improvements and to maintain adequate standards of service, as well as to exercise the routine functions of management.[1]

But the government has reserved the right to set the over-all pattern of transport competition. For it determines when and where new transport facilities are needed and the conditions under which the concerns occupying the field may compete for traffic.[2]

The federal government's treatment of this basic aspect of transport organization has been anachronistic, substantively defective, and is now lacking in unity of purpose. There are major conflicts between regulatory standards and objectives applicable to rail, motor, and water agencies as set forth in the Interstate Commerce Act and those prescribed for aviation under the Civil Aeronautics Act.[3]

### I. THE INTERSTATE COMMERCE ACT

No person may conduct a for-hire business in interstate commerce by rail, highway, water facilities, or pipeline without the legal authorization of the Interstate Commerce Commission. By granting or withholding certificates of public necessity and convenience and operating permits, the government attempts to exercise positive control over the supply of transportation and the standards of competition. However, as we shall observe below, the effort has not proved particularly successful. In the first place, except for air transportation, this method of transport control has been applied to the several transport media too late to affect materially the development of their physical structure and operating pattern. And, in each case, the concerns already occupying the field were permitted to continue operation without any affirmative demonstration

---

[1] Hiring and firing, scheduling of service, solicitation of traffic, etc.

[2] Control over rate competition is dealt with in Chap. 12, and supervision over transport co-ordination and integration is discussed in Chap. 14.

[3] There is a similar lack of unity between the purposes of the Civil Aeronautics Act and the Merchant Marine Act with respect to foreign transportation. This problem is dealt with in Chap. 7.

of public need for their service. Moreover, with respect to motor and water transportation, only common and contract carriers are required to obtain certificates and permits, leaving extensive private operations unregulated.

*Railroad construction and abandonment.* Prior to adoption of the Transportation Act of 1920, the federal government exercised no direct control over the construction and abandonment of railway lines. Under that act the Interstate Commerce Commission was empowered to grant or deny any railroad the right to construct new lines, to extend or abandon existing facilities, or to acquire additional right of ways. Full discretion was delegated to the Commission for the administration of these controls. For the only statutory standard provided was that "the present or future public convenience and necessity" should be served by any proposed extension of service or abandonment of facilities.[4] So far as railroad transportation is concerned, this particular phase of public control has been significant primarily with respect to the abandonment of facilities.[5] For by 1920 the period of extensive railroad expansion was over. Since then structural adjustments have come mainly in the form of abandoning obsolete trackage.[6]

*Highway and water transportation.* With passage of the Motor Carrier Act, 1935,[7] Congress undertook for the first time positive direction over the physical expansion and detailed operating pattern of a rapidly expanding transportation busi-

[4] *Interstate Commerce Acts Annotated,* Vol. 9, p. 7296.

[5] "The Interstate Commerce Commission since 1920 has authorized the abandonment of 70 percent more mileage than it has authorized to be constructed." Memorandum on "Consolidation of the Rail Transportation Facilities of the United States into a Single System for Ownership and Operation under Private Management," submitted by ICC Commissioner Miller in 1938 to the Senate Committee on Interstate Commerce, p. 3 (mimeo.).

Although the Commission may, under certain circumstances, order a rail carrier to extend its facilities, the rise of competitive agencies has made the use of such power unnecessary. See: *Interstate Commerce Commission Activities, 1887-1937,* p. 193.

[6] Railroad mileage reached the peak of 254,037 miles in 1916. Since that date continuous abandonments have reduced the total to 226,696 miles of "first track"—miles owned by various carriers. *I.C.C. Statistics of Railways, 1917,* p. 12, and the same, *1945,* p. 4.

[7] 49 Stat. 543, approved Aug. 9, 1935.

ness. Since June 1, 1935 no person may legally establish a new common or contract carrier operation in interstate commerce by highway, or alter an existing operation without express authorization from the Interstate Commerce Commission.

An applicant for a certificate of public necessity and convenience must assume the burden of proving to the Commission that he is "fit, willing, and able properly to perform the service proposed" and to conform to all the provisions of the Motor Carrier Act. He must also satisfy the Commission that "the proposed service, to the extent to be authorized by the certificate, is or will be required by the present or future public convenience and necessity."[8]

An applicant for a permit to conduct contract carrier operations must also demonstrate fitness, willingness, and ability to perform the contract service proposed, and that the operation "to the extent authorized by the permit, will be consistent with the public interest and the national transportation policy declared in this act."[9]

Under the Transportation Act of 1940, the inauguration of new common or contract carrier services by water is controlled by standards that are identical in wording and intent with those prescribed in the Motor Carrier Act of 1935.[10]

It should be noted that the assertion of this plenary authority over the right of individuals to enter the for-hire business of highway and water transportation did not result in any drastic rearrangement of the operating and competitive patterns that had been developed in those industries up to the time that regulation was imposed. In both enactments, the concerns that were in bona fide operation on specified dates were authorized to continue the same service without any further showing as to public need or otherwise.[11]

Moreover, the Commission is specifically precluded from attaching to any certificates or permits, terms or conditions that would restrict the right of the carrier to add equipment,

[8] *Interstate Commerce Acts Annotated,* Vol. 10, p. 7988.
[9] The same, Vol. 11, p. 9467.
[10] The same, p. 9634.
[11] The same, sec. 206 (a), p. 9404; 209 (a), p. 9459; and 309, p. 9627.

facilities, or contracts over the routes authorized "as the development of the business and the demands of the public shall require."[12]

In addition numerous types of carriers and operations are exempted either in whole or in part from the certificate and permit provisions of the act. For example, vehicles used by a farmer for the transportation of his agricultural commodities, products, and supplies are exempted, as are "for-hire" vehicles when used in carrying livestock, fish, or unprocessed agricultural commodities.[13] Important segments of water transportation are also exempted from certificate and permit control. Thus, complete exemption is provided for transportation of liquid cargoes in bulk, and for transportation of commodities in bulk when not more than three such commodities are carried in the cargo space of a single vessel.[14] Such major gaps in legal jurisdiction as represented by these exemptions raise considerable doubt regarding the validity and feasibility of the controls the government has undertaken in this field. In reality certificate and permit regulations are effective only for common and contract carriers which constitute a small portion of the total domestic highway and water transportation system.

Since 1935 the processing of motor carrier applications for operating rights has bulked large in the Commission's work. By the end of 1947 it had disposed of all but about 3,000 of the 155,000 applications filed since the act became effective. Almost 90,000 of this total represented so-called "grandfather clause" applications involving only one determination by the Commission: whether or not the carriers were in "bona fide" operations on a specific date. (See table p. 190.)

---

[12] The same, Vol. 10, sec. 208 (a), p. 8021; sec. 209 (b), p. 8057; and sec. 309 (d), Vol. 11, p. 9633.

[13] Other exemptions include school buses, certain types of taxicab operations, vehicles used in national park service, in newspaper distribution, and incidental to air transportation.

[14] Other types of exemptions include contract carriers not competing with rail and motor carriers, water operators engaged in terminal services, or in contract arrangements with rail, express, motor, or other water carriers and those operating within the limits of a single harbor or between places in contiguous harbors.

STATUS OF APPLICATIONS FOR OPERATING RIGHTS FILED BY MOTOR
CARRIERS WITH THE INTERSTATE COMMERCE COMMISSION
TO OCTOBER 31, 1947[a]

| | Cumulative to Oct. 31, 1947 |
|---|---|
| "Grandfather" applications filed on and prior to Feb. 12, 1936 | 82,770 |
| "Grandfather" applications filed after Feb. 12, 1936 | 6,781 |
| Applications for authority to institute new operations | 29,604 |
| Applications for authority to conduct broker operations | 1,379 |
| Statements under second proviso (sec. 206 (a)) | 5,366 |
| Applications for temporary authority under secs. 210 (a) and 204 (f) | 29,198 |
| Applications for exemption of one-state operations under sec. 204a (4a) | 118 |
| Total applications received | 155,216 |
| Applications approved | 54,801 |
| Applications denied, dismissed, or withdrawn | 97,719 |
| Applications pending | 2,696 |

[a] *61st Annual Report of the Interstate Commerce Commission, 1947*, p. 114.

The extreme complexity of the motor carrier operating
pattern that has been given legal status through this process is
indicated by the fact that the certificates, permits, and licenses
issued by the ICC characteristically contain the following types
of specifications:

(1) The legal characteristics of the service authorized—common or
contract; (2) the routes over which or the territories in which such
operations may be conducted; (3) the points to and from, or to or
from, which a carrier may render the specified type of service along
such routes or in such territories; (4) the commodities or classes of
commodities which a carrier may transport for compensation in
interstate commerce; and (5) in the case of motor carriers the degree
to which physical movement of vehicles is tied to specific highway
routes. The class of shippers or type of industry that a carrier may
serve is sometimes designated, especially in contract-carrier permits
of motor carriers; and provisions stating the size of the shipment
that may be accepted, the season during which transportation may
be conducted, the type of equipment that may be utilized, and the
type of container that may be used for accepted shipments of the
authorized commodities are not uncommon.[15]

[15] Board of Investigation and Research, *Federal Regulatory Restrictions upon
Motor and Water Carriers*, S. Doc. 78, 79 Cong. 1 sess. (1944), p. 5. This re-

In dealing with the more than 30,000 applications to institute permanent new motor carrier operations, the Commission has been forced to formulate standards at least a bit more specific than those provided by statute. Manifestly, little practical guidance is afforded by a standard that directs the Commission to approve the applications for the inauguration of a new service when a proposed common carrier operation is found to be required by the "present or future public convenience and necessity" and when a proposed contract service is found to be "consistent with the public interest." Although the Commission has encountered great difficulty in reducing these vague standards to anything approaching quantitative precision, there is no evidence that its discretion has been used to produce results at variance with those contemplated by the law.

The Commission has recently summarized as follows its policy with respect to the inauguration of new motor-carrier services:

> We have frequently stated that this question, in substance, is whether the new operation or service will provide a useful public service, responsive to a public demand or need; whether this purpose can and will be served as well by existing carriers; and whether it can be served by applicant in a specific operation without endangering or impairing the operations of existing carriers, contrary to the public interest. . . . We have consistently adhered to the view that existing carriers are entitled to handle any available traffic which they can handle economically and efficiently, and that the promotion of sound economic conditions in the motor-carrier industry would be jeopardized by allowing new operators to enter a field in competition with existing carriers who are furnishing adequate and efficient service.[16]

In view of the legislative history of the Motor Carrier Act and the declared purpose of that regulatory statute (see Chapter IX), the Commission would seem to have no alternative but to follow

---

port, prepared by Dr. James C. Nelson, represents the only comprehensive effort that has been made to date to analyze the standards applied by the ICC in passing upon such applications and to evaluate the long-range implications of this regulatory policy.

[16] *The Squaw Transit Co. Common Carrier Application*, 48 M.C.C. 17, 21, decided Mar. 1, 1948.

this general policy. The application of such restrictive standards, of course, tends to protect established carriers against the potential competition of those who would inaugurate new service. For it is difficult for anyone to demonstrate abstractly that a proposed innovation will afford better or cheaper services than those provided by the enterprises already occupying the field. There is therefore inherent in the regulatory process a tendency to resist experimentation and consequently to slow down technological progress. This is particularly true when the burden of proving that existing ways of performing transport service are adequate or outmoded is placed upon the applicant who wishes to inaugurate a new or different kind of transport facility.[17]

For this reason, some observers have questioned the long-range wisdom of applying severe limitations to the operating rights of an essentially small-scale industry, particularly one whose chief competitive advantage lies in flexibility.[18] For example, the relatively small portion of total truck transportation subject to the ICC regulation is divided among more than 20,000 companies classified as follows:

|  | Property Carriers | Passenger Carriers | Total |
|---|---|---|---|
| Common, issued certificates under sec. 206 or 207 | 16,020[19] | 1,386[19] | 17,406[19] |
| Common under second proviso of sec. 206 (a) | 1,840 | 197 | 2,037 |
| Contract, issued permits under sec. 209 | 3,178 | 14 | 3,192 |
| "Grandfather," no final authority issued | 34 | 3 | 37 |
| Late "Grandfather," no final authority issued | 24 | 6 | 30 |
| Total carriers | 21,096 | 1,606 | 22,702 |
| Brokers issued licenses under sec. 211 of this act | 81 | 84 | 165 |

[17] In this connection it is important to remember that the motor transport industry is made up predominantly of small businesses. About 26 per cent of the "trucking companies" authorized by the ICC to operate in interstate commerce have only one truck; and 92 per cent operate fewer than ten trucks; only 7 per cent of the companies have annual gross operating revenues of $100,000 or more, and they operate only an average of 29 vehicles. Statement of Edward M. Welliver, American Trucking Associations, Inc., before a subcommittee of the House Small Business Committee, June 10, 1948, p. 2 mimeo.

[18] ". . . it might well be questioned whether the adjustments in truck service that are always necessary to meet changing shipper needs can be made

As already noted, in 1940 the Commission was given the same statutory authority over operating rights of water carriers as it has exercised over motor carriers since 1935. As with motor carrier operating rights, the bulk of the Commission's water carrier work has involved disposal of the so-called "grandfather clause" applications. (See table below.)

WATER CARRIER APPLICATIONS FILED SINCE PART III OF INTERSTATE COMMERCE ACT BECAME EFFECTIVE UNTIL OCTOBER 31, 1946[a]

Applications filed to October 31, 1946:

| | |
|---|---|
| For authority to continue operations under "grandfather" clause .... | 775 |
| For authority for new operations .............................. | 116 |
| For authority to continue (formerly exempted) operations by small craft | 17 |
| For exemption .............................................. | 419 |
| For authority to extend operations ............................ | 9 |
| For temporary authority ...................................... | 269 |
| Total ................................................... | 1,605 |

[a] *60th Annual Report of Interstate Commerce Commission 1946*, p. 117.

There is some evidence that the Commission has applied less severe tests of the need for additional water carrier services than in the case of motor carriers.[20] Thus 123 certificates to inaugu-

smoothly and quickly when commodities, points, and routes are closely controlled, even allowing for temporary authorities. A related question is whether by protecting established carriers from actual or potential competition by new entrants greater or less ingenuity will be applied in management and in the search for new procedures and devices to improve efficiency. The concern expressed by some opponents of comprehensive regulation of motor carriers was not merely that small truckers would be handicapped, but that the general use of motor vehicles in intercity traffic would not be fully explored." S. Doc. 78, 79 Cong. 1 sess., p. 15.

[19] 273 carriers of property and 26 carriers of passengers also conduct some additional operations under the second proviso of sec. 206 (a). *61st Annual Report of the Interstate Commerce Commission, 1947*, p. 114.

[20] Nelson's study of this subject indicated that ". . . regulated water carriers on domestic waterways have been controlled by the Commission far less restrictively than intercity motor carriers of property. The more liberal point of view evidenced by Division 4 and the entire Commission as to water carriers does not appear to be a result of specific legislative direction. The 'grandfather' and other entry provisions applying to water carriers are similar, if not identical, to those applicable to motor carriers. Moreover, since the general purposes for public control are quite similar in both cases, it seems clear either that the two industries have been considered as presenting radically different regulatory problems or that the Commission has recognized that it has gone too far in suppressing competition in the motor field." S. Doc. 78, 79 Cong. 1 sess. p. 266.

rate new operations have been approved as against 57 denied; and 249 orders granting temporary operating authority were issued as against 70 orders denying such authority. (See

DISPOSITION BY THE ICC OF APPLICATIONS FILED
BY WATER CARRIERS FOR OPERATING RIGHTS[a]

|  | Cumulative Total Nov. 1, 1941- Oct. 31, 1948 |
|---|---|
| **Certificates issued:** | |
| Authorizing continuance under "grandfather" clause | 417 |
| Authorizing new operations | 123 |
| Authorizing small craft operations | 3 |
| Exemption granted | 3 |
| **Permits issued:** | |
| Authorizing continuance under "grandfather" clause | 88 |
| Authorizing new operations | 21 |
| **Orders issued:** | |
| Granting temporary authority | 249 |
| Extending temporary authority | 130 |
| Granting exemption | 23 |
| **Substitution applications:** | |
| Approved | 51 |
| **Applications dismissed or denied:** | |
| For exemption | 135 |
| For authority to continue operation under "grandfather" clause | 420 |
| For authority for new operations | 57 |
| For authority for small-craft operation | 8 |
| For temporary authority | 70 |
| For authority to extend operation | 18 |
| Total | 1,816 |
| Applications pending | 27 |

[a] Annual Reports of the Interstate Commerce Commission for 1948, p. 131; 1947, p. 145; 1946, p. 118; 1945, p. 116; 1944, p. 102; 1943, p. 130; 1942, p. 139.

table above.) However, it is evident that the Commission is applying the same general principles and is seeking the same transportation objective in the administration of both sets of controls. The primary purpose is to prevent an oversupply of transportation services in any given area, and consequent undermining of the carriers' financial stability. Thus in a most recent case, the Commission denied the application of a water common carrier for extension of its service to include the transportation of commodities generally between designated Pacific Coast and Gulf ports. The application was denied because the Commission found that "the traffic available at present or in the foreseeable future is not sufficient fully to utilize the vessel space" of the carriers already serving the Gulf intercoastal trade.[21] The Commission also observed that "an additional competitive service under the conditions shown by this record might so diffuse the available traffic as to result in uneconomical operation detrimental to all concerned."[22]

There has been considerable controversy over the need for liberalizing the statutory standards governing operating rights.[23] The important question, however, is whether the control program as presently constituted and administered actually works effectively "to eliminate destructive competition not only within each form but also between or among the different forms of carriage."[24]

The purpose is to prevent the establishment of more transport enterprises than can be supported by available or anticipated traffic and to guarantee that service once instituted will not be arbitrarily withdrawn from the communities and industries that have become dependent upon it. And the ultimate objective is to facilitate the economic allocation of available traffic by the maintenance of fair competition among those concerns authorized to operate.

[21] *Arrow Line Extension—Gulf Ports*, ICC No. W-384 (Sub-No. 1), decided June 11, 1948, Sheet 12 (mimeo.)

[22] The same.

[23] One study of this problem concludes: "The general conclusion of this study is that both the war effort and normal transportation needs would be furthered by a substantial liberalization in the operating authority of interstate motor carriers of property. Since it is not practicable, either in terms of the time or effort required, to attempt to achieve the desirable relaxation of certificate and permit restrictions by the case-by-case procedure under present statutory provisions and this procedure would involve endless wrangling, specific legislation would be appropriate to clarify the situation and to direct the Commission to take the necessary steps toward this objective." S. Doc. 78, 79 Cong. 1 sess., p. 301.

[24] *Eastern-Central Motor Carriers Association v. U. S.*, 321 U.S. 194, decided Feb. 7, 1944.

But as we have seen, large segments of motor and water transportation are subject only to limited controls affecting safety. And the lack of jurisdiction over scheduling of service by the regulated carriers vitiates certificate and permit supervision as a device for preventing an oversupply of service on authorized routes. An even greater deficiency originates in the divorcement of certificate control from the planning and provision of physical facilities. Various executive agencies of the federal government decide when and where additional airports, highways, and waterways are needed to meet transportation requirements. Other agencies, principally independent regulatory commissions, decide whether or not the public "necessity and convenience" will be served by permitting particular classes of carriers to provide transportation service over these physical facilities. As we have seen in Part I of this study, the agencies which provide the facilities have no direct legislative or administrative contact with the commissions which authorize or deny their use.

The federal government's attempt to control the supply of transport services as one means of making competition work effectively is also complicated by major conflicts at the regulatory level. In its specialized treatment of air transportation, the government has departed sharply from the economic and legal standards of transport performance imposed on other media under the Interstate Commerce Act.

## II. CIVIL AERONAUTICS ACT OF 1938

With the adoption of the aeronautics act, the federal government assumed authority and responsibility for evolving a satisfactory route and competitive pattern for air transportation. No person may enter the business of air transportation, extend a service, or abandon a service without authorization of the Civil Aeronautics Board.[25]

[25] However, under the terms of the 1938 act, operating authorizations were issued as a matter of right for routes served by an air carrier continuously from May 14 to Aug. 22, 1938. The only exception was when the Board found such service to be inadequate or inefficient. Sec. 401 (e) (1), Civil Aeronautics Act, 1938, 52 Stat. 988.

Before authorizing a new or additional air route or service, the Board must find that such service is required by the "public convenience and necessity."[26] Operating authorizations for service between the United States and foreign countries, whether issued to foreign flag carriers in the form of "permits," or to American flag carriers in the form of "certificates," become effective only after approval by the president of the United States, as well as the Civil Aeronautics Board. The State Department conducts negotiations with foreign governments to obtain the intergovernmental agreements necessary to carry on the business operations authorized in the certificates and permits.[27]

*Declaration of policy and CAB interpretation.* The Declaration of Policy attached to the Civil Aeronautics Act adds very little precision to the intangible standard of "public convenience and necessity" which is supposed to guide the Board in its development of air transportation. According to the Board: "This declaration of policy makes the present and future needs of the commerce of the United States, the Postal service, and the national defense the primary criteria by which we determine whether a particular proposal meets public convenience and necessity."[28] Presumably of lesser importance is the congressional declaration in favor of maintaining competition "to the extent necessary to assure the sound development of an air transportation system adequate to our national needs."[29]

Such declarations and standards are, of course, meaningless until given more specific administrative interpretation and application. As a first step in this difficult process, the Board stated its "position" with respect to the authorization of new or additional services as follows:

Obviously in the light of these standards, [Declaration of Policy, sections 2 and 401 of the 1938 act] it was not the Congressional

[26] Sec. 401 (d) (1), 52 Stat. 987.
[27] "Agreements have been concluded with most of the countries to which United States-flag lines are certificated. Both the Chicago agreement and the various bilateral agreements negotiated provide for exchange of commercial operating rights on a reciprocal basis." *Statement of Civil Aeronautics Board before the President's Air Policy Commission,* Oct. 27, 1947, p. 16 (mimeo.).
[28] The same.
[29] The same.

intent that the air transportation system of the country should be "frozen" to its present pattern. On the other hand, it is equally apparent that Congress intended the Authority to exercise a firm control over the expansion of air transportation routes in order to prevent the scramble for routes which might occur under a "laissez faire" policy. Congress, in defining the problem, clearly intended to avoid the duplication of transportation facilities and services, the wasteful competitive practices, such as the opening of nonproductive routes, and other uneconomic results which characterized the development of other modes of transportation prior to the time of their governmental regulation.[30]

This statement was made in connection with the "first new route case" decided by the Board. In a series of subsequent leading cases, the CAB developed the following somewhat more tangible criteria to govern its determination on new route applications:

. . . (1) whether the new service will serve a useful public purpose, responsive to a public need; (2) whether this purpose can and will be served as well by existing lines or carriers; (3) whether it can be served by the applicant without impairing the operations of existing carriers contrary to the public interest; and (4) whether the cost of the proposed service to the government will be outweighed by the benefit which will accrue to the public from the new service.[31]

It will be observed that there is a striking similarity between the objectives of national transportation policy as expressed in the Interstate Commerce Act and those set forth in the Civil Aeronautics Act. Moreover, both responsible regulatory agencies have adopted similar standards to govern their administrative application of the substantive provisions of the respective acts. But despite these surface similarities, there are underlying and irreconcilable differences between the long-run objectives and the administrative methods of these government programs.

*Comparison of objectives.* The Interstate Commerce Commission, as noted above, must administer its control over operating rights in the light of general transportation requirements. Thus, it must recognize and preserve the "inherent advantages" of each form of transportation subject to its jurisdic-

[30] *Duluth-Twin Cities Operation,* 1 C.A.A. 573, 577 (1940).
[31] *Red Bluff Operation,* 1 C.A.A. 778 (1940); and the *St. Louis-Nashville-Muscle Shoals Operation,* 1 C.A.A. 792 (1940).

tion; it must promote safe, adequate, economical, and efficient service and foster sound financial conditions for the regulated carriers; and it must encourage the establishment and maintenance of reasonable charges for transportation services without unjust discrimination or unfair or destructive competitive practices. The ultimate purpose is to develop, co-ordinate, and preserve *a national transportation system* by water, highway, and rail, as well as other means "adequate to meet the needs of the commerce of the United States, of the Postal Service, and of the national defense."

In contrast to this situation, the Civil Aeronautics Board is given a single and unqualified responsibility: to promote the development of air transportation. Moreover, the Board is equipped with a powerful set of tools for this purpose. Not only does it have full authority to mold the corporate and operating pattern of the industry, but solvency of the enterprise may be underwritten by financial subsidies in the form of air-mail payments.

Under these circumstances, it would appear that the Board has had an unprecedented opportunity and facilities to assure orderly and sound development of air transportation. The CAB recognized from the outset that Congress intended it to "exercise a firm control over the expansion of air transportation routes" in order to avoid duplication of facilities, wasteful competition, and "other uneconomic results which characterized the development of other modes of transportation prior to the time of their governmental regulation."[32] It is therefore surprising to find that air transportation now exhibits most of the operating characteristics that were frozen into the structure of "other modes of transportation prior to their time of governmental regulation."[33] Among the most significant of these characteristics are: (1) overexpansion of routes and unsound pricing policies; and (2) extension of operations into areas of

[32] *Duluth-Twin Cities Operation*, 1 C.A.A. 573, 577 (1940).
[33] As pointed out in Chap. 13, the ICC has been attempting unsuccessfully since 1920 to rearrange the corporate and operating structure of the railroads into a balanced and unified system. The task has been vastly complicated by the fact that long before 1920 gross imperfections had become frozen into the physical structure by generations of competitive and speculative railroad building.

least relative advantage. Although found throughout the air transport industry, these defects have widely varying significance with respect to trunk-line as compared with feeder-line operations.

### III. OVEREXPANSION OF TRUNK-LINE AIR ROUTES

Historically, the period of rapid expansion in the life cycle of transportation agencies has always been characterized by a "scramble for routes" leading to excess and duplicating facilities, and to general instability of rates and service. One of the major objectives of the Civil Aeronautics Act was to prevent such a development in air transportation.[34] However, it seems apparent that the Board has not achieved impressive results in this undertaking.

In the first place, the air transportation industry which was supposed to be restrained by the government from inaugurating unneccessary and duplicating services complains of excessive competition:

We believe in competition, especially under the policy outlined in the Civil Aeronautics Act of 1938, which is designed to develop the scheduled airline industry by promotion of clean and constructive competition. It is the general consensus of opinion, however, that there is in some cases too much duplication in routes, lines and services. In the past six months the fact has been shown that there is more air competition between certain important centers than there is rail competition.[35]

[34] One commentator has aptly characterized the point as follows: "To summarize is to risk inaccuracy. But it is reasonably fair to say that the Congressional decision of 1938 amounted to a determination that a new agency of five men, vested with sweeping authority, should see to it that an infant transport industry, of more than passing importance to our military power, should be spared the evils of overbuilding, wasteful competitive warfare, bankruptcies, rate discrimination, and business piracy which, in surface transportation, had concerned Congress for many years before it took remedial action. If any of these evils were to appear in the air as they had on earth it would be due to the faulty judgment of five men, not of Congress. That is just about the substance of the Civil Aeronautics Act." Howard C. Westwood, "Choice of the Air Carrier for New Air Transport Routes," *The George Washington Law Review*, Vol. 16, December 1947, p. 2.

[35] Address of Vice Admiral E. S. Land, President, Air Transport Association of America, before Society of Automotive Engineers, summer meeting at French Lick, Indiana, June 10, 1948, p. 5 (mimeo.).

With respect to this issue, the President's Air Policy Commission recently observed that: "The present air transportation system has not developed as expected before and during the war," and that "there is . . . widespread confusion as to the principles which guide the Civil Aeronautics Board in its route determinations."[36] Pending clarification of these principles, the Commission recommended that the Civil Aeronautics Board "defer for a short time decisions in new route certification cases."[37]

The Civil Aeronautics Board maintains, however, that its authorization of new routes has been specifically designed to guard against excessive competition. Although recognizing that competition may contribute to improved service and technological development, the Board states that:

. . . it has never followed a doctrine of direct duplication of existing services or what some of the carriers like to call "competition for competition's sake." Except in the unusual instances where it has been necessary to make extensions of existing lines to common traffic gateways for the establishment of through long-haul connections or the improvement of weak route structures of small carriers by their extension to strong traffic terminals, the Board has avoided direct point-to-point competition even on strong routes. Rather, the Board's general policy has been one of terminal-to-terminal competition. It has provided alternative routes between two major points by competing carriers where sufficient traffic is available to support both carriers on an economical basis.[38]

In the practical application of these standards, however, the Board claims that it has been hampered by what is termed a "conflict between the original route pattern and technological aviation progress."[39] This conflict is said to stem from the inheritance in 1938 of an "illogical route pattern."[40]

[36] *Survival in the Air Age,* A Report by the President's Air Policy Commission (1948), p. 110.
[37] The same.
[38] *Statement of Civil Aeronautics Board before the President's Air Policy Commission,* p. 18.
[39] The same, p. 13.
[40] It will be recalled that the CAB was required to authorize the continued operation of any carrier that was providing bona fide service as of the effective date of the 1938 act.

*The illogical route pattern.* The pattern was made up of three size groups defined as follows: (1) the relatively large, inter-regional, or transcontinental carriers, commonly known as the "Big Four";[41] (2) intermediate-size regional carriers;[42] and (3) relatively small regional carriers.

During the thirties, according to the Board, this structural organization of the industry was reasonably well-adapted to current technology. For the flying equipment of that period (dominated by the DC-3) was in general "better suited for regional than long-haul operations, although by the end of the 1930's, currently obtainable flying equipment had become over-large for efficient operation on some of the small regional routes."[43]

Recently, particularly since 1945, the range and carrying capacity of aircraft have increased sharply. Such equipment could not be utilized efficiently on strictly regional routes dominated by short-hauls and requiring relatively high frequency of schedules in order to attract traffic.

Because of these developments, the Board was presumably faced with three choices: (1) permit or force absorption of the regional carriers by the Big Four carriers that already had routes adapted to modern technology; (2) retain the obsolete regional route pattern and compensate for the resulting uneconomic operation by increased mail subsidy; or (3) permit the regional carriers to extend and adjust their operating routes so as to take advantage of modern flying equipment.

Obviously the Board has attempted to resolve the conflict between the inherited route pattern and the demands of technological progress by authorizing the obsolescent regional carriers to extend their range of operation. This is clearly indicated by the fact that the certified air routes for the so-called "trunk-line" carriers have increased from 39,267 miles in 1938 to 115,484 miles in 1948. (See table p. 203.)

[41] American Airlines, Eastern Air Lines, Transcontinental and Western, and United Air Lines.

[42] Represented by Northwest, Braniff, Pennsylvania-Central, Chicago & Southern, and Western.

[43] *Statement of Civil Aeronautics Board before the President's Air Policy Commission,* p. 13.

Of major significance is the fact that over 63 per cent of the total ten-year increase in route miles has occurred since the end of 1945. It was during this period that the CAB faced the problem of adjusting the route pattern to the striking technological changes that had been hastened by wartime aviation experi-

CHANGES IN CERTIFICATED AIR ROUTE MILES,
DOMESTIC AND INTERNATIONAL 1938-48[a]

| | Domestic | | | | | | International and Overseas | |
| | Trunk Lines[b] | | Feeder Lines[c] | | Total | | | |
| Year | Increase | Total | Increase | Total | Increase | Total | Increase or Decrease | Total |
|---|---|---|---|---|---|---|---|---|
| 1938 .. | | 39,267 | | | | 39,267 | | 31,067 |
| 1939 .. | | 39,782 | | | 515 | 39,782 | 9,061 | 40,128 |
| 1940 .. | | 44,643 | | | 4,861 | 44,643 | 18,651 | 58,779 |
| 1941 .. | | 46,453 | | | 1,810 | 46,453 | 14,931 | 73,710 |
| 1942 .. | | 49,297 | | | 2,844 | 49,297 | 23,657 | 97,369 |
| 1943 .. | | 54,502 | | | 5,205 | 54,502 | —6,517 | 90,852 |
| 1944 .. | | 62,937 | | | 8,435 | 62,937 | —5,886 | 84,966 |
| 1945 .. | | 67,149 | | | 4,212 | 67,149 | 22,612 | 107,578 |
| 1946 ... | | 79,485 | | 12,043 | 24,379 | 91,528 | 67,910 | 175,488 |
| 1947 ..32,301 | | 111,786 | 3,955 | 15,998 | 36,220 | 127,748 | —4,576 | 170,912 |
| 1948 .. 3,698 | | 115,484 | 7,090 | 23,088 | 10,824 | 138,572 | 7,381 | 178,293 |

[a] Official mileage records of Tariffs and Service Division, Civil Aeronautics Board.
[b] Includes helicopter, pick-up, and air commuting routes.
[c] First feeder routes established in March 1946.

ence. In view of the standards adopted by the Board (noted above), it must be assumed that these extensions and adjustments were granted in order to promote the sound development of air transportation and on the specific finding that the authorized services could be supported "on an economical basis" by existing or expected traffic.

*The financial consequences of overexpansion.* That the assumptions and projections noted above proved distressingly erroneous is indicated by the fact that the *net profit* of the domestic trunk-line air carriers dropped from approximately 17 million dollars in 1945 to a deficit of some 5 millions in 1948.

(See App. A, Table 12.) Stated another way, the operating profit[44] dropped from approximately 34 millions in 1945 to 2 millions in 1948. This striking deterioration in financial position indicates that fundamental errors in business judgment were made. (1) The size of the total market, or the airline portion of that market was grossly overestimated; (2) costs were seriously underestimated; or (3) service was improperly priced.

Although total traffic increased at an impressive rate, it is clear that management overestimated demand. Thus, revenue passenger-miles (now the predominant source of carrier income) rose from about 3.3 billions in 1945 to 5.8 billions in 1948, an increase of 80 per cent. But capacity, measured by available seat-miles, was increased 164 per cent during the same period. (See chart p. 205.)

Meanwhile, capital outlays for equipment and operating costs were increasing at a much faster rate than anticipated. As an industry spokesman has pointed out:

These [postwar] planes were at the planning stage in 1944. One type was then estimated to cost five and one-half times the cost of a new prewar DC-3. When the first of these planes was delivered in 1946, instead of a cost estimated in 1944 at $550,000, there was a price tag reading $800,000. In other words, the new plane would carry less than three times the number of passengers as the DC-3, but the price of the new plane was eight times the 1940 purchase price of a DC-3.[45]

In addition, direct flying costs and all other operating costs were increasing at unanticipated rates. Operating expense per plane-mile rose from 87 cents in 1945 to $1.20 in 1947, an increase of 37.9 per cent. Between the same dates, operating revenue per revenue plane-mile increased only 8.7 per cent—from $1.04 to $1.13. (See App. A, Table 12.)

In the face of these unfavorable cost and utilization trends, the airlines lowered their fares from an average of 5.35 cents per passenger-mile in 1944 to 5.06 cents in 1947, a reduction of approximately 5 per cent. This reduction was not compelled by

[44] Eliminates the effect of federal taxes.
[45] Address of Vice Admiral E. S. Land, p. 2.

competitive price cuts. For during the same period railroad, parlor, and sleeping car fares were raised from 2.43 cents to 2.74 cents per passenger-mile. (See table p. 206.) Nor were the airlines under any pressure to reduce fares because of potential

SELECTED MILEAGE AND FINANCIAL DATA FOR
DOMESTIC AIR CARRIERS, 1938-48[a]

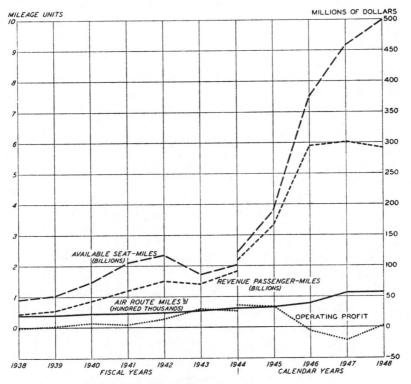

[a] See App. A, Table 12 for supporting data.
[b] Air route miles data are for calendar years throughout.

diversion of traffic to the railroads. From a wartime peak of over 90 billion passenger-miles in 1944, railroad pullman and intercity coach traffic had dropped more than 50 per cent by 1947. Sleeping and parlor car travel, the type most highly competitive with air service, decreased approximately the same per cent. (See table p. 207.) This loss of traffic was occurring at ap-

REVENUE PER PASSENGER MILE 1940-48[a]

(In cents per mile)

| Year | Domestic Airlines | Coach (other than commuta- tion)[b] | Parlor and Sleeping Cars[b] |
|---|---|---|---|
| 1940 .............. | 5.07 | 1.67 | 2.30 |
| 1941 .............. | 5.04 | 1.64 | 2.28 |
| 1942 .............. | 5.28 | 1.77 | 2.40 |
| 1943 .............. | 5.27 | 1.74 | 2.39 |
| 1944 .............. | 5.35 | 1.70 | 2.43 |
| 1945 .............. | 4.95 | 1.71 | 2.39 |
| 1946 .............. | 4.63 | 1.82 | 2.45 |
| 1947 .............. | 5.06 | 2.02 | 2.74 |
| 1948 .............. | 5.75 | 2.29 | 3.01 |
| *Percentage Change* | | | |
| *1944-47* ............*−5.4* | | +18.8 | +12.8 |
| *1944-48* ............*+6.9* | | +34.7 | +23.9 |

[a] Data for airlines from CAA, *Statistical Handbook of Civil Aviation, 1948*, p. 68. Coach and parlor and sleeping cars: 1940-47, ICC *Statistics of Railways in the United States*, Table 52; 1948, ICC Statement M-250, December 1948.

[b] Changes in these averages result not only from changes in the basic fare and in the proportions of pullman and coach traffic, excursion traffic, and half-fare traffic, but also from the loss of more short-distance than long-distance traffic where the latter pays lower rates per mile than the former.

proximately the same time that airline passenger volume was expanding by 80 per cent.

The net result of these combined miscalculations regarding market and pricing[46] was an operating deficit of some 20 million dollars, for domestic trunk-line carriers in 1947. The 1948 financial situation showed some improvement. Although revenue passenger-miles declined about 3 per cent in the first quarter of 1948 by comparison with the same period of 1947, passenger revenues increased 15 per cent as a result of an upward adjustment of fares. This improvement, together with increased revenue from other sources, particularly air freight, resulted in a

[46] A recent comment of an airline official is significant on this point: "One reason why the airlines lose money is that they have mistakenly and consistently tried to offer premium merchandise at bargain basement prices. It is axiomatic that no concern can sell below cost for long and stay in business." Statement of Warren Lee Pierson, Chairman of the Board of Trans World Airline, Aug. 12, 1948.

REVENUE PASSENGER MILES, CLASS I RAILROADS 1940-48[a]

(In millions of miles)

| Year | Coach (Excluding commutation) | Sleeping and Parlor Car | Total |
|---|---|---|---|
| 1940 | 12,485 | 7,288 | 19,773 |
| 1941 | 16,106 | 9,166 | 25,272 |
| 1942 | 30,910 | 17,853 | 48,763 |
| 1943 | 57,907 | 24,675 | 82,582 |
| 1944 | 63,288 | 26,944 | 90,232 |
| 1945 | 59,415 | 26,912 | 86,327 |
| 1946 | 39,039 | 19,801 | 58,840 |
| 1947 | 27,660 | 12,261 | 39,921 |
| 1948 | 24,315 | 11,015 | 35,330 |
| *Percentage Change* | | | |
| *1944-46* | –38.3 | –26.5 | –34.8 |
| *1944-47* | –56.3 | –54.5 | –55.8 |
| *1944-48* | –61.6 | –59.1 | –60.8 |

[a] 1940-47 data from ICC *Statistics of Railways in the United States*, Table 52; 1948 data from ICC Statement M-250, December 1948.

net loss of 5 million dollars in 1948, compared to a loss of over 20 millions in 1947.

The fact remains, however, that the financial condition of the domestic certificated air carriers is far from satisfactory. For a deteriorated financial situation is, with a few outstanding exceptions, characteristic of the entire industry. In 1947, for example, only four of the 16 domestic trunk-line carriers produced enough operating revenue to cover operating expense. And only one of these four carriers fell into the classification of the "Big Five." This spotty financial situation continued into 1948 for again only one carrier of the "Big Five" reported an operating profit, and ten of the 16 domestic trunk-line carriers had an operating ratio of over 100 per cent. (See table p. 208.)

*Evaluation of program.* As a preface to evaluating this phase of the government's aviation program, it must be borne in mind that the operating records and results under consideration here refer to an industry that enjoys substantial public aid, both of a direct and indirect nature. Thus the "operating expense" re-

OPERATING REVENUES AND NET PROFIT AND OPERATING RATIOS FOR
DOMESTIC AIR CARRIERS, 1948[a]

(Dollar figures are in thousands)

| Airline | Total Operating Revenue | Net Profit or Loss | Ratio of Operating Revenues to Operating Expenses (Per cent) |
|---|---|---|---|
| Trunk Lines: | | | |
| American | 85,744 | 2,597 def. | 98.04 |
| Braniff | 13,509 | 420 | 105.16 |
| Chicago & Southern | 8,432 | 446 | 108.14 |
| Colonial | 3,582 | 46 def. | 100.74 |
| Continental | 4,879 | 184 | 106.11 |
| Delta | 14,365 | 858 | 109.04 |
| Eastern | 65,586 | 2,406 | 108.90 |
| Inland | 2,271 | 116 | 108.64 |
| Mid-Continent | 6,920 | 104 | 103.00 |
| National | 7,376 | 1,718 def. | 82.48 |
| Northeast | 4,644 | 531 def. | 90.91 |
| Northwest | 23,250 | 2,066 def. | 89.80 |
| Capital | 23,325 | 124 | 103.71 |
| T.W.A. | 61,868 | 1,135 def. | 101.10 |
| United | 73,400 | 1,588 def. | 98.11 |
| Western | 8,201 | 24 | 99.34 |
| Feeder Lines: | | | |
| All American | 984 | 149 def. | 91.87 |
| Challenger | 1,150 | 168 def. | 91.80 |
| Florida | 759 | 18 def. | 109.84 |
| Los Angeles | 372 | 4 def. | 107.43 |
| Monarch | 1,435 | 129 def. | 97.32 |
| Pioneer | 2,985 | 120 | 109.15 |
| Southwest | 2,364 | 28 def. | 103.74 |
| Trans-Texas | 1,551 | 6 def. | 107.62 |
| West Coast | 1,023 | 326 def. | 79.08 |
| Piedmont[b] | 1,467 | 70 def. | 100.17 |
| Wisconsin Central[c] | 705 | 37 def. | 95.31 |
| Robinson Airlines[d] | 195 | 106 def. | 75.04 |
| Empire | 1,303 | 283 | 148.77 |
| Territorial | | | |
| Caribbean Atlantic | 606 | 3 def. | 100.44 |
| Hawaiian | 4,044 | 105 | 105.60 |
| Total | 428,295 | 5,535 def. | |

[a] CAB *Recurrent Report of Financial Data,* 4th quarter, 1948.
[b] Inaugurated Feb. 20, 1948.
[c] Inaugurated Feb. 24, 1948.
[d] Inaugurated Sept. 19, 1948.

ported by the carriers reflects only a portion of the total actual cost incurred in providing the service. An accurate economic accounting would include an appropriate allocation of the public expenditures made for airways and airports, as well as air-mail payments that exceed payment for service rendered. Only in this way would it be possible to make a definitive evaluation of the total cost, and, therefore, of the wisdom of the public policy being pursued with respect to this industry. However, the operating results produced to date raise specific questions with respect to the validity and feasibility of the entire program. One important question is whether or not it is theoretically feasible or administratively possible for the government to develop and maintain sound economic conditions in an industry through a continuing program of direct financial subsidies.[47]

On the basis of the preceding analysis we must conclude that administration of the Civil Aeronautics Act by the CAB has produced only one affirmative result. It has underwritten and accelerated expansion of the industry's route coverage and operating capacity. But it must be emphasized that the primary purpose of the act was to guide this development into a balanced and orderly operating pattern and to maintain sound economic conditions in the industry, presumably with a view to minimizing the amount of public subsidy required for its support.

The plenary powers given to the Board over the right to establish or alter air transport services were specifically designed to avoid the monumental mistakes of past transportation policy. We describe elsewhere (Chapter XV) the stubborn nature of the railroad consolidation problem inherited in 1920 because of the government's failure to control the pattern of railroad expansion during the preceding thirty years. The initial objective of the Civil Aeronautics Act was to prevent a similar development in the field of air transportation.

By reference to that test, the results achieved so far under the

[47] The corollary and equally important issue relates to the impact of such a policy, whether it fails or succeeds, on other segments of the transportation system and on other phases of regulatory action. This issue is discussed at the end of the present chapter.

Civil Aeronautics Act must be rated as unsatisfactory. For the Civil Aeronautics Board has not succeeded in preventing the development of excessive air transport capacity, nor has it evolved a balanced corporate and operating structure for the industry. Several reasons of doubtful validity have been advanced for this failure. The President's Air Policy Commission, for example, concluded that the observed confusion and uneconomic route pattern had resulted from the fact that, "a body which is under the constant pressure of daily decisions of case after case cannot accomplish the careful planning which the development of a national route pattern demands."[48]

This explanation, if valid, suggests that the government has undertaken an impossible task. For the Civil Aeronautics Board was given a single and unqualified statutory responsibility: to promote the orderly and sound development of air transportation. To date the Board has focused its energies on the control of air route patterns. It has not been burdened with problems of rate discrimination, bankruptcy, and financial reorganization; the co-ordination of unlike carriers; and minimum rate control. These are the types of problems that introduce extreme complexities into the regulatory process. In any event, as we have noted above, the Civil Aeronautics Board does not concede that its performance has been marred by any lack of long-range planning or policy standards. On the contrary, it contends that new route authorizations have been carefully designed to prevent wasteful competition.

Somewhat more persuasive is the implication that the Board's task was made futile at the outset by inheritance of an illogical route pattern. But this does not bear up under close scrutiny. Although the predominantly regional character of the original pattern was made functionally obsolete by rapid technological advances in flying equipment, the Board made generous use of its authority to add and adjust new routes as a means of correcting for this factor. Thus, in a ten-year period, it added almost 100,000 air route miles to the 39,000 "frozen" into the pattern under the grandfather clause of the 1938 act—an

[48] *Survival in the Air Age,* p. 110.

increase of over 250 per cent. Since it had full authority to give or withhold operating rights, it must be assumed that the Board took such action to correct the deficiencies of the original pattern and to expand the industry on an orderly and sound basis.[49]

We must therefore conclude that neither the pressure of work nor the inherited route pattern offers a satisfactory explanation of the difficulties encountered by the CAB in its effort to adjust the supply of air-transport services to effective traffic demands. On the contrary, the task has been complicated from the outset by a defective control system and by the corroding effects of subsidies.

Defective control system. The Board in reality has no control over the amount of air transportation service that can be offered to the public at any given time. The law states that:

No term, condition, or limitation of a certificate shall restrict the right of an air carrier to add to or change schedules, equipment, accommodations, and facilities for performing the authorized transportation and service as the development of the business and the demands of the public shall require.[50]

Under these circumstances, a route and competitive pattern properly adjusted to the present and expected volume of traffic can be thrown out of balance in short order by the multiplication of schedules or by stepping up the individual carrying capacity of the plane. This is precisely what has occurred since the end of the war. Ordinarily the development of excess capacity would lead to rate-cutting which would in turn bring to bear the minimum rate power of the regulatory agency.[51] But, when an agency, as in the case of the CAB, is under statutory mandate to promote the development of a transport medium by the use of direct financial aid, there is a natural reluctance to take any restrictive action that would lead to over-all retrenchment in

[49] "New trunk-line routes authorized since 1938 have been largely improvement in or additions to this basic statutory grandfather route pattern." *Statement of the Civil Aeronautics Board before the President's Air Policy Commission*, p. 15.

[50] Sec. 401 (f), Civil Aeronautics Act of 1938, 52 Stat. 989.

[51] As noted below, this control device is used extensively by the Interstate Commerce Commission in controlling the competitive standards of rail, highway, and water agencies.

the industry. It is simpler and perhaps more in accord with the intent of the act to support the excess capacity by the use of subsidy payments. The process tends to become circular and eventually self-defeating unless restricted by the application of rigid standards of what constitutes "honest, economical and efficient management."

Corroding effects of subsidies. The fatal defect in the promotional program for air transportation stems from the inherent difficulty of determining what constitutes honest, economical, and efficient management in a subsidized industry. By definition, the adoption of a subsidy policy discards the inexorable and historic test of managerial efficiency—the ability to survive in a competitive market. This places on the regulatory agency a heavy responsibility for developing substitute and measurable standards. At this point a redundant process is set in motion. As with any other economic activity, the ultimate efficiency of transportation enterprises is measured by three factors: (1) correct evaluation of the need for a particular service at the time and place chosen for its establishment; (2) accurate measurement of effective demand for the service as the basis for deciding when and at what rate to expand or retrench; and (3) correct pricing, as measured by cost, quality of service, and elasticity of consumer demand.

In the type of program administered by the CAB, however, initial authority and final responsibility for these basic determinations are hopelessly divided between government and private enterprise.[52] Government decides who shall inaugurate a new transport enterprise, the areas to be served, and when and where the service may be extended. As a basis for authorizing or denying operating rights, it must necessarily make its own estimates of the aggregate present and future demand for transportation service and decide what portion of that demand will express an effective preference for air transportation as compared with alternative forms. Government also has final author-

[52] We use the term in this connection advisedly. As indicated later, all regulation of private enterprise involves a large, but not necessarily fatal, degree of divided responsibility.

ity over pricing policies. However, if private enterprise is to be given more than academic status in this undertaking, significant areas of managerial discretion must be left to the private operators. At the minimum, they must be given initial responsibility for estimating the size of the transportation market and considerable freedom to determine general pricing policy. And it is especially important that they be assigned primary responsibility for technological progress in the industry.

Under such an arrangement the regulatory agency must determine whether or not these responsibilities are being exercised in accordance with the legal standards of "honest, economical, and efficient management." This task has perplexed the regulators ever since the concept was expressly incorporated in the Transportation Act, 1920. The Interstate Commerce Commission, for example, has been forced into a rather untenable position in dealing with the matter.[53] As to principle, the Commission has repeatedly observed that "we are not managers of the railroads."[54] It has also stated that "to go into the question of efficiency of management in a thoroughly effective way would necessitate an organization of experts especially qualified to investigate the numerous and complex phases of railroad management" and would "in some degree duplicate the work of the technical staff of the railroads."[55] Nevertheless, as Commissioner Eastman candidly admitted, the Commission was constantly faced with the task of deciding whether or not specific proposed lines of action did in fact constitute the exercise of "sound business judgment."[56]

The Civil Aeronautics Board faces an even more difficult problem. It may and should be held directly accountable to the taxpayer for stewardship of the public funds used in the promotion of air transportation. Thus, if it places chief reliance on managerial judgment to determine the rate at which air transportation shall expand, the type of equipment to be used,

[53] The problem is discussed in more detail in Chap. 13.
[54] *Fifteen Per Cent Case, 1931,* 178 I.C.C. 539, 576.
[55] *36th Annual Report of the Interstate Commerce Commission, 1922,* p. 25.
[56] Concurring opinion of Commissioner Eastman in *Fifteen Per Cent Case, 1937-38 (Ex Parte No. 123),* 226 I.C.C. 41, 152.

and the rates to be charged for the service, only to discover later that those judgments were faulty, the general taxpayer will be called upon to underwrite the error. In fact, the CAB has proposed paying a total of almost 8 million dollars ($7,808,000) to the carriers in the form of retroactive increased mail rates for the year 1948 to cover their operating losses for the year.[57] By contrast, the main impact of any errors made by the ICC in assessing the efficiency of railroad management falls on the individuals who have assumed the risk of investing their private capital in the enterprise.

This constitutes the core of the problem under discussion. The controlling fact is that the presence of a subsidy backstop dilutes the main forces that tend to make management prudent and efficient. The compelling motive for efficient management in any self-supporting enterprise is to keep revenues and costs balanced in such a way as to preserve the original capital investment and realize at least as good a return as could have been expected from some alternative use of that capital. The penalty of any major miscalculations is the loss of income or investment. To the extent that the managers of any private enterprise are released from these disciplines, managerial efforts inevitably tend to become diffused and the exercise of judgment less precise.

The diffusion of effort comes about naturally enough because the industry's future depends quite as much upon the ability of the managers to persuade government to supply improved airports and airways as it does upon the more orthodox aspects of managerial efficiency. The tendency toward less precision in business judgment is just as natural but operates in a more subtle way. Any enterprise that operates in a competitive field must assume the risks inherent in technological progress, or stagnate. This is particularly true where, as with air transportation, operating techniques and equipment are changing rapidly. Under these circumstances, the ordinary hazards of predicting

---

[57] CAB Economic Program for 1949, Statement of Policy, Feb. 21, 1949, CAB Release No. 49-13, p. 6, and Summary of Orders Issued to Implement Civil Aeronautics Board Statement of Policy, Feb. 25, 1949 (mimeo.).

future costs and the potential market are enhanced by the impulse to confuse consumer interest with effective demand. When this attitude becomes dominant, a period of speculative overexpansion is foreshadowed. Nothing short of a sharp retrenchment in general business activity or a strong restraining influence on the part of the regulatory agency can prevent such overexpansion and the ensuing financial difficulty. Neither of these forces became operative. As noted by the President's Air Policy Commission:

Most of the air lines are in financial difficulties for a number of reasons. Both their management and Government aviation officials were overoptimistic as to the volume of postwar passenger traffic. Starved for both airplanes and personnel during the war, the lines hired large numbers of new people when the war ended, ordered many new airplanes and in several instances made what may prove to have been unwise route extensions.[58]

Moreover, it is evident that the CAB did not develop any acute concern regarding the extent of overexpansion in the industry until after the distressing operating deficits of 1947 had been recorded. For as late as the third quarter of 1947, the CAB apparently was disturbed over the reduction of profit rather than over the prospects of substantial industry-wide deficit.

The end of the war marked the beginning of a period during which the domestic airline industry has been expanding at an unprecedented rate, which will undoubtedly continue for several years. This expansion has taken the form of increased service on existing routes and the inauguration of service on new routes and was made possible by the increased availability of both aircraft and personnel resulting from sharp reductions in military requirements. To effect the foregoing expansion, the airlines have recruited large numbers of new personnel who had to be trained before their assignment to productive duties, facilities had to be enlarged, and additional capital had to be acquired to finance the expanded operations. These factors had the effect of materially reducing the profits which would normally have resulted from the increased traffic carried by the airlines during the fiscal year 1946.[59]

[58] *Survival in the Air Age*, p. 99.
[59] *Annual Report of the Civil Aeronautics Board, 1946*, p. 8.

There is no suggestion in this official comment that management had displayed either imprudence or inefficiency in service extension, large additions to personnel, or capital investment for new equipment. Yet a few months later, apparently on the basis of the same operating record, the CAB, in effect, charged the managements of four of the five major airlines with general inefficiency for the year ended September 30, 1947. In a major air-mail rate case decided March 1948, the Board observed that for the 1947 operating period Eastern Air Lines "was the only carrier which reported a profit before federal income taxes. It is believed that each of the four other carriers[60] had at least as favorable an opportunity to earn reasonable profits as did Eastern during this 12-month period."[61] On the basis of this controlling finding, the Board had no alternative but to attribute the extreme variations in operating results to variations in managerial competence:

With the exception of the rising price level, which affected all air carriers as well as other industries, the principal differences in operating results among the five carriers whose mail rates are being reviewed herein are factors resulting from management decisions for which the stock-holders should properly hold management responsible. Certain of these management decisions which resulted in temporary reductions in earnings or even in temporary losses might very well have a long-run beneficial effect upon the future earnings status of a particular carrier. But regardless of this factor, the approximate equality of opportunity of each of these five carriers to earn a fair profit is amply supported by the facts.[62]

If each of the five carriers had an approximate "equality of opportunity" to earn a fair profit during this period, the extreme variations in actual financial results can be explained only on the basis of relative managerial competence ranging from high efficiency to gross mismanagement. For the rate of return on average invested capital ranged from 5.6 per cent for Eastern Air Lines to a theoretically negative return of almost 17 per cent for TWA. (See table p. 216.)

[60] Northwest, United Air Lines, American Airlines, and TWA.
[61] CAB, *Statement of Tentative Findings and Conclusions*, Docket Nos. 3309, 3021, 3211, 2849, 3014, adopted Mar. 29, 1948, p. 33 (mimeo.).
[62] The same, p. 34.

Under these circumstances it might be assumed that the CAB would have taken decisive and, if necessary, drastic action to locate and remove the causes of the observed variations in managerial efficiency. Instead, the Board merely made the legal finding that "under conditions of economical and efficient management, in the future period the five carriers in this proceeding do not have any need for mail compensation over and above a fair and reasonable service rate."[63]

RATE OF RETURN—NET INCOME AFTER TAXES AS PER CENT OF AVERAGE INVESTED CAPITAL "BIG FIVE" AIR CARRIERS

| Carrier | 1947[a] | Future Estimate Reflecting Effect of Increased Rates[b] |
|---------|---------|---------------------------------------------------------|
| American | −2.93 | 7.63 |
| Eastern | 5.60 | 36.11 |
| Northwest | −6.20 | 11.87 |
| T.W.A. | −16.77 | 12.65 |
| United | −7.37 | 8.14 |

[a] Figured on 1947 yearly net profit or loss figures and investment figures for 9 months ended Sept. 30, 1947. Income figure from CAB *Recurrent Report of Financial Data,* 4th quarter 1947. Investment figure from CAB, *Statement of Tentative Findings and Conclusions,* Docket Nos. 3309, 3021, 3211, 2849, 3014, adopted Mar. 29, 1948, App. 2 (mimeo.).

[b] The same, p. 68.

It is clear that under this interpretation uneven earning power of the trunk-line carriers cannot be corrected by use of mail payments. For, the estimated operating results for the "future period" reflect great variations in the earnings of the individual carriers, all of which, according to the official findings, have an equal opportunity under honest, economical, and efficient management to earn a "fair profit."

The so-called "service rate" prescribed by the Board for carrying mail, together with other revenue will produce a rate of return on invested capital varying from 36 per cent for Eastern Air Lines to 7.6 per cent for American Airlines. (See table above.) Manifestly, if a return of 8 per cent for one carrier constitutes reasonable earnings, 36 per cent for a similarly situated carrier constitutes an exorbitant profit.

[63] The same, p. 57.

It is therefore apparent that the Civil Aeronautics Act as administered to date has failed to produce a balanced corporate operating structure for the industry as contemplated by the law. The Board has been unable, through control of operating rights, to adjust the supply of air transport facilities to the effective public demand for that service. Nor has the agency, in the face of critical overextension of the industry, been able to restore a balanced operating pattern. The net results of these failures is a general condition of financial instability throughout the air transportation industry, a situation in direct variance with the declared objectives of the Civil Aeronautics Act.

Up to this point we have considered only the overexpansion of routes and services with reference to the so-called trunk-line air carriers. Before attempting further evaluation of government action in this field, we must review another phase of the CAB program for air promotion. Analysis of the so-called "feeder route" experiment indicates that equally serious policy errors are being made here by an attempt to project air transportation into areas of least relative advantage.

#### IV. FEEDER ROUTES—EXTENSION INTO AREAS OF LEAST RELATIVE ADVANTAGE

In carrying out its statutory responsibility to promote and develop air transportation, the CAB has chosen to make a sharp distinction between the policies and methods applied to trunk-line or long-haul operation as compared with the feeder or characteristically short-haul type of service. In effect, it has segregated the latter type of operation for experimental treatment and has utilized air-mail payments determined on a "need" basis as a means of financing the experiment.

At the outset it was decided that the operating technique and managerial methods of the trunk-line carriers were not properly adapted for the conduct of this experiment. Thus in the first decision dealing in a clear-cut manner with the feeder route problem, the Board authorized the operation of a new carrier in preference to an established firm using conventional equipment. It placed emphasis on the difficulty that would be encountered in developing satisfactory traffic volume in the sparsely settled area involved and observed that:

Greater effort and the exercise of managerial ingenuity may be expected from an independent local operator whose continuation in the air transportation business will be dependent upon the successful development of traffic on the routes and the operation of the service on an adequate and an economical basis.[64]

Under the general guidance of this policy, ten feeder lines have been authorized and the coverage of feeder routes has been expanded from 12,043 miles in 1946 to 23,088 in 1948. (See table p. 203.)

Before inaugurating this experiment, the Board conducted a general investigation as a result of which it concluded that: ". . . the provision of a short-haul and local service with aircraft will be, in a very great measure, an experimental operation, and constitutes a problem with respect to which we have little or no information of a factual nature."[65]

Presumably the Board has moved ahead on this experiment on the assumption that the cost of financial subsidies will be justified by the development of significant operating information together with the resultant benefits to the communities served. It is difficult, however, to find any rational basis either for the timing of this experiment or for the underlying assumption regarding its potential experimental value. In the first place, late in 1947 the CAB stated that "today there is no certificated air-craft ideally situated to operation on purely regional routes."[66] It is not made clear how valid experimental results can be expected to emerge from the subsidized operations of technically ill-adapted equipment on routes of admittedly submarginal traffic prospects.

The second and more important question, however, relates to the assumption that the experiment would reveal the appro-

[64] Rocky Mountain States Air Service, 6 CAB 695, 737, decided Mar. 28, 1946.

[65] Local, Feeder, and Pickup Air Service, 6 CAB 1, 3 (1944).

[66] Statement of the Civil Aeronautics Board before the President's Air Policy Commission, p. 13.

priate economic role of air transportation in the field of short-haul or "local-feeder" transportation. In launching this experiment, the Board called attention to the fact that its legal obligation and authority was limited to furthering the interests of air transportation:

The statutory duty of this Board to promote and develop air transportation must be construed in harmony with its statutory obligation to regulate air transportation in such manner as to recognize and preserve its inherent advantages and to foster sound economic conditions in the industry.[67]

Thus the Board had no responsibility to determine or even give weight to the effect on existing transport agencies which could be expected from the introduction of a new and competitive air transport service. But the CAB could not avoid making an estimate of the amount of traffic that the new air service might be able to divert from the established carriers:

With respect to public acceptance of local-feeder services, our greatest difficulty is in reaching a sound judgment on the extent to which the various forms of surface transportation facilities will offer more attractive means of conveyance between small cities separated by relatively short distances. Despite the boundless enthusiasm shown by the cities to be on the air map of the country, the tickets will be paid for by individuals, each acting on his own judgment as to whether he can reach his destination more conveniently by the train, bus, private automobile, or the airline.[68]

It will be observed that in this reference to shipper-choice, emphasis is placed on the relative *convenience* of the service offered by the various transport agencies. No mention is made of relative total cost of providing these alternative services. The only point at which cost calculation entered into the determination was in connection with fixing the amount of mail pay subsidy required to support the experimental operation:

As in all new-route cases, consideration must be given to the anticipated financial cost to the Government in the requirements of mail compensation. Because of the low traffic potential of the smaller cities and towns to be served by the local-feeder services and the

[67] *Rocky Mountain States Air Service,* 6 CAB 695, 730 (1946).
[68] The same.

intense competition to which they will undoubtedly be subjected by rail and highway transportation, economy of operation must be a primary concern of local-feeder service operators if the cost to the Government is to be kept within reasonable limits.[69]

The results produced to date by this experiment raise considerable doubt as to whether or not the costs to the government are being kept within "reasonable limits." For example, in a recent mail pay case, one member of the Board observed that:

An examination of the reports filed with the Board by the feeder airlines discloses such limited amount of patronage on some of the feeder routes as to raise serious doubt whether the value of the service being performed by some of these carriers is commensurate with the cost to the Government.[70]

This observation was based in part on the "increasing costliness of the experiment," and in part on developing evidence that the air traffic potential of some of the routes had been fundamentally miscalculated.

As to the first of these points, the Board has found it desirable or necessary to increase substantially the amount of mail pay subsidy for all the authorized feeder routes. Originally, temporary mail pay rates were established on the basis of 25 cents per plane-mile. The rate was then increased to 35 cents per plane-mile, and subsequently to 60 cents per plane-mile for the first six months' period of operation with a provision for a decrease of 5 cents per plane-mile for each succeeding three months' period with a minimum of 35 cents per plane-mile.[71]

On the basis of the mail pay in effect for 1947, some startling results were produced with respect to the division of feeder-line operating costs between the general taxpayer and the patrons who found the new air service more "convenient" than

[69] The same, p. 731.

[70] Dissenting opinion of CAB member Harlee Branch in *Monarch Air Lines, Inc.*, CAB Docket No. 2741, decided Apr. 5, 1948, p. 2 (mimeo.).

[71] Pioneer Airlines is the only feeder carrier operating at a permanent rate (as of April 1948). The original rate for this carrier was fixed at 25 cents per plane-mile and was subsequently raised to 45 cents. The same, p. 1.

other means of travel. Disregarding the carriers that were not in operation for the full year, we find that in some cases the general taxpayer is being called upon to pay four times as much for an air ride as the actual passenger who has chosen that service on the basis of competitive fares. Thus, the individuals who chose to patronize Empire Airlines during 1947 paid to the company an average of $11.59 for their tickets. During the same period the average payment made by the government to that company in the form of mail pay amounted

PASSENGER LOAD, MAIL PAY PER PASSENGER, AND AVERAGE
PASSENGER TICKET, ALL FEEDER LINES, 1947[a]

| Lines | Average Passenger Load | Average Mail Pay per Passenger | Average Passenger Ticket |
|---|---|---|---|
| Challenger[b] ................4.50 | | $32.58 | $12.84 |
| Empire ....................2.76 | | 40.29 | 11.59 |
| Florida[c] ..................1.33 | | 55.11 | 6.91 |
| Monarch ..................3.30 | | 35.85 | 12.13 |
| Pioneer ..................7.72 | | 16.40 | 12.37 |
| Southwest ................8.30 | | 9.19 | 7.95 |
| Trans-Texas[d] .............1.42 | | 87.34 | 10.05 |
| West Coast ...............6.15 | | 9.63 | 6.90 |
| Average ................5.65 | | 17.47 | 9.61 |

[a] Adapted from dissenting opinion of CAB member Branch in *Monarch Air Lines, Inc.*, CAB Docket No. 2741, decided Apr. 5, 1948 (mimeo.).
[b] Inaugurated May 3, 1947.
[c] Inaugurated Jan. 10, 1947. Operations discontinued by order of the CAB Mar. 7, 1949.
[d] Inaugurated Oct. 11, 1947.

to $40.29 per passenger. (See table above.) Results from other companies indicated wide variations, but in each case the amount paid per passenger in the form of mail pay was greater than the average amount paid to the company by the passenger through the purchase of air transport tickets.

Despite this substantial amount of government support, seven of the thirteen feeder airlines failed in 1948 to cover operating expenses by operating revenues. (See table p. 208). It was primarily on the basis of this record that one member of the Civil Aeronautics Board raised the question as to:

. . . whether it is not the duty of the Board in the public interest to make some reexamination of those feeder operations which after a period of months—in one or two cases after operations have been conducted for more than a year—show an almost infinitesimal amount of public patronage and an ever-mounting cost to the Government.[72]

The growing public cost of underwriting the feeder-line experiment emphasizes the fundamental policy error that permeates the entire undertaking. As we have already indicated, the true competitive role of air transportation in the short-haul or "intercommunity" field of service cannot be determined by offering the shipper or traveler a choice between a heavily subsidized new service as against established carriers that must charge rates reflecting total economic costs. Such an experiment can demonstrate nothing but the obvious: that other aspects of the service being equal or similar, traffic will be diverted from the self-supporting to the subsidized carrier. For it is axiomatic that the individual shipper or traveler as a practical matter will patronize the agency offering the lowest actual rate. It is immaterial that such a rate may be relatively low only because he, along with other general taxpayers, is bearing indirectly a major part of the total cost of performing the service.

There is also inherent in this type of experimentation the probability that a long-run disservice will be done the entire industry by inducing expansion into areas of least relative advantage. For example, the CAB's efforts to extend air transportation into the short-haul field apparently have ignored the costly experience in the field of highway transportation. In the latter case there was an early tendency to overextend the range of trucking services in particular into the field of long-distance movements where for most commodities the truck has no particular advantage in cost, speed, or flexibility.

The same tendency to overextend beyond the range of natural advantage is evident in air transportation except that the direction of overextension is reversed. However, from the standpoint of public policy there is a fundamental difference

[72] Dissenting opinion of CAB member Branch in the same, p. 1.

between the two situations. The financial losses incurred in the overexpansion of trucking operations have been borne by the private operator and have forced retrenchment. In contrast, the growing losses associated with the air transport experiment are borne by the public treasury, thus making it unnecessary to retrench or abandon services to the extent indicated by operation results.[73]

In addition to the issues discussed above, the feeder-line experiment raises important problems with respect to other phases of government action in the transportation field. It will be recalled that the federal policies administered by the Interstate Commerce Commission are dedicated to the co-ordination of transport services by highway, water, and rail; to the prevention of destructive competition; and to the adjustment of supply to effective demand. Thus, new truck and bus operations may be inaugurated only after showing that existing service (by all means of surface transport) is inadequate to meet public need. By contrast, as just pointed out, the CAB has no obligation or authority to consider the over-all adequacy of existing services in its program to promote air feeder-lines. Calculation of the comparative total cost of performing a particular service by air as compared with another medium occurs, if at all, only in connection with estimating the amount of subsidy that will be required to support the feeder lines.

In connection with this problem, it is important to recall that the federal government has for many years played an important role in the development of highway transportation designed especially to serve short-haul or "intercommunity" transportation needs. Moreover, the national government is now committed to the expenditure of more than one billion

[73] It should be noted, however, that recent action indicates some tightening of CAB policy with respect to subsidizing feeder airlines. Thus, on March 7, 1949, the CAB ordered Florida Airways, Inc., to discontinue operations on the grounds that the route served "is an uneconomical route, that no substantial increase in nonmail revenues can be expected in the reasonably foreseeable future and that further expenditures of public funds will not avail to develop it into a route that can be operated at a reasonable cost to the Government commensurate with the service rendered." *Florida Airways, Inc.*, CAB Docket No. 3511, decided Mar. 7, 1949, p. 9, (mimeo.).

dollars for the years 1949 and 1950 in federal aid to the states for highway improvement. This is in addition to the 1.5 billion dollars authorized under the act of 1944. Presumably all of these expenditures are intended to make highway transportation—an essentially short-haul service—more efficient, convenient, and safer.

During the past quarter of a century, every community has been given access to improved and costly highway facilities. The individual has the choice of using a private automobile or truck, a common carrier or contract carrier truck, or a common carrier bus. So far as the movement of people is concerned, especially in the so-called intercommunity type of service, it is well to recall that common carrier scheduled bus operation now serves every city and village of the country and even makes a multiplicity of local stops to accommodate rural residents.

Before embarking on an ambitious and potentially expensive program for the extension of air transportation into the field of local service—at public expense—it would, therefore, appear to be wise public policy to determine whether or not any need exists for additional expenditure of public funds in this segment of the transportation system. The final test should be based on comparative total cost, relative efficiency, and economy.

## V. SUMMARY

The analysis in this chapter indicates that the government has met with indifferent success in its attempt to adjust transport supply to effective demand by means of control over the establishment and abandonment of transport enterprises. This area of control was designed to supplement and strengthen the regulation of rates and quality of service. But the control over transport supply has been rendered more or less ineffective because of three major defects:

1. *The controls were, in major instances, asserted too late.* Thus, Congress made railroad expansion and abandonment subject to regulation in 1920, long after such characteristics as duplication of physical facilities and variation in earning power

had become embedded in the railroad operating and corporate structure. Moreover, by 1920 the period of railroad expansion had long since passed. Consequently, the control over the right and obligation to operate railroad enterprises served primarily to retard the abandonment of obsolete facilities. For it gave communities, shippers, and other special interests a legal device for resisting and postponing the orderly adjustment of the railroad structure to the new competitive era. This occurred even though the protesting groups had already transferred their patronage to other modes of transportation.

2. *The regulatory agencies were given incomplete and otherwise imperfect statutory jurisdiction.* This is particularly true with respect to the operating controls imposed after 1935 on highway, air, and water agencies. The gaps in regulatory jurisdiction are of two main kinds. In the first place, the regulatory controls have been limited to the so-called "for-hire" portions of highway and water transportation (common and contract carriers). Moreover, important portions of the for-hire industry are exempted by statute from the obligation to demonstrate public need for their service.

Since the bulk of all freight and passenger movement by highway and inland waterways is in the hands of the private and exempted for-hire operators, the regulatory agency is left at the outset with an extremely limited jurisdiction. Manifestly, no agency can be expected to effect an accurate adjustment between the supply of transport service and the demand for that service when the bulk of the operating capacity, either actual or potential, lies beyond its control.

Lack of jurisdiction over the scheduling of service constitutes the second major reason why the regulatory agencies have been unable to make effective use of operating certificate and permit controls. In reality, as matters now stand, regulatory agencies authorize and control "route patterns" rather than the volume of service to be supplied to the public over those routes. This follows from the fact that the agencies are specifically precluded by law from controlling the number of schedules that may be operated over an approved route. Thus, the aggregate volume of service available to the public may be changed at will by the authorized operators through the simple device of adjusting the number and capacity of vehicles utilized in the service. This factor accounts in part for the inability of the Civil Aeronautics Board to prevent overexpansion in the air transportation industry.

3. *Effective control of air transport development has been complicated by a policy of subsidization.* The proponents of continued subsidization of air transportation contend that the industry has not yet reached maturity. Consequently, it must be conceded that by taking jurisdiction over operating rights in 1938, the government had ample opportunity to affirmatively direct the sound development of aviation. The declared objective was to avoid the historical evils of overexpansion, duplication of facilities, and variation in earning power.

Although the Civil Aeronautics Board since 1938 has concentrated on the control of the air route patterns, the aviation industry is now characterized by financial instability and defective operating structure. One major explanation for this situation lies in a gross miscalculation by industry and government of the air transportation market. Availability of subsidies in the form of air-mail payments appears to have been a major factor in the formulation of these erroneous business and regulatory judgments. For these subsidies have tended to weaken the disciplines ordinarily imposed on managerial efficiency by the threat of bankruptcy. In consequence there has been an inclination on the part of industry and government agencies alike to expand the air route pattern far beyond the dictates of prudent business management.

We must therefore conclude that existing controls over the right and obligation to operate are not effective devices for advancing the public interest in adequate transportation service at reasonable price. The declared objective of the program could be realized only by adding to the present system plenary and specific control over scheduling and type of equipment. Moreover, it would be necessary to make the regulatory coverage complete by withdrawal of current exemptions and by extending controls to private operations. Any such system of regulation would leave little leeway for the effective play of competitive forces and would therefore make the continuing role of private enterprise in this field of doubtful validity or utility.

In final analysis, current government regulation of the right and obligation to operate transport enterprises serves primarily to maintain some degree of corporate stability in the field of transportation by protecting established enterprises against would-be competitors. To this extent, government action serves the owners of the protected enterprises more directly than shippers or the general public. Certainly, operating controls are not necessary to guarantee an adequate supply of transport facilities since, in practice, they are used primarily to limit the number of firms that would otherwise enter the field. And the program has proved incapable of exercising effective control over the volume or quality of service available to the public. This means that the effectiveness of the government's regulatory program is mainly dependent on the results of rate regulation. The scope of public action in this field, together with the policy issues encountered, is dealt with in the next three chapters.

## CHAPTER XI

## RATE REGULATION AND DISCRIMINATION

From the outset, rate regulation has constituted the core of federal action in the field of transport control. However, the scope and purpose of such regulation has changed materially from time to time in accordance with varying regulatory objectives and new patterns of transport organization and competition. From 1887 to 1920 rate control was designed primarily to restrain the monopoly power then possessed by the railroads to levy discriminatory and exorbitant charges against the shipping public.

From 1920 to the mid-1930's the railroads remained the chief object of federal rate regulation, but a positive concern for the financial welfare of the carriers was made an integral part of national policy. Although the previous prohibitions against unduly discriminatory and excessive charging were retained in the law, the Interstate Commerce Commission was, in effect, directed to adjust the general level of rates in such a way that the carriers would be permitted to earn a fair return on their transport investment. The period from 1935 to date has been marked by the extension to all other major forms of domestic transportation of the pattern and standards of rate regulation previously applied to the railroads.[1]

There are three major objectives of contemporary rate control: (1) to prevent public carriers from discriminating between individuals and communities in the matter of prices and service; (2) to allocate traffic among the competing carriers in accordance with the relative efficiency and economy of each; and (3) to "maintain" the financial solvency of the regulated carriers.

Regulatory agencies have encountered difficulty in the attempt to realize these stated objectives of national policy because: (1) there are important conflicts between the nondis-

[1] Ocean shipping and international aviation—where foreign competition constitutes an important factor—are not subject to similar types of federal rate regulation.

229

criminatory standards of regulation on the one hand and the effect of promotional policies on the other; (2) the fact that some transport agencies are subsidized while others are not makes it difficult to allocate traffic among competing agencies through the use of minimum rate controls; (3) the assumption by government of positive responsibility for the financial well-being of the carriers has in reality tended to act as a drag on managerial initiative and has retarded necessary adjustments of prices (rates) to changing costs and the traffic conditions.

The present chapter focuses on the first of these three problems: namely, the conflict between objectives of nondiscrimination as the effects of promotional action.

### I. THE CONCEPT OF NONDISCRIMINATORY TREATMENT

Public resentment against the ability of the railroads to discriminate among individual shippers and communities in the matter of rates and service constituted one of the main reasons for adoption in 1887 of the original "Act to Regulate Commerce."[2] That statute made it mandatory for common carriers engaged in the interstate transportation of persons and property exclusively by rail, or jointly by rail and water,[3] to make only "reasonable and just" charges for the service offered to the public. The act specifically prohibited "unjust discriminations" and any form of "undue or unreasonable preference."[4] Unjust discrimination was broadly defined as the exaction by the carrier of varying rates from different persons for "a like and contemporaneous service in the transportation of a like kind of traffic under substantially similar circumstances and conditions."[5]

One special form of particularly offensive discrimination was

[2] 24 Stat. 379.
[3] In the latter case, only if the joint service was being furnished under arrangement for a continuous shipment, or if both facilities were under a common control or management.
[4] Interstate Commerce Acts Annotated, Vol. 9, pp. 6955, 7345, 7386. The present law reads: "All charges made for any service rendered or to be rendered in the transportation of passengers or property . . . , or in connection therewith, shall be just and reasonable, and every unjust and unreasonable charge for such service or any part thereof is prohibited and declared to be unlawful." The same, p. 7008.
[5] The same, sec. 2, p. 7335.

specifically prohibited. Under the provisions of the so-called "long and short haul" clause of the act,[6] it was declared unlawful for a carrier to charge more in the aggregate for a shorter than for a longer haul where the former is included within the latter, is over the same line, and in the same direction, and where a like kind of property is transported under "substantially similar circumstances and conditions." The Interstate Commerce Commission, however, was empowered in "special cases" to exempt carriers from the operation of that section.[7]

*Statutory requirements apply to all transport agencies.* The fundamental prohibitions against discrimination and undue preference have been carried forward in all subsequent railroad legislation and, with the extension of regulatory coverage, have been made similarly applicable to other forms of transportation. All carriers subject to federal regulation are now uniformly required to file with the regulatory agency, print, and keep open for public inspection, tariffs showing rates, fares, and charges for the particular transportation service being offered by that carrier. Such rates and rules governing standards of service can be changed only after filing revised tariffs. The revised rates become effective only after the lapse of a statutory period, and if not suspended in the meantime by the regulatory commission for investigation as to reasonableness. Motor carriers since 1935, and domestic water carriers since 1940, have been subject to the provisions of the Interstate Commerce Act which has long prohibited any form of railroad discrimination:

It shall be unlawful for any common carrier subject to the provisions of this part to make, give, or cause any undue or unreasonable preference or advantage to any particular person, company, firm, corporation, association, locality, port, port district, gateway, transit point, region, district, territory, or any particular description of traffic, in any respect whatsoever.[8]

[6] The same, Vol. 11, sec. 4, p. 9163.
[7] Generally referred to as "fourth section relief" cases. The primary contemporary significance of this provision is in connection with railroad applications to the ICC for permission to reduce rates where water competition is effective without making similar reduction for a similar service that is beyond the reach of effective water competition. Discussed under sec. 2 of this Chapter.
[8] *Interstate Commerce Acts Annotated,* Vol. 11, p. 9147. The act contains similar requirements with respect to motor carriers, sec. 216 (b); and water

With respect to discrimination, the Civil Aeronautics Act of 1938 provides that:

No air carrier or foreign air carrier shall make, give, or cause any undue or unreasonable preference or advantage to any particular person, port, locality, or description of traffic in air transportation in any respect whatsoever or subject any particular person, port, locality, or description of traffic in air transportation to any unjust discrimination or any undue or unreasonable prejudice or disadvantage in any respect whatsoever.[9]

Controls of a similar nature affecting ocean shipping originated with the Shipping Act of 1916.[10] United States citizens engaged in common carrier operations by water in foreign commerce may not charge or collect any rate or fare that is unjustly discriminatory between shippers or ports, or unjustly prejudicial to exporters of the United States as compared with their foreign competitors. Every carrier and person subject to the act is required to establish, observe, and enforce just and reasonable regulations and practices relating to or connected with the receiving, handling, stowing, or loading of property. Whenever the regulatory authority (now the Maritime Commission) finds that any such regulation or practice is unjust or unreasonable, it may determine, prescribe, and enforce a just and reasonable regulation or practice.

These unequivocal standards of nondiscriminatory treatment in the provision of transportation services supply the integrating force of federal transport regulation as now constituted. Through the universal application of such standards, government in effect has declared that private individuals and concerns who undertake to provide the public with essential transport services must observe rigid rules of fair, just, and reasonable behavior. Thus so far as declaration of policy is concerned, Congress has been governed by an exacting code of political ethics. The basic purpose is to make the transportation

---

carriers, sec. 305 (b). The terms "region, district, territory" were added by the Transportation Act of 1940 apparently in order to ensure that these prohibitions were applicable to the interterritorial freight rate problem.

[9] 52 Stat. 993, sec. 404 (b).

[10] 39 Stat. 728.

system, as a whole, function as an impartial service agency for the national economy. Neither rates nor standards of service are to be used by government or by private enterprise as a means of advancing the interests of one region or sector of the economy to the prejudice or disadvantage of any other.

*Interterritorial discrimination.* Occasionally, special groups have attempted to breach this governing principle of transport regulation. But the Interstate Commerce Commission in a long line of decisions has endeavored to apply impartially the declared statutory theory of nondiscrimination.[11] Some of the most complex and controversial proceedings in regulatory history involve efforts of the Interstate Commerce Commission to make the transportation system supply similar service to the various regions of the country at the lowest rate consistent with variable costs. In all such cases the Commission has required the removal of interterritorial rate differentials that were found not justified by actual variations in the cost of performing the service. In the most recent application of this standard, the Commission in effect held the general system of railroad freight classification to be unreasonable and unduly prejudicial.[12] The railroads were given the option of promulgating a uniform freight classification for the entire country, or having one imposed by the ICC. The carriers elected to revise their system of freight classification.[13] Pending this action, the Commission ordered a 10 per

[11] For example, the Hoch-Smith resolution approved Jan. 30, 1925, instructed the ICC in adjusting freight rates to consider "insofar as it is legally possible" the conditions which "at any time prevail in our several industries." (48 Stat. 801). This specific instruction by Congress was inspired primarily because of the depressed conditions in agriculture and by the desire to alleviate those conditions through favorable transportation rates. However, the Commission maintained that this resolution added no standards for rate making that had not already been embodied in statutes and judicial interpretation. This position was upheld by the Supreme Court in *Ann Arbor Railroad Company, et al., v. U. S. et al.*, 281 U. S. 658 (1930).

[12] In 1939 the Commission instituted on its own motion two investigations regarding the lawfulness of the existing rate making standards for interstate railroad class freight rates. (*Class Rate Investigation, 1939*, Docket No. 28300, and *Consolidated Freight Classification*, Docket No. 28310.) The two inquiries were consolidated and decided May 15, 1945: 262 I.C.C. 447-766.

[13] For a description of the existing railroad rate structure indicating the methods by which rates are formulated, the significance of interterritorial rate relationships, etc., see: Board of Investigation and Research, *Report on Interterritorial Freight Rates*, H. Doc. 303, 78 Cong. 1 sess.

cent increase in rates within Eastern Territory, together with a 10 percent reduction of all class rates in and between Southern and Western Trunk-Lines and Southwestern territories, and between those territories on the one hand and Official (Eastern) Territory on the other.

The validity and legality of this order was challenged by the carriers, but the Commission's decision was eventually sustained by the courts. The Supreme Court pointed out that the Interstate Commerce Act (section 3 [1]) "does not dictate a policy of national uniformity in rates; it only requires that the lack of uniformity in rates among and between territories be justified by territorial conditions."[14]

The interests that protested the Commission's order placed considerable emphasis on the fact that a relatively small volume of interterritorial freight moves on so-called class rates.[15] It was therefore contended that unjust or unreasonable discrimination could not result from "paper rates." The Court rejected this argument with the following observation:

The Commission's over-all conclusion was that the classifications in force and the class rates computed from them harbor inequities which result in unlawful discriminations in favor of Official Territory and against the other territories. The fact that relatively small amounts of freight move by class rates proves not that the regional and territorial discrimination is slight, but that the rate structure as constituted holds no promise of affording the various regions or territories that parity of treatment which territorial conditions warrant. The Commission in substance concluded that that result could not be achieved unless traffic was, in the main, moved on class rates.[16]

[14] New York et al., v. U. S. et al., 331 U. S. 284, 350, decided May 12, 1947. The Court also observed that: "The inquiry of the Commission into the effect of class rates on the economic development of Southern, Southwestern, and Western Trunk-Line territories took a wide range. It concluded that prejudice to the territories in question had been established. We think that finding is supported by substantial evidence." The same, p. 310.

[15] Class rates are established in the form of a schedule which shows the price per 100 pounds of moving first-class freight over every possible combination of routes and distances. The cost of moving commodities rated other than first class is fixed by stated percentage relations to the cost of first-class movement. For various reasons, primarily considerations of competition and the desire to develop traffic, the bulk of carload freight (approximately 94 per cent in 1942) moves on three other types of ratings: exception rates, commodity rates, and column rates.

[16] New York et al., v. U. S. et al., 331 U. S. 284, 309.

Some groups have interpreted the Commission's decision in this case as the first step in a trend toward the use of rate regulation as a device for equalizing the social and economic status of various regions of the country.[17] Thus, an official spokesman for the organized shippers of the nation observed:

We are not so rooted to traditions and attached to the patterns of the past that we should oppose progress in the methods of transportation or in the arts of rate making. But for all the reasons that make for free enterprise as against a managed economy, it seems of highest importance to resist measures and programs designed to treat transportation as a vehicle for bringing about social and economic changes rather than a servant of commerce and to deprive private managements of carriers of the responsibility and prerogative of designing and maintaining rates suited to the needs of the patrons and of the public.[18]

The fact is, however, that nothing in the Commission's decision, nor in the Supreme Court's approval of that decision, can be interpreted as an effort to distort the proper function of transportation. On the contrary, the stated purpose was to guarantee that transportation would serve its true function as a "servant of commerce" by removing artificial rate barriers to the interregional flow of goods.

As the Supreme Court has stated: "Discriminatory rates are but one form of trade barriers."[19] The purpose of the Commission's order requiring the establishment of nondiscriminatory class rates was to achieve the equality of treatment guaranteed under the Interstate Commerce Act. Moreover, the standards of that act encompassed potential, as well as actual, discriminations. It will be recalled that the Transportation Act of 1940 broadened the prohibitions against discrimination to include regions and territories as well as the individual shippers. On this point the Court observed:

If a showing of discrimination against a territory or region were dependent on a showing of actual discrimination against shippers

[17] A wide range of views on this problem will be found in Duke University, *Law and Contemporary Problems*, Vol. 12, No. 3, Summer 1947.

[18] From address of John S. Burchmore, Counsel for National Industrial Traffic League, before Chicago Association of Commerce and Industry. Quoted in *Traffic World*, June 7, 1947, p. 1765.

[19] *Georgia v. Pennsylvania Railroad Company*, 324 U. S. 439, 450.

located in these sections, the case could never be made out where discriminatory rates had proved to be such effective trade barriers as to prevent the establishment of industries in those outlying regions. If that were the test, then the 1940 amendment to Section 3 (1) would not have achieved its purpose. We cannot attribute such futility to the effort made by Congress to make regions, districts and territories, as well as shippers, the beneficiaries of its antidiscrimination policy expressed in Section 3 (1).[20]

It is therefore evident that the concept of nondiscriminatory treatment is firmly imbedded in the regulatory program. Moreover, so far as the railroads are concerned, the Interstate Commerce Commission has not only the power but the will to protect individuals, communities, and economic regions against any semblance of price or service discrimination. In addition, the Interstate Commerce Commission has consistently refused to require railroad rate equalization solely to compensate for the natural competitive handicaps of a particular shipper.[21] However, the Commission has been rendered powerless to apply these standards uniformly throughout the transportation system. For Congress has seen fit to pursue promotional policies that deliberately create regional preferences and give rise to competitive inequalities among transportation agencies. As a result, the ethical standards of regulation looking toward nondiscriminatory treatment of individuals and communities and toward fair and impartial regulation of transport agencies are violated by the objectives and results of promotional action.

## II. CONFLICT BETWEEN NONDISCRIMINATORY STANDARDS AND PROMOTIONAL ACTION

This problem arises in an acute form in connection with the Commission's responsibility for establishing through routes, joint rates, and rate differentials between rail and water carriers. The resultant issues illustrate more sharply than any other specific aspect of the transportation problem the irreconcilable conflict between the promotional program of the national gov-

---

[20] *New York et al.*, v. *U. S. et al.*, 331 U. S. 284, 308.
[21] *Great Lakes Steel Corp.* v. *Ahnapee and Western Ry. Co., et al.*, I.C.C. Docket No. 29139, decided May 17, 1948, sheet 3 (mimeo.).

ernment and the declared purposes of regulatory policy. The basic issue of long standing is to what extent and under what standards of rate regulation the railroads should be forced to serve as the vehicle for distributing the benefits of waterway subsidies to interior points not directly served by water transportation.

*Use of railroads as vehicle for distributing water subsidies.* In a recent report on an investigation of rail and barge joint rates,[22] the Commission concluded that:

Viewing the facts before us in the light of the clear Congressional policy with respect to water transportation on the Mississippi River and its tributaries we conclude that joint barge-and-rail routes and rates generally are necessary and desirable in the public interest and differentials between such rates and all-rail rates are justified.[23]

In this report the Commission has at last put aside the legal and statistical legerdemain that had previously obscured the essential issues. It made three controlling findings with respect to: (1) the objectives of congressional policy in the field of water transportation on the Mississippi and its tributaries; (2) the nature of the public interest in the maintenance of joint barge and rail routes and rates; and (3) the justification for the establishment of differentials between such rates and all-rail rates.

Congressional policy regarding river transportation. On this point the Commission concluded in effect that Congress intends to pursue indefinitely its policy of furnishing subsidized transportation to the Mississippi Valley area. For more than a quarter of a century, progressively larger amounts of public funds have been spent for river and harbor development in that area, and for maintenance of the federally owned Inland Waterways Corporation. (See Chapter V.)

The Commission notes that in carrying out this program Con-

---

[22] This investigation was instituted by the Commission on its own motion in March 1935. The hearings continued intermittently for 8 years during which period a record of 16,440 pages and about 1,500 exhibits was developed. And as the examiner pointed out: "During the period covered by the hearings there were far-reaching changes in commercial and transportation conditions. For that reason much of the evidence, particularly that in the earlier part of the record, is of little or no present significance." Examiner's Report in I.C.C. Docket No. 26712, *Rail and Barge Joint Rates,* Sheet 13, (mimeo.).

[23] *Rail and Barge Joint Rates,* 270 I.C.C. 591, 613, decided July 7, 1948.

gress has been influenced by the Mississippi Valley Association whose object is to "promote the economic welfare of the Mississippi Valley States *and of the nation* by developing the economic resources and promoting the commerce of the Mississippi Valley."[24] The association contends that high transportation costs have held back the normal development of industry and population in the Mississippi Valley, and that:

This handicap can be removed in large degree through the development and use of inland water transportation. The extent to which these benefits can be spread throughout the interior will depend upon the extent to which favorable joint rates and services are established and maintained.[25]

It is clear that this rationalization for the use of subsidized transportation to promote sectional interests has been given explicit expression in federal action. Although originally established to demonstrate the feasibility and economy of privately operated water transportation, the Inland Waterways Corporation has in reality deteriorated into a device for regulating railroad rates.

Under the Denison Act of 1928,[26] the Commission was required to issue a certificate of necessity and convenience to any common carrier that desired to establish transportation service on the Mississippi and Warrior Rivers or their tributaries. It then became the duty of the Commission to require all connecting railroads to establish through routes and joint rates with the certificated water carriers. Unlike the provisions of the Transportation Act of 1920, regulating the extension or abandonment of railroad service, the Commission was given no authority under the Denison Act to determine the public need for additional common carrier service by water. On the contrary, the single purpose was to overcome the natural geographic limitations of water transportation by forcing the railroads to

---

[24] The same, p. 607. Italics supplied.
[25] The same.
[26] 45 Stat. 978. This act also authorized the secretary of war who was then technically responsible for management of the Inland Waterways Corporation to extend service to the tributaries of the Mississippi (other than the Ohio) and to other connecting waterways.

make available their facilities to feed traffic into the government-supported water transport system.

Public interest in differential rail-barge rate. Spokesmen for the Mississippi Valley interests insisted (and Congress acquiesced) that the "benefits" of public subsidy for water transportation should be widely diffused. In short, it was realized at an early date that the application of general tax funds for purely sectional development would become vulnerable to attack on the basis of gross regional discrimination and would consequently lose public support. Thus a congressional committee reporting on the legislation that became the Denison Act observed that:

The hearings on this bill convinced the committee that legislation somewhat drastic is now not only needed but is necessary in order to fully carry out the purpose for creating the Inland Waterways Corporation, and to realize the benefits of the policy of Congress manifested by the large expenditures made for the improvement of our inland waterways.

Paragraph (e) of the bill was carefully prepared to accomplish this purpose. If enacted into law, it is believed by the committee that it will immediately result in overcoming the reluctance of many of the railroads to cooperate with the Inland Waterways Corporation, and will aid in bringing about such through routes, joint rates, and fair division of joint rates as *will afford to the people of a large part of the country the economies of cheaper transportation by water.*[27]

It is therefore evident that in 1928 Congress recognized that the so-called "economies of cheaper transportation by water" resulted directly from the government's expenditure for river and harbor improvement, and that it expected those "economies" to be made available to shippers at interior points as well as those located on improved waterways. Consequently, it was necessary to enable these shippers to move commodities between two points by combination rail and water facilities at a joint rail-water rate differentially lower than the all-rail rate between the same two points. And since the railroads naturally displayed no enthusiasm for voluntarily delivering traffic to

[27] Report of the House Committee on Interstate and Foreign Commerce cited in *Rail and Barge Joint Rates*, 270 I.C.C. 609-10. Italics supplied.

their subsidized water competitors, Congress decided to require co-operation with its waterway policy.

Although the Denison Act was repealed by the Transportation Act of 1940, there has been no change in the basic purpose of congressional policy regarding waterway promotion. The Interstate Commerce Act now authorizes the Commission to establish through routes and joint rates applicable to transportation by water carriers and railroads and:

> In the case of a through route, where one of the carriers is a common carrier by water, the commission *shall* prescribe such reasonable differentials as it may find to be justified between all-rail rates and the joint rates in connection with such common carrier by water.[28]

Moreover, there remains in effect the provision of the Inland Waterways Corporation providing that the government operation of the barge service shall continue until (among other things) "there shall have been published and filed . . . such joint tariffs with rail carriers as shall make generally available the privileges of joint rail and water transportation upon terms reasonably fair to both rail and water carriers."[29]

Under these circumstances, the Commission has concluded that existing law requires the establishment of joint water-rail rates lower than corresponding all-rail rates when it finds such differences "to be justified."

Justification for differentials. The railroads contended that the Commission is under obligation to establish differentials only on proof that the cost of barge-rail service is less than the cost of corresponding all-rail service. The Commission rejected this argument although acknowledging that it "derives some dramatic force from the fact that in the past the proponents of barge transportation have strongly asserted a cost advantage on the part of the barge lines."[30] However, the Commission's report leaves considerable room for doubt as to precisely what stand-

[28] *Interstate Commerce Acts Annotated,* Vol. 11, p. 9619, sec. 307 (d). This section as passed by the House contains the word *may,* but the word *shall* was substituted by the Senate and House Conference Committee. Italics supplied.
[29] Denison Act 1928, 45 Stat. 978, sec. 3 (c).
[30] *Rail and Barge Joint Rates,* 270 I.C.C. 591, 610.

ards are applied in determining when rate differentials are justified.

Strict application of relative cost standards would afford no basis for the Commission's conclusions in the case under consideration, namely: that differentials between joint barge-rail rates and all-rail rates are justified in the public interest. For ICC cost experts reached the general conclusion:

. . . that the cost for the joint rail-barge routing is greater than that for the direct all-rail routing. Important factors contributing to this result are the relatively high cost for barge terminal operations and the added terminal handlings incurred on joint rail-barge traffic.[31]

This evidence is dismissed by the Commission with two observations. First, it points out that in earlier reports dealing with the same issues, lower cost of barge service was stressed as an important reason for such differentials, but "in no instance did we decline to prescribe or approve differential rates because the economy thereof had not been affirmatively shown."[32] Second, the Commission stresses the fact that the cases in which cost considerations were given important weight antedated the enactment of section 307 (d) of the Transportation Act of 1940, (described above). And the Commission adds that: "Neither the wording nor the legislative history of that section supports the conclusion that differentials are justified only where there is such an affirmative showing."[33]

The Commission also disagrees with the railroad interpretation of the relationship between the national transportation policy and the rail-barge differential rate issue. An essential part of the railroad position in this matter is that the establishment of rate differentials on any basis other than relative cost would contravene, in three important particulars, the policy declaration of the Interstate Commerce Act:

1. It would fail to recognize and preserve the "inherent advantage" of all-rail transportation over joint barge-rail service.

[31] The same, p. 604.
[32] The same, p. 611.
[33] The same.

2. Sound economic conditions in transportation and among the several carriers would not be fostered.

3. Undue preference and advantage would accrue to the shippers who benefit directly from the differential rates by comparison with those who are not in a geographical position to use barge transportation.

By way of elaborating the latter point, the railroads insist that differential rates are "economically unsound because they tend to divert traffic from all-rail routes over which it can be handled most advantageously and thus increase the economic burden on the transportation system as a whole."[34]

The railroads are in reality challenging the Commission to choose between : (1) carrying out the declared regulatory policy of Congress as expressed in the Interstate Commerce Act, or (2) adhering to congressional policy (as interpreted by the ICC) with respect to the promotion of water transportation. Clearly the Commission has chosen the latter course for it stated:

> We are unable to accept this argument [presented by the railroads] based on the national transportation policy. In the past several years Federal [the government-owned Federal Barge Line] has received continuing consideration by congressional committees on appropriations as well as others. It definitely appears from that consideration that Federal is deemed to be performing a pioneering function for the purpose among others of demonstrating the advantages of joint barge-and-rail transportation in the belief that such service eventually will prove to be economical. It is not for us to say that the experiment should now come to an end.[35]

Thus the Commission has concluded that it must continue to serve as the administrative vehicle for carrying out two diametrically opposed policies of Congress. With one hand it must apply impartially to all forms of transportation under its jurisdiction the statute prescribing nondiscriminatory treatment, to the end that no individual community or region shall enjoy an artificial advantage over any other by virtue of preferential transportation rates and services. At the same time the Commission apparently feels obligated to serve as the instrument for

[34] The same.
[35] The same, pp. 611-12.

carrying out another policy of Congress that deliberately seeks to use subsidized water transportation as a means of giving preferential treatment to one region of the country through the two-fold device of depressing railroad rates and shifting a portion of water transportation costs from the shippers of that region to the general taxpayer.

There can be no other conclusion with respect to the Commission's own interpretation of its obligation to carry out congressional policy in the field of waterway promotion. First, with respect to the effect of water subsidies on railroad rates, the Commission found that in the light of the legislative history of the Inland Waterways Corporation Act the term "privileges of joint rail and barge transportation must be understood as referring to barge and rail rates lower than all-rail rates."[36] And in support of this interpretation, the Commission cites the following statement of the House Appropriations Committee:

> In determining the value to the people of the operation of the barge lines consideration must be given to the effect on the rates of railroad transportation, the vast benefits of which cannot be estimated and which are not limited to the immediate areas of the rivers.[37]

Second, with respect to the factor of regional preference, the Commission observes that the Mississippi Valley Association, whose object was to "promote the economic welfare of the Mississippi Valley States," has "exercised a potent influence on Congressional policy with respect to barge transportation in the Mississippi Valley."[38] The Commission discovered further support for this finding in a recent statement of a House committee dealing with continuation of the Inland Waterways Corporation:

> It is apparent that the privately owned barge lines will not initiate service on the Missouri River. . . .
> Barge service is of great importance to the communities on the Missouri River. Rail transportation is costly from these interior

[36] The same, p. 610.
[37] Report of the House Committee on Appropriations on Government Corporations Appropriation Bill, 1947, as cited in 270 I.C.C. 591, 610, note 19.
[38] The same, p. 609.

points and it is difficult for them to compete with communities which are closer to their markets. The Panama Canal increased their competition by cutting transportation costs from the Pacific coast. Thus, their markets were further restricted. The railroads then, to compete with the Canal, initiated water-compelled rates from the west coast to Chicago so that it costs less to ship some commodities to and from Chicago from and to the west coast than it does in the case of certain Midwest communities.

By lowering transportation costs, barge service will give this area access to new markets and sources of supply.[39]

We do not intend to suggest by this analysis of the rail-barge rate problem that it would be appropriate for the Commission to ignore or override a historic and cherished policy of Congress—one calculated to produce discrimination between individual forms of transportation and regional preference. On the contrary, we have attempted only to document the fact that no regulatory agency can be expected to administer with impartiality and integrity, congressional policies that are inherently contradictory and irreconcilable.

If Congress expects the Commission to enforce impartially the ethically rigid provisions of the Interstate Commerce Act and to foster sound economic conditions in transportation generally, it must adjust promotional and subsidy policy to the attainment of these regulatory objectives. In short, the government must withdraw the regional preferences that inhere in its current program for the promotion of barge transportation. By this action Congress will raise the standard of its own performance to the level of responsibility and equity demanded of privately owned transportation enterprises. The objective is not merely to realize some abstract goal of consistency and equity in national policy. Rather the purpose is to make it possible for transportation to serve its true function: the provision of economical and dependable service to all sections of the country and to all shippers without discrimination in rates or quality of performance.

[39] Report to the House Appropriations Committee by the House Small Business Committee, dated May 14, 1947, relating to the Inland Waterways Corporation, as cited in the same, p. 612.

To this end it is essential that public regulation accord each of the transportation agencies an equal opportunity to compete for traffic on the basis of economic standards of relative cost and quality of service. But here, as in the case of discrimination discussed above, we find that the government's subsidy policy interferes with its regulatory effort to maintain fair standards of interagency competition through the device of rate control. This problem is analyzed in the next chapter.

## CHAPTER XII

## RATE REGULATION AND FAIR COMPETITION

As a logical corollary to the control of transport competition by limiting the right to enter or withdraw from the business, Congress has attempted to stabilize transport competition by rate regulation. Individual concerns are no longer free to adjust at will the physical pattern of their operations by seeking customers in new territories, abandoning unprofitable operations, or withdrawing from the service altogether. Consequently, survival as a business enterprise is controlled largely by price and service competition. For this becomes the controlling element in the allocation of available traffic among the carriers authorized to serve a given territory. Manifestly, if it is unsound to determine the adequacy of transportation supply by unrestrained competition, it is equally unsound to depend upon unrestricted price competition as the arbiter of economic survival.

We have already noted above the statutory rate standards that are designed primarily to prevent undue discrimination between individuals and places. Another and equally important aspect of rate control is in effect designed to guide the allocation of traffic among competing agencies in accordance with the relative cost and service characteristics of each agency.[1]

In the analysis of this problem it will be necessary to distinguish between the policies and decisions of the Interstate Commerce Commission and the Civil Aeronautics Board, since the latter agency has only recently entered the field of minimum rate control and has dealt with specialized problems.

### I. INTERSTATE COMMERCE COMMISSION ADMINISTRATION OF COMPETITIVE RATES

The power to prescribe reasonable minimum rates was first given to the ICC in the Transportation Act of 1920 to prevent "destructive competition," thereby avoiding dissipation of car-

[1] Regulation of the general level of rates is considered in Chap. 13.

rier revenue and discriminatory charging.[2] During the 1920's the Commission used its minimum rate power sparingly.[3] But, with the broadening of interagency competition and the extension of regulation to all principal agencies, the control of minimum rates has become a major problem for the Commission. The issues had already become acute before full authority over water transportation was added to the Commission's jurisdiction in 1940. Thus in 1939, Commissioner Eastman observed that:

The chief questions by which the Commission is confronted in the adjustment of rates of competing forms of transportation are whether and how and to what extent it should exercise its authority to prescribe minimum reasonable rates.[4]

He went on to note that:

The competition between the different modes of transportation is, of course, affected very materially by the extent to which public aid or subsidy is given, directly or indirectly, to each. Very complicated questions of fact and of public policy are presented by this matter, but they have not been committed to the Commission for determination or consideration, and we must take the situation as it exists in this respect regardless of what it should be.[5]

This observation goes to the heart of the minimum rate problem. Manifestly, rate control cannot be used effectively to determine how total available traffic shall be allocated among competing agencies if the regulatory authority is unable to develop a measurable standard of what constitutes a reasonable minimum rate. In the quest for such a standard, relative cost of performing a given service has assumed increasing impor-

[2] It will be recalled that the rule of rate making prescribed by sec. 15a of the 1920 act contemplated that the carriers would be permitted to earn "an aggregate annual net railway operating income equal, as nearly as may be, to a fair return upon the aggregate value of the railway property of such carriers held for and used in the service of transportation." *Interstate Commerce Acts Annotated*, Vol. 3, p. 2077.

[3] *Petroleum and Petroleum Products, California to Arizona*, 241 I.C.C. 21, 41.

[4] Joseph B. Eastman, Chairman, Interstate Commerce Commission, "The Transportation Problem," *The American Economic Review*, Pt. 2, Supplement, March 1940, p. 126.

[5] The same.

tance.[6] But the Commission has encountered great difficulty in the attempt to make practical application of this technique.

*Technical problems of cost-finding.* At the outset, the Commission is confronted with the fact that the "costs" with which it must deal are not comparable. This arises from the fact that the rates of some agencies, must, in the long run, cover total economic costs of providing all services while the rates of other carriers reflect varying portions of such costs. For example, railroads and pipelines, being privately owned and financed throughout, must maintain a rate structure that will produce sufficient revenue on the average to pay all operating costs, including maintenance and depreciation of equipment and fixed plant and property taxes. In addition, the rate structure must provide enough net operating revenue to pay interest charges on debt, and to maintain credit or supply new capital requirements out of earnings.

By contrast, other carriers, because they use publicly owned facilities, are enabled to offer services at rates which cover only a portion of corresponding costs. Water carrier rates, for example, do not reflect any of the costs incurred by government for the construction and maintenance of river and harbor facilities, and aids to navigation. Airlines enjoy relatively free use of publicly provided airports and airways, and, in addition, are eligible for direct financial aids in the form of air-mail payments. Highway users, on the other hand, pay substantial amounts in the form of user charges for support of publicly provided highways. But it is by no means certain that heavy vehicles used in intercity motor carrier operations contribute enough in user taxes to compensate for the added capital and maintenance costs incurred in their behalf. For these reasons it follows that under current government promotional policies,[7]

[6] For example, Commissioner Eastman observed that the "Commission is concentrating attention on the subject of cost finding, and has recruited a small staff of experts for this purpose." (The same, p. 127.) That "small staff" has since been materially expanded (33 positions were allocated to cost finding for fiscal year 1949) and the cost finding function has been given recognized status by the recent creation of a "Bureau of Accounts and Cost Finding."

[7] This subject is dealt with extensively in Pt. 1.

the economic allocation of traffic among the competing agencies cannot be achieved by strict application of relative cost standards in the regulation of minimum rates.

The second difficulty encountered in using cost standards for minimum rate control arises because of the technical obstacles to accurate cost finding in any complex industry. This is particularly true of railroad operation where a substantial portion of total cost is incurred in common for the movement of a wide variety of commodities.

As the Commission has observed:

If the minimum rate making power were intended by Congress to be used only in cases where the rate assailed had been proven with arithmetical exactitude to be less than the cost of service, the grant of that power would be ineffectual, because such a test of exact cost of service is impracticable of application to specific rates on a single commodity, and this has been recognized by the Supreme Court of the United States.[8]

Under such circumstances, the allocation of common costs to the movement of a particular commodity is necessarily based on a rather arbitrary formula or on estimates.[9] The resultant problems of cost finding have been accentuated by the character of interagency competition that has developed in recent years. Certain motor carriers, for example, specialize in the transporta-

---

[8] *Salt Cases of 1923*, 92 I.C.C. 388, 410.

[9] The theoretical aspects of cost determination so far as transportation rate making is concerned have been well-stated as follows:

"The significance of cost of service as opposed to value of service in rate making may be briefly summed up as follows: Cost-of-service considerations go principally to the apportionment of the (long-run variable) costs. Value-of-service or demand considerations go to the apportionment of the constant and joint costs.

"The assignment of the variable costs is fundamentally based on the relative use which the traffic in question makes of the carrier's plant and facilities. The apportionment of the constant costs is fundamentally based on a weighing of the effect which the rates themselves would have upon the movement of the traffic and the carrier's revenues. Of far-reaching significance in this latter connection has been the recognition and application of the principle that by reducing the rates on traffic having expansible (elastic) traffic volume, the contribution to the constant costs or revenue needs can be increased, within limits, beyond that attainable by limiting rate differentiation strictly to cost-of-service considerations." Ford K. Edwards, "Cost Analysis in Transportation," *American Economic Review*, Vol. 37, May 1947, p. 461.

tion of single commodities such as petroleum, household goods, and new automobiles. Any attempt to make direct comparison between such direct costs and the allocated costs of moving similar products by rail, in combination with numerous other commodities gives rise to sharp technical controversy.

And finally, the so-called value-of-service as contrasted with the cost-of-service concept of rate making has exerted a powerful influence in the development of the general rate structure with which the Interstate Commerce Commission must deal in deciding individual rate cases.[10]

Under these circumstances, it is not surprising to find that the Commission has followed a cautious and empirical course in the administration of minimum rate controls.[11] But what is more important, it is becoming increasingly apparent that there are inherent conflicts between: (1) the regulatory effort to achieve economic allocation of traffic by use of minimum rate control, and (2) government promotional programs which enable some carriers to base rates on partial costs. This problem has recently been highlighted by rate cases dealing with competitive conflicts between the railroads and barge lines.

*Rail-barge competition and the subsidy issue.* We noted

[10] The following statement of this development has the virtue of precision and accuracy:

"In the past, cost of service lurked in the background in the fixing of railroad rates, but the railroads used only rule-of-thumb methods in determining such cost and were chiefly interested in it from the standpoint of results in the aggregate. In fixing rates on a particular kind of traffic, they were more interested in what it would bear. More euphemistically, this has come to be known as giving consideration to the value of the service. The highest rates in relation to the cost of service were, I think, and speaking broadly, the carload rates on commodities capable of fairly heavy loading and of relatively high value. The present widespread competition from other modes of transportation, both public and private, has brought cost of service into the foreground and given it a much greater degree of importance. In adjusting rates between competing forms of transportation, specific knowledge of respective costs of service, so far as it is attainable, seems essential." Eastman, *American Economic Review*, p. 126.

[11] For example, that agency stated:

"Discretion and flexibility of judgment within reasonable limits have always attended the use of costs in the making of rates. Costs alone do not determine the maximum limits of rates. Neither do they control the contours of rate scales or fix the relations between rates or between rate scales. Other factors along with costs must be considered and given due weight in these aspects of rate making." *Class Rate Investigation, 1939*, 262 I.C.C. 447, 693.

above that the existence of subsidized transportation further complicates the inherently difficult task of allocating traffic by means of rate regulation. The issues of public policy involved in this troublesome problem have recently been brought into sharp focus by the Supreme Court which stated that:

It is . . . not within the province of the Commission to adjust rates, either to equalize the transportation cost of barge shippers with that of shippers who do not have access to barge service or to protect the traffic of railroads from barge competition. For Congress left the Commission no discretionary power to approve any type of rate which would reduce the "inherent advantage" of barge transportation in whole or in part.[12]

Thus, in effect, the Commission is under mandate to preserve the so-called "inherent advantages" of water competition regardless of whether those advantages stem from operating efficiency or from the fact that a substantial part of the cost of water transportation is borne by the general taxpayer and therefore not reflected in the rate charged the shipper. The Commission alluded to the bearing of this situation on its rate responsibilities:

In recent years, a comprehensive inland waterway system has been developed, largely at public expense, in connection with the Mississippi River and its tributaries, certain rivers in Alabama, and the intracoastal canals. The present proceeding is important not only as to the particular traffic under consideration but also insofar as it may provide administrative standards which may be used as guides in fitting barge transportation into the general rate structure, particularly on grain and grain products, under the governing statutory provisions, in fairness to all concerned, and in the public interest generally.[13]

The case under consideration involves the reshipment of grain from Chicago to eastern destinations by rail where the original movement of the grain from the producing areas to Chicago is by barge. It illustrates clearly the manner in which subsidized water transportation rates tend to erode the entire

[12] *Interstate Commerce Commission* v. *Mechling et al.*, 330 U.S. 567, 579, decided Mar. 31, 1947.
[13] *Grain Proportionals, Ex-Barge to Official Territory*, 262 I.C.C. 7, 10.

railroad rate structure, even in the areas not served by water transportation. On this point, the Commission found that:

The barge-rail rates are far below the all-rail rates from the same and other Illinois origins. This is an inequitable situation giving rise to requests for reductions in the all-rail rates from the Illinois and central territory origins, and it is difficult to see, with such extreme disparities, how such requests could properly be denied. . . . [T]here is a substantial production of corn in central territory. While the farmers therein did not appear at the hearing to show that they were hurt by this situation, such evidence was adduced by others in the same relative position. . . . This is what is meant by the statement . . . that the present ex-barge proportionals from Chicago jeopardize the all-rail rate structure.[14]

The background of this extended controversy is as follows: for many years before 1939, the railroads serving the Eastern Territory had applied to grain reshipped at Chicago to eastern points, a proportional rate 8½ cents lower than their local rates, regardless of whether the grain entered Chicago from western points by means of rail, barge, or lake. The result was that the barge-rail rates from a western point to eastern destinations were considerably below the all-rail rates from those points—the difference being accounted for by the lower rate over the barge portion of the through route. Consequently, when barge service from western grain localities in Chicago was resumed after 1933, there occurred a marked diversion of grain traffic from the railroads to water.[15]

In 1939 the eastern railroads filed schedules with the ICC imposing on so-called "ex-barge" grain the local rate from Chicago east, but allowing grain coming into Chicago by rail or lake to move to eastern destinations by rail 8½ cents per hundred pounds lower than the local rates from Chicago east. As the Court points out:

The result of this rate schedule would have been that, although barge lines could still have carried grain from the west to Chicago much more cheaply than the railroads could, by the time the grain

[14] The same, p. 20.
[15] Barge service from the grain section west of Chicago to that city was available from 1886 to 1907. It was discontinued in that year and not resumed until 1933. The same.

had been reshipped to New York or other eastern points, the barge-rail carriage would have been more expensive to the shipper than all-rail carriage. This would have put the barge lines at a competitive disadvantage with railroads in barge-served localities.[16]

After lengthy litigation in which the court did not pass on the legality of the rate differential under consideration,[17] the Commission found that the 8½ cent higher rate for ex-barge grain as proposed by the railroads in 1939 was unlawful and required cancellation of the proposed rate schedules. However, the Commission found that a rate on ex-barge grain from Chicago east 3 cents per hundred pounds higher than rates for ex-rail grain would be reasonable and lawful. And it provided that its order requiring cancellation of the originally proposed schedule was "without prejudice to the filing of new schedules in conformity with the findings herein."[18]

The rate schedule approved by implication would permit grain to move into eastern territory by combination of barge and rail shipment at a slightly lower rate than the all-rail movement. Such a rate differential was considered justified by the Commission since it would have permitted ex-barge grain "a fair opportunity to move in competition with lake-rail and all-rail traffic."[19] However, the Supreme Court condemned this arrangement because it meant that: ". . . the through barge-rail transportation would cost more than it would have if the through rates had accurately reflected the cheaper in-bound barge rates."[20]

We have dealt with this case at some length because it brings into sharp perspective one of the fatal defects in our current transportation policy. It demonstrates conclusively that rate regulation cannot be depended upon to remove the distorting and discriminatory elements that are injected into the transportation rate structure by government subsidies. The case

[16] 330 U. S. 567, 571.
[17] See 248 I.C.C. 307, *Interstate Commerce Commission* v. *Inland Waterways Corporation*, 319 U. S. 671.
[18] 262 I.C.C. 7, 33.
[19] The same, p. 29.
[20] 330 U. S. 567, 572.

under consideration represents an effort on the part of the ICC to protect railroad traffic from the eroding effects of subsidized water competition. The futility of the attempt is indicated not only by judicial disapproval but by the oblique character of the technique used by the ICC.

Traffic and revenues of the affected western carriers could not be protected by ordering a direct increase in the barge rates.[21] For the barge rates in question did not constitute unfair competition, being compensatory in the technical sense of covering all of the costs actually incurred by the water common carriers.[22] Apparently, the only course open to the Commission was to increase the rail rate on the Chicago-to-the-east combined barge-rail movement thus reducing the competitive advantage of the barge operators and tending to shift traffic to the western rail carriers. As to the validity of this indirect technique for equalizing competitive opportunity, the Supreme Court observed that: "If the western railroads need relief from the competition of barges, that is a question wholly unrelated to the rates of eastern roads."[23]

Although this dictum constitutes a rather narrow interpretation of general regulatory policy,[24] it represents current doctrine. And it is evident that the full Commission must now adopt the approach advocated by a dissenting opinion of one Commissioner in the original decision.

The only real solution of the problem, if any solution is called for, is to establish minimum rates for the boats and barges operating on the Illinois Waterway so as to protect the western rail lines against the competition thus created. These western railroads, however, have not made out such a case on this record. The boat lines are apparently prospering under the rates which they are now charging,

[21] See above discussion of the principles laid down by the ICC on this matter.

[22] The Commission found that "the barge rates yield fair returns to the barge carriers, and, for the purpose of this proceeding, may be accepted as reasonable." 262 I.C.C. 7, 19.

[23] 330 U. S. 567, 579.

[24] Justice Jackson dissented and Justice Frankfurter concurred in the dissenting opinion. The dissent was based primarily on the contention that the Court's decision deprived the Commission of "these discretionary powers to adjust through rates to general shipping conditions and rate structures." The same, p. 585.

and there seems to be no reason for putting a floor under those rates.[25]

But this "solution" actually guarantees that traffic will continue to be allocated on the basis of artificial standards.[26] This follows from the fact that a rate may be "compensatory" for barge operators and still fail by a wide margin to cover the full cost of performing that service, since general taxpayers rather than the shippers are bearing the cost of improving and maintaining the waterways and other necessary aids to navigation.

So long as this situation prevails, the regulatory agency is rendered powerless to guide the allocation of traffic between competing rail and water agencies in accordance with true relative costs and quality of service.

The situation is quite different where competitive rates must reflect the full cost of service. Thus, because motor carriers pay substantial fees for the use of publicly provided highways, the Commission has more nearly approximated the goal of fair and economical competition in the regulation of road-rail rates than in the case of rail-water competition. Moreover, the Commission has effectively prevented the type of rate competition that results only in the diversion of traffic from one carrier to another and the dissipation of transportation revenue.

*Dissipation of carrier revenue.* On this issue, the Commission has said, in effect, that no rail carrier may reduce a rate on a given commodity where the sole purpose and effect is to divert traffic from one carrier to another within a given rate group. The doctrine was invoked in order to prevent rate wars that

---

[25] 262 I.C.C. 7, 34.

[26] This is indicated by a recent decision of the ICC relative to the same type of problem. (An investigation of the rate structure in *Grain To, From and Within Southern Territory,* 270 I.C.C. 713-721, decided July 7, 1948.) The Commission reversed a previous decision that had prescribed proportional rates on ex-barge traffic from the major gateways to the south, which in some instances were higher than rates on corresponding traffic moving all-rail. In a current report, the Commission concluded that the ex-barge rates should not exceed those "concurrently applicable on ex-rail grain from those gateways to the same destinations." (The same, p. 720.) The Supreme Court's decision in the Mechling case discussed above was cited as a major reason for the Commission's reversal of its previous order.

would tend to "needlessly sacrifice the carriers' revenue." In the Lake Cargo Coal Case, for example, the petitioning rail carriers maintained that the proposed rates were above out-of-pocket cost and that it was their duty to stockholders and patrons "to initiate rates with a view to meeting competitive conditions and protecting their traffic, and that in publishing these rates they exercised a managerial function which belongs to them."[27]

The Commission disapproved the proposed rate reduction on the grounds that it could not permit one carrier to disrupt the entire interrelated rate structure.[28] Although the Commission's order in this case was set aside on other grounds, its right was upheld to prescribe minimum rates "to prevent ruinous rate wars and to guarantee reasonable earnings not only to the carriers affected but also to competing carriers who may labor under higher cost of doing business."[29]

Moreover, in recent cases involving highway and rail competition, the Commission has been reasonably successful in maintaining the so-called inherent advantage of rival carriers by the use of minimum rate regulation.

*Rate control and inherent advantage.* The Interstate Commerce Commission is required to administer its rate authority with a view to preserving the inherent advantage of each regulated carrier. However, the Commission has not interpreted this provision as a mandate to hold the rates of one carrier at an arbitrarily high level for the sole purpose of enabling another carrier (with higher costs) to compete for a share of the traffic.

One practical application of this principle is that the ICC will not force the railroads to raise a compensatory rate on a particular product in order to permit the higher-cost motor carriers to share the traffic. This issue was dealt with in the controversy between rail and motor carriers over rates on

[27] *Lake Cargo Coal,* 139 I.C.C. 367, 372. In this case the Chesapeake and Ohio and various other railroads serving that area proposed to reduce freight rates on bituminous coal from West Virginia mine areas to transshipment points at Toledo and Sandusky, Ohio.

[28] The same, p. 393.

[29] *Anchor Coal Co.,* v. *United States,* 25 Federal (2nd) 62.

petroleum products moving from points in California to points in Arizona. Motor carrier costs for this operation exceeded those of the rail carriers. But the motor carriers contended that the rail rates should be raised to a point above the level of motor carrier costs in order to permit the latter to participate in the movement. This contention was rejected by the ICC on the grounds that such action would "disregard the admonition of both the Interstate Commerce Act and the Motor Carrier Act to give due consideration 'to the need in the public interest of adequate and efficient . . . transportation service at the lowest possible cost consistent with the furnishing of such service.' "[30]

This decision was made under a rule of rate making that directed the ICC to "give due consideration, among other factors, *to the effect of rates on the movement of traffic;* to the need, in the public interest, of adequate and efficient railway transportation service at the lowest cost consistent with the furnishing of such service. . . ."[31] The Transportation Act of 1940 amended the rule of rate making and placed considerable emphasis on the maintenance of the "inherent advantages" of each form of transportation subject to the regulation. For this reason certain carriers have recently contended that rate regulation should be used by the Commission as a device for allocating traffic to each agency on the basis of its peculiar service characteristics rather than relative cost.[32]

The ICC, however, rejected this interpretation of the 1940 amendments and, in the exercise of its minimum rate powers,

[30] *Petroleum and Petroleum Products, Calif. to Ariz.,* 241 I.C.C. 21, 43.

[31] Amended by the Emergency Railroad Transportation Act, 1933, 48 Stat. 220. The Motor Carrier Act, 1935, carried similar standards of rate making. Italics supplied.

[32] Summarized by the Commission as follows:
"The trucking association contends, in effect, that we should now give less weight than in the past to costs of operation and competition as criteria of reasonableness, where we have under consideration the rates of competing modes of transportation subject to our jurisdiction. It insists that we should now consider the inherent advantage in respect of service of each such mode of transportation as paramount to other factors, prescribe rates necessary to preserve such advantage, and prevent other modes of transportation from attempting to overcome it by reducing their rates to out-of-pocket cost bases." *New Automobiles in Interstate Commerce,* decided Feb. 6, 1945, 259 I.C.C. 475, 539.

has continued to place major emphasis on relative cost.[33] Under this version of its statutory responsibility, the Commission has recently refused to restrain the railroads from reducing rates on new automobiles in their effort to halt the diversion of traffic to the motor carriers.[34]

The case under discussion also illustrates the intimate interrelationship among all phases of rate regulation under highly competitive conditions. For example, the most intensive rail-highway competition for automobile traffic is in the short haul from the manufacturing and assembling areas to the points of retail distribution. Highway competition is relatively less effective on the long rail movement from the Detroit manufacturing center to the more distant points of assembly or retail distribution.

Beginning in 1931, the railroads in an effort to protect their new automobile traffic against this increasing competition had established special commodity rates on the short-haul traffic (competitive) considerably lower proportionally than the class rates on the long-haul movement. This type of pricing naturally raises the question of discrimination—that is, whether or not the railroads are charging more than a reasonable rate on a

[33] " . . . it is of interest that the rule of rate making in section 15a has been recently amended so as to require us, in the exercise of our authority to prescribe just and reasonable rates, to 'give due consideration, among other factors, to the effect of rates upon the movement of traffic *by the carrier or carriers for which the rates are prescribed.* . . .' This admonition is repeated in sections 216 (i) and 307 (f), containing rules for rate making relating to motor and water carriers, respectively. The words which have been italicized for emphasis are of particular interest. They were not in either of the bills originally passed by the Senate and the House of Representatives but were added by the committee of conference. Their meaning, supported also by the legislative history, seems to be that no carrier should be required to maintain rates which would be unreasonable, judged by other standards, for the purpose of protecting the traffic of a competitor." *Seatrain Lines, Inc.,* v. *Akron, C. and Y. Ry. Co.,* 243 I.C.C. 199, 214.

[34] "It is obvious that rate reductions cannot be halted by the prescription of minimum rates unless the existing rates have fallen below a reasonable minimum level. According to the cost studies, the rates of the several forms of transportation are generally compensatory, except in scattered instances. Within reasonable limits the public is entitled to the reduced rates brought by competition. There is no showing that the rate structures under consideration threaten the financial stability of the carriers." *New Automobiles in Interstate Commerce,* 259 I.C.C. 475, 538.

noncompetitive traffic in order to compensate for losses incurred on the traffic moving under competitively reduced rates.[35] To guard against such possible discriminatory situations, the Commission prescribed a maximum reasonable rate and minimum loading requirements for the rail movement of new automobiles in carload lots.[36]

So far in this chapter we have considered only the problems encountered by the ICC in maintaining fair competition among rail, inland waterway, and highway transport agencies. Postwar developments have raised similar issues with respect to government policy affecting coastal and intercoastal shipping. And the problem has been further complicated by considerations of national security.

*Rail-coastal water competition and national security issues.* The attempt to restore coastal and intercoastal shipping to prewar status has again brought into prominence policy questions relating to rate and service competition between the railroads and coastal shipping enterprises.

For many years, low operating costs of the shipping companies made possible satisfactory earnings at rates considerably below the general level of rail charges for similar movements. As a general proposition, the railroads could not lawfully make selective rate reductions on commodities subject to effective competition of coastal shippers, for such reductions would normally violate the "long and short haul" clause of the Interstate Commerce Act (sec. 4) which makes it unlawful for a carrier to charge more in the aggregate for a shorter than for a longer haul where the service is being rendered under "substantially similar circumstances and conditions." However, the Commission was empowered in "special cases" to exempt carriers from the application of that provision.

[35] Development of the competitive rate structure for the movement of new automobiles since 1931 is described in the same, pp. 494-99.

[36] The same, p. 556. This case was set for rehearing and the portion dealing with maximum reasonable rail rates was amended by increasing the prescribed maximum from 75 to 85 per cent of corresponding first class rates and by reducing the minimum carloading requirements from 12,000 to 10,000 pounds. *New Automobiles in Interstate Commerce*, 263 I.C.C. 771, 781, decided Nov. 13, 1945.

Over a period of years, the Commission was persuaded to grant a substantial number of applications for relief from the fourth section prohibitions, thus giving the railroads greater freedom to meet the relatively unregulated water competition.[37] For example, with respect to the West Coast situation, the Commission granted substantial relief to the affected rail carriers in 1927,[38] and subsequently enlarged the coverage of that relief, observing that:

> The water competitive conditions along the Pacific coast necessitate the maintenance of rail rates on a basis lower than a reasonable maximum level to enable the rail carriers to participate in the port-to-port traffic. This is also true to a less extent on traffic to or from adjacent interior points.[39]

In 1946 the Maritime Commission and the War Shipping Administration, acting as operators of government-owned ships,[40] petitioned the Interstate Commerce Commission to investigate the reasonableness of railroad rates and practices insofar as they were competitive with domestic water carriers,[41] alleging that such rates were in violation of the Interstate Commerce Act in the following respects:

> . . . in many instances they are lower than necessary to meet water competition; many represent excessive reductions below normal rates; in some instances they are lower than rates heretofore condemned by the Commission because they did not meet the criteria established by the Commission of reasonably compensatory rates. Many existing competitive rates were authorized by the Commission

[37] It will be recalled that prior to 1940 the Interstate Commerce Commission had no jurisdiction over the rates, operating rights, or practices of water transportation.

[38] *Pacific Coast Fourth Section Applications*, 129 I.C.C. 3.

[39] *Pacific Coast Fourth Section Applications*, 190 I.C.C. 273, 285, decided Dec. 15, 1932.

[40] The War Shipping Administration was absorbed by the Maritime Commission on Sept. 1, 1946. In the meantime, the ICC had granted temporary authorization to the War Shipping Administration to conduct coastal and intercoastal water transport services. *War Shipping Administration Temporary Authority Application*, 260 I.C.C. 589.

[41] The request dated Mar. 21, 1946, signed by acting chairman of the U. S. Maritime Commission and acting administrator of the War Shipping Administration, carries the title: "Before the Interstate Commerce Commission—Petition —An Investigation into the Lawfulness and Reasonableness of Water Competitive Railroad Rates and Practices" (mimeo.).

to grant relief from the requirements of the Fourth Section of the Interstate Commerce Act, which relief is no longer justified in view of interim increases in transportation costs and other changed conditions.[42]

The Maritime Commission went on to say that:

As a result of these competitive practices the United States is now faced with a serious threat of annihilation, or at least very drastic curtailment, of water transportation in the domestic trades. The volume of tonnage handled by the water carriers is but a small fraction of the tonnage handled by the railroads. To the latter, with their huge reserves of non-competitive traffic, the gain or loss of such tonnage cannot be very significant, but to the water carriers it is a matter of life or death. The loss to them of this tonnage creates a threat of extinction—which . . . constitutes a grave menace to the nation.[43]

Although attributing the financial difficulties of the water lines partly to sharp increases in postwar operating costs, the Maritime Commission noted that even prior to the war the general economic condition of the water lines was unsound. Thus between 1928 and 1938, an aggregate deficit (after depreciation) of more than 40 million dollars had been suffered by some 42 major water lines.[44] And as late as 1940 the financial prospects were so unpromising that some operators withdrew from the service altogether. Having attributed the unsound finances of the water lines primarily to "depressed rail rates" and "repressive practices" of the railroads, the Commission was "compelled to the conclusion that successful and profitable operation of domestic shipping in the post-war period is not possible, even under the most favorable traffic conditions, unless readjustments are made in competitive rail rates to permit vitally necessary readjustments in water rates."[45]

The Interstate Commerce Commission found that the request of the maritime agency was so vague and generalized that an investigation based on the allegations of the petition

[42] The same, pp. 4-5.
[43] The same, p. 11.
[44] United States Maritime Commission, *Economic Survey of Coastwise and Intercoastal Shipping* (1939).
[45] Maritime Commission petition to the ICC, p. 3.

would be neither practical nor legal. Consequently, in May 1946 the ICC notified the petitioning agency that "more detailed precise reference to the rates sought to be involved was necessary."[46]

In the meantime, the ICC on its own motion reopened "virtually all" outstanding orders under the long and short haul provisions of section 4 involving water competition. In a countrywide order (July 19, 1946) the railroads were directed "to show cause" why outstanding relief that had been granted in the applications enumerated in the order should not be modified or vacated. As a result of this order,[47] about 40 rail carriers consented to rescission of outstanding relief; continuation of relief was ordered in 19 applications; and 32 others were set for hearing.[48] Subsequent hearings and ICC orders resulted in setting aside additional fourth section orders of long standing.[49]

The Commission's recent review of the rail-water competitive problem has not been limited to fourth section relief cases. The issue has been broadened to include investigation of transcontinental rail rates that are competitive with coastal and intercoastal shipping, as well as rail rates from interior points to certain Gulf and Pacific ports.[50] In the latter case the ICC went beyond the request of the Maritime Commission by including an investigation of the level of water rates as well as rail rates.

The issues that have arisen in these cases and the administrative performance of the Commission in disposing of them are significant for the purposes of this study for three reasons:

1. It has been demonstrated that the Commission will not

[46] *All-Rail Commodity Rates between Calif., Oreg., and Wash.*, 268 I.C.C. 515, 518, decided June 26, 1947.

[47] It involved 65 proceedings embracing 95 applications.

[48] *61st Annual Report of the Interstate Commerce Commission, 1947*, pp. 47-50.

[49] For example in *All-Rail Commodity Rates between Calif., Oreg., and Wash.*, 268 I.C.C. 515-46, the Commission vacated and set aside Fourth Section Orders Nos. 10425, 10688, 10722, 11365, and 14115. These orders embraced 15 "Pacific Coast Fourth Section Applications."

[50] The same, p. 518.

permit the railroads to use fourth section relief as an artificial device to stifle water competition. Outstanding relief orders have been vacated when the Commission has found that the "special conditions" on which the orders were originally based no longer prevail.

2. The Commission will not use its minimum rate powers for the sole purpose of requiring increases in the rates of one type of carrier in order to permit another type to participate in the traffic. Thus in the Citrus Fruit Case, the Commission refused to require an increase in compensatory railroad rates on these products even though the water lines contended that they could not compete effectively with the railroads at such rates.[51]

Apparently the Maritime Commission concurs in this interpretation of the ICC's responsibility, for the former agency objects primarily to rail rates that are "unreasonably low" per se, that is, not compensatory to the railroads.[52] It will be noted that the Commission has applied the same standards of minimum rate control to rail-water competition that have been generally used in controlling rail-highway competition. (See analysis of rates on new automobiles above.)

3. The apparently grave postwar competitive disabilities of coastal and intercoastal shipping present issues regarding national security requirements. According to the Maritime Commission, railroad competition threatens domestic water transportation with "annihilation, or at least very drastic curtailment." Although the Interstate Commerce Commission has taken positive steps to enforce the statutory requirements for fair competitive rates and practices between rail and water agencies, major issues remain unsolved. As Commissioner Aitchison stated with reference to the Commission's investigation of rail and water rates:

The questions presented in these proceedings are of major importance. They involve the broad question of the national policy

---

[51] *Citrus Fruit from Florida to North Atlantic Ports,* 266 I.C.C. 627, 635.
[52] 268 I.C.C. 515, 518.

concerning competition between rail and water carriers. There is wide divergence of opinion between shippers and carriers, as well as government agencies . . . as to what that policy is or should be.[53]

The major current difficulty arises because the relative cost position of the two competing agencies has apparently been reversed. Thus, until recently water transportation has generally been considered as having "inherent advantage" over rail transportation because of lower relative costs.[54] If coastal and intercoastal shipping cannot attract any substantial volume of traffic on the basis of regulated rate and service competition, the maintenance of a merchant marine adequate for the national defense will become progressively more difficult.

The controlling fact is that over 60 per cent of the tonnage of the prewar merchant marine was employed in the protected coastal and intercoastal operations. Consequently, if it develops that domestic shipping can no longer make any substantial contribution to the merchant marine deemed essential to national security, demand will undoubtedly arise for further subsidization of domestic shipping. As noted elsewhere, coastal and intercoastal operators, although ineligible for direct construction and operating subsidies under the Merchant Marine Act of 1936, have long been protected from foreign competition. And they enjoy a substantial amount of subsidy resulting from the purchase of government-owned vessels at nominal rates and various preferred credit arrangements. Therefore, additional subsidization would necessarily take the form of direct financial aid from the government.

Such a policy might contribute to national security insofar as an adequate merchant marine is concerned, but it would create even more serious problems with respect to other forms

[53] Statement of Clyde B. Aitchison, Chairman, Interstate Commerce Commission in *Proposed Amendments to the Ship Sales Act of 1946*, Hearings before the Subcommittee on Ship Sales, Charters, and Lay-ups of the House Committee on Merchant Marine and Fisheries, 80 Cong. 1 sess., 1947, p. 542.

[54] As Commissioner Aitchison observed: "This is now disputed as a matter of fact, even by one of the departments of the Government [Maritime Commission]. . . ." The same, p. 543.

of domestic transportation. In the light of our recent war experience, no one can seriously contend that the economic and financial health of the domestic water carriers or any other transport agency is more important to the effective prosecution of war than is the maintenance of an efficient railroad system.[55]

The railroads are already subject to a substantial amount of subsidized competition. Manifestly, if the range and effectiveness of this competition is extended, the government will sooner or later be faced with a "railroad crisis." For no privately owned and financed enterprise can permanently survive the erosion of traffic and revenue that results from heavy and continuing subsidization of its competitors. Eventually, the government would have to choose between extending compensating subsidies to the railroads or transferring them to public ownership or its equivalent.

We have already seen how subsidies for waterways work against equitable regulation of competitive rail-water rates. Similar problems are emerging in air transport regulation.

## II. RATE REGULATION UNDER THE CIVIL AERONAUTICS ACT

Air transportation is governed by statutory rate standards that correspond to those applicable to other forms of transportation. However, as previously noted, there are two essential differences between the purposes and practical effect of rate regulation as administered by the Civil Aeronautics Board and the Interstate Commerce Commission, respectively.

*Contrast between ICC and CAB rate regulation.* First, the CAB controls air transport rates with the single purpose of promoting the development of air transportation. It need consider only the effect of rate levels on the aggregate revenues of the air transportation industry and the effect of rate relationships on the competitive position of one airline as compared with another. By contrast, the Interstate Commerce Commission, in addition to being charged with similar responsibilities

---

[55] See Pt. 1 for discussion of relative importance of transportation agencies to national security.

for railroad, highway, water, and pipeline transportation, is under statutory obligation to maintain fair standards of rate and service competition among all these agencies.

Second, the CAB has available in the form of mail payments a positive device for controlling pricing policy in the field of air transportation. For this reason it has great flexibility in rate determination, and, to the extent that it sees fit, can materially influence the rate and direction of development in the industry by giving or withholding mail subsidies. The ICC is not equipped with any corresponding administrative tool and must administer its rate making responsibility within the limits set by interagency competition, general economic conditions, and in accordance with accepted principles of public utility regulation.

Until recently the Civil Aeronautics Board has concentrated on the establishment of route patterns and administration of air-mail payments. As a general rule, the airlines have been left free to set passenger fares and quality of service in accordance with managerial estimates of effective demand for the service. However, the postwar expansion of air transportation into the cargo field forced the CAB into the area of minimum rate control. It was thereby confronted with the perennially troublesome problem of defining destructive rate competition.

*Air cargo and minimum rate control.* Air freight transportation is a product of the postwar era. Wartime experience proved the feasibility of moving cargo by air, and subsequent improvement in aircraft efficiency and cargo-handling practices suggested that rates could be reduced to a level that would attract a considerable volume of traffic. The commercial prospect was sufficiently promising so that a group of newly-formed carriers inaugurated exclusive freight services without making any claim for direct government support in the form of mail payments.

Although not permitted to offer regular common carrier service, these all-cargo carriers accounted for approximately one half of the freight handled by the domestic air transport industry during 1947. The publication in mid-1947 of legal tariffs showing the details of air cargo rates for certificated and non-certificated carriers set off a rate war between the established carriers (the certificated passenger and air-mail companies) and the new enterprises specializing in air cargo. Resultant rate reductions were of substantial proportions and were instituted in the face of generally rising price trends and at the same time that rates on other traffic were being raised.

As a result of these developments, the Civil Aeronautics Board launched an investigation in October 1947 to determine whether or not the air cargo rates contained in specified air freight tariffs were "unjust or unreasonable, or unjustly discriminatory, or unduly preferential, or unduly prejudicial."[56] After lengthy hearings the Board concluded that:

. . . many of the existing rates were established almost wholly on the basis of competitive considerations and that the entire freight rate structures of a number of the most directly competitive carriers in relation to cost are so low as to endanger the sound development of air freight and to undermine the financial condition of the carriers.[57]

In the course of its deliberations the CAB explored the various concepts of rate making, ranging from a unique "no-cost theory"[58] to the familiar standards of fully allocated costs and value of service. With respect to the function of cost finding and allocation in "sound rate making" policy, the Board observed that:

It is a commonly accepted principle in all transportation rate making and a requirement to insure the continued existence of any transportation service that the rate levels have a reasonable relationship to attainable cost levels.

We are of the opinion that economic considerations do not demand that at all times the rates for any class of traffic or type of service must cover the fully allocated cost of carrying that traffic or providing that service; rather that rates must at all times be reasonably related to costs. The tests of reasonableness must include recognition of variations in the ability of traffic to carry a full share of

[56] *Air Freight Forwarder Assn. et al.*, Motions, 8 C.A.B. 469, 476, decided Oct. 2, 1947.

[57] *Air Freight Rate Investigation*, C.A.B. Docket No. 1705 et al., decided Apr. 21, 1948, p. 5 (mimeo.).

[58] The same, p. 8. Apparently some of the smaller certificated carriers contended in effect that freight should be carried free in the unused cargo space of passenger flights.

costs at different stages in the development of that traffic, the effect of low rates in generating new traffic and the resultant effect of increased volume on reductions in unit costs.

But belief in the justifiableness of promotional rates does not lead to endorsement of rates which are uneconomic in character and depart from all regard for cost.[59]

It would appear, therefore, that the Board favored the use of a relative cost standard in the solution of this competitive problem. It is clear, however, that neither the Board nor members of the industry had anticipated the need for accurate cost data. For example, the Board found that all the cost estimates submitted by industry had defects, "most of which were frankly admitted by their sponsors." And it also observed "that the development of more reliable cost data will become increasingly necessary as the air freight service expands."[60]

In the absence of any better standards, the Board eventually concluded that "the costs of the non-certificated carriers, constituting as they do the only pure freight cost available, are the most usable guide to the determination of the reasonableness of the rates under investigation."[61] It therefore prescribed legal minimum cargo rates for the entire industry closely approximating those previously published by the all-cargo carriers. The Board's decision was obviously influenced by its desire to protect the all-cargo experiment from possible suppression by the established carriers. On this point it observed that the entry of the specialized carriers into the air freight field without dependence on direct government subsidy "constitutes an experiment of great importance to the public as a test of whether a specialized air freight industry can be developed on the basis of its own economic ability to exist."[62]

Two aspects of this case are of primary interest from the standpoint of general transportation policy and administrative organization. First, as long as one segment of the air transportation industry is subsidized directly—or is eligible for subsidy—

[59] The same, p. 7.
[60] The same, p. 10.
[61] The same, p. 14.
[62] The same, p. 6.

and another is attempting to operate on a self-supporting basis, any effort to control competitive rates on the basis of relative cost cannot hope to achieve the precision and authority necessary to make cost finding an effective regulatory tool. While giving official approval to cost standards, the Board in reality would be forced to resolve the competitive issues by the exercise of more or less arbitrary judgment.

For example, considerable doubt exists regarding the accuracy of the term "service rate" used by the Board to characterize the current basis of air-mail payments for major airlines. The CAB contends that "the argument that the tariffs filed by the certificated carriers are supported by mail subsidies is wholly unsound."[63] The Board points out that the chief competitors of the all-cargo carriers do receive 45 cents a ton-mile for the carriage of the mails but that this is a "service rate— a rate designed and determined to compensate them only for the costs of carrying the mail plus reasonable compensation upon the investment devoted to that service."[64]

On this question, the Post Office Department has asserted that: "While the use of this connotation, at the present time may have applicability for some of the so-called service rate carriers, this situation has certainly been far from true in the past."[65] In support of its assertion, the Department points out that the admitted cost of handling mail in 1944 was 20.6 cents per ton-mile, yet the service rate in effect at that time was 60 cents a ton-mile. Moreover, United Air Lines is now petitioning the Board for a mail pay rate of $1.25 per ton-mile. "Such a request must include a demand for substantial subsidy."[66]

We are not primarily interested in the quantitative aspects of the debate between these two official agencies. The point is

[63] 8 C.A.B. 469, 473.
[64] The same. As indicated in Chap. 10, in March 1948 the CAB increased the rate of air-mail payment for the so-called Big Five carriers resulting in an estimated effective rate ranging from 55.7 to 70.9 cents per ton-mile.
[65] *Brief of the Post Office Department to the Civil Aeronautics Board,* in Docket No. 1705 et al., (*Air Freight Rate Case*), Mar. 25, 1948, p. 7 (mimeo.)
[66] The same.

that we are here witnessing the development of another area of government regulation where potential or actual subsidy injects controversy, speculation, and instability into the public control over transport enterprises.

The second significant aspect of the air cargo case relates to the long-range competitive relations between air transportation and other media in the freight field. If the anticipated expansion of air cargo occurs, some way must be found to establish equitable standards of rate and service competition among air, railroad, and highway agencies. As noted above, the Interstate Commerce Commission in discharging its responsibility with respect to rail, highway, and water agencies has been forced to give increasing weight to cost standards as a guide to competitive rate control. The Civil Aeronautics Board is moving in the same direction.[67] But so long as these standards are administered in separate agencies and complicated by subsidy consideration, there is no assurance that traffic will in reality be allocated among competing agencies in accordance with relative efficiency and economy.

### III. SUMMARY

It would seem evident from the analysis up to this point that uniformly fair standards of transport competition cannot be maintained under current federal policies. Some forms of transportation enjoy the free or partially free use of publicly financed facilities. Others must finance their entire plant from operating revenues. As a result, competitive rates do not in all cases reflect the total real costs of performing the service. Shippers are interested in comparative rates rather than relative economic costs. Traffic therefore tends to be allocated in accordance with the amount of government aid enjoyed by each agency rather than on the basis of true relative cost and quality of service.

[67] The CAB did not inaugurate specialized cost analysis work until December 1946. During fiscal year 1947-48 five positions were budgeted for this work, with an increase to nine for fiscal year 1948-49. So far, the cost analysis work is limited to the certificated carriers. (Information supplied by Civil Aeronautics Board Information Division.)

There appears to be only one valid and direct solution for this problem. The rates of all competing agencies must be made to reflect the true economic cost of performing transportation services. Such cost must cover the capital and maintenance expenditures made by government in providing physical facilities and service as well as the operating and capital costs incurred by private enterprises that actually provide the transportation services to the public.

If private enterprise in transportation is to be maintained, this principle of user support must be uniformly applied to all forms of transport that compete for traffic in the domestic market. A superficially persuasive case can be made for government subsidies as the most dependable way to meet certain national security requirements. But in most instances it will be found on close analysis that one subsidy begets another. In the long run, more problems are created than are solved.

## CHAPTER XIII

## RATE REGULATION AND RAILROAD EARNINGS

In the two preceding chapters we have discussed the types of rate regulation that are primarily designed to prevent discrimination and to set the standards of fair competition. Of course, all forms of regulation affect the financial condition of the carriers. Thus, since 1906, when the Interstate Commerce Commission was first given power to prescribe maximum rates for the future, there has been a steady expansion of federal power over the financial fortunes of transport agencies.[1] However, it was not until 1920 that the government assumed positive responsibility for adjusting the general level of transportation rates with a view of satisfying the revenue needs of the carriers. The effect of this type of public control on railroad earnings is the subject of the present chapter.

Between 1920 and 1933 the Commission was, in effect, directed by the statutory rule of rate making to adjust the general level of railroad rates in such a way as to permit the carriers to earn a fair return on their investment.[2] This period was characterized not only by a beneficent attitude on the part of the government with respect to the legal rights of the carriers to fair earnings, but by an assumption that the railroads retained a practical monopoly in the domestic transportation field.

The Emergency Railroad Transportation Act of 1933 abandoned any official idea of attaining quantitative precision in general rate regulation. The act adopted a new general rule of rate making which, in effect, discarded the idea that rates could be adjusted by governmental action so as to provide some

---

[1] Under the Hepburn Act of 1906 (34 Stat. 589), the Commission for the first time was expressly vested with power to "determine and prescribe by order a [railroad] rate, regulation, or practice for the future." *Interstate Commerce Acts Annotated,* Vol. 1, p. 79. However, it was not until 1910 with passage of the Mann-Elkin Act (36 Stat. 539) that the Commission was empowered to suspend new rate schedules filed by the carriers pending investigation of their reasonableness.

[2] Set by the ICC at 5.75 per cent of fair value.

specific rate of return upon a precisely measured property valuation. The criteria substituted were highly generalized providing merely that:

. . . In the exercise of its power to prescribe just and reasonable rates the commission shall give due consideration, among other factors, to the effect of rates on the movement of traffic; to the need, in the public interest, of adequate and efficient railway transportation service at the lowest cost consistent with the furnishing of such service; and to the need of revenues sufficient to enable the carriers, under honest, economical, and efficient management, to provide such service.[3]

In 1940 the portion of the rule of rate making dealing with the effect of rates on traffic movement was amended to read:

. . . In the exercise of its power to prescribe just and reasonable rates the commission shall give due consideration, among other factors, to the effect of rates on the movement of traffic *by the carrier or carriers for which the rates are prescribed;* . . .[4]

The manifest purpose of this statutory restriction on the Commission's discretion was to assure water and motor carriers that the Commission would not be permitted to establish arbitrarily high rates for water and highway services in order to protect rail traffic and revenues.

### I. THE COMMISSION ASSUMES FUNCTIONS OF MANAGEMENT

In reality, the congressional attempts to write tangible standards into the rule of rate making have had little practical effect on the Commission's handling of so-called revenue rate cases. From 1920 to date the Commission, regardless of variations in the rule of rate making, has in effect served as the board of directors for the nation's railroads with respect to general pricing policies. In performing this function the Commission has consistently reserved the right to substitute its business judgment for that of railroad management.

With only one exception since 1920, the Commission has de-

---

[3] Sec. 15a (2), *Interstate Commerce Acts Annotated,* Vol. 9, p. 7708.
[4] The same, Vol. 11, p. 9281. Italics added. The Interstate Commerce Act now includes comparable provisions applicable to motor carriers under Pt. 2, sec. 216 (i) and to carriers by water under Pt. 3, sec. 307 (f).

cided general rate (revenue) cases on the basis of its own judgment regarding the probable effect of particular rate adjustments on: (1) the general economy of the country, (2) the competitive position of the railroads, and (3) public relations of the railroads. The one exception is found in the first general rate case to come before the Commission after passage of the 1920 act. Under the influence of the positive congressional mandate and generally good business conditions, the Commission granted freight and passenger rate increases in amounts calculated to produce a 6 per cent return on the aggregate fair value of the carriers' property.[5] Apparently, at that time it found no reason to question the business judgment of the carriers as to the probability of securing the authorized amount of increased revenues from the level of charges proposed. However, in every subsequent general rate case of any significance, the Commission has interpreted its responsibility to maintain "just and reasonable" rates as a sweeping congressional mandate to protect both the railroad industry and the general economy from the possible results of what was deemed to be imprudent managerial pricing policies.

Thus when the 1921 recession cut into railroad earnings, the Commission ordered a general rate reduction stating that: "High rates do not necessarily mean high revenues, for, if the public can not or will not ship in normal volume, less revenue may result than from lower rates."[6] On other occasions the ICC has refused to grant requested rate increases because the carriers failed to demonstrate the existence of any financial emergency. This holding was made despite the fact that the *requested* level of rates was sufficient only to produce the "legal" rate of return amounting to 5.75 per cent on the value of the railroad properties affected.[7]

Throughout the thirties the Commission used its authority freely to impose on railroad management rate policies which were deemed best adapted to current economic conditions and

[5] *Increased Rates, 1920,* 58 I.C.C. 220-260 (1920).
[6] *Reduced Rates, 1922,* 68 I.C.C. 676, 732.
[7] *Revenues in Western District,* 113 I.C.C. 3-43 (1926).

the long-run interests of the railroads. In 1938, for example, the Commission severely criticized the pricing policies adopted by the carriers during the early stages of the depression.

In 1931, at a time when traffic and the general price level both were falling every day and competition with other forms of transportation was growing apace, the railroads sought a horizontal increase of 15 percent in all rates. In the circumstances we found that rates so increased would be unjust and unreasonable, but we did authorize a comprehensive system of lesser emergency surcharges.[8]

Obviously, the Commission's dictum that the level of rates requested by the carriers would be "unjust and unreasonable" was not based on a finding of excessive profits, for the expected earnings would have fallen short of a satisfactory, much less "legal," rate of return on the official valuation of the carriers' property. On the contrary, the Commission disapproved because it felt that the carriers were displaying bad business judgment by attempting to extract added revenue from the shipping public under the prevailing circumstances. According to the ICC, the railroad pricing policy was defective because:

(1) . . . at a time when transportation costs are of vital consequence to every industry it will stimulate new competitive forces already rapidly developing; (2) . . . it will alienate or impair the friendly feeling toward the railroads on the part of the people of the country which is essential to adequate legislation for their protection and the proper regulation of all forms of transportation in the public interest, and (3) . . . it will disturb business conditions and an already shell-shocked industry, and accelerate the tendency toward a localization of production.[9]

Growing sensitivity of the transportation rate structure to competitive forces eventually became one of the dominant factors in the Commission's rate policy. In 1938 it observed that:

. . . particularly since the enactment of the motor carrier act in 1935, our opportunities for observation have been multiplied in intensity and scope, and the keenness of competition continually has forced on our attention the effect of increased or reduced charges in

---

[8] *52nd Annual Report of the Interstate Commerce Commission, 1938,* p. 6.
[9] *Fifteen Percent Case, 1931,* 178 I.C.C. 539, 575.

influencing the movement of traffic by one or another of the several competing forms of transport agencies.[10]

In final analysis the Commission took the position that it could discharge its statutory standards for maintaining "just and reasonable" rates through no other process than by weighing the carriers' revenue needs against "the probable effect of increases of the existing rates upon the future movement of traffic, as developed by consideration of the ability or willingness of individual shipping interests to meet such increased costs."[11] All important revenue cases presented to the Commission in the postwar period have involved identical issues. And the Commission has continued to function as a board of directors for the railroads in matters affecting general rate policies.

Before analyzing the issues of transportation policy created by the situation just described, it should be noted that for some curious reason the Commission contends that its administration of general rate cases involves no infringement of managerial functions.

We have often referred to the fact that we are not managers of the railroads and have taken the position that we ought not to interfere with those who are entrusted with management on matters which are not controlled by law but must be determined in the last analysis by wise administrative policy and judgment. That is still our view.[12]

But the record shows that the Commission reserves the right to decide what constitutes the exercise of "wise" business judgment. For example, in the 1931 decision referred to above, the Commission explains in the following terms the substitution of its own judgment for that of the carriers with respect to the effect of general economic conditions on the productivity of given rate levels:

But here reliance upon the judgment of the executives as to the

[10] *Fifteen Percent Case 1937-1938* (Ex Parte 123), 226 I.C.C. 41, 78.
[11] The same.
[12] *Fifteen Percent Case, 1931,* 178 I.C.C. 539, 576.

revenue effect of an increase in rates is much weakened by their failure to adduce any substantial reasons for their judgment and the definite withholding of the best available information on this point in their possession, namely, the information of their traffic departments. . . .

On the other hand we have a mass of definite and concrete evidence from the shippers on this point of revenue effect which stands in the record uncontradicted by anything other than general assertions. Five of our members heard this evidence, although none heard it all, and they had the opportunity of appraising the character and sincerity of the witnesses. In our opinion, this evidence is entitled to great weight.[13]

A more forthright explanation of the dilemma faced by the Commission in revenue cases was supplied by the late Commissioner Joseph B. Eastman:

We have said that . . . "it is no part of our duty to interfere with management in the fixing of rates when the question is only one of what is wise or unwise in the exercise of sound business judgment." The difficulty here is that I am left by the record in great doubt as to whether the proposal to increase all rates 15 percent is an exercise of the "sound business judgment" of the managements.[14]

In final analysis then, the Commission does not grant as a matter of right the prerogative of private management to exercise its own business judgment on matters which the Commission admits can be decided only by the application of "wise administrative policy and judgment." On the contrary, the carriers are permitted to translate their business judgment into general rate policies only through the process of convincing the Commission that such managerial judgments are sound.

If for some reason spokesmen for the carriers fail to convince a majority of the 11 commissioners that a particular rate proposal will not contribute unduly either to inflation or deflation; will not divert traffic to the railroads' competitors; or will not unduly offend public opinion, the record shows that the Commission will substitute its judgment for that of management and

[13] The same.
[14] Concurring opinion of Commissioner Eastman in *Fifteen Percent Case*, *1937-38*, 226 I.C.C. 41, 152.

adjust the rate levels accordingly.[15] We can find no alternative interpretation of the Commission's official record in dealing with general level rate cases.

## II. SIGNIFICANCE OF DIVIDED AUTHORITY
### OVER BUSINESS DECISIONS

The division of authority and responsibility over general rate policies has produced serious problems. First, the attempt of the Commission to discharge exacting managerial responsibilities by the use of inflexible and legalistic procedures has resulted in intolerable delays in disposing of general rate cases. The immediate consequence has been a serious impairment of the carriers' financial position. Second, the division of responsibility threatens the long-term prospects for survival of the carriers as privately financed enterprises.

*Procedural delays and immediate financial consequences.* The Interstate Commerce Commission has gained an enviable reputation for procedural impartiality. It has been punctilious in permitting anyone with a legitimate interest in a particular case to have a full and fair hearing before the Commission. This effort to adhere to statutory requirements for a fair hearing and thus to avoid reversal of decisions by the courts has gradually led the Commission into a legalistic and ponderous method of conducting its business.

The traditional ICC hearing, patterned on the procedure of the common law court, although characterized by excessive "advocacy," slowness, and high cost, apparently worked fairly well for the restrictive type of regulation that was administered by the ICC prior to 1920. And, as a former commissioner observed, the procedure was "comfortable" for all concerned. But growth in the scope and complexity of the Commission's work made the traditional procedure unworkable.

This form of procedure, unmodified, results in records of unbear-

---

[15] We are not here concerned with the complex issues of rate relationships that complicate all general rate cases. A proposal to make a horizontal percentage increase in the general level of rates inevitably brings into question large numbers of rate adjustments previously prescribed by the Commission dealing both with maximum reasonable individual rates and rate relationships.

able size, and inevitably results in the consumption of so much time as to defeat the primary purpose for which the administrative agency was created, when a nation-wide or even a great issue of lesser scope is to be heard and determined. If the controversies before the Commission are to be settled well and with even reasonable promptness, the traditional type of "hearing" must be modernized or a substitute found. Always we must have in mind that the Constitution and the Act must be observed, and that the procedure is fair, and is recognized by the public as being fair. In some way the volume of the records must be condensed, and the time consumed in making the facts known of record must be shortened, while preserving the essentials insisted upon by law.[16]

Under the pressure of an increasing workload the Commission has for many years been attempting to break away from the inflexibilities of the traditional hearing. It has made an important discovery, although belatedly, that the "common-law court system of trial is not always a suitable pattern for an administrative hearing—and often is quite unsuitable and must be modified materially."[17] But despite procedural improvement, the Commission has not succeeded in developing any method of disposing of general rate cases, or others embracing major issues, with any acceptable degree of expedition.

Because of rapidly increasing material and labor costs since the end of the war, delay in obtaining compensating adjustments in rates has been especially serious to the railroads. The Commission's treatment of two recent general freight rate cases clearly indicates the nature of the managerial responsibility assumed by the Commission and the resulting financial implications for the railroads.

1946 Increased Freight Rates (Ex Parte 162). On April 3, 1946 the railroad operating brotherhoods (15 nonoperating and 3 operating) received an arbitration award granting a substantial increase in hourly wage rates. The bulk of this increase was made retroactively effective to January 1, 1946.[18]

[16] Address of Commissioner Clyde B. Aitchison, Chairman, Interstate Commerce Commission, before Chicago Chapter of the Association of ICC Practitioners, Nov. 7, 1947, Palmer House, Chicago.

[17] The same.

[18] National Mediation Board Case A-2215 Arb. 61 and 62. The final settle-

The resultant increase in total railroad labor costs for 1946 was estimated at 680 million dollars.

In order to compensate for known and anticipated increases in labor and materials costs, the railroads filed on April 15, 1946, a petition for an increase of approximately 22 per cent in the general level of freight rates. After so-called "emergency hearings," the Commission on June 20 granted an interim increase of approximately 6 per cent to become effective July 1, 1946.[19] (See Appendix A, Table 13.) Extensive hearings and arguments on the permanent aspect of the case were held regionally and in Washington from July 22 to September 26, 1946. Finally, on December 5, 1946 the Commission granted an additional 11.5 per cent increase in the general level of freight rates to become effective January 1, 1947.[20]

Thus a full year had elapsed between the time the railroads felt the impact of increased costs and the date on which they were permitted by the ICC to increase freight rates by anything like a corresponding amount. It is difficult to find an adequate explanation for this extreme time lag. For the controlling facts were so strikingly clear that any prolonged and formal hearing designed to "inform the Commission as to the facts" was not only unnecessary but was destined to produce delay.

What did the Commission learn from the July-September hearings that was not or could not have been determined from the May hearings? In short, what facts or circumstances justified a 17 per cent increase in freight rates effective January 1, 1947, as against a 6 per cent increase effective July 1, 1946? The two major elements of cost, labor and materials, that controlled the December decision were known as firmly in June as in December. The only major speculative element was the anticipated level of traffic. The carriers' traffic estimate for the last half of 1946 indicated that the railroads as a whole, and

---

ment of the wage dispute was made on May 25, 1946, and provided for a 16-cents-per-hour increase retroactive to between January 1 and May 21, and for an 18½-cents-per-hour increase effective from May 22, 1946.

[19] Increased Railway Rates, Fares, and Charges, 264 I.C.C. 695-752.

[20] Increased Railway Rates, Fares, and Charges, 266 I.C.C. 537-623.

particularly certain carriers, could escape serious financial difficulties only by an immediate and substantial increase in the general level of their rates.

In fact the Commission's delay in deciding these cases obviously contributed to the financial deterioration of the regulated carriers. Between January 1, 1946 and January 1, 1947, the working capital of Class I railroads was reduced from approximately 1,643 million dollars to 1,257 million dollars, or 23.5 per cent. A substantial amount of this reduction was occasioned by the extreme distortion in cost-price relations brought about by the Commission's unhurried handling of the rate case.[21] And despite near-capacity operations, Class I carriers as a whole realized a return of only 2.75 per cent on their investment. This compared with a rate of 2.23 per cent for the 1930-34 period which includes three of the most disastrous operating years in modern railroad history. (See chart p. 282.)

Moreover, this average figure does not reveal the true impact of the 1946 cost-price relations on individual railroads, for in that year, 29 of the 131 Class I railroads failed to earn fixed charges (suffered a deficit of net income).[22] And, even though total railroad capitalization had been scaled down extensively as a result of financial reorganization, almost one half (45 per cent) of the total amount of stock outstanding in 1946 failed to yield any dividends. Although of less serious immediate consequence, the 1946 difficulties of the railroads in attaining rate adjustments were experienced again in 1947.

1947 Increased Freight Rates (*Ex Parte 166*). Against the background of unsatisfactory 1946 financial results and rapidly increasing operating costs during the first half of 1947, the carriers filed another petition for increased freight rates on July 3, 1947. (See Appendix A, Table 15.) The petition was set for hearing by the ICC for September 9, 1947. In the meantime,

[21] It will be remembered that during the same period the announcement of wage increases for other industries where industry-wide bargaining prevailed (steel, coal, automobiles, etc.) was almost invariably followed immediately by announcement of compensating price increases.

[22] This includes the New York Central and the Pennsylvania Railroad, two of the nation's largest carriers.

sharp increases had occurred in the cost of major railroad operating supplies. Also, an arbitration board had awarded the nonoperating railroad employees a substantial increase in wage rates effective September 1, 1947.[23]

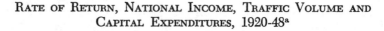

RATE OF RETURN, NATIONAL INCOME, TRAFFIC VOLUME AND CAPITAL EXPENDITURES, 1920-48[a]

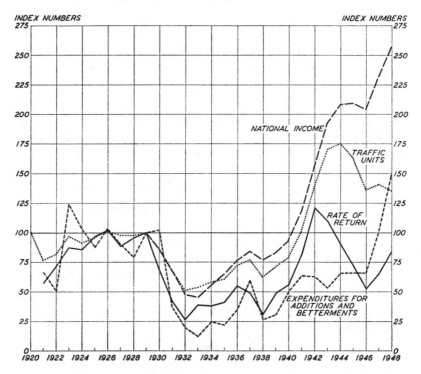

[a] See App. A, Table 14 for supporting data.

An amended railroad petition called for an increase in the general level of freight charges amounting to approximately 27 per cent. Again the carriers as a whole were faced with an emergency situation, one requiring a prompt restoration of balance between income and outgo.[24] Consequently, their

[23] National Mediation Board Case A-2595, Arb. 91.

[24] The seriousness of the plight confronting the individual carriers was dramatized by the position of the New York, New Haven and Hartford. In September

spokesmen concentrated on obtaining promptly an interim increase of 10 per cent. The initial hearings before the ICC were devoted largely to argument on this point. This was clearly an expedient to avoid repetition of the 1946 experience—not an admission that the requested 27 per cent increase was a mere bargaining figure. Carrier witnesses contended that even though the interim increase of 10 per cent were granted by the Commission and made effective September 15, 1947 (six days after opening of the hearing), the amount of revenue produced would compensate the carriers only for added pay-roll and material costs incurred after July 3, 1947. In short, even with the interim increase, the financial position of the carriers at the end of 1947 would be the same as it would have been had the wage and cost levels of July 3, 1946, prevailed during the remainder of the year.

The interim decision of the Commission granting the carriers an increase of approximately 8.9 per cent was made October 6, effective October 13. After further extensive hearing and argument, the Commission on December 29, 1947, issued a second interim report modifying the earlier interim order by authorizing a general increase of 20 per cent in the basic rates, effective January 5, 1948. And in a supplemental report adopted April 13, 1948, the Commission authorized general increases in the basic rates of 30 per cent within Eastern Territory; 25 per cent within Southern Territory and from, to, and within Zone 1 of Western Trunk-Line Territory, and also interterritorially, and 20 per cent within the remainder of Western Territory, subject to stated limitations as maxima.[25] These increases superseded the two previous interim authorizations and brought the total increase in basic freight rates authorized by the Commission on the basis of *Ex Parte 166* proceedings up

---

1947 this carrier was emerging from financial reorganization after 12 years of operating in the hands of the courts. Despite a substantial reduction in total capitalizations (approximately 17 per cent), the New Haven had no prospect of earning fixed charges at existing rates during the first quarter of its operation as a "solvent carrier." Revised statement of Howard S. Palmer, Trustee and President of the New York, New Haven and Hartford Railroad Company, for the hearing before ICC Division 2, Sept. 9, 1947, in *Ex Parte No. 166* (mimeo.).

[25] *Increased Freight Rates, 1947*, 270 I.C.C. 93, 98, decided Apr. 13, 1948.

to approximately the level originally requested by the carriers in the supplemental and amended petition of September 5, 1947.[26]

The fact remains that the relief requested on the basis of September 1947 labor and operating costs was not realized by the carriers until May 1, 1948—a lag of about eight months. The "final" report on *Ex Parte 166* was not issued until July 27, 1948—or almost eleven months after the original petition was filed. Although interim relief of less than 10 per cent was effective during the last two and one-half months of 1947, the financial results for the entire year 1947 were only slightly better than 1946. The average rate of return increased from 2.75 per cent to 3.41 per cent. (See Appendix A, Table 14.) Again the average figure obscures the plight of individual companies. Approximately the same number of carriers (33 in 1947 as compared with 26 in 1946) failed to make fixed charges and 38 of the Class I carriers earned less than 2 per cent on their investment. (See chart p. 337.)

A similar pattern of lag between rising costs and rate adjustments occurred during 1948. Negotiations for increased rates of pay, changes in the work week and working conditions resulted in additions to the railroad labor costs at an estimated rate of 650.6 million dollars annually.[27]

[26] The Commission issued a "final" report on further consideration on July 27, 1948, which would increase Class I railroad revenues from freight about 67.4 million dollars on an annual basis above the rates in effect as a result of three interim increases. In this report, the Commission prescribed an increase of 15 per cent in charges for protective services, instead of 10 per cent as previously authorized, and increased the maxima on many commodities. There was a reduction in permitted increase from 25 per cent to 22½ per cent in rates between Western Territory other than Zone I of Western Trunk-Line Territory and Zone I of Western Trunk-Line Territory. *Increased Freight Rates, 1947*, 270 I.C.C. 403-72, decided July 27, 1948.

[27] These are preliminary data from Association of American Railroads. Figure includes additional pay-roll taxes due to increase in the rate of tax effective Jan. 1, 1949.

Agreements were reached with conductors and railway trainmen on Oct. 4, 1948, and with the nonoperating organizations on Mar. 20, 1949. The Emergency Board to investigate the dispute of the nonoperating employees was created on Oct. 18, 1948, and the recommendations of the Board for higher rates of pay and a shorter work week were issued Dec. 17, 1948. However, actual settlement of this dispute was held up due to unsettled issues regarding

In order to compensate for these added labor and other operating costs, the carriers filed with the Interstate Commerce Commission on October 1, 1948, a petition for an 8 per cent increase in the general level of freight rates. On October 12 this petition was amended, requesting a 13 per cent permanent increase with an 8 per cent interim adjustment. The interim aspect of this case was decided by the Commission on December 29, 1948, with the granting of a 4 to 6 per cent increase.[28] At this date (July 1949) the requested 13 per cent permanent increase has not been decided by the Commission. (See Appendix A, Table 17.)

Although the latest rate increases were not reflected in 1948 operations, the apparent financial position of the Class I carriers for that year showed some improvement over 1947. The rate of return on net investment increased to 4.38 per cent (based on investment at beginning of 1948). And only 19 roads reported net deficits as against 33 in 1947, while aggregate net income rose from 490.4 million dollars to 700 millions. However, on the basis of rates now in effect (May 1949) and making allowance for increased labor costs, it is estimated that net income will drop to 497 million dollars in 1949 and that the rate of return will fall to 3.1 per cent.[29]

We must therefore conclude from this analysis of recent general rate cases that regulatory delays are responsible in no small measure for the relatively poor financial record made by the railroads in the immediate postwar period. This situation cannot be viewed merely as an adverse development for rail-

---

monthly rated employees and yardmasters. At the request of the unions and railroads, the Board reconvened in March to mediate this matter and the application of the five-day week to working conditions. Agreement, based on these and the December recommendations, was reached Mar. 20, 1949. (See App. A, Table 16.)

[28] The interim increases vary within territories from 4 per cent in Western Territory other than Zone 1 of that territory to 6 per cent within Eastern and Southern Territory. *Increased Freight Rates, 1948,* 272 I.C.C. 295-720, decided Dec. 29, 1948.

[29] Income data from ICC *Monthly Comment on Transportation Statistics,* Mar. 11, 1949, p. 1, 1948 rate of return and 1949 estimates from *Ex Parte 168, Increased Freight Rates 1948,* Carriers' Exhibit No. 34 (witness J. H. Parmelee), before the Interstate Commerce Commission, Mar. 1, 1949, pp. 11 and 15A.

road security holders who are experiencing only moderate returns in the midst of unprecedented levels of general economic activity. On the contrary, failure of the railroad industry to participate in the generally high level of postwar industrial profits raises doubts as to the long-run financial prospects of the carriers.

*Procedural delays and long-term financial implications.* Accurate evaluation of this problem requires that we keep in mind the public interest in the maintenance of an efficient and progressive railroad system. As the Supreme Court has said:

> Congress has long made the maintenance and development of an economical and efficient railroad system a matter of primary national concern. Its legislation must be read with this purpose in mind. In keeping with this purpose Congress has often recognized that the nation's railroads should have sound corporate and financial structures and has taken appropriate steps to this end.[30]

And, as the ICC has recently observed:

> It is clear to us . . . that increasing costs of operation now pose and unchecked will continue to pose a serious threat to the maintenance of adequate transportation service; that the railroads as a whole, and many of the most important railroads of the country in particular, are definitely facing such a threat at the present time; that the public vitally needs an efficient transportation service, and imperatively demands a transportation system that is adequate for the national defense in any emergency.[31]

There seems to be little doubt that in the predictable future the main burden of war-generated traffic will be carried by the railroads as it has in the past. For this reason alone, the system must at all times be maintained in a high state of physical and operating efficiency with sufficient flexibility to permit rapid increase in carrying capacity.

The record indicates conclusively that earnings or credit posi-

---

[30] *Seaboard Air Line Railroad Company, appellant, v. John M. Daniel as Attorney General of the State of South Carolina, and W. P. Blackwell, as Secretary of the State of South Carolina, Appellees*, U. S. Supreme Court No. 390—October term, 1947, decided Feb. 16, 1948, p. 6.

[31] *Increased Freight Rates, 1947, Ex Parte 166*, 269 I.C.C. 33, 53, decided Oct. 7, 1947.

tion adequate to finance necessary additions and betterments have been realized in the past only during relatively brief periods of high level economic activity. Being peculiarly sensitive to the ups and downs of the business cycle, the railroads invariably encounter severe financial difficulties in depression periods. Obversely, high earnings have always been associated with high levels of general business activity.[32] Thus, the precipitous drop in traffic volume from an index number of 100 in 1929 to an extreme low of 51 in 1932, is sufficient to account for the critical condition of railroad earnings during the early phases of the depression. For the index of national income dropped correspondingly to about 48. (See chart p. 282.)

Railroad recovery persistently lagged behind general business recovery during the 1930's, but by 1942 war-generated traffic had pushed the index of traffic volume to 141 and the rate of return index to 121. However, since that period there has occurred a substantial deterioration in the railroad position. By 1946 the index of earnings had dropped from 129 to about 53, while the index of total traffic volume remained only a few points below the 1942 level. Earnings for 1948 showed considerable recovery as a result of increased freight rates. But the index of traffic volume continued to decline as a result of freight traffic diversion to competitors and a precipitous drop in passenger traffic. (See chart p. 282.)

Rigidity of railroad rates clearly constituted one of the major difficulties. It is also significant that, compared with other important sectors of the economy, the railroads have realized only minor benefits from increased volume of business. Between 1939 and 1947, railroad production (freight ton-miles) increased 118 per cent and aggregate value (freight revenue) only 136 per cent. In striking contrast to this record, the aggregate value of manufacturing production increased 248 per cent while volume

[32] The primary explanation is found in the high proportion of fixed to total costs that characterize railroad operations, combined with the fact that the bulk of railroad service consists in moving what others produce and consume. When traffic drops abruptly, it is impossible to make corresponding downward adjustments in overhead costs, with the result that unit costs rise as traffic declines. For the same reason, up to the point of full utilization of available capacity, there is a tendency for unit costs to decline as traffic volume increases.

of production was increasing only 82 per cent. An even more impressive inflation occurred in the price of agricultural products as indicated by a 27 per cent increase in production accompanied by a 272 per cent increase in agricultural value of

PERCENTAGE CHANGE IN PHYSICAL QUANTITIES PRODUCED OR
EXCHANGED AND IN THEIR AGGREGATE VALUES, 1939-47[a]

| | Increase, 1939-47[b] | |
| --- | --- | --- |
| | Physical Quantity | Aggregate Value |
| Agricultural production | 27[c] | 272[c] |
| Mineral production | 46 | 156 |
| Manufacturing production | 82 | 248 |
| Construction activity | 34 | 150 |
| Revenue freight (ton miles) | 118 | 136 |
| Retail sales | 73 | 226 |
| Consumer expenditures | 54 | 156 |
| Employment in manufacturing[d] | 70 | 248 |
| Employment in mining[d] | 34 | 171 |

[a] Adapted from: Frederick C. Mills, *The Structure of Postwar Prices*, National Bureau of Economic Research, Occasional Paper 27, July 1948, Table 1, p. 2.

[b] Fourth quarter of 1947.

[c] Increase from 1939 to 1947. The movement for net farm income between these dates is 242.

[d] Employment is here measured in man-hours. The corresponding increase in number of production workers is 57 per cent in manufacturing, 3 per cent in mining.

product. (See table above.) The sharp difference between the experience from 1939 to 1947 of the railroads on the one hand and other major areas of the economy on the other is explained by one fact. The price of railroad service is rigidly controlled by public authority while other industries are free to adjust price to current demand.

The current financial and operating positions of the railroads therefore present a striking paradox. The railroads are now operating at approximately their practical freight capacity.[33]

[33] It is true that the railroad *passenger* deficit in 1946 and 1947 constituted a heavy drain on the operating income derived from freight service. However, this was nothing new in railroad experience, and the extent of the drain was accurately anticipated by the carriers in the advance rate applications filed with the Commission during those years.

Yet their operating ratios and net earnings are reminiscent of a period when general business stagnation and low traffic levels afforded ample explanation for unsatisfactory financial results. Most disturbing is the unfavorable trend in the factors which condition railroad credit. For years the general experience of the railroad stockholders has tended to discourage the flow of new equity capital into the railroad industry. And the unprecedented volume of peacetime business enjoyed by the carriers since 1945 has done little to restore the railroad credit position. In 1946 about 45 per cent of outstanding railroad stock failed to receive any dividends. This compares with less than 30 per cent during the 1925-29 period. (See chart below.)

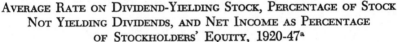

AVERAGE RATE ON DIVIDEND-YIELDING STOCK, PERCENTAGE OF STOCK NOT YIELDING DIVIDENDS, AND NET INCOME AS PERCENTAGE OF STOCKHOLDERS' EQUITY, 1920-47[a]

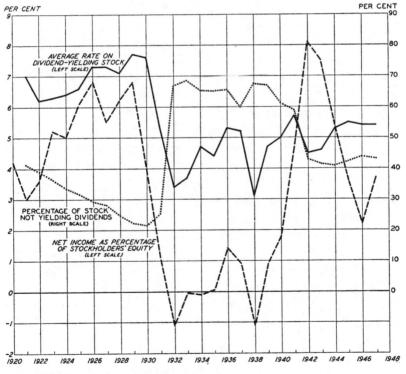

[a] See App. A, Table 18 for supporting data.

In this connection it is significant that by 1946 the bulk of railroad bankruptcy reorganizations had been completed. These reorganizations wiped out large amounts of stock and generally scaled down fixed charges. Yet in a peak traffic year the owners of almost one half of the stock in an industry recently purged of excess capitalization failed to receive any return of their equity.[34]

Moreover, the modest 1946 rate of 5.4 per cent on dividend-yielding stock was achieved only because the carriers paid dividends amounting to 84 per cent of their aggregate net income. In the 1925-29 period, characterized by high fixed interest charges, less than 60 per cent of net income was required on the average to produce a 7 per cent rate on dividend-yielding stocks.

In final analysis, return on stockholders' equity has become so erratic that the railroad industry as a whole cannot obtain necessary new capital through equity financing. There was no net income for four of the ten years between 1930 and 1940. And the return on stockholders' equity has declined from a wartime peak of 8 per cent in 1942 to about 2 per cent in 1946. (See chart p. 289.) This compares with a pre-depression rate ranging from 5.5 to 6.8 per cent (1925-29).

Reversal of the historic relationships between railroad prosperity and the level of business activity creates a grave problem of public policy. For, if the carriers are not permitted to realize high earnings in the midst of general economic prosperity, their prospects for continued solvency are indeed poor. It will be impossible to maintain and improve the railroad plant at the rate necessary to meet intensive competition and to assure the availability of stand-by capacity for national security purposes.

The record indicates clearly that the railroads were able to carry the unprecedented traffic load of World War II primarily because of the heavy capital investments for additions and betterments that were made during the 1920's. Between 1921 and

---

[34] It should be borne in mind that all railroad financial reorganizations must be approved by the ICC. Presumably the drastic scaling down of capital structures was required in order to assure that the reduced charges could be supported by expected traffic and earnings.

1940 the carriers made gross expenditures amounting to 10.5 billion dollars for additions and betterments to the railroad plant. Of this amount some 7.7 billions, or almost 74 per cent, was expended between 1921 and 1930. (See Appendix A, Table 14.) Less than 10 per cent of such expenditures was made during the major depression years 1931-35.

The timing and amount of expenditure for additions and betterments was, of course, controlled by the level of earnings. Thus the ten-year period 1921-30, in which almost three fourths of gross expenditures were concentrated, accounted for two thirds of the net operating income earned during the entire twenty-year period 1921-40. Although about 15 per cent of the aggregate operating income for the twenty-year period was earned in the five years between 1931 and 1935, less than 10 per cent of the aggregate expenditures for additions and betterments was made during that period. The explanation is that, as depression forces reduced revenue, interest and other fixed charges consumed correspondingly larger proportions of a decreasing net operating income, leaving less net income for reinvestment or to sustain credit.

Exceptionally high railroad earnings of World War II resulted only to a limited extent in accelerated capital expenditures for railroad improvement. Wartime scarcities of labor and materials necessitated a rigid allocation program that held railroad maintenance and replacement to minimum requirements. Although the rate of return for the four wartime years, 1941-45, was slightly higher than the best previous five-year experience, the index of wartime expenditures for additions and betterments ranged between 53 and 65 based on a 1929 index of 100. (See chart p. 282.)

Moreover, the high wartime earnings did not provide any substantial reserve for future capital investment. It is true that railroad indebtedness was reduced substantially and working capital was built up with a view to future investment. However, as noted above, the extremely rapid rise in postwar labor and material costs, combined with the lag in rate adjustments, dissipated these reserves. At the same time the increasing cost of new equipment and other replacement materials, such as steel rail and wood ties, tended to further decrease the amount of real capital improvement that could be effected by the declining net operating income.

As a result, the bulk of postwar additions and betterments to the railroad plant had been in the form of improved equipment rather than modernization of the right of way and other physical properties. Thus in 1948 only 27 per cent of gross expenditures was for additions and betterments to road and structures. This was the lowest ratio since 1923. (See table below.)

GROSS EXPENDITURES FOR ADDITIONS AND BETTERMENTS TO RAILWAY
PROPERTY, CLASS I RAILWAYS, 1923-47[a]

(In thousands of dollars)

| Average for Period | Equipment | Roadway and Structures | Total | Roadway and Structures as Per Cent of Total |
|---|---|---|---|---|
| 1923-30 ........$380,993 | | $461,721 | $ 842,714 | 54.8 |
| 1931-35 ........ 59,254 | | 147,559 | 206,813 | 71.3 |
| 1936-40 ........ 200,536 | | 144,843 | 345,379 | 41.9 |
| 1941-45 ........ 323,186 | | 207,872 | 531,058 | 39.1 |
| 1946 ........ 319,017 | | 242,940 | 561,957 | 43.2 |
| 1947 ........ 565,901 | | 298,788 | 864,689 | 34.6 |
| 1948 ........ 924,084 | | 344,929 | 1,269,013 | 27.2 |

[a] Adapted from Carriers' Exhibit 34 (J. H. Parmalee testimony) *Ex Parte 168*, Sheet 35, before the Interstate Commerce Commission, Mar. 1, 1949.

Because of almost universal interchangeability, railroad rolling stock can be purchased with relatively small cash outlay through the use of so-called equipment trust certificates bearing a low rate of interest. However, this form of financing is not available for the equally necessary modernization of the roadbed, terminals, and other fixed property. For these purposes earnings must be sufficiently high either to provide the necessary funds for reinvestment or to make equity financing feasible. Obtaining necessary new capital by increasing long-term indebtedness is clearly undesirable. For that course would only intensify the vulnerability of railroad operation to cyclical fluctuations.[35]

It seems clear then that in the interest of preserving a financially stable, efficient, and progressive railroad system, some way must be found to remove all unnecessary obstacles to the prompt adjustment between the operating costs incurred by the carriers and the level of rates paid by the public. Otherwise the carriers will be unable to realize a sufficiently high level of earnings during periods of business prosperity to tide them over recurring traffic and profit famines.

But the record demonstrates conclusively that so long as the Commission exercises its discretion to review and decide general rate cases in the capacity of board of directors for the railroad industry, expedition will not be attained. It is equally certain from the experience of more than a quarter of a century that the Commission will continue to encroach on managerial functions so long as its present legal jurisdiction remains unchanged. Consequently, if the impasse is to be broken, it appears that statutory restraint must be placed on the Commission's control over the general level of railroad rates. The question is: Can this be done without jeopardizing the valid objectives of modern rate regulation?

### III. IS THERE NEED FOR CONTINUING ICC CONTROL OVER THE GENERAL LEVEL OF RATES?

Before any satisfactory answer to this query can be presented, we must determine what the Commission is actually attempting to achieve through its current treatment of general rate cases, and why the process is so time-consuming. Regarding the mechanical aspects of this problem the Commission has observed that:

[35] It is agreed that the extreme financial difficulties encountered by the railroads during the 1930's were caused in part by the high proportion of fixed debt in the railroad capital structure. The financial reorganization of approximately one third of the nation's railroad mileage, stemming from bankruptcies and receiverships incurred during the 1930's, resulted in a substantial reduction of fixed interest charges for Class I railroads. Any move to increase the proportion of fixed interest debt in the total railroad capitalization would be generally considered unsound.

Our procedure is in some respects slower and more cumbersome than we would like. In the exercise of the administrative process we are bound by the law of the land. We have learned by experience, as a result of many court reviews of our decisions, that we must exercise great care in the making of records and in the drafting of our reports. Those who seek reductions in railroad rates, however, have suffered much more severely from delays than have the railroads when seeking increases. The latter proceedings have been expedited at the expense of other work, and have been heard and decided as rapidly as their complexity and importance would permit. The industries and people of the country are vitally affected by nation-wide, horizontal increases in rates. They are entitled to a fair hearing before such increases are approved. They cannot be heard in the twinkling of an eye, and the evidence submitted must be considered.[36]

No one will contend that shippers should not have a "fair hearing," nor that complex rate cases can be heard "in the twinkling of an eye." However, it is obvious that the regulatory process will remain slow and cumbersome so long as the Commission's conception of a "fair hearing" permits wide-ranging debate and speculation over such matters as: (1) the elasticity of demand for railroad service; (2) the basic theory of business cycles; and (3) the direction and intensity of inflationary forces, and the Commission's responsibility for restraining those forces.

It is difficult to understand why the Commission considers these subjects relevant, much less indispensable, to deciding whether or not the carriers need additional revenue in order to maintain their plant and service at an adequate level. But the fact remains that a major portion of the hearing time, and presumably the Commission's deliberations in its recent rate cases, has been devoted to these essentially managerial questions and economic theories—matters that are inherently unsuited to solution by legalistic procedure. Thus, a distressingly large part of the total time spent in the extensive hearings on the 1947 rate case discussed above, *Ex Parte No. 166*, was devoted to shipper testimony designed to persuade the Commission that:

1. The carriers were not entitled to any increased revenue either because they were inefficiently or uneconomically oper-

---

[36] *52nd Annual Report of the Interstate Commerce Commission, 1938*, p. 8.

ated, or because predicted increases in traffic volume would generate adequate revenue at existing rates.

2. The carriers should be denied the requested increase except to the extent required to prevent bankruptcy. Thus the spokesman for the National Industrial Traffic League urged that the owners of the railroads should forego temporarily any return on investment, thereby contributing to control of the inflationary spiral.[37] In effect, the shippers who had promptly passed on to the railroads and other consumers the increased cost of producing steel, coal, lumber, petroleum, and other materials asked the Interstate Commerce Commission to refuse to permit the carriers to take corresponding action with respect to their increased costs.

3. The carriers' requested rate increase should be denied in part, or adjusted by the Commission, because the specific advances proposed would not produce any additional net revenue, but would only divert traffic to competitive agencies.

There was little prospect that the most extreme of these shipper arguments would influence the Commission. They appear to have been advanced solely to achieve maximum delay in the final decision of the case, thus avoiding increased freight charges in the meantime.[38] For the Commission has on many occasions appropriately rejected irrelevant arguments advanced by special interests. Thus in the 1947 advance rate case, the Commission dismissed the contention that rate regulation should be used as a vehicle for breaking or controlling the inflationary spiral.

It has been strongly urged upon us by the responsible authorities that any increase in freight rates and charges at the present time

[37] "About two weeks ago, as a member of the Commission, I listened to several distinguished gentlemen representing some of the great industries of the nation. They argued that to grant the railroads an increase in rates would add to the inflationary spiral that the country now finds itself in. Many were the arguments made why rates should not be increased. One distinguished gentleman, representing an outstanding industrial institution, advocated that the railroads should be required to use up their cash on hand before the increases were granted." Address of Commissioner R. F. Mitchell before the annual meeting of the American Short Line Railroad Association, New York, Oct. 21, 1947.

[38] Unlike railroad wage awards, freight rate increases are never made retroactive to the date when the carriers' proposals for advances are suspended for investigation by the Commission. Thus it is clearly to the advantage of shippers to delay as long as possible an inevitable increase in freight rates.

might stimulate already existing inflationary forces. But in our judgment that factor is outweighed by the necessity of keeping the carriers, in the face of higher costs of operation, in a reasonably healthy condition in order that they may maintain their credit, procure additional equipment which is now urgently needed, and rehabilitate and improve their properties generally to take care of the demand of the public for adequate transportation service.[39]

The significance of this episode lies in the fact that critical hearing time was consumed in dealing with an issue beyond the control of the Commission. It should be obvious that the manipulation of railroad rates cannot materially affect the course of inflation or deflation in an economy where the bulk of all prices are not subject to governmental control. In 1946 and 1947 the income produced by Class I railroads accounted respectively for only 3.01 and 2.89 per cent of the total national income.[40] Moreover, freight charges constitute a relatively small and decreasing portion of wholesale prices. For example, in 1946 freight charges constituted 5.46 per cent of the wholesale prices at destination of commodities transported by rail as against 8.4 per cent in 1939.[41]

Despite the manifest implications of these facts, the Commission laboriously heard testimony and deliberated on the question and eventually formed a "judgment" that the need for controlling existing inflationary forces was "outweighed" by the necessity for keeping the carriers solvent.

So long as the Commission finds it desirable or necessary under its statutory responsibility to hear evidence and formulate judgments on such matters through the process of "fair hearing," we can look forward to continuing rigidities in the regulatory process with the attendant unsatisfactory implications for the financial health of the railroads. Under peak levels of traffic, such as prevail today, the carriers will not be permitted to build up any substantial financial reserves to compensate for

[39] *Increased Freight Rates, 1947,* 269 I.C.C. 33, 53, decided Oct. 6, 1947.
[40] Interstate Commerce Commission, *Monthly Comment on Transportation Statistics,* Mar. 11, 1948, p. 6.
[41] *Freight Revenue and Wholesale Value of Commodities Transported on Class I Steam Railways in the United States, Calendar Year 1946,* ICC Statement 4823 issued Sept. 21, 1948 (mimeo.).

sharp declines in traffic. And, if the Commission follows precedent, the carriers in any future depressed situation will not be permitted to exercise their own business judgment in deciding the effect on their revenues of particular rate adjustments. As noted above, in the 1922, 1931, and 1937 general rate cases the Commission consistently reserved the right to determine whether, or the extent to which, the economy as a whole or particular industries under depression conditions could stand increases in transportation costs.

The extension of ICC jurisdiction into the field of business management has occasioned repeated efforts on the part of railroad management to obtain statutory restrictions on the ICC rate making powers. This controversy became a major issue in the legislative deliberations leading to the passage of the Transportation Act of 1940. In that connection the Commission summarized its differences with railroad management in the following terms:

It is evident that the railroads want a rule which will be divorced from the requirement of section 1 that rates be "just and reasonable," except for the proviso that the Commission shall have "reasonable latitude to modify or adjust any particular rate which it may find to be unreasonable or unjustly discriminatory and to prescribe different rates for different sections of the country." In both the original and the present section 15a, the rule has been linked with the requirement of section 1 that rates be "just and reasonable." It has given the Commission certain standards to apply in enforcing that requirement, but without eliminating from consideration other matters which have always, by well-settled principles of law, been regarded as relevant and of weight in determining what is "just and reasonable." In particular, the railroads want the Commission precluded from consideration of the "effect of the rates on the movement of traffic."[42]

In final analysis the Commission did not relish the reduction in authority and official prestige that would have resulted from the railroad's proposal:

Apparently the thought is that under such a revised rule, if the

[42] Letter from ICC Legislative Committee to Clarence F. Lea, Chairman of House Committee on Interstate and Foreign Commerce in *Omnibus Transportation Bill*, Hearings on H.R. 2531 and 4862, 76 Cong. 1 sess., Pt. 4, p. 1565.

Commission is asked to permit a general increase in rates, it will have no other option than to grant permission, provided it is shown that existing revenues are not adequate to support needed credit and to provide investors with a reasonable return, and it does not appear that the proposed increase will yield more revenue than is needed for these purposes. In other words, our function is to become that of "mere computers," a conclusion which we repudiated in *Reduced Rates, 1922*, 68 I.C.C. 676.[43]

This statement seems only to obscure the central issue. The fact that the ICC in 1922 repudiated the role of rate computer is irrelevant to a solution of the issues posed by the carriers in 1939. The Commission has repeatedly acknowledged that the near-monopoly once held by the railroads has been replaced by intensive and almost universal competition. Even at current high levels of traffic, interagency competition is so effective that the railroads hesitate even to *propose* general rate increases that would provide adequate revenue. For example, in a recent case the chief traffic witness for the railroads stated:

May I also again remind you that this increase as here requested does not provide for the required cushion to furnish the money to make up the deferred maintenance, or even to stop the accumulation of additional deferred maintenance, on some of the most important railroad properties in the United States. From a rather broad experience and service on various railroads and in various sections of the country, may I say that in my very carefully considered judgment, this increase, even if granted promptly, is still inadequate to meet the full needs of the railroads under the present conditions and the problems facing them to revamp their equipment and service to properly meet the demands and requirements of the public as they will be in the next few years.[44]

The admitted inadequacy of the carriers' own rate proposal was attributed by the railroad spokesman to the fear of diverting traffic to competitors. Initial responsibility for formulating railroad rate policies rests directly on the chief traffic officers of the carriers. It was pointed out however, that in discharging these responsibilities:

[43] The same.
[44] Testimony of Walter S. Franklin, Vice President in Charge of Traffic, The Pennsylvania Railroad Company, in ICC Docket *Ex Parte No. 166, Increased Freight Rates, 1947*, p. 35 (mimeo.).

These officers are keenly aware of the danger of pricing the railroads out of their market. The Chief Traffic Officers are constantly reminded of that fact by their own junior officers, and, of course, by the shippers. The Chief Traffic Officers have been too cautious in their proposals, relying too much on what the Operating Officers could accomplish as to savings and the rapidity with which these savings could be put into effect.[45]

This extreme sensitivity to the competitive effect of rate increases creates a natural tendency to place the burden of increases on the traffic that is least vulnerable to competition. In the 1947 freight rate increase, the carriers found it necessary to except several important commodities from the general percentage increase. The reasons for exempting specified products of agriculture from the full burden of the general percentage increase was explained as follows:

With respect to cotton, the originating railroads deemed it necessary to preserve origin relationships. This together with truck and water competition made it expedient to propose a maximum of 10 cents per 100 pounds.

On fresh fruits and vegetables a maximum of 20 cents per 100 pounds is proposed in order to preserve relationships from the main producing areas to the chief consuming markets in eastern territory. There is keen competition among the various growers. Competition from other forms of transportation, particularly truck, was another factor that had considerable influence. Notwithstanding their desire to apply the general increases the railroads chiefly concerned with this traffic are firmly of the conviction that they could not consistently propose anything higher than the maximum suggested.[46]

This tendency to shift the railroad freight burden to the least competitive commodities offers the real explanation for the Commission's desire to retain rigid control over general rate cases. This situation was neatly summarized by the Commission in 1938:

Opposed to the opinion of the railroads and investors that larger increases should have been permitted stands the sincere conviction of a large proportion of those who ship freight that many of the rates have become too high for either the railroads' or the public's

[45] The same, p. 34.
[46] The same, p. 12.

health. The railroads have made much of the fact that average ton-mile revenue fell each year from 1923 to 1937, and that in the latter year it was only 31.5 percent above the 1916 level. Such comparisons are misleading, for the fall in the average since 1923 has been caused largely by the fact that in recent years the railroads have voluntarily reduced many rates to meet highway, water, and pipe-line competition, and have increased the severity of competition between themselves. *The rates, however, on the traffic which still is affected little, if at all, by such competition have stayed up. It is of these non-competitive rates that shippers complain.*[47]

From this and other statements on the same subject, it seems clear that the Commission's objective is to protect both the railroads and the shippers from the effects of intensive but uneven competition. But on careful analysis, the Commission appears to have assumed a responsibility that is of questionable validity.

The unavoidable facts are that the generous and aggressive assistance of the federal government has developed during the last quarter of a century competitive agencies that have revolutionized transport organization and pricing. If the railroads are to survive in private ownership, their rate structure must be adjusted to the facts of the new competitive organization. In the areas of service where competition is pervasive and effective, railroad rates must be adjusted to the level necessary to meet that competition, or the traffic will be lost permanently. Under these circumstances the railroads would be imprudent if they did not adjust such rates to the level that would cover out-of-pocket costs and make any contribution, however small, to fixed charges. As already observed above, the Commission has full power, through its minimum rate control, to decide how these competitive rate situations shall be adjusted in the interests of maintaining over-all adequacy in the transportation system.

Having made the rate reductions necessary to meet competitive conditions, the carriers have no alternative but to raise rates on the less competitive traffic to a higher level than would be necessary if all traffic could be made to contribute uniformly to total railroad costs, including a return on capital.

[47] *52nd Annual Report of the Interstate Commerce Commission, 1938,* p. 7. Italics supplied.

If railroad management is to retain any of the essential functions of business control, it must be permitted to exercise its own judgment as to how far these rates can be raised without driving traffic away. In making these decisions, railroad management will, of course, be circumscribed by the prohibitions against undue discrimination and against realizing an exorbitant rate of return on its total capital investment. For it will be recalled that no one, including the railroads, has seriously proposed diluting the Commission's authority over undue discrimination and preference, nor the abandonment of the historical concepts of a fair return on fair value. But within these limits the rate structure must be adapted to the facts of contemporary transport organization. This means that rate relationships, regulatory concepts, and market structure that were developed to fit monopoly situations must be abandoned.

Under these circumstances, it appears that a progressively larger portion of aggregate railroad revenue must be derived from those areas of service in which the railroads have the greatest *relative* advantage over their competitors. In practice, this means that the rates on commodities least subject to interagency competition will tend to move away from cost standards, while the rates on highly competitive traffic will move inexorably in the direction of actual cost of performing the service. In short, some industries, sections of the country, and individuals will enjoy sharply reduced transportation costs as a result of the new competition, while those remaining primarily dependent on railroad service will be adversely affected.

It will be recalled that to a substantial extent the character, amount, and physical location of this new competition have been dictated by government action involving the financing and provision of transport facilities. Consequently, any effort on the part of the ICC to retard or prevent this inevitable adjustment of the rate structure to new conditions could have only one result—the eventual bankruptcy of the railroads.[48]

---

[48] As we shall point out below, the withdrawal of public subsidies for selected transport agencies would by no means remove all of the competitive pressure on the railroads. Thus, to a considerable extent, the effectiveness of the new competition results from inherent economies of joint use (such as joint use of

It is primarily for this reason that the railroads, as noted above, lay stress on the desirability of relieving the Commission of any responsibility or authority for considering "the effect of the rates on the movement of traffic." The Commission's complaint that such an amendment to the present rule of rate making (section 15a, Interstate Commerce Act) would reduce its function to that of "mere computers" appears to be considerably overdrawn. Such revision would leave the Commission with full control over minimum rates of all major transport agencies; plenary power over all forms of undue discrimination and preference, including the extremely complex interterritorial freight rate problem and responsibility for determining the value of railroad property.[49]

As a matter of fact, the Commission would be left with ample authority to protect the public against the exercise of any vestiges of monoply power on the part of the railroads, and with effective tools to control the standards of competition so far as the minimum level of rates is concerned. Moreover, the validity of individual rate adjustments would come within the purview of its control over unjust discrimination. The proposed amend-

the highways by trucks and private automobiles) and from relative service advantages of the new forms of transportation. One of the most burdensome aspects of current railroad operations is found in the heavy passenger deficit that must be made up by high freight rates. The most important single factor in the deterioration of railroad passenger business has been the diversion from rail to private automobile. Yet very little, if any, of this diversion is explained by the effect of public subsidies since the principle of user support for highway development forms the basis for highway taxation in all states. Consequently, in the absence of some revolutionary technological improvement in railroad passenger service, it appears that so long as the railroads are required or attempt to maintain passenger schedules, the freight service will be required to carry a substantial burden of passenger deficits.

[49] For example, in the *Fifteen Percent Case, 1937-1938*, the Commission observed that: "Consideration of the need of the applicants for sufficient revenues to enable them to provide such transportation service as is contemplated in section 15a of the act necessarily requires that the fair value of their property be taken into account. Even though the applicants are not here asserting a constitutional right to a fair return of any definite amount, it is necessary for us to inquire into the question of the value of the property employed in performing the service, both because of its bearing upon the economic cost of performing the service, and because of the duty we are under to avoid putting rates upon a basis which would compel the use of the property without just compensation, although the Constitution does not protect against all business hazards, *Montana Public Service Comm. v. Great Northern Utilities Co.*, 289 U.S. 130." 226 I.C.C. 41, 60.

ment would produce only one major change. There would no longer be any occasion for the Commission to take endless testimony on general economic trends, inflationary forces, and the ability of particular industries to bear additional transportation costs. For the full and final responsibility for gauging the effective demand for various classes of railroad service would be placed with private management where it belongs.

Apparently the Commission does not object on principle to restoring to management full control over maximum rates. A rather cryptic statement on this issue would seem to indicate that it seeks only to share with management the onus of increased rates:

> The railroads have proposed changes in section 15a of the Interstate Commerce Act, for the purpose of limiting our discretion in passing upon rate increases, so that upon proof of low earnings approval of such increases would necessarily follow. We do not favor such an amendment, but suggest that the simple way to accomplish the real result desired would be to limit our authority to the fixing of minimum rates and the removal of unjust discrimination (using this term in its broad sense), leaving maximum rates to the discretion of the railroads. We venture to believe, however, that if such a change were made, the railroads would make limited use of the freedom so accorded. It is one thing to increase rates where the Government, through this Commission shares the responsibility, and it is quite another thing for the managements, under present competitive conditions, to accept sole responsibility.[50]

We are left in considerable doubt as to the precise manner in which government "shares . . . responsibility" with management. Certainly no financial liability is involved. When the Interstate Commerce Commission miscalculates economic trends or demand factors, railroad owners and creditors suffer the full financial consequences. The federal treasury does not make deficiency appropriations for railroad owners. Consequently, there seems to be no reason to believe that divesting the Commission of jurisdiction over the general level of rates would tend to increase the financial risks of railroad owners. On the contrary,

[50] *52nd Annual Report of the Interstate Commerce Commission, 1938*, p. 20, note.

the owners would gain by a system under which private management could be held clearly accountable for satisfactory results. They could more effectively control the quality of management than under a system of "shared responsibility." As matters now stand, neither government nor private management can be held firmly accountable for efficiency and progress in railroad transportation.

The restoration to private management of greater flexibility in the matter of general policies would be facilitated by the elimination of the extreme variations in the earning power of individual railroads. This situation, resulting from historical imperfections in the railroad corporate and operating structure, constitutes one of the major arguments for continuing the Commission's present authority over the general level of rates. The Commission is under constant pressure to hold the general level of railroad rates at a point which produces starvation earnings for many carriers because any higher level would produce unconscionable earnings for others. The origin and current status of this special problem in the field of transportation is explored in Chapter XV dealing with railroad consolidation.

# CHAPTER XIV

# CO-ORDINATION AND INTEGRATION

As already noted, control over the establishment of new transport enterprises was not asserted until after the physical operating pattern and the structure of corporate ownership had taken definite form. At the time restrictions on expansion were imposed,[1] the affected transport agencies had reached widely varying stages in their life cycles. And it was recognized that the relatively uncontrolled corporate development of these agencies had given rise to defective organization and extreme variations in the earning prospects (and therefore survival) of individual carriers. In order to avoid repetition of this experience, standards were prescribed for the orderly co-ordination and integration of individual concerns. To this end, statutory provision has been made for two main types of structural rearrangement:[2] (1) the combination of similar types of carriers through outright consolidation or acquisition of control;[3] and (2) the ownership or control of one type of carrier by another.

Administrative jurisdiction over these two forms of transport

---

[1] 1920 for railroads; 1935 for motor carriers; 1938 for air transport; and 1940 for domestic waterways.

[2] Co-ordination of service is also attained by the establishment of through routes and rates. The Transportation Act of 1940 added considerably to the regulatory provisions governing the establishment of through routes and rates among transportation agencies. The Declaration of Policy attached to that act stresses the attainment of transport co-ordination by the establishment of through routes and rates among the regulated carriers. Thus the ICC is empowered to require the establishment of such routes between railroad, pipeline, and rail-water lines on the one hand, and common carriers by water on the other. However, common carriers by water are not required to establish through routes with motor common carriers.

The provisions of the act governing through routes of motor carriers, as related to other carriers, remain as written in the Motor Carrier Act of 1935. Under these provisions common carriers of passengers by motor vehicle are required to establish reasonable through routes with other such carriers. Common carriers of property are not required to establish through routes with other common carriers.

The most controversial aspect of this problem is discussed in connection with rail-barge through routes and joint rates. (Chap. 12.)

[3] Railroad consolidation and acquisition of control are dealt with as a special problem in Chap. 15.

integration and co-ordination is divided between the Interstate Commerce Commission and the Civil Aeronautics Board. And current statutes provide different standards to govern the combination of individual units within a given form of transportation (carriers of like form) as contrasted with the acquisition of one type of carrier by another.

## I. COMBINATION OF LIKE CARRIERS

Any railroad, motor carrier, or water carrier,[4] or two or more carriers jointly seeking "to acquire control of another through ownership of its stock or otherwise" must present an application to the Interstate Commerce Commission. If the Commission finds that the proposed transaction "will be consistent with the public interest, it shall enter an order approving and authorizing such transaction, upon the terms and conditions and with the modifications, so found to be just and reasonable."[5]

The ICC has used this authority constructively to permit combination of motor carriers into more effective operating units. For example, in a leading case it permitted a combination of 17 previously independent motor carriers into a single company (Associated Transport, Inc.) on the grounds that such integration would produce operating economies and consequent improvement of service to the public. This action was taken despite the fact that such combination obviously tended to reduce to some extent the effectiveness of transport competition within the area affected. However, the Commission's judgment was upheld by the Supreme Court with the observation that:

. . . Whatever may be the case with respect either to other kinds of transactions by or among carriers or to consolidations of different types of carriers, there can be little doubt that the Commission is not to measure proposals for all-rail or all-motor consolidations by the standards of the anti-trust laws. Congress authorized such consolidations because it recognized that in some circumstances they were appropriate for effectuation of the national transportation

---

[4] ". . . the term 'carrier' means a carrier by railroad and an express company . . .; a motor carrier . . .; and a water carrier. . . ." Sec. 5 (13) *Interstate Commerce Acts Annotated,* Vol. 11, p. 9217.

[5] The same, sec. 5 (2)(b), p. 9180.

policy. It was informed that this policy would be furthered by "encouraging the organization of stronger units" in the motor carrier industry. And in authorizing those consolidations it did not import the general policies of the anti-trust laws as a measure of their permissibility.[6]

Manifestly, Congress has given the Commission great responsibility and wide discretion with respect to transport integration. It must determine how much intra-agency competition is desirable. But what is more important, it must make certain that each unification will further the national objective of interagency co-ordination. As the courts pointed out:

. . . the Commission must estimate the scope and appraise the effects of the curtailment of competition which will result from the proposed consolidation and consider them along with the advantages of improved service, safer operation, lower costs, etc., to determine whether the consolidation will assist in effectuating the over-all transportation policy. Resolving these considerations is a complex task which requires extensive facilities, expert judgment and considerable knowledge of the transportation industry. Congress left that task to the Commission "to the end that the wisdom and experience of that Commission may be used not only in connection with this form of transportation, but in its coordination of all other forms."[7]

It will be observed that the CAB is not required to give similar consideration to general transportation objectives when passing on air transport unifications. An air carrier seeking to acquire control of another air carrier through consolidation, merger, purchase, lease, or operating contract must present an application to the Civil Aeronautics Board. Approval is mandatory unless the Board finds that the proposed transaction (1) "will not be consistent with the public interest . . ."; or (2) that it would "result in creating a monopoly or monopolies

[6] *McLean Trucking Company* v. *U. S.*, 321 U.S. 67, 83. Justice Douglas, in a dissenting opinion, contended that the Commission had misinterpreted the congressional intent governing consolidations, stating that: ". . . proper interpretation of the Act (Interstate Commerce Act, Section 5) requires the Commission to give greater weight to the standards of competition than it has done here." The same, p. 92.

[7] The same, p. 87.

and thereby restrain competition or jeopardize *another air carrier*" not involved in the transaction.[8]

## II. COMBINATION OF DISSIMILAR CARRIERS

The statutory standards for the combination of a rail carrier and a motor carrier are the same as those stated above for a combination of two rail, motor, or water carriers, with the added requirement that the proposed transaction must enable the rail carrier "to use service by motor vehicle to public advantage in its operations and will not unduly restrain competition."[9]

Similar statutory provisions govern the integration of other forms of transportation with air carriers. Thus the Civil Aeronautics Act provides that the application of a surface carrier to acquire control of an air transport enterprise may be granted if the proposed transaction "will promote the public interest by enabling such carrier other than air carrier to use aircraft to public advantage in its operation and will not restrain competition."[10]

Although operating under these comparable statutory provisions, the ICC and the CAB have placed fundamentally different interpretations on their authority and responsibility with respect to the integration of unlike carriers.

*The ICC interpretation.* In the administration of this type of transport integration, the ICC has felt obligated to approve unifications that offer reasonable prospects of improving transportation services. Thus railroads have been given considerable freedom to substitute highway services for rail operations within the areas already served by a particular railroad. In a leading case the Commission found that:

The proof is convincing that over some of the routes in question the railroad can "use service by motor vehicle to public advantage in its operations." The motor vehicle can undoubtedly be used as a very valuable auxiliary or adjunct to railroad service, particularly less-than-carload service, and the many opportunities for such use here have been pointed out of record and are clear. Such coordina-

[8] Sec. 408 (b), Civil Aeronautics Act, 1938 (52 Stat. 1001). Italics added.
[9] Sec. 5 (2)(b) *Interstate Commerce Acts Annotated*, Vol. 11, p. 9180.
[10] Sec. 408 (b) Civil Aeronautics Act, 1938 (52 Stat. 1002).

tion of rail and motor-vehicle operations should be encouraged. The result will be a new form of service which should prove of much public advantage. Nor do we believe that the creation of this new form of service will "unduly restrain competition." On the contrary, it should have the opposite effect.[11]

However, in the exercise of its discretion to attach reasonable "terms and conditions" to the authorization, the Commission specified that:

. . . the service to be rendered by the Barker Motor Freight, Incorporated . . . be confined to service auxiliary and supplementary to that performed by the Pennsylvania Railroad Company in its rail operations and in territory parallel and adjacent to its rail lines.[12]

*The CAB interpretation.* Although administering identical standards governing integration of dissimilar carriers, the practical effect of CAB interpretation differs radically from that applied by the ICC. Where the latter agency has used its discretion to encourage transport co-ordination, the CAB has for all practical purposes excluded surface carriers from any participation in air transportation. This policy is reflected in the unsuccessful efforts of both rail and ocean shipping enterprises to utilize aviation as a modern supplement to established services.

Experience of steamship companies. After numerous individual and unsuccessful attempts to obtain certificates to engage in air transportation, several steamship companies requested the CAB to institute a general review of policies that had been formulated to govern the participation of American steamship companies in foreign and overseas air transportation.[13]

The Board held that a general investigation would "serve no useful purpose," since hearings on pending applications of steamship companies for operating certificates would afford opportunity "to present pertinent proof and data along the lines suggested by the petitioners."[14] The occasion was used by

[11] *Pennsylvania Truck Lines, Inc., Control—Barker*, 1 M.C.C. 101, 111 (1936).
[12] The same, p. 113.
[13] *Petition of American President Lines, Ltd.*, filed with the CAB July 31, 1946 (mimeo.).
[14] *American President Lines, Ltd., et al., Petition*, 7 C.A.B. 799, 807-08, decided Mar. 19, 1947.

the Board, however, to clarify its position with respect to the question: "What relationship does the law permit to exist between air transportation and other forms of transportation, that is, between air carriers and common carriers other than air carriers?"[15]

In previous cases the CAB had taken the position that a surface carrier seeking to enter air transportation, whether by acquisition of an existing operation or inauguration of a new service, was subject to the unification section of the act. (Sec. 408 (b).) As already noted, this section requires affirmative showing that the public interest will be promoted by enabling the surface carrier to improve service through use of aviation. In line with the ICC interpretation, the CAB had construed the standard to mean that proposed air service should be supplementary and auxiliary to the surface carriers' operation.[16]

Upon reconsideration in the investigation under discussion, the Board abandoned this position in part by holding compliance with section 401 (regulating the issuance of certificates to *air carriers*) to be the only legal condition necessary to the grant of a certificate for a surface carrier to engage in air transportation. This revised interpretation appears to have only legalistic significance. For the Board still looks to the unification section (sec. 408) for one of the important statutory standards to be considered in dealing with surface carrier applications, holding that it has

. . . the power and the duty in a proceeding under section 401 to limit the entry of a surface carrier into air transportation to operations which would enable such surface carrier to use aircraft to public advantage in its surface transport operation unless the record of the case were to reveal that the public interest required service by a surface carrier regardless of the circumstance that it was a surface carrier.[17]

The interpretations of the Board prior to 1947 have been characterized as a "story of cumulative error" under which

[15] The same, p. 800.
[16] This doctrine subsequently restated was first enunciated in *American Export Lines, Control—Amer. Export Air*, 3 C.A.B. 619 (1942).
[17] 7 C.A.B. 799, 804.

. . . surface carriers have consistently been denied the right to engage in air transportation, always on the basis of a finding that some other air carrier was better fitted for engaging in the particular task than the surface carrier, or that the particular air transportation sought was not warranted by public convenience and necessity.[18]

Recent action of the CAB with respect to rail transportation indicates that the "technical correction" of the legal interpretation will not make it any easier for surface carriers to enter the field of air transportation.

*Railroad experience.* On July 1, 1946, the Santa Fe Skyway, Inc., a subsidiary of the Atchison, Topeka and Santa Fe Railway Company, began operating between New York and California and intermediate points as a contract carrier of air freight. Suspension of operations was announced early in 1948 because the CAB had refused to permit the rail subsidiary to operate as a common carrier pending final disposition of its application for a certificate of convenience and necessity.[19] Such interim authorization was permissible under the Board's regulations[20] and had been granted to a number of noncertified air cargo carriers. But similar exemption was denied the rail-affiliated air carrier on the grounds that continued operation as a noncertified cargo carrier "would render Santa Fe in violation of the Civil Aeronautics Act unless (a) Santa Fe were to divest itself of control of Skyway within the meaning of Section 408 of the Act, or (b) prior Board approval were obtained of the acquisition of control of Skyway by Santa Fe within the purview of Section 408 of the Act. . . ."[21]

The Santa Fe Railway contends that the decision in this case reflects a fixed assumption that entry of surface carriers would hinder development of air transportation. Spokesmen for the

[18] Concurring opinion of Chairman Landis in the same, p. 814.
[19] On Nov. 8, 1946, Santa Fe Skyway, Inc., filed with the CAB an application for a certificate to engage in the transportation of property and mail as a common carrier by air.
[20] CAB Economic Regulation No. 292.5. Santa Fe Skyway filed application for exemption on May 12, 1947.
[21] *Santa Fe Skyway, Inc., and the Atchison, Topeka and Santa Fe Railway Company,* CAB Docket No. 2930, decided Dec. 5, 1947.

railroad also hold that the Board's ". . . discriminatory policy against surface carriers can only be changed by amendment of the Civil Aeronautics Act to make it clear that surface carrier applicants before the Board are to receive the same consideration as other applicants for air certificates."[22]

Whether the Board's action in this case constitutes a "discriminatory policy" or merely a rigidly technical interpretation of the law need not concern us here. The important point is that the current dispersion of authority and responsibility is producing diametrically opposed results from identical regulatory statutes.

This outcome should occasion no surprise. For, when one agency is given responsibility for the promotion of an individual form of transportation, there is a natural tendency to resist physical or service co-ordination with competitive agencies. A cult of separatism inevitably arises. The fostered industry becomes obsessed with the need for maintaining its "integrity" and develops the myth that its problems are so unique and technical as to defy comprehension by other than "master minds."

This sense of aloofness from the general run of transportation problems and agencies finds expression in active resistance to any form of administrative or policy co-ordination. Having become accustomed to specialized and preferential treatment from government, the air transport industry wants no part of any program of transport integration:

> We of aviation do not want to submit ourselves to such an all-seeing master [a consolidated regulatory agency]. Ours is an industry requiring intensive technical knowledge and an abundance of "know-how". . . .
> The mechanics of aviation, and its problems are, compared with those of other forms of transportation, as dissimilar as day and night.
> Men do not discuss aviation and railroading, and the merchant marine, and pipe lines in the same breath, in the same terms. They are not the same, and the men dealing with these various forms of transportation are not the same. They are wholly different types.

[22] Release from Santa Fe Railway News Bureau, Jan. 12, 1948.

Aviation requires peculiar skills, peculiar planning skills, peculiar maintenance skills and peculiar getting-the-business skills. We are the embodiment of American free enterprise; we are the result of it. And in the transportation field, we are the anathema of monopoly.[23]

The normal inclination is to dismiss these observations as evidences of the growing pains of a young and vigorous industry. However, the observations assume significance when it is realized that they constitute the only reasons that can be advanced in support of the existing segregation of air transport from other transportation agencies. Thus, the case for the continued specialized and preferential treatment of air transportation for regulatory and promotional purposes rests on the following contentions:

1. That air transportation is young and vigorous; is manned by young and vigorous executives, and that this situation is somehow significant in forming public policy with respect to that form of transportation. One may readily grant the youth and virility of air transport companies and their personnel and at the same time fail to discover in that situation any compelling or even good reason for setting air transportation aside from other forms of transportation so far as public regulation is concerned. Certainly, aviation interests do not intend to cling indefinitely to the self-deprecating appeals for preferential treatment based on the "infant industry" argument. As we have noted, their public attitude is quite different, not that of an adolescent but that of a maturing young giant having no fear for the future in an unrestricted competitive market.

It might also be noted in passing that commercial highway transportation is both young and vigorous. But this fact did not persuade Congress to set up a separate regulatory agency to give specialized attention to motor carriers.

2. The second argument is that the operating techniques and problems of air transportation differ so fundamentally from

[23] Stuart G. Tipton, "Air Transport and Free Enterprise," *The Commercial and Financial Chronicle*, Aug. 30, 1945, p. 956. An address before the Aviation Industry Forum, New York Board of Trade. At this time Mr. Tipton was Acting President of the Air Transport Association of America.

those encountered in other transport media that "men do not discuss aviation and railroading and the merchant marine and pipe lines in the same breath, in the same terms."

This assertion is, of course, specious. One need only scan the flood of papers produced for presentation at aviation forums since the war's end to note that railroad, bus, truck, passenger automobile, and ocean shipping transportation play a predominant role in the speculation and planning of aviation interests.[24] Speculation regarding relative money costs, relative speed, and relative attractiveness of service, run like a refrain through all discussion of aviation's future. Any other situation would be utterly unrealistic. For the only normal function of aviation, in common with all other transport media, is to move people and goods from one place to another at the lowest real cost compatible with optimum convenience, safety, and speed. The "highway," rolling stock, and operating techniques differ somewhat from agency to agency, and the type and degree of technical training required for satisfactory personnel have distinguishing characteristics. But there the differences stop.

Retention of the current policy of dealing with air transportation in a regulatory vacuum because of the technical intricacies of the method of transportation itself can lead only to mischievous results. It confuses the fact that different transport media have widely varying technical characteristics with the fact that all transport agencies are designed for the same purpose of transporting persons and goods. The technical differences among transport agencies must, of course, be taken into account in the provision of facilities and the engineering of their use. But the similarities of the several transport agencies with respect to their *function* must be recognized if the regulatory objective of fair interagency competition and non-discriminatory treatment is to be achieved.

Arguments in favor of isolating air transportation from the regulation of other forms had considerable plausibility at a time when the new transport medium had no significant place

---

[24] Recall also CAB absorption with competitive relations in air feeder cases discussed above.

in the transportation system. But continued separation at this stage in the growth of air transport serves no useful purpose. On the contrary, it places innumerable difficulties in the way of assuring the shipping and traveling public of the most effective use of the transportation system as a whole. To put off this inevitable fusion on the ground that it is "not yet time" will merely compound the difficulties which are being nurtured under present policy. Protracted delay might well fasten onto this new industry the types of structural and operating weakness that for many years have handicapped the railroads' efforts to deal with modern competition.

# CHAPTER XV

# THE PROBLEM OF RAILROAD CONSOLIDATION

By 1920 several generations of unrestrained building had produced a railroad system characterized by duplication of facilities and extreme variations in the earning power of its individual units. The Transportation Act of 1920 attempted to deal with this problem through permissive pooling of revenue, consolidation of individual companies into a limited number of balanced systems, and by other types of approved unifications. Governmental efforts to reshuffle the corporate and operating structure of the railroads into a balanced and unified system constitute perhaps the most signal failure in the history of transport regulation. In major respects this failure stems from legislative reluctance to tackle the problem of overexpansion at a time when preventive measures might have been effective.

## I. BACKGROUND OF THE PROBLEM

The undisciplined way in which the railroad system had been permitted and encouraged to develop during its period of early expansion was generally recognized as involving a waste of capital. Moreover, the resulting excesses in competitive operation led to gross discrimination in rates and service. However, the recognized evils of the situation were defended on the ground that any other course "would assuredly have retarded the building up of the country in comparison with the progress attained under freedom from legislative restrictions."[1] The manifestly injurious effects were viewed as "in the nature of a mortgage handed down for payment to the present generation as its share of the price paid for making habitable and building up our vast domain at a rate of progress never equalled in any other country."[2]

During deliberation on the initial act to regulate commerce (1887), Congress was counseled by some witnesses to take

[1] S. Rept. 46, 49 Cong. 1 sess., Pt. I (1885-86), p. 5.
[2] The same.

positive action that would avoid handing down another "transportation mortgage" to the next generation. Those advisers urged that sound public policy would attack the problem at its source by asserting positive direction over the future expansion of railroad facilities and over inter-line competition.[3]

This advice was rejected by Congress. As a matter of fact, the cumulative effect of government action between 1887 and 1920 was to force railroad expansion into uneconomical and wasteful patterns. Under the 1887 Act to Regulate Commerce, all forms of railroad pooling were prohibited and the Sherman Antitrust Act of 1890[4] was interpreted by the courts as prohibiting any form of concerted action by the carriers tending to restrain competition. Thus in leading rate conference cases, the Supreme Court ruled that the antitrust law made railroad rate agreements illegal regardless of the "reasonableness" or "justness" of the rates involved.[5] Moreover, organized attempts to effect combinations of competing railroad lines by direct unification were arrested in 1907 by enforcement of the antitrust law.[6]

As a result of these prohibitions against concerted or co-operative action, the carriers intensified competition by physical expansion into each other's traffic territory. Between 1890 and 1916 the railway network increased from 163,597 to about 254,000 miles.[7] This growth, in contrast to that occurring prior to 1890 tended to duplicate facilities rather than to open up new territory or provide new facilities. It consisted largely in the construction of feeder lines, connecting lines, and spurs.

The natural corollary of unprogramed growth of rail facilities was wasteful cross-hauling, circuitous routing, and un-co-ordinated terminal operation. By 1920 this pattern had become frozen into the corporate structure of the railroads, managerial policies, property rights, and trade channels. Conse-

[3] The same, p. 44. See particularly the testimony of Simon Sterne.
[4] 26 Stat. 209.
[5] *United States* v. *Trans-Missouri Freight Association,* 166 U.S. 290 (1897); and *United States* v. *Joint Traffic Association,* 171 U.S. 505 (1898).
[6] *Northern Securities Company* v. *United States,* 193 U.S. 197.
[7] *ICC Statistics of Railways in the United States, 1891,* p. 14; the same, 1917, p. 12.

quently, the consolidation program of 1920 was launched in an unpromising environment.

## II. CONSOLIDATION AND RECAPTURE UNDER THE 1920 ACT

Under the Transportation Act, 1920, the Interstate Commerce Commission was, in effect, instructed to adjust the general level of rates in such a way that the carriers as a whole and on the average would be permitted to earn a fair return on the value of their transportation property. The situation of the weak and strong railroads was to be dealt with on the short-run basis by the recapture of excess earnings. The idea was to force favorably situated carriers to serve as the financial benefactors of the weak roads. However, the long-range solution was to be achieved through the physical consolidation of the weak and strong roads into a limited number of balanced systems.

*Defects of the program.* The Commission was instructed by Congress to prepare and adopt "as soon as practicable . . . a plan for the consolidation of the railway properties of the continental United States into a limited number of systems."[8] Specifically, it was instructed to arrange the various systems so that:

. . . the cost of transportation as between competitive systems and as related to the values of the properties through which the service is rendered shall be the same, so far as practicable, so that these systems can employ uniform rates in the movement of competitive traffic and under efficient management earn substantially the same rate of return upon the value of their respective railway properties.[9]

This proposed solution of the co-ordination problem proved ineffective and largely futile for two reasons. In the first place, the restrictive standards prescribed by the act tended to defeat the objective of railroad unification. The Commission was, in effect, directed to formulate a consolidation scheme that would not disturb competitive relations and channels of trade any more than necessary. Thus, emphasis was placed upon the maintenance of existing operating and corporate relationships

[8] Sec. 5 (2) *Interstate Commerce Acts Annotated,* Vol. 9, p. 7438.
[9] The same.

despite the fact that the major purpose of unification was to reduce the waste arising out of a poorly balanced system.

The second major weakness stemmed from the fact that initiative and final decision with respect to railroad consolidation was left in the hands of railroad management. The Commission was directed to formulate a general plan of consolidation, but it was not given power to require conformity by the individual carriers. Naturally, the stockholders of prosperous roads could see no personal advantage in diluting their earnings by merging with weak lines. But as the Commission observed, precisely this was required as a practical matter.[10]

*Failure of the consolidation program.* The fact is that the provisions of the 1920 act did not achieve the desired results of rearranging the railroads into balanced systems that could "employ uniform rates in the movement of traffic and under efficient management earn substantially the same rate of return on the value of their . . . railway properties." As one student of this problem has observed:

However attractive the idea of combining strong and weak roads may have seemed to the legislators, in practice the strong carriers shunned necessitous roads and instead took over properties which offered immediate profit or provided some strategic advantage to the acquiring carrier.[11]

But failure of the program is explained by several factors other than basic defects of the statutory provisions. Although Congress emphasized expedition, the Commission did not promulgate a "final plan" of consolidation until 1929.[12] Throughout

---

[10] "The primary purpose of consolidation, as we understand it, is to effect, subject to certain requirements as to preservation of competition and of existing routes where practicable, an amalgamation between the weak and the strong roads so as to produce systems which, while perhaps not as strong as some of the existing properties, will be stronger than the average of the weaker roads to be consolidated; and there is no conceivable way by which that objective may be attained except by allocating to the same system both strong and weak roads." *Consolidation of Railroads,* 185 I.C.C. 403, 420 (1932).

[11] William M. Leonard, *Railroad Consolidation under the Transportation Act of 1920* (1946), p. 264.

[12] *Consolidation of Railroads,* 159 I.C.C. 522 (1929). This plan differed from that tentatively proposed in 1921 mainly in the recognition given in the former to the consolidations which had, in effect, been accomplished in the interim through authorized acquisitions of control.

this period the agency repeatedly expressed doubt "as to the wisdom of the provisions of the law which now require us to adopt a complete plan to which all future consolidations must conform."[13] However, in 1929, the Commission finally decided to "comply as far as possible with the mandate of the law" since Congress had refused to amend the original provisions.[14]

In the meantime, partial unification was taking place under other provisions of the act which permitted one carrier to acquire control of another through lease or by purchase of stock subject to Commission approval. Regarding the significance of this development, the Federal Coordinator observed in 1934 that: ". . . The delay in adopting a plan prevented the consummation of consolidations in the technical legal sense, but did not prevent the accomplishment of the same virtual result in other ways."[15] This interpretation is open to question. For by approving partial unifications the Commission made progressively more difficult the attainment of the ultimate objective of integration through physical consolidation. Some of the approved mergers subsequently proved to be "uneconomical and ruinous."[16] But of more importance they tended to accentuate and rigidify the undesirable pattern of weak and strong roads.

*Shift of emphasis to transport co-ordination, 1933.* The disruptive impact of depression forces in the early thirties again focused attention on the structural and financial weakness of the railroad system. Through emergency legislation enacted in 1933[17] an attempt was made to eliminate the more obvious defects of the consolidation devices contained in the 1920 act.[18] But for all practical purposes the idea of general consolidation

[13] *39th Annual Report of the Interstate Commerce Commission, 1925*, p. 13.

[14] *43rd Annual Report of the Interstate Commerce Commission, 1929*, p. 87.

[15] Federal Coordinator of Transportation, *Regulation of Railroads*, S. Doc. 119, 73 Cong. 2 sess. (1934), p. 22.

[16] Leonard, *Railroad Consolidation*, p. 267.

[17] The Emergency Railroad Transportation Act, 1933 (48 Stat. 211).

[18] This legislation eliminated the differences in the statutory conditions under which acquisitions and consolidations could be approved and subjected all devices for acquiring control of carriers, including the holding company technique, to ICC jurisdiction.

was subordinated to a radically different attack on the problem of competitive waste in transportation.

Recognizing the failure of direct Commission action in this field, the 1933 legislation set up a temporary office of "Federal Coordinator of Transportation" and, in effect, instructed this agency, among other things:

To encourage and promote or require action on the part of the carriers and of subsidiaries subject to the Interstate Commerce Act . . . which will avoid unnecessary duplication of services and facilities . . . and permit the joint use of terminals and trackage. . . .[19]

For a variety of reasons the Coordinator failed to achieve any tangible results in the direction of compulsory co-ordination or consolidation of physical transport facilities.[20] This office was permitted to lapse in 1936, and full responsibility for consolidation and acquisition of control reverted to the Interstate Commerce Commission.

### III. PRESENT STATUS OF CONSOLIDATION PROGRAM

In 1940 the Commission was relieved of any further responsibility for the preparation of a general plan of railroad consolidation. However, the Commission apparently attaches little importance to this amendment:

Inasmuch as the plan of consolidation can readily be, and upon several occasions has been, changed to permit unifications for which it did not provide, and inasmuch as in eastern territory at least, it now provides for consolidations which substantially reflected the

---

[19] 48 Stat. 211, sec. 4.

[20] Actually the efforts of the Coordinator were concentrated on research and investigation and on recommendations for new regulatory programs affecting highway and water transportation. In reviewing the work of his office, the Coordinator at one point stated:

"In the discussion of the Act prior to its enactment attention had been particularly directed to forms of waste which involved unnecessary duplication or multiplication of operations, and to projects for the elimination of such waste, like the unification or joint use of terminal facilities or the pooling of trains or traffic. Upon consideration it seemed to the Coordinator that there were even more important forms of waste growing out of failure to adjust operations, equipment, service, and rates to the new conditions which had been created by the tremendous development of competing forms of transportation. . . ." *Fourth Report of the Federal Coordinator of Transportation on Transportation Legislation,* H. Doc. 394, 74 Cong. 2 sess. (1936), p. 35.

combined judgment of the leading railroad executives in that territory, there seems little reason to believe that such a change in the law will be very fruitful of results.[21]

As the case now stands, the Commission may approve any proposed railroad acquisition or consolidation (one railroad by another) if it finds that the proposed transaction, as modified or qualified by the Commission, is "consistent with the public interest."[22] In passing upon such proposals, the Commission is directed to give weight to the following considerations among others:

(1) The effect of the proposed transaction upon adequate transportation service to the public; (2) the effect upon the public interest of the inclusion, or failure to include, other railroads in the territory involved in the proposed transaction; (3) the total fixed charges resulting from the proposed transaction; and (4) the interest of the carrier employees affected.[23]

It will be observed that the 1940 amendment removed the previous requirement that consolidations should not unduly interfere with the maintenance of competition and channels of commerce. But there is little reason to believe that the course of railroad consolidation will be very much different under the 1940 act than it was under the 1920 law. For Congress has failed to recognize the inescapable conclusion that effective railroad consolidation cannot be achieved on a voluntary basis. Experience has demonstrated that some private interest inevitably conflicts with the objectives of any sound consolidation plan. The Commission has power to require the inclusion of weak carriers in any particular consolidation proposal. But the initiating railroads have no obligation to accept the modified plan. Moreover, it is unnatural to expect the owners of a financially strong carrier voluntarily to dilute their equity by absorbing a weak and therefore high-cost carrier, even though such action would serve the general public interest in the maintenance of sound transport conditions.[24]

---

[21] 53rd Annual Report of the Interstate Commerce Commission, 1939, p. 15.
[22] Sec. 5 (2)(b), Interstate Commerce Acts Annotated, Vol. 11, p. 9180.
[23] The same, sec. 5 (2)(c).
[24] ". . . the Act has not got at the salient defects of earlier legislation, which

Ordinarily, consolidation proposals of any significance are opposed by organized labor and affected shippers, as well as by investors and railroad management. Labor fears reduction of total employment, since most estimates attribute approximately 60 per cent of potential saving from consolidation to reduction in the amount of labor required to produce a satisfactory level of service. This apprehension is apparently unabated by the fact that the Commission is directed, as a condition of its approval of any consolidation or acquisition transaction, to "require a fair and equitable arrangement to protect the interests of the railroad employees affected."[25]

Industries and communities which have grown up around and are dependent upon established patterns of railroad service and rates usually contend that consolidation would leave them stranded or dependent upon a single rail line. Such opposition is not firmly grounded. Under modern transport conditions, the most rigid type of railroad consolidation would not deprive any community of adequate service. Each would enjoy the competition of railroad and highway agencies at the minimum, and most would be served by rail, air, and highway. A substantial number would have direct access to rail, highway, air, and water services. Moreover, as noted above, the regulatory agency is fully equipped with power to prevent discriminatory pricing as well as other types of undue preference.

It is, of course, true that effective railroad consolidation would produce temporary dislocations and inconveniences, and even permanent rearrangements of the accustomed relationships between transport services and shippers. It would also involve some drastic reshuffling of corporate relationships and

---

all grew out of the fact that Congress has tried to promote consolidation on a voluntary and competitive basis and yet achieve objectives contrary to the conflicting hopes and aspirations of the persons and interests which alone have the power to initiate the projects, viz., rail executives and investors." Ralph L. Dewey, "The Transportation Act of 1940," *American Economic Review*, Vol. 31 (1941), p. 22.

[25] Sec. 5 (2)(f), *Interstate Commerce Acts Annotated*, Vol. 11, p. 9181. Actually, the law prescribes specific standards which, in effect, protect workers from any worsening in their positions for a period of four years from the effective date of any consolidation order.

executive positions. But, none of these considerations should be allowed to obscure the fact that systematic consolidation is essential to transportation progress.

### IV. THE NEED FOR CONSOLIDATION

There is a growing body of evidence which indicates that solution of the consolidation problem is indispensable not only to the long-term improvement of railroad efficiency but to orderly rate regulation as well.

*Relation to railroad efficiency.* Contemporary competition together with the progressive pressure of rising costs on revenues makes railroad survival in private ownership dependent upon the elimination of all drags on operating efficiency. Differences of opinion exist as to how consolidations should be achieved and who is to blame for the failure to achieve it. But railroad executives are generally agreed that systematic consolidation would tend to modernize the railroad industry and increase efficiency. For example, one executive has recently observed:

> Through federal negation of steps taken in the early days of the past century toward consolidating the railways into a few great systems and by subsequently interposing additional legal regulatory and procedural obstacles in the path of their corporate amalgamation, the railways today, alone among the great industries of America, are not organized for mass production.[26]

Moreover, the official organization for the railroad industry has recently emphasized the inadequacies of informal "coordination" as a device for improving the general competitive position of the industry:

> While . . . there has been considerable progress in consolidation through voluntary action of the railroad companies, it falls short of anything like a complete consolidation of the railroads of the country into a limited number of systems. Much of the progress along these lines represents a closer integration of properties which for many years had been related to one another in some form or other. . . . *The future of the railroad industry depends to a consider-*

[26] John W. Barriger (President, Monon Railroad), "Streamlining Railroads for Mass Production of Transportation," an address delivered before the American Association of Railroad Superintendents, Chicago, Ill., June 5, 1947.

*able extent upon its ability to so reduce its costs as to enable it to prosper under a level of rates which competition will force upon it together with the volume of traffic necessary to produce adequate revenues.* Moreover, important savings lie in the field of necessary capital expenditures which the railroads must make to meet post-war conditions. These expenditures will be on a high cost level and there is more necessity than ever that they be concentrated to the very best advantage of the industry as a whole. "Coordination" of independently owned facilities is helpful, but for well-known reasons, falls short of meeting the situation.[27]

It seems clear then that railroad efficiency and perhaps survival in a competitive transportation era will be determined by the outcome of consolidation efforts. Manifestly, the operating pattern and corporate structure must be re-cast along lines that will permit full exploitation of modern technology in order to produce the lowest cost and most efficient transportation service.

*Rate regulation and the weak and strong problem.* It will be recalled that the original goal of railroad consolidation as set forth in the Transportation Act, 1920 was to rearrange the nation's carriers into a limited number of balanced systems. The systems were to be so constituted that the individual carriers assigned to each would have reasonably comparable operating costs. Uniform rates would therefore produce similar rates of return on invested capital. Approximation of these objectives has been achieved only with respect to rate uniformity. And, in view of the extreme disparities in the operating costs of individual carriers, all competing for the same traffic, rate uniformity has produced incongruous results with respect to relative earnings and has continuously embarrassed the regulatory process.

The basic problem arises in connection with the Commis-

[27] Association of American Railroads, *Consolidation of Railroads* (1945), p. 31. (Italics added.) A presidential committee had pointed out several years before: "Those who have had experience in rail transportation recognize that the only true coordination is that which is brought about through consolidation. The practical difficulties which inhere in coordination are absent in consolidation." *Report of Committee Appointed September 20, 1938, by the President of the United States to Submit Recommendations Upon the General Transportation Situation* (Committee of Six), Dec. 23, 1938, p. 31.

sion's effort to regulate the general level of railroad rates in such a way that all carriers will be able to survive financially without, at the same time, enabling some roads to realize exorbitant rates of return on their capital investment. So far, the effort has proved futile, although the Commission has applied a wide range of techniques and theories in the search for a solution.

At an early stage the Commission merely closed its eyes to the wide disparities in the earnings of individual carriers and assumed that the independent units in reality constituted one operating system. Thus in 1914 the Commission observed that:

The financial condition of the various railroads composing the 35 systems varies greatly, as disclosed by their net corporate income as well as by their net operating income. The condition of some of them is so prosperous that they clearly do not need a higher net income; the condition of others is such as to preclude the expectation of a return upon outstanding capital stock or the possibility of raising much additional capital without a thorough reorganization. . . .

*Treating as one road the 35 railway systems* that have joined in this application for our approval of a so-called 5 percent advance in their freight charges, we have reached the conclusion that their net operating income is insufficient and should be increased.[28]

The attempt to solve the problem by imagining the existence of a single railroad system was set aside by the Transportation Act of 1920, which, as already noted, sought to solve the issue eventually by actual consolidation. In the meantime, rates were to be set at a level which would provide a reasonable rate of return for the industry as a whole; and excessive profits, resulting from unbalanced earning power of individual carriers, were to be "recaptured." The latter was viewed solely as a temporary expedient pending the recasting of the carriers into a small number of balanced systems. However, the recapture experiment became entangled in litigation over the elements of value that should enter into the construction of a rate base. And since the consolidation program had failed, the recapture device was abandoned in 1933.

[28] *The Five Percent Case*, 31 I.C.C. 351, 384, decided July 29, 1914 (Italics added).

*Commission experiment with pooling of revenue.* Left without any direct method of dealing with the problem of weak and strong railroads, the Commission turned to experiments with the pooling of carrier revenue.[29] The first major attempt in this direction was made in 1931 without success; another equally unsatisfactory effort was made in 1937. Apparently, pooling has now been abandoned by the Commission as a method of dealing with the weak and strong road problem.

Fifteen Percent Case of 1931. In this case the Commission denied the carriers' application for a general 15 per cent increase in the level of rates but allowed the imposition of so-called "surcharges" on specified commodities. The increases allowed were made conditional upon the submission by the carriers of a plan for the "division among them of the gross proceeds derived from the increase."[30]

Protesting that the pooling conditions prescribed by the Commission were unlawful and unworkable, the carriers applied for the substitution of a lending plan. Although not "prepared to admit that the construction placed upon section 5 (1) of the act by counsel for the carriers" was correct, the Commission conceded that "the language contained in that paragraph is not sufficiently definite to exclude differences in views concerning its meaning."[31]

[29] Before enactment of the original act to regulate commerce in 1887, it was common practice for the carriers to pool revenue and traffic in an effort to avoid ruinous rate wars. This practice was declared illegal in all forms by sec. 5 of the 1887 act, and was also declared in violation of the Sherman Antitrust Act of 1890. (*U.S.* v. *Trans-Missouri Freight Association,* 166 U.S. 290.) The Transportation Act, 1920 gave the Commission authority to approve pooling arrangements under certain conditions. However, the carriers asked the Commission to approve such agreements "only in a very few instances of limited scope." 179 I.C.C. 215, 227. From dissenting opinion of Commissioner Eastman in Supplemental Report on Reconsideration of 178 I.C.C. 539, *Fifteen Percent Case, 1931.*

[30] "The applicants apparently recognize that at this time it is futile to increase rates with the object of reaching 5.75 per cent on the value of their properties as a whole. The practical limitation of what the traffic will bear and continue to move by rail must be given consideration. Clearly any practicable increase, unaccompanied by a pooling provision, might not prevent threatened default in the fixed interest obligations of some of the carriers. On the other hand, a smaller increase in the aggregate revenue, marshalled for the benefit of the carriers in need, will tend to stabilize the industry. We shall provide for such marshalling." *Fifteen Percent Case, 1931,* 178 I.C.C. 539, 579-80.

[31] 179 I.C.C. 215, 218.

In the face of these objections and ambiguities of the law, the Commission modified its original report "to the extent of relieving the carriers from the necessity of complying with the pooling plan therein described."[32] This left the carriers free to apply their own lending plan since the Commission took no responsibility for prescribing or approving its terms. However, the Commission observed that: ". . . We rely on them to apply the funds to be derived from the authorized increases in rates in aid of financially weak railroads in accordance with the purposes expressed in our original report. . . ."[33] By this action the Commission, in effect, abandoned the attempt to force the pooling of carrier revenue. Commissioner Eastman pointed out in his dissent, since the majority decision left the matter "wholly within the discretion of the carriers," there was no assurance that the purpose of the original order would be realized.[34]

The 1937 pooling experiment. Despite the complete failure of the Commission's 1931 attempt to impose a general pooling system on the carriers, another effort along similar lines was made in 1937. In the General Commodity Rate Increases Case of that year, the Commission was again faced with the weak and strong road problem, highlighted as usual by the relative affluence of the coal carriers. Of the estimated 53.6 million dollars to be derived from the proposed increases, 31.4 millions would come from the transportation of coal and coke; and of the latter amount bituminous coal alone would account for 26.9 million dollars.[35]

The ICC further observed that of the 26.9 million dollars estimated to be derived from increases on bituminous coal, the Pocahontas region would receive some 6.3 million dollars, or 23 per cent of the total. But the embarrassing fact was that the three principal railroads of the so-called Pocahontas region were in no need of additional revenue. In 1936 they earned 9 per cent on aggregate investment as shown by their own books.

[32] The same, p. 219.
[33] The same.
[34] The same, p. 221.
[35] *General Commodity Rate Increases*, 1937, 223 I.C.C. 657, 740.

The Commission was therfore forced to admit that if those carriers alone were under consideration there would not be "a shadow of justification for permitting an increase in their freight rates on coal, which constitutes the bulk of their traffic."[36] Again, the Commission was caught in the dilemma of competitive rate structures. The situation was such that "unless the Pocahontas rates are increased, many of the most important rates of other lines in the eastern district and perhaps some of the rates elsewhere cannot, as a practical matter, be increased."[37]

In other words, the charges made for similar services must be practically uniform because keen competition exists between the railroads in all areas of the country and for all types of traffic. Moreover, the unit cost of moving particular types of traffic varies widely among individual carriers in the same territories. Consequently, any effort on the part of the Commission to allow "needy carriers" (high-cost) to raise rates on competitive traffic without at the same time permitting (or requiring) similar increases for the opulent (low-cost) roads would result in further impoverishment of the weak lines. For such a rate structure would tend to divert traffic from the high- to the low-cost roads.

On many occasions, the Commission's conscience has been "shocked" by this coexistence of carrier opulence and poverty under presumably fair, just and reasonable rate structures prescribed by that body. The specific aspect of the coal case that disturbed the Commission was the fact that, in setting a level of rates adequate to support the less fortunately situated railroads, the revenues of the Pocahontas lines would be "swollen by more than $6,000,000 which they do not need and which will not be used for any betterment of the general railroad situation."[38]

The Commission observed that "by appropriate resort to the pooling and division of earnings which the act permits, such

[36] The same, p. 741.
[37] The same, p. 745.
[38] The same.

unfortunate results could be avoided."[39] However, it was thought unwise to require such a pooling arrangement since the "possibilities in this direction were not canvassed *in the present record*."[40] Under these circumstances, the regulatory agency adopted the expedient of placing a time limit on its findings with respect to bituminous coal rates. The obvious purpose of this device was to persuade the carriers to present to the Commission some voluntary pooling scheme.[41] No one has been able to explain why the Commission believed that the Pocahontas lines would come forward with such a scheme to aid their competitors.

The cases discussed above illustrate the manner in which the weak and strong railroad problem has plagued the rate-making process for more than a quarter of a century. To a limited extent, the division of joint rates can be used to deal with the situation.[42] Mandatory pooling of revenue could also be used effectively in certain circumstances if Congress were inclined to give the commission the necessary authority.[43] And occasionally the traffic pattern is such that rate differentials can be used to give one set of carriers needed rate increases without at the same time enabling others to make excessive earnings.[44]

[39] The same.

[40] The same. (Italics added.)

[41] "The truth is, as the report shows, that the time limit is placed on the approval of increases upon bituminous coal with the expectation that some coercion will thereafter be exercised by someone to induce the Pocahontas lines to pool their coal revenue, and distribute part of it to other less strong lines." The same p. 759, dissenting opinion of Commissioner Aitchison.

[42] The Commission has power to divide the revenues derived from joint rates among the participating carriers in accordance with financial need rather than in the portion of the transportation work performed. *New England Divisions*, 66 I.C.C. 196 (1922). There are, however, severe practical limitations of the extent to which this device can be used as a general solution for the weak and strong problem. See D. Philip Locklin, *Economics of Transportation* (revised ed. 1944), p. 430.

[43] Although the ICC recommended that provisions for mandatory pooling be incorporated in the Transportation Act of 1940, such action was not taken. Consequently, that agency is as powerless now as before to deal with the weak and strong road problem through direct pooling requirements.

[44] For example, in *Ex Parte 166*, Interim Decision of Oct. 6, 1947, the Commission allowed a 10-cents-per-ton increase on iron ore ex-lake but allowed no increase on movements to the upper lake ports. However, this solution was not entirely satisfactory for it penalized several "weak" ore-carrying roads.

But these devices do not reach to the root-cause of the trouble. At best they would serve to compensate in a tortuous way for basic imperfections in the corporate and operating organization of the railroad industry. In order to correct the situation at the source, the individual units must be physically rearranged to eliminate wasteful duplication of facilities and to make possible the most efficient use of equipment. And there must be actual merging of corporate and financial structures in order to make the earnings of the merged unit available for needed investment in additions and betterments on any part of the system.

*Unifications have not solved weak and strong road problems.* Some contend that the acquisitions and mergers effectuated under the terms of the Transportation Act, 1920 have integrated the railroad structure as effectively as though consolidation had taken place under the Commission's general plan. The Federal Coordinator of Transportation, for example, contended that:

> By resort to long-term leases, often accompanied by complete stock ownership, properties were tied together about as tightly as if they had been technically consolidated, and lesser degrees of control were also effected. Much more was done in this way than is commonly supposed.[45]

It is true that there has been a definite trend to the centralization of railroad control into fewer companies. Thus between 1920 and 1940 the total number of railroads reporting to the ICC decreased from 882 to 541. The number of Class I roads reporting to the ICC decreased from 186 to 133.[46] Centralization of control was also furthered by stock ownership. By 1940 such control had developed to the point that 58 Class I railroads, constituting 20 systems, accounted for 80 per cent of total operating revenues of Class I railroads and 77 per cent of road miles operated.[47] Since that date further consolidation, arising primarily out of reorganization plans, has increased the degree of centralized control.[48]

[45] S. Doc. 119, 73 Cong. 2 sess., p. 22.
[46] Association of American Railroads, *Consolidation of Railroads* (1945), p. 17.
[47] The same.
[48] For the classification of railroads into "systems" as defined by the ICC, see *ICC Statistics of Railways in the United States,* annual issues.

This marked trend since 1920 toward centralization of control does not mean that the original objectives of physical consolidation for purposes of ownership and management have been achieved. For these unifications do not constitute the limited number of systems with balanced earning power contemplated under the Transportation Act, 1920.[49] Nor do the constituent parts of the system actually operate as integrated corporations with respect to the pooling of earnings. Thus the excess earnings of a strong road in the system are not available either to make up the deficits incurred by the weaker parts of the system or for reinvestment in additions and betterments for the weak lines.

The chief advantage realized from the grouping of individual carriers into railroad systems has been in the handling of interchange traffic and in facilitating the division of revenues from joint services. While this obviously makes for improved service and some economy, it does not go to the heart of the weak and strong problem. It does not eliminate the waste involved in duplicating terminals and parallel routes. Nor has the system of grouping provided any solution for the problem of rate regulation, for the historic pattern of variations in earnings persists.

During the fairly representative prewar period of 1939-41, the rate of return on net investment[50] of Class I carriers averaged 3.25 per cent. However, the actual range was from a high of 19 per cent for one carrier to a deficit for 11. Twenty-one carriers had a rate of return on investment of 6 per cent and higher. These carriers accounted for only 7 per cent of the net investment and about 9 per cent of the transportation work done (as measured by operating revenue). However, they earned almost 17 per cent of the net operating income of all Class I carriers, almost 40 per cent of the net income, and paid over 52 per cent of all dividends declared. (See chart p. 333.)

At the other extreme, 50 carriers showing a rate of return ranging from 2 to 4 per cent accounted for over 72 per cent of

[49] As noted above, railroad management concedes that the carriers are not properly organized today to take full advantage of the efficiencies which would flow from rapid and orderly adoption of railroad technological advances.

[50] Depreciated investment in railway property plus cash and materials and supplies.

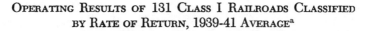

# OPERATING RESULTS OF 131 CLASS I RAILROADS CLASSIFIED BY RATE OF RETURN, 1939-41 AVERAGE[a]

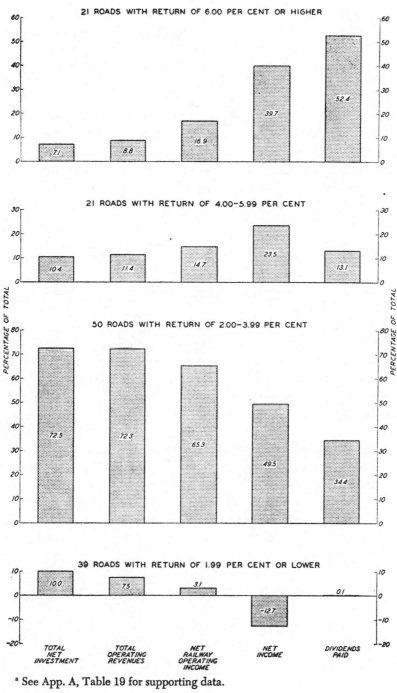

[a] See App. A, Table 19 for supporting data.

333

total investment and transportation work done. But they earned only 65 per cent of the net operating income and less than 50 per cent of the net income, and accounted for only 34 per cent of the dividends paid. The 39 carriers earning less than a 2 per cent return accounted for 10 per cent of the investment and 7.5 per cent of the operating revenues, yet earned only 3 per cent of the operating income and suffered a net loss for the period.

It is significant that operating results for the 1939-41 period reveal equally wide variations between the average earnings of the so-called railroad systems, and also among the individual carriers within any one system. Of the 19 systems composed of 66 carriers, only 2, containing 9 roads, exceeded a 4 per cent rate of return. These two systems accounted for less than 14 per cent of the total investment and over 14 per cent of the transportation work done. But they earned 21.5 per cent of net operating income, almost 41 per cent of the net income, and accounted for over 42 per cent of dividends paid. (See chart p. 335.)

In contrast, the 15 systems composed of 50 carriers having a return varying from 2 to 4 per cent accounted for 82 per cent of the investment and almost 83 per cent of the operating revenues. But they earned less than 67 per cent of the net income and accounted for less than 58 per cent of dividends paid. Although a few systems showed fairly even distribution of earnings among the carriers composing the system, most reveal a wide disparity. For example, there was wide variation of earnings among the 8 carriers of the Missouri Pacific system with the rate of return ranging from more than 9 per cent for one carrier to a deficit for another. The rate of return among the 9 units of the Atlantic Coast Line system varied from a high of over 7 per cent for one carrier to a deficit for another. (See Appendix A, Table 20.)

*Improved capital structure has not solved the problem.* The disparity in earnings persists, although the capital structure of a large number of important carriers has been drastically revised in recent years through reorganization proceedings.[51] Thus

[51] As of 1938, 38 Class I carriers accounting for approximately 77,119 miles

## OPERATING RESULTS OF 19 SYSTEMS (COMPRISING 66 CARRIERS) CLASSIFIED BY RATE OF RETURN, 1939-41 AVERAGE[a]

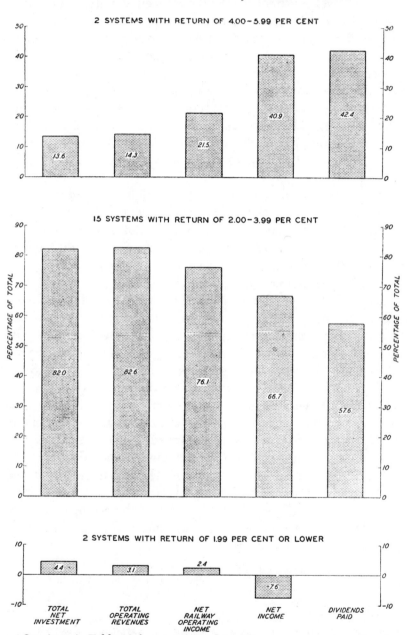

2 SYSTEMS WITH RETURN OF 4.00–5.99 PER CENT

15 SYSTEMS WITH RETURN OF 2.00–3.99 PER CENT

2 SYSTEMS WITH RETURN OF 1.99 PER CENT OR LOWER

[a] See App. A, Table 19 for supporting data. There were no systems showing a rate of return of 6 per cent or higher.

335

the rate level in effect in 1947 produced variations in actual earnings of individual companies, ranging from a high of almost 26 per cent return on net investment for one carrier to a deficit for 16 carriers. (The average for all Class I railroads was 3.41 per cent.) Twenty-nine railroads showed a rate of return of 6 per cent or more and accounted for less than 10 per cent of the total investment and for 10.8 per cent of the transportation work done. However, they earned almost 23 per cent of the net railway operating income, 29 per cent of the net income, and paid 35 per cent of all dividends declared by Class I railroads. (See chart p. 337.)

At the other extreme, 38 carriers earning a rate of return of less than 2 per cent accounted for 29 per cent of the total investment and about 28 per cent of the transportation work done. But they earned less than 9 per cent of the net operating income, accounted for less than 7 per cent of the dividends paid, and as a group suffered a net loss for the year.

As in the earlier period (1939-41) there was almost as much variation among the 19 railroad systems (composed of 60 Class I carriers) as there was among the individual carriers. Six systems, made up of 21 Class I carriers, earned a return varying from 4 to 6 per cent. These systems accounted for about 28 per cent of both the total investment and the transportation work. They earned over 44 per cent of the net operating income, 58.6 per cent of the net income, and paid over 50 per cent of the dividends declared by all system carriers. (See chart p. 338.)

At the other end of the scale, 6 systems, composed of 19 roads, earned less than a 2 per cent return. These systems accounted for over 41 per cent of both total investment and transportation work, but earned less than 22 per cent of the net operating income, only 9 per cent of the net income, and paid 18 per cent of the aggregate dividends.

---

were undergoing financial reorganization brought about by bankruptcy or receivership. At the end of 1947, this figure had been reduced to 18,631 miles and only 17 Class I railroads remained in the process of reorganization. A comparison of the capital structure of the 21 reorganized roads just prior to the date they were taken into the hands of the court with the capital structure set up under the reorganization plans reveals that these reorganizations resulted in scaling down the capitalization of the affected carriers by approximately 1,380 million dollars, or 33.4 per cent, and a drastic reduction of fixed charges.

## OPERATING RESULTS OF 127 CLASS I RAILROADS (REPRESENTING 131 CARRIERS) CLASSIFIED BY RATE OF RETURN, 1947[a]

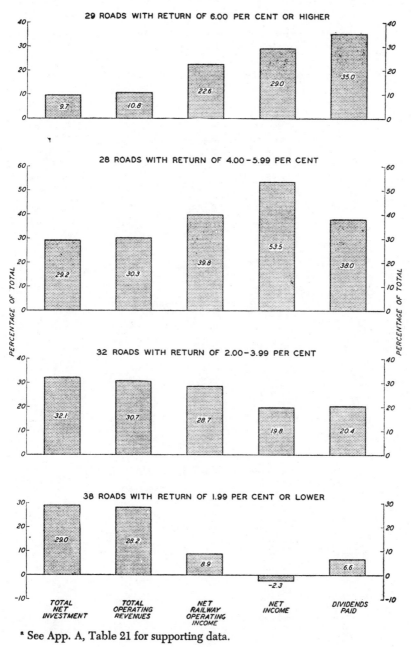

[a] See App. A, Table 21 for supporting data.

# OPERATING RESULTS OF 19 SYSTEMS (COMPRISING 60 RAILROADS) CLASSIFIED BY RATE OF RETURN, 1947[a]

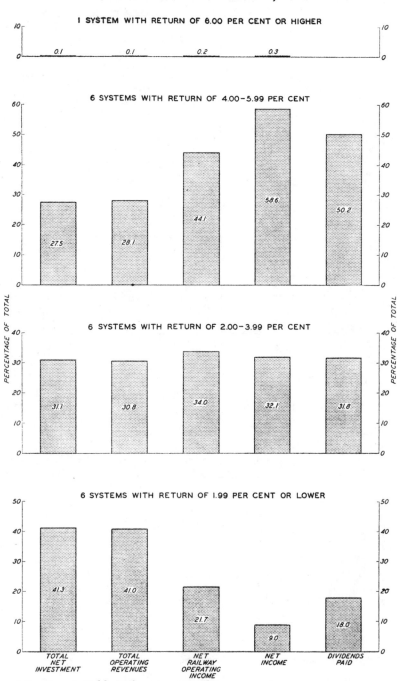

[a] See App. A, Table 21 for supporting data.

## V. THE NEED FOR REVISION OF CONSOLIDATION POLICY AND REASSIGNMENT OF ADMINISTRATIVE RESPONSIBILITY

From the above review we have seen that railroad consolidation in this country has had a stormy and largely futile career. The government has struggled for almost three decades in an effort to deal with the weak and strong railroad problem. Costly and protracted experiments have been conducted with such devices as voluntary consolidation in accordance with an official "general plan"; recapture of excess earnings; and pooling of revenues.

It has also been shown that, in the interest both of improved railroad efficiency and rational rate regulation, some effective means must be found to rearrange the corporate and operating structure of the carriers. However, it is equally clear that this objective is not likely to be attained without drastic revision of policy and reassignment of administrative responsibility. Two basic requirements must be met if substantial progress is to be made in the direction of systematic railroad consolidation:

1. There must be legislative recognition of the fact that the voluntary program has failed and that systematic railroad consolidation can be effected only in accordance with a general plan.

2. The Interstate Commerce Commission should not be given responsibility for the formulation of such a plan.

*Failure of voluntary program and need for a general plan of consolidation.* It will be recalled that the Interstate Commerce Commission, as well as the interested parties, viewed the statutory requirements for a general plan of consolidation as a deterrent to railroad unification. Thus a special presidential committee representing railroad management and labor reported in 1938:

The fact that consolidation of railroads has not been carried out to an even greater extent is, in our opinion, ascribable to two factors. Prior to 1920 it was retarded by the prohibitions of the anti-trust acts. Since that date it has been hampered by the unduly restrictive provisions of section 5 of the Interstate Commerce Act with their requirement for a rigid plan developed in accordance with a prescribed formula, which militates against any results that are not highly artificial and unattractive.

We do not think the country is ready for any compulsory system of consolidations. Whether ultimate resort must be had to the principle of compulsion is a question which we think it better to defer until after there has been an opportunity to see what can be accomplished if the railroads are relieved from these limitations and restrictions.[52]

The so-called restrictive features referred to above were largely removed by the Transportation Act of 1940. However, as we have already noted, there is little reason to believe that effective railroad consolidation will be advanced by relieving the Commission of responsibility for formulating a general plan of unification. Actually, this action on the part of Congress constitutes an official abandonment of "a comprehensive and planned system of consolidations."[53] By relieving the ICC of the obligation to prepare a general plan and to see that voluntary proposals made by the carriers conform to the plan, Congress has validated the Commission's traditional policy of leisurely and empirically settling each case and issue "on its own merit."

Apparently Congress has failed to realize that the case-by-case approach to the problem of railroad consolidation is both theoretically and technically defective. The sole purpose of a general plan of consolidation is to provide the framework within which the individual carriers may be arranged to provide the maximum operating economy, and consequently the lowest possible transportation cost. If, as contended by the Commission, the formulation of such a plan is not feasible, how can it be seriously argued that the recognized objectives of consolidation can better be achieved through piecemeal approval or rejection of individual consolidation proposals? By what standards or tests does the Commission decide in each of these individual cases whether or not the specific unification proposal is in the public interest? Certainly it must take into account the effect of the proposed consolidation upon traffic

---

[52] *Report of the Committee Appointed September 20, 1938, by the President of the United States to Submit Recommendations upon the General Transportation Situation* (Committee of Six), Dec. 23, 1938, p. 31.

[53] Leonard, *Railroad Consolidation*, pp. 253-54.

flow in the area involved, the impact upon agricultural, manufacturing, commercial, and labor interests and the interagency competitive situation.

Manifestly, no sensible decision with respect to these matters can be reached in a given case prior to deciding whether or not the specific proposal is superior to some alternative arrangement of the carriers in the territory or region involved. Thus specific decision cannot be made with respect to a single proposal in the absence of an over-all and previously determined program indicating how all the related parts should be fitted into an effectively operating unit.[54]

In reality, the Commission's experience during the course of two decades has not proved that a general plan of consolidation acts as a deterrent to railroad unification. On the contrary, it has only served to underscore the fundamental defect of dependence on voluntary action. For the Commission's difficulties arose primarily because of the inherent conflicts between the requirements of a sound general plan of consolidation and the immediate self-interest of individual carriers. Naturally, voluntary proposals will be advanced only by the carriers that stand to profit from the regrouping provided in the general plan. And just as naturally, the adversely affected roads will not join in the proposal. Stalemate results unless the interested group of carriers is able to gain sufficient financial control over the dissenting units to command their "co-operation."[55]

In this connection it will be recalled that the Federal Coordinator of Transportation in 1934 recommended against compulsory consolidation on the grounds that: "It would precipitate a controversy in which many railroads, many communities, and labor would join with equal vigor and from which it would be

[54] It is, of course, conceivable that the Commission contemplates a thorough study of the entire transportation problem of an area in the course of deciding each voluntary consolidation proposal that is presented. Such a procedure, although acknowledging the feasibility of formulating a general plan, would be wasteful in the extreme.

[55] The competitive bidding for carrier control that occurred during the late 1920's and early 1930's in anticipation of the promulgation of the Commission's "final plan" of consolidation affords ample evidence of the financial evils associated with such practices.

difficult to emerge."[56] He warned, however, that a choice would have to be made eventually between government ownership or railroad consolidation unless carrier management improved operating efficiency through voluntary means:

> Much will depend upon the railroad managements. They are of one mind in opposition to public ownership and operation, and in general they are against grand consolidation plans. One or the other of these remedies, however, will eventually be applied, unless the managements are able to remedy present ills in some other way. This alternative, if it is possible, can only take the form of a better organization of the railroad industry which will enable them to deal collectively and effectively with matters which concern them all. The managements must pull together instead of pulling against each other in a great variety of different directions. The difficulties are great, and I am not at all sure that they can be surmounted. The tendency to cling to assumed individual advantages in preference to those which would be gained by coordination or correlation is ingrained, and it may be impossible to overcome.[57]

Experience since 1934 indicates that the Coordinator's forebodings were well founded regarding the inability of railroad management to put aside "individual advantages" for the common good. Thus the accumulated evidence of more than a quarter of a century demonstrates that some form of compulsion will be required to break through the stubborn and effective opposition that has been concentrated on the consolidation program by special-interest groups. This does not necessarily mean that the government must launch immediately a program of outright compulsory consolidation. A middle course, under which the power of government would be used only to bring dissenting minorities into line, offers sufficient prospect of success to justify a trial. Under such an arrangement initiative for proposing railroad unifications would be left with management; but approval of individual proposals would not be left contingent on unanimous acceptance by all the carriers involved. On the contrary, it could be provided by statute that any consolidation proposals carrying the assent of a prescribed percentage

[56] S. Doc. 119, 73 Cong. 2 sess., p. 30.
[57] The same, p. 33.

of the aggregate amount of securities outstanding for the carriers involved would be approved if the Commission found that the rearrangement would be in the public interest and would otherwise conform to the provisions of the statute. The dissenting interests would then be required to exchange their securities for those of the new corporation on the terms provided by the consolidation plan and approved by the Commission.

The specific purpose of this proposal is to leave the leadership and the major work of consolidation with railroad management. In the knowledge that government authority stands ready to deal with minority interests that could otherwise block any voluntary proposals, the constructive elements in the railroad industry would have an incentive to initiate plans for modernization of the railroad structure.

It has been argued in the past that the national government has no power to effect such a proposal. However, at this juncture there appears to be little doubt that such a statute, if properly drafted, would be upheld by the courts.[58] Moreover, there are precedents for this type of combined compulsory and voluntary procedure. For example, a recent enactment provides for the "voluntary" reorganization of the railroad financial structures.[59] However, a substantial element of compulsion is involved. For, if the Interstate Commerce Commission finds that a proposed modification of the financial structure of a carrier has been approved by a specified percentage of the holders of outstanding securities, it is directed to approve the proposed alteration on the terms and conditions deemed "just and reasonable."

Whether federal incorporation of the railroads would be the most effective device for effectuating carrier unification is a question that should be considered carefully in the drafting of a revised consolidation statute.

If Congress is willing to be guided by the evidence at hand

[58] For example, as early as 1933, Leslie Craven concluded from an intensive study of the subject that Congress has the constitutional power to compel consolidation of interstate commerce carriers by railroad. See the same, App. 3, p. 98.

[59] Public Law 478, 80 Cong. 2 sess., approved Apr. 9, 1948.

and to provide the statutory basis for compulsory railroad consolidation, it necessarily follows that a general plan must be formulated to guide the corporate rearrangement of the carriers. It appears that the Interstate Commerce Commission should not be assigned any direct responsibility for the formulation of such a plan.

*Responsibility for formulating general consolidation plan.* There are two compelling reasons why responsibility for the formulation of a general consolidation plan should not be vested again in the Interstate Commerce Commission. In the first place, that agency is antagonistic to the general program. But of greater importance, the environment, procedural tempo, and philosophic convictions of the Commission offer at best a hostile administrative setting for effective performance of the function.

*Hostile administrative setting.* It will be recalled that during the greater part of two decades the Commission made repeated efforts to obtain congressional release from responsibility for promulgating a general plan of railroad consolidation. It considered the task onerous, impractical, and unsuited to its empirical methods. Under these circumstances, it is unrealistic to assume that the task would now be done either well or expeditiously. The tendency as before would be to give priority to the more pressing problems of rate regulation and to let the consolidation work muddle along as it did between 1920 and 1940.

Close observers of the Commission's performance have for many years been concerned over the increasing administrative burden and the consequent interference with the quality of its major regulatory functions. Thus, as early as 1931, Sharfman pointed out that:

. . . the very dominance of the Commission in the regulatory scheme, and the tremendous expansion of its functions and activities, have resulted in administrative difficulties which threaten the effectiveness of its labors. . . . The very fact that the Commission has succeeded in maintaining a high tradition of performance, despite its strikingly extensive calendar of activities, has led to its utilization as a sort of service department of the Federal Government in all matters directly or remotely related to the sphere of its primary jurisdiction.

But this approach has resulted in serious embarrassment. . . . Both thoroughness of consideration and promptness of decision, which are presumed to characterize the administrative method of control, tend to become very difficult, if not impossible, of attainment.[60]

It is significant that this evaluation of the Commission's administrative performance was made years before the extensive responsibilities for motor carrier, water, and freight forwarder regulation were added to the Commission's workload. And we have already indicated by reference to the long delays in disposing of current general revenue cases that the Commission has so far failed to discover any feasible method of dealing expeditiously with its major tasks.

Under these circumstances, it is imperative that functions not integrally related to the appropriate performance of the Commission's major responsibilities be assigned elsewhere. This is particularly true where, as in the case of formulating a consolidation plan, the problems are more directly related to the promotional aspects of national activity than to the regulatory responsibilities assigned to the Commission.

Relation between the consolidation plan and promotional programs. When responsibility for promulgating a general plan of railroad consolidation was vested in the Interstate Commerce Commission in 1920, the problem was limited to railroad transportation. Intercity highway transportation was in its infancy; inland water transportation was moribund; and the feasibility of air transportation was yet to be demonstrated. There was therefore some validity to the assumption that the Commission could formulate a sound consolidation plan on the theory that the future needs of interstate commerce were to be met almost exclusively by railroad transportation.

By 1933 when the "final" consolidation plan was promulgated, this assumption had long since become invalid. As indicated in Part I of this study, the federal government had in the intervening period assumed a definitive role in a vast expansion of competitive transport facilities. Not only had this competition rendered a large portion of the railroad plant functionally ob-

[60] I. L. Sharfman, *The Interstate Commerce Commission* (1931), Vol. 1, pp. 8-9.

solete, making abandonment inevitable, it had reduced previously essential mileage to a marginal status. Although retaining some economic value, much of this marginal plant had:

. . . nothing to warrant continued operation except the fact that it has attracted local interests who feel that their very existence depends upon it, but whose transportation needs could be as well if not better served today by non-rail carriers, trackage rights over competing railroads and in other ways.[61]

The net result of the multiplication of transport facilities was the failure of the railroad traffic to keep pace with the advancing volume of physical production. As the Commission observed:

. . . the chief reason for this has been the growth of competitive forms of transportation. Not only have the railroads lost since 1929 a continually increasing share of the total traffic to these competitors, but they have also found it necessary, in order to retain much other traffic, to make competitive reductions in their rates and fares.[62]

One of the major purposes of systematic railroad consolidation is to adjust the corporate and operating structure of the carriers to these new competitive forces. Consequently, any workable program for railroad consolidation must be formulated with expedition, and actual corporate rearrangement of the carriers must be effected with a minimum of delay. Otherwise the general plan will be obsolete before it is promulgated.

It is also essential that the plan be formulated with full knowledge of, and provision for, the impact of government promotional programs. Manifestly, there can be no permanent value to any plan for railroad consolidation that does not recognize the competitive implications of current and projected public expenditures that are designed to improve the range and quality of highway, air, and water services.

It is equally important that these promotional programs of the national government be tested by reference, among other

---

[61] "Consolidation of the Rail Transportation Facilities of the United States into a Single System for Ownership and Operation under Private Management," Memorandum from ICC Commissioner Miller to the Senate Committee on Interstate Commerce, Mar. 31, 1938, p. 3 (mimeo.).

[62] General Commodity Rate Increases, 1937, 223 I.C.C. 657, 731-32.

standards, to their combined effect on railroad transportation. Attainment of both objectives would be facilitated by vesting in one administrative agency full authority and responsibility for these organically related lines of government action. Such an agency would have exclusive power to initiate long-range improvement programs with respect to each major form of transportation. It would also have the corollary responsibility of assuring that all related government programs were moving in the direction of improved transportation service at the lowest possible cost in the long run.

In summary, there is persuasive evidence that the public interest will be served by effective railroad consolidation, and that such consolidation can be attained without intolerable delay only by compulsory action. The methods necessary to achieve effective consolidation will involve some drastic re-arrangement of government organization and procedure and will present formidable administrative problems. The technical complexities of the task are accentuated by the fact that, if the problem is to be solved at all, it must be attacked as a whole and disposed of within a fixed and relatively short period.

The alternative is to muddle along indefinitely with discredited concepts and methods—a route that promises to end in government ownership.

# PART III
## REVISION OF NATIONAL POLICY

# CHAPTER XVI

## CRITICAL DEFECTS OF NATIONAL TRANSPORTATION POLICY

Federal activities exert a profound influence on the provision and management of transportation services. But the various promotional and regulatory programs are loosely organized and not governed by any coherent set of principles. In final analysis, government policy in this field is characterized by defects in the programing and expenditure of public funds, unattainable regulatory objectives, and indeterminate division of authority and responsibility between government and private management.

In the private sector, where the financial condition of the majority of carriers is notoriously weak, private management has been guilty of ill-advised expansion, failure to achieve maximum economy, and lack of alertness to the possibilities of the newer forms of transportation. Communities and other interested groups have multiplied these problems in numerous ways; for example, by tenaciously resisting the abandonment of obsolete plant and service. Removal of these and other drags on progress will, of course, be necessary if we are to achieve the desirable volume and quality of transport service at the lowest possible cost. But some of the most critical present and prospective weaknesses in the transportation system are attributable to defects in the policy and administrative organization of the national government.

Expenditures for the provision of transportation facilities are authorized with no consideration for over-all transportation requirements or the relationships among transport agencies. The result has been an improvident use of public funds and a failure to program in accordance with priority of need. The use of general taxes rather than user charges to finance these facilities has resulted in an uneconomic distribution of traffic and consequently a misapplication of productive resources. In addition,

351

failure to consider the problems and possibilities of the railroad system in conjunction with the planning of public transportation facilities has prevented the realization of maximum benefits and maximum economy.

It has been noted, too, that Congress has not succeeded in welding the various phases of regulatory and promotional programs into an economically sound and efficiently administered transportation policy. It has set as one regulatory goal the fair and impartial treatment of transportation enterprises and has imposed on them the obligation to provide service without discrimination or preference between individuals and communities. At the same time, it has been deliberately discriminatory in the varying degree of public aid extended to the several transport agencies. It has charged two separate regulatory agencies with responsibility for preventing wasteful and destructive competitive practices in transportation, by rate regulation and by controlling entry and abandonment of business operations. At the same time, it has given other branches of government the power to determine independently the character of physical transport facilities, their location and capacity, and the rates at which they shall be expanded.

Conflict between policy objectives and actual practice is likewise found in the regulatory process itself. Congress has directed that the general level of rates be regulated in such a way that carriers under honest and efficient management may obtain the revenues required to provide a transportation plant adequate for the needs of commerce and national security. But the process has become so encumbered with procedural rigidities that in practice the benevolent intent serves only to delay the adjustments of rates to changing economic conditions, thereby producing financial embarrassment for the carriers affected.

The net result of these diffuse programs is that government restricts with one hand and promotes with the other. It applies control devices appropriate to the regulation of monopoly and simultaneously attempts to enforce competition. Responsibility is so widely and vaguely divided that no branch of government can be charged with the deficiencies of public action in this field. What is more important, the cumulative effect of the federal program is a division of authority between government and private enterprise such that neither can be held firmly accountable for efficiency and technical progress in transportation.

The provision of a dependable and adequate supply of transportation services is so vital to economic health and national security that any failure on the part of government and private enterprise working jointly to supply adequate transportation would necessarily lead to the assumption of full responsibility by government. This follows from the elementary fact that important segments of the total transportation plant can be provided proficiently only by government. Consequently, if government action cannot be reconciled to the motivating forces of the private enterprise system, the sector occupied by the latter will gradually contract and the benefits of this joint arrangement will be lost.

### I. DEFECTS IN PROGRAMING AND PUBLIC EXPENDITURE POLICIES

The federal government has spent some 30 billion dollars for the provision of transportation facilities and services in little over three decades. These outlays, augmented in some cases by state and local matching and maintenance expenditures, have been a major factor in determining the nature and extent of the transportation system.

Despite the physical accomplishments which such expenditures have made possible, it cannot be said that maximum progress has been made toward providing efficient and economical transportation service. Major defects in promotional policy have caused federal achievements to fall far short of potential goals. Federal activity has been marked by vague objectives, questionable methods of economic justification, narrowly conceived programing of expenditures, unsound financial policy, and defective administrative management.

Basically, the weakness in federal policy is the failure to

recognize that the ultimate objective is to achieve the best possible transportation system for the movement of persons and goods. Because different treatment of the several transportation agencies has been required throughout the history of federal transportation development, it has been assumed that for this reason the needs of each transportation agency should be considered in isolation. The result has been neglect of over-all transportation objectives and failure to view the transportation problem as a whole. Instead there has been a preoccupation with the individual problems of individual transportation agencies.

The interrelationships among transportation agencies are generally ignored by federal policy. The fact remains, however, that these relationships are basic to the determination of economic justification, to the establishment of priorities for public expenditure, and to realistic consideration of the impacts of federal transportation activity. Failure to think or act in terms of over-all transportation requirements has meant that no individual or agency has been in a position to weigh, for example, the relative financial needs of waterways and airways, or to evaluate the net results of all the various federal transportation undertakings. This failure has meant either outright waste of public funds or the loss of opportunity to achieve full benefits from public expenditure.

Recent trends indicate a continuing expansion of federal responsibility in the field of transportation. The upward trend in the scope and magnitude of federal transportation activity stresses more than ever before the need for assuring that the expenditure of federal funds is directed to the desired objectives. Since the war, national transportation activity has expanded to include a vastly augmented responsibility for roads and streets, which has more than doubled the prewar mileage of facilities eligible for federal funds. A new federal-aid program for airport development and an entirely new concept of air navigation aids have likewise been included in the category of federal projects; and plans for the development of merchant marine and river and harbor programs suggest new high levels of peacetime activity.

Moreover, the physical needs of our transportation system today are very extensive, including the heavy requirements for maintaining and replacing existing facilities and the tremendous demands for modernization. Our principal highways are grossly inadequate to accommodate current levels of motor traffic and bold concepts of design will be required to supplant the orthodox and often inadequate approach to the highway problem. The installation of an all-weather airways system, basic to the safety and regularity of air transportation, is another program demanding early completion. Modernization and consolidation of terminals are needs long overdue, especially since these facilities account for a high percentage of the time and money cost of transportation.

*In view of the magnitude of transportation requirements, the role of the federal government must be clearly defined and the relative importance of projects objectively assessed.* Consideration must be given to the degree of national importance which attaches to various aspects of the transportation program in order that federal action may be concentrated on projects best adapted to federal action and most urgently needed from the standpoint of the country as a whole. There is no apparent basis for the relative emphasis now placed on the several transportation agencies by federal promotional programs, and in some cases the desirability of any participation on the part of the federal government is open to question. Even where legitimate federal objectives are involved, justification of federal participation is often so vague that the merits of the program are difficult to judge. In the case of alleged national defense requirements, for example, no attempt is made to impose upon the military the responsibility for stating in specific terms what their needs may be.

An attempt must be made, therefore, to establish a more definitive federal role in this field. The size and character of federal programs must be determined with reference to specific national objectives. There must be a careful appraisal of the various transportation projects to be accomplished in order that the greatest needs and the most appropriate priorities may be agreed upon. These determinations cannot be made in a vacuum for each form of transportation, but only through consideration of the needs of the transportation system as a whole.

*More uniform procedures must be adopted for carrying out federal transportation activities.* The growth of federal transportation activity in separate compartments has resulted in a diversity of procedure and a failure to view at once the several aspects of federal transportation policy. Waterway proposals, for example, are submitted to Congress by interested groups or individuals, and their economic justification is determined by a branch of the military establishment which has no responsibility or concern for transportation needs as a whole. The Congress then makes the final determination of the individual projects to be included in the river and harbor program and appropriates funds to cover their construction, maintenance, and operation. In the case of federal aid for highways, the planning of a desirable program is a state function, but all projects must be contained in a limited system of eligible routes selected with federal approval. Federal funds for highway purposes are allocated among the individual states on the basis of a specific formula prescribed in the law; and these funds are limited to construction purposes and must be matched by the states.

There are numerous other procedural variations among the several federal promotional programs. All federal highway aid is channeled through the states, whereas airport aids may be granted directly to local units. Federal authorizations for highways constitute contractual obligations which are made available in full through subsequent appropriations, whereas authorizations for other transportation projects may or may not be appropriated. Operating subsidies for ocean shipping are granted in the form of direct payments to ship operators, while in the case of airlines these subsidies are included in payments for the carriage of the mail.

*There has been a lack of effective transportation planning for national defense.* Failure to plan the development and organization of transportation facilities to meet the emergency requirements of war has been another serious defect in federal policy.

That the results have not been disastrous may be attributed to the fortunate circumstances which have afforded us the time and opportunity to devise emergency procedures. During the last war we were able, after the start of hostilities, to establish a central agency in the federal government and to experiment until effective procedures had been developed. Likewise we were able to compensate for lack of foresight by creating with prodigious effort a shipbuilding industry and merchant fleet, a new pipeline network, a synthetic rubber industry, a rationing system, and other emergency solutions. The success which attended these efforts was fortunately great enough to overcome the failure to anticipate their importance. But tremendous risks were involved in gambling with the transportation system.

The prospect that another war would strike without warning and that extensive destruction would be suffered by our country, including its transportation system, makes it even clearer that the good fortune which has thus far brought victory cannot be relied upon in the future. It will be necessary to have in being at the beginning of any future conflict the transportation facilities necessary to carry us through; and the operating pattern and organization capable of assuring effective operations. Unless these plans are laid during peacetime, and the machinery established for their prosecution, it would be folly to expect the war-supporting economy to be adequately sustained.

In summary, the programing of public transportation facilities is characterized by differences, discrepancies, and omissions which are inevitable when the transportation problem is looked upon as a variety of separate problems. There are no uniform standards by which federal agencies may determine economic justification, no over-all estimates of traffic needs and trends upon which to judge needs and priorities, no uniformity with regard to the manner of establishing plans, and no opportunity for physical integration of facilities. There is no consistency with respect to the distribution of federal funds, the character of federal aid, and the extent of nonfederal participation.

*There is need for revising financial policy.* One of the fundamental difficulties of national transportation policy stems from the fact that railroad and pipeline facilities are privately owned and financed, whereas the basic facilities required for transportation by air, water, and highway are publicly provided and financed for the most part through general taxation. These public expenditures provide varying degrees of aid to owners and users of private transportation equipment, who compete with the operators of privately financed facilities as well as among themselves. Since the cost paid for the operation of equipment over the public ways reflects only part of the true cost of providing the service, the choice of transportation method made by consumers and shippers is not based on relative economy, but only on that part of the cost not defrayed by subsidy. In other words, the degree to which these several forms of transportation are patronized, and the nature and extent of public and private investments in transportation facilities and equipment, are determinations which often reflect the generosity and unevenness of legislative appropriations rather than an agency's own ability to attract traffic at rates which will cover cost.

An economic development of transportation and a productive use of resources, therefore, call for the financing of public facilities through charges levied on the users. The achievement of self-support by this device, however, will not completely overcome the financial inequalities between privately owned railroads and publicly provided facilities. Furthermore, in some cases only partial user support may be possible due to the need for general fund expenditure to promote objectives which might otherwise be unattainable. But, insofar as we can approach a condition of self-support, we will move closer to an allocation of traffic based on relative economy, and therefore to an allocation of resources designed to achieve maximum results at minimum cost.

It is not contended that the federal government has no right or obligation to invest general tax funds in transportation facilities; on the contrary, there are circumstances in which such a use of public funds is warranted and necessary. As pointed out earlier, such federal objectives as assuring adequate facilities for national defense or promoting uniformity or minimum standards among the several states may be legitimate objects of federal expenditure. Wherever possible, however, user charges afford the best means of paying the transportation bill. For, in addition to the desirability of including transportation costs in the final determination of prices, and of avoiding the distorting effects of subsidy, user charges have additional merits which further the attainment of transportation objectives. Direct charges for transportation services are a useful expedient in lieu of general taxes because they provide a continuing source of revenue on a fairly predictable basis, as the productivity of the gasoline tax for highways attests. This financial continuity in turn serves as a basis for long-range budgeting and affords a means of preserving capital investments.

User taxes also reduce the amount of waste which occurs in the development of transport facilities, for the beneficiaries who urge the provision of transportation facilites know they must pay the bill, and they are therefore more prudent in the type and extent of the proposals they submit. For example, the uneconomic expansion of inland waterway facilities would not continue at the present rate if those who espoused them knew that they would be held responsible for their support. Finally, in view of the magnitude of federal transportation expenditures, user revenues are to be preferred over general taxes as a means of promoting fairness between general taxpayers and the users who benefit directly from transportation developments. The ability to identify the users of public transportation facilities, and to measure the extent of their use, makes such direct financing possible.

*As a general principle, transportation facilities should be financed through tolls or other special charges imposed on the users.* The precise methods to be applied in collecting these revenues, and the possibilities of achieving self-support, are considerations which must be determined for each form of transportation and in some cases for individual projects. Investigations of this nature should be included in the transportation research conducted by the federal government.

*Exclusion of the railroads from federal transportation development precludes effective programing.* Federal policy raises the question not only of the financial inequalities created between privately and publicly provided facilities, but of the wisdom of excluding from federal transportation development all consideration for the physical condition and service potentials of the railroad plant. During the decade ahead, public agencies will participate in large-scale development of air, highway, and water transportation facilities. These developments cannot be intelligently programed without consideration of the future role to be played by the railroads, the impact of public policies on the financial and physical condition of rail links, and the opportunities for supplanting rail services or physically co-ordinating them with other transportation agencies.

To illustrate, today a phenomenal increase is taking place in the volume of motor traffic and in the physical requirements of highway modernization to accommodate this trend. One of the factors adding substantially to these physical needs is the spectacular increase in heavy truck transport. The rise in intercity truck traffic can be attributed either to the lower costs or the better service afforded by highway transportation compared to rail; and these advantages may be due to one or more of several causes. The truck may be in a favored position owing to technical advantages over the railroads. Or its advantage may be due to favorable treatment by government, in the form of either subsidy or preferential tax and regulatory policy. On the other hand, the relative position of highway and rail carriers may be due to remediable defects in the railroad system itself, including the failure to consolidate or modernize.

From a national standpoint the question is to what extent funds should be spent to accommodate further shifting of freight traffic from rail to highway, and to what extent steps should be taken to achieve better and more economical railroad service. Today there is no other alternative than to neglect the possibilities of railroad modernization, regardless of where this course may lead. The probability is, however, that it will lead to further loss of traffic by the railroads, higher rates of expenditure for alternate highway facilities, further deterioration of the railroads, and ultimate public support of essential railroad services.

There is no suggestion here that the inevitable shift of certain classes of traffic from the railroads owing to technological change should be resisted. It is merely pointed out that for certain types of work, particularly long haul and mass movement of freight, the railroad system is technically well-adapted. The relative economy of rail transportation in this sector is substantial; and it is essential that these facilities be maintained for national defense purposes. Nevertheless, current national policy fails to recognize these considerations. The federal government undertakes extensive tax-supported promotional programs which create unfair competitive disadvantages for the railroads; it then attempts to accommodate the resulting shift of traffic by further expanding these public investments. At the same time it evades the minimum responsibility of compelling corporate and operating revisions in the railroad system.

There are many examples of the futility of attempting to formulate a physical program for national transportation development when the role of railroad transportation is excluded from consideration. Revisions in methods of financing public facilities, relaxation of railroad regulation, and the consolidation of railroad facilities would in combination materially improve the long-run financial outlook, hence physical condition, of the railroad system. But the hiatus between railroads and other transport facilities would continue to impose an unnatural obstacle to over-all transportation developments in the interest of both the users of transportation facilities and the general taxpayer. The government must therefore keep under continuous scrutiny the advantages and disadvantages of the present admixture of privately and publicly provided facilities, the implications of ultimate government ownership of the railroads, and the practicability, as an alternate solution, of government ownership of basic railroad facilities for lease to private operators.

## II. CONFLICT BETWEEN PROMOTIONAL ACTION AND REGULATORY PROGRAM

The keystone of the federal government's regulatory program is the maintenance of fair competition among transport enterprises. All regulatory statutes carry prohibitions against discriminatory rates or service. And all explicitly reject monopolistic organization of transportation by declaring that the "inherent advantages" of each mode of transport shall be preserved.

It has not been assumed that fair competition will be achieved in this field through automatic processes. On the contrary, the government exercises affirmative control over rates, route patterns, and the corporate structure of the industry. The underlying theory of our national regulatory scheme is to preserve workable competition. The end purpose is to afford each transport medium an opportunity to find its area of usefulness on the basis of relative efficiency and quality of service. Free consumer choice, guided by rate and service competition, would then allocate the available traffic equitably and economically among the several forms of transportation and their constituent operating units.

But the government has failed to provide the economic environment and administrative machinery essential to the successful operation of such a system. In fact it seems clear that under the current diversity of policy and organizational arrangements the dominant objectives of transport regulation cannot be attained. The promotional and subsidy phases of government action interfere with the economic allocation of traffic, and the diffusion of regulatory responsibility leads to competitive inequalities, over-expansion of transportation facilities, and un-co-ordinated services.

*Rate competition does not produce an economic allocation of traffic among transportation agencies.* It is axiomatic that an effective pricing mechanism constitutes the mainspring of a competitive system. By the same token, to the extent that the operation of the mechanism is distorted either by private manipulation or government interference, competition becomes unreliable as the arbiter of economic survival.

Government policy now contemplates that the respective roles to be played by each agency in the transportation economy will be determined in the main by price and service competition. Regulatory agencies, however, have been given the power to see that such competition does not become "destructive." Thus the Interstate Commerce Commission determines by minimum rate regulation the extent to which rail, motor, and water carriers may adjust prices in order to hold their traffic or tap the market of a competitor, and control over the rates of air carriers is vested in the Civil Aeronautics Board.

It is obvious that traffic will not be allocated among competing agencies in accordance with relative economy unless the rates under question reflect true economic costs and unless both agencies apply uniform standards of evaluating service factors. But we have observed that neither of these conditions obtains. The existence of preferential government subsidies renders futile much of the regulatory effort to use minimum rate regulation in order to achieve an equality of "competitive opportunity" among the various transport agencies. The main difficulty is that the "costs" with which the commissions deal are not comparable, since the rates of some agencies must in the long run cover total economic costs while the rates of other carriers reflect varying portions of such costs. The rate structure of the privately financed railroads and pipelines must, of course, produce sufficient net operating revenue to pay all operating expenses plus sufficient net income to meet interest charges and provide for new capital requirements. Other carriers, notably water operators and airlines, by virtue of their use of publicly financed facilities are able competitively to offer service at rates which cover only a portion of total costs.

When several agencies are competing for a given volume of traffic under such circumstances, the one striving to recoup total costs will inevitably suffer an erosion of its rate structure. For obviously the shippers' concern is with comparative rates rather than with total economic costs. If the quality of service is comparable, the shipper will give his business to subsidized and therefore low-rate carriers even though the total real cost, including that paid by the general taxpayer, exceeds the rates charged by the self-supporting carrier.

A self-supporting enterprise such as the railroads can cope with this situation only by reducing rates or improving service. In the effort to prevent traffic diversion, rates on the commodities that are most vulnerable to competition will tend toward the level of out-of-pocket costs. Revenue required to obtain the level of earnings needed to induce new capital into the industry can then be secured only by increasing rates on the less vulnerable traffic. This, in turn, will further expose such traffic to competition and the processes of erosion will continue.

Manifestly, no privately financed enterprise can survive if a large portion of its rate structure covers only out-of-pocket costs. If that agency possesses at any given time a substantial managerial or technical superiority, erosion of the rate structure may be retarded. The process may also be slowed down by recurring periods of economic activity which generate enough traffic for all agencies, thus lessening the intensity of rate competition. But these uncertain prospects hold little attraction for the private investor to commit his capital to the modernization of the railroad industry.

The chief hazard is the element of uncertainty. Under current national policy, neither railroad management nor prospective private investors can gauge with any accuracy the future scope and intent of the government program of financial assistance for other transportation agencies. Until 1944, for example, it appeared that the federal role in highway development had become fairly well stabilized, both as to the amount of financial assistance to be advanced and the class of roads on which such funds were to be expended. Since that time, however, federal appropriations for highway improvement have been greatly expanded, and eligibility for the application of such funds has been extended from a limited federal-aid system to include city streets and secondary roads. Appropriations for river and harbor improvements continue to mount. And the proponents of aviation development are urging large-scale and long-range federal expenditures for improved airports and airways. None of these expenditure programs carries any terminal date, nor any specific policy of self-liquidation.

Under such circumstances, the essential requirements for attracting long-range new capital investment into the railroad industry are absent. There is no assurance that the plant or equipment so provided will have an opportunity to compete for the nation's transportation business on a basis of equality with the agencies singled out by government for preferential as-' sistance. On the contrary, it seems certain that the uneconomic allocation of traffic will continue to drain away the financial strength of the unsubsidized enterprises such as the railroads. Policy declarations in favor of impartial regulation and fair competition implemented by minimum rate regulation cannot as a practical matter correct the distorting effects of public subsidy. This situation not only introduces maladjustments into a competitive system, but it threatens to destroy the moral foundations of public regulation.

*Regulation is unable to prevent unfairness and discrimination.* From the outset the statutory requirements that public carriers shall charge only "reasonable and just" rates and shall serve all communities and shippers without unjust discrimination or preference have constituted the core of transport regulation. Through the universal application of these standards, government in effect has declared that private individuals and concerns undertaking to provide the public with essential transportation services must observe rigid rules of fair, just, and reasonable behavior.

In the regulatory sphere of government action, then, Congress has been guided by an exacting code of political ethics. The objective is to make the transportation system function as an impartial service agency for the national economy. The clear implication is that neither rates nor standards of service shall be used by government or by private enterprise as a means of advancing the interest of one region or sector of the economy to the prejudice or disadvantage of any other. Yet, government transport subsidies have introduced an insidious type of discrimination into the transportation system.

*In effect, government-created discrimination has been substituted for that formerly exercised by private monopoly.* Such discrimination arises for two primary reasons. First, the government distributes its financial aids unevenly among regions and types of carriers. Second, the coexistence of both publicly subsidized and self-supporting carriers in a highly competitive transport system forces the latter into discriminatory rate making in order to survive. The most glaring example of the uneconomic distribution of government assistance is found in the promotion and subsidization of water transportation.

For many years the federal government has provided improved waterways without direct cost to the users. Because of the physical limitations of water transportation, the assumed benefits of these promotional expenditures can be realized directly only by the shippers and communities that have access to improved waterways. In order to avoid the patent regional preference involved in this program, Congress has in effect required the privately owned railroads to serve as the vehicle for the distribution of waterway subsidies to interior points not directly served by water transportation. Specifically, the Interstate Commerce Commission has recently found that the "clear Congressional policy with respect to water transportation of the Mississippi River and its tributaries" requires the railroads to establish joint barge and rail routes to permit movement of goods via these routes at rates differentially lower than the all-rail rate for similar movements. The net result is the diversion of traffic from the railroads to the subsidized water operation. And in the process, the communities and shippers that are in a position to use this partially subsidized joint service gain, at the expense of the general taxpayer, a competitive advantage over other shippers who must continue to use all-rail service to the same markets.

The second major element of discrimination introduced by federal waterway promotion stems from the effect of subsidized competition on the general financial position of the railroads. In the effort to compensate for the revenue lost to their subsidized competitors, the railroads in order to survive must attempt to raise rates on the traffic least affected by such competition. Thus another discriminatory element is introduced into the rate structure. For the shippers who are not in a position to utilize subsidized water competition are placed at a double disadvantage. As taxpayers they must contribute to the cost of improving waterways which they cannot use, and at the same time they must pay higher railroad rates in order to compensate for the railroad's loss of revenue to subsidized water transportation.

In the attempt to carry out the inherently antagonistic policies enunciated by Congress, the Interstate Commerce Commission is placed in an anomalous position. With the one hand it must apply impartially to all forms of transportation under its jurisdiction a statute designed to guarantee that no individual or region shall enjoy an artificial advantage over any other by virtue of preferential transportation rates and service. At the same time, the Commission has been obligated to serve as an instrument for carrying out another policy of Congress which deliberately uses subsidized transportation as a means of rendering discriminatory assistance to individuals, regions, and forms of transportation. Manifestly, no regulatory agency can be expected to administer with uniform impartiality and integrity congressional policies which are inherently contradictory and irreconcilable.

We must conclude therefore, that if Congress expects the Commission to enforce impartially the ethically rigid provisions of the Interstate Commerce Act, and intends to retain the concept of fair and workable competition as the keystone of transport regulation, promotional and subsidy policies must be revised. The first step, as already noted, is to assess against the direct user rather than against the general taxpayer the major cost of providing and maintaining transport facilities. This revision alone, however, will not suffice to remove all the major deficiencies of national policy. For the divison of regulatory responsibility creates other and equally important problems.

The federal government has assumed broad jurisdiction over the physical pattern and corporate structure of the transportation plant. Through a series of enactments, Congress has vested in regulatory commissions wide discretion in determining who should enter the transportation business, the routes to be served, the conditions under which service may be expanded or abandoned, as well as the validity of proposed mergers and unifications of transportation enterprises. The vaguely defined but clearly implied three-fold purpose is:

(1) to prevent overexpansion of the total transportation plant, thereby avoiding instability and competitive waste;

(2) to allot to each form of transportation the type of work for which it is best fitted, thereby preserving the "inherent advantage" of the new as well as the older media.

(3) where justified by considerations of operating economy, to permit integration and co-ordination of the several forms of transportation.

We have found, however, that faulty organization and policy work against the achievement of these objectives. Division of regulatory authority and responsibility among several independent regulatory commissions, aggravated by a policy of selective subsidization, creates the major problem.

*Government effort to promote the sound development of commercial aviation by specialized regulation and subsidies has led to overexpansion and financial instability.* Specialized regulatory policy and a special administrative organization have been provided for air transportation. The underlying contention has been that sound economic development of aviation could be achieved most speedily by a sympathetic attitude on the part of government administrators; by undivided attention to the technical problems of aviation; and by direct financial assistance to compensate for immaturity. It was assumed that the Civil Aeronautics Authority would be able to develop an economically sound route pattern, thereby avoiding the wasteful duplication of facilities and financial instability that had characterized the evolution of other transportation agencies, particularly the railroads. And it was further assumed that direct operating subsidies in connection with air-mail payments would provide financial stability and assist the industry in finding its proper place in the transportation world.

We find, however, that a full decade of fostering and special care on the part of the federal government has not produced the results anticipated. In reality, air transportation has in a remarkably short period exhibited the familiar attributes of unplanned competitive development: physical overexpansion, miscalculation of the available market for its service, wide variation in the earning power of individual companies, and general financial instability. The primary explanation for this miscarriage of benevolent government intent is found in a gross miscalculation by industry and government of the air transportation market.

It is clear that the presence of a subsidy backstop has contributed to the formulation of these erroneous business and regulatory judgments. For money subsidies have tended to weaken the disciplines ordinarily imposed on managerial efficiency by threat of bankruptcy. The result has been an inclination on the part of industry and government agencies alike to expand the air route pattern far beyond the dictates of prudent business management. Overexpansion produces financial instability in the aided industry, followed by demands for further financial assistance to "bail out" the distressed carriers. In the meantime, the goal of achieving fair and workable competition becomes more remote.

*Division of regulatory authority also makes it more difficult to achieve the goal of transportation economy through appropriate integration.* The federal government is now committed to a general policy of permitting one carrier to acquire control of another, to use the facilities of another type of transportation in its own business when it can be shown that such integration will contribute to operating economy. However, as in the case of rate and certificate control, administrative jurisdiction over this phase of the regulatory program is divided between the Interstate Commerce Commission and the Civil Aeronautics Board. Although operating under comparable statutory provisions, these regulatory agencies have made fundamentally different interpretations of their authority and responsibility with respect to the integration of unlike carriers. The Interstate Commerce Commission, for example, has felt obligated to approve unifications that offer reasonable prospects of improved transportation services. Thus railroads have been given considerable freedom to substitute highway for rail operations within the areas already served by a particular carrier.

The Civil Aeronautics Board, on the other hand, has for all practical purposes used its administrative discretion to exclude surface carriers from any participation in air transportation. This policy is reflected in the unsuccessful efforts of both rail and ocean shipping enterprises to use aviation as a modern supplement to established services.

Such an outcome should occasion no surprise. For, when one agency is given responsibility for the promotion of an individual form of transportation, there is a natural tendency to resist physical or service co-ordination with competing agencies. This tendency stems from the specious assumption that air transportation must be dealt with in a regulatory vacuum because of the technical intricacies of the method of transportation itself. The technical differences among transport agencies must, of course, be taken into account in the provision of facilities and the engineering of their use. But each of the several transport agencies has the same function of transporting persons and goods, and this must be recognized if the regulatory objective of interagency competition and nondiscriminatory treatment is to be achieved.

Arguments in favor of segregating air transportation from the regulation of other forms were more persuasive when the new transport medium had no significant place in the transportation system. But continued separation in this stage of the growth of air transport serves no useful purpose. On the contrary, it places innumerable difficulties in the way of assuring the shipping and traveling public of the most effective use of the transportation system as a whole.

We have therefore concluded that the national government

cannot confidently rely on workable competition as the keystone of its transportation program without drastic changes both in policy and procedure. Three specific revisions are required:

1. Explicit and consistent economic standards should govern the future legislative programing of public expenditures for basic transportation facilities. And each expenditure proposal should be evaluated with reference to total transportation needs.

2. The major costs of providing and maintaining public facilities should be assessed directly against the transportation agencies which demand and use them rather than against the general taxpayer.

3. The regulation of all major competitive transport agencies should be administered under uniform standards of public need, rate competition, and obligation to serve the public without preference or discrimination. Experience has demonstrated that to achieve this objective, regulatory authority should be centered in a single agency.

There is no other way to assure in the long run the economic allocation of traffic in view of the fact that it has been found desirable and necessary for government to provide some types of basic facilities. And by the same token workable competition cannot be maintained between privately financed transportation enterprises and those media which are enabled to use publicly financed physical plants, unless the test of relative cost and efficiency is permitted to govern the allocation of traffic. To this end, the rates of competing agencies must be required to reflect the total economic costs of performing transportation services. Moreover, each form of transportation should be given an equality of opportunity to serve the transportation market.

### III. INTRUSION OF REGULATION INTO FUNCTIONS OF MANAGEMENT

Other defects in national transportation policy stem from the failure of the government to modernize its regulatory program.

Regulatory controls which were asserted in order to make private monopoly amenable to the public interest have been carried over into an era characterized by universal and intensive transport competition. Some of these controls reach deeply into the functions of business management, creating divided responsibility and undesirable government interference. This problem arises primarily in connection with the type of rate regulation that controls the general level of railroad revenues.

In the exercise of its power to regulate rates, the Interstate Commerce Commission since 1920 has assumed some of the most important functions of private management. It has gone far beyond the restrictive aspects of rate making designed to prevent discrimination and destructive rate cutting. Thus in deciding rate cases involving the general level of railroad rates, it has consistently reserved the right to formulate and act on its own judgment regarding the probable effect of particular rate adjustments on: (1) the general economy of the country, (2) the competitive position of the railroads, and (3) public relations of the railroads.

In the exercise of this type of regulatory authority the Commission is attempting to protect the railroads against the possible consequences of unsound managerial judgment. Thus in periods of depression, it has refused to allow rate increases on the theory that the railroads might price themselves out of the market and aggravate deflationary forces. In periods of business boom the Commission has delayed increases on the theory that rapidly advancing transportation costs would contribute inflationary pressures. At other times the regulatory body has felt that particular rate increases would tend to divert traffic from the railroads to their competitors, thereby worsening the railroad financial position. Although the declared purpose of this authoritative control is to protect railroad revenues, the practical results have been unsatisfactory for the carriers.

*Delays inherent in the regulatory procedure have been damaging to the railroad financial position.* In the effort to maintain its well-deserved reputation for impartiality, the Commission has been punctilious in permitting anyone with a legitimate interest in a particular case to have a full and fair hearing. This procedural policy has inevitably led the Commission into a legalistic, and at times ponderous, method of conducting its business. Although procedural improvement has been effected, the Commission has not yet succeeded in disposing of general rate cases with expedition. The inescapable fact is that a judicialized procedure, consisting of testimony by innumerable parties with a financial stake in the outcome, cross-examination, controversy among lawyers over the meaning of terms, exclusion of evidence on legalistic bases, and oral argument, is not only unwieldy but singularly ineffective as a means of arriving at sound business judgments.

Because of these regulatory rigidities, and the resulting lag between increasing costs and revenue, the carriers as a whole have not benefited substantially from the general postwar prosperity. In fact, the current financial and operating position of the railroads stands in striking contrast to the prosperous condition of other industries. The carriers are now operating at approximately their practical freight capacity. Yet their operating ratios and net earnings are reminiscent of the period when general business stagnation and low traffic levels afforded ample explanation for unsatisfactory financial results.

This reversal of the historic relationship between railroad prosperity and the general level of business activity creates a grave problem of public policy. For if the carriers are not permitted to realize high earnings in the midst of general economic prosperity, their prospects for continued solvency are poor. The record indicates clearly that without high earnings at the peak of the business cycle to compensate for inevitable losses during depression, it will be impossible to maintain and improve the railroad plant at the rate necessary to meet intensive competition and to assure the standby capacity necessary for national security.

It seems clear, then, that in the interest of preserving a financially stable, efficient, and progressive railroad system, some way must be found to remove unnecessary obstacles to prompt adjustment between carrier operating costs and the level of rates paid for the service.

*A larger measure of discretion over general pricing policy should be restored to railroad management.* If railroad management is to retain any of the essential functions of business control, it must be permitted to exercise its own judgment as to how far rates can be raised without driving traffic away. It must also be permitted to judge what particular type of pricing policy and rate structure is best adapted to a strengthening of the railroad competitive position. This proposal does not contemplate any change in the Commission's present authority over minimum rate regulation, nor any dilution of the prohibitions against discrimination. The sole purpose is to remove from the Commission's extensive duties any obligation to protect the carriers against the consequences of alleged bad business judgment, or to share with the carriers the onus of raising transportation rates. Under a competitive organization of the transportation system, it is no longer necessary for public authority to assume the burden of such control. For experience indicates that regulatory agencies are inherently ill-adapted to the exercise of managerial functions and cannot be held directly responsible for decisions that prove financially injurious to the regulated industry.

The restoration of a better balance between government and private enterprise in the matter of general rate levels could be effected by two simple amendments to the rule of rate making contained in the Interstate Commerce Act. First, in disposing of general rate cases, the Commission should be relieved of any authority or responsibility for considering the "effect of the rates on the movement of traffic." Second, the amended rule should make it mandatory for the Commission to grant advances on the simple showing by the carriers that substantial increases in operating costs have been incurred. Subsequent hearings could then deal with the intricate question of rate relationships and any questions that might arise with respect to excessive earnings by individual carriers.

These amendments would leave the Commission with ample authority to protect the public against the exercise of any vestiges of monopoly power on the part of the railroads, and with adequate power to control the standards of competition by minimum rate regulation. The proposed amendments would thus produce only one major change. There would no longer be any occasion for the Commission to take prolonged testimony on general economic trends, inflationary forces, and the ability of particular industries to bear additional transportation costs. Final responsibility for gauging the effective demand for various classes of railroad service would thus be placed with private management.

Restoration to private management of greater initiative in the matter of general rate policies would be facilitated by the elimination of major imperfections in the railroad corporate and operating structure. For these imperfections result in extreme variation in the earning power of individual railroads and constitute one of the few remaining arguments for continuing the Commission's present authority over the general level of rates. The Commission is under constant pressure to hold the general level of railroad rates at a point which produces starvation earnings for many carriers because any higher level would produce unconscionable earnings for some railroads.

### IV. RAILROAD CONSOLIDATION AND THE ROLE OF THE NATIONAL GOVERNMENT

It is generally agreed that the operating pattern and corporate structure of the railroads must be recast along lines which will permit exploitation of modern technology in order to produce the lowest cost and most efficient transportation service. And it is also apparent that such rearrangement can be achieved only through systematic railroad consolidation. Such expedients as co-ordination and integration, if soundly directed, may produce some operating economies. But they do not go to the root of the weak and strong railroad problem. Such arrangements leave intact an operating and corporate pattern that was developed before the railroads were faced with service competition throughout the entire range of their operations.

*For more than a quarter of a century the federal government has attempted to deal with the problem of railroad consolidation by voluntary methods.* The initiative for proposing the regrouping of railroads into more economic operating units has been left to railroad management, and the final decision with respect to the validity of such proposals has been vested in the Interstate Commerce Commission. Until 1940 the Commission was required to consider individual unification proposals within the framework of the general plan of railroad consolidation. The Transportation Act of 1940, however, relieved the Commission of any obligation to formulate and keep current a general plan of consolidation. Initiative for proposing consolidation was left with railroad management.

We have observed that contrary to what was contemplated by the Transportation Act of 1920, the voluntary system has not resulted in a systematic regrouping of the nation's railroads into a limited number of systems with reasonably balanced earning power. The major obstacle has been the reluctance on the part of the strong, favorably situated carriers, voluntarily to assume the financial liabilities of the weak roads. Such resistance undoubtedly could be overcome to some extent by outright abandonment of marginal facilities. But the powerful opposition of the affected communities, labor groups, and investors has placed obstacles in the way of this solution.

*The record indicates that some form of compulsion will be necessary if railroad consolidation is to be realized without interminable delay.* There is a possibility that the necessary degree of compulsion would be provided by a middle course under which the power of government would be used only to bring dissenting minorities into line. Initiative for proposing railroad unification would be left wth management. But it could be provided by statute that any consolidation proposals carrying the assent of a prescribed percentage of the aggregate amount of securities outstanding for the carriers involved would be approved if the Commission found that the rearrangement would be in the public interest and would otherwise conform to the provisions of the statute. The dissenting interests would then be required to exchange their securities for those of the new corporation on the terms provided by the consolidation plan and approved by the Commission. In the knowledge that government authority stands ready to deal with minority interests that could otherwise block any voluntary proposals, the constructive elements in the railroad industry would have an incentive to initiate plans for modernization of the railroad structure.

## V. SUMMARY

It seems clear from the foregoing analysis of major defects in policy that government action in this field must be governed by a more coherent set of principles if we are to move in the direction of transport efficiency and technological progress.

1. National transportation policy must be unified, made internally consistent, and directed toward a tangible and economically sound goal.

2. Regulatory standards which control the inauguration, operating pattern, and abandonment of transport enterprises must be made uniform and equally applicable to all forms of transportation. And the administration of these controls must be correlated with government programing and provision of physical facilities.

3. If the potential contributions of the private enterprise system are to be realized, available traffic must be allocated among the competing forms of transportation in accordance with economic standards of price and service competition. This means at the minimum that all rates must reflect the true economic cost of performing transportation service. Where a portion of the transportation plant is supplied initially by government, workable competition can be maintained only if the cost of providing and maintaining such facilities is charged

against the direct users rather than against the general taxpayer.

4. Initiative and responsibility for basic managerial decisions must be restored to private enterprise, particularly with respect to general pricing policy of the railroads.

5. Authority and leadership of government must be used more effectively in dealing with the problem of railroad consolidation.

6. Congress must formulate a clear and concise policy with respect to the transportation program required for national security.

# CHAPTER XVII

## REORGANIZATION OF FEDERAL TRANSPORTATION AGENCIES

Enumeration of the defects in federal transportation policy makes it clear that basic policy revisions will be necessary if the goals of maximum achievement and economy are to be attained. Changes in policy, however, cannot be effected without the necessary organizational tools. Once the desired policy is determined, accompanying changes in government organization not only help to make the goal possible but tend also to promote the realization of policy objectives by creating an environment favorable to them.

### I. PAST REORGANIZATIONS AND PROPOSALS

The existing organization of federal transportation functions indicates clearly that federal administration has not been guided by principle; and the historic instability of federal transportation agencies suggests that the organizational solutions happened upon to date have been inadequate to cope with basic transportation problems. Agencies have been shifted and reshifted without any apparent consideration of the nature of their functions, and generally without regard for the facts of interagency relationships. And numerous special commissions and study groups have been appointed to study the transportation problem and to recommend revisions in transportation policy and administration.

To illustrate, the administration of air transportation policy was originally lodged in the Post Office Department, later in the Bureau of Air Commerce and the Interstate Commerce Commission, then in the independent Civil Aeronautics Authority. Aviation policy at present is carried out by the Civil Aeronautics Administration of the Department of Commerce and the independent Civil Aeronautics Board. During these changes in administration, the aviation safety function has shifted from the

379

three-fold supervision of the Post Office, Bureau of Air Commerce, and Interstate Commerce Commission to the joint responsibility of the Civil Aeronautics Authority and an independent Air Safety Board. Aviation safety matters now are shared by the Civil Aeronautics Administration and the Civil Aeronautics Board.

This administrative evolution was marked by considerable contention and disagreement on the part of interested agencies. In 1935 the president suggested that the ICC be given regulatory power over air transportation, and legislation was introduced to amend the Interstate Commerce Act accordingly. The bill did not come to a vote in that session of Congress, and the final outcome of congressional action was to unify aviation responsibilities in the Civil Aeronautics Authority. Dissatisfaction with this setup led, two years later, to the present CAA and CAB organizations.

Activities in the field of water transportation have undergone similar organizational changes. The United States Shipping Board operated independently until 1933, when it was abolished and its functions transferred to the Shipping Bureau and Merchant Fleet Corporation in the Department of Commerce. In 1936 the independent United States Maritime Commission took over these functions, with proviso for transfer of regulatory powers to the ICC;[1] but in 1938 an amendment to the 1936 act[2] withdrew authorization for the transfer. Yet two years later the Transportation Act of 1940 transferred by statute from the Maritime Commission to the ICC all regulatory controls over water transportation except ocean shipping and noncontiguous territory operations.[3] Next, to meet war requirements, the War Shipping Administration was created by Executive Order in 1942,[4] and, to aid in restoring peacetime conditions in the merchant marine, the Merchant Ship Sales Act was passed in 1946. The Inland Waterways Corporation was originally set up under

---

[1] Sec. 204 (b) of the Merchant Marine Act of 1936, 49 Stat. 1987.
[2] 52 Stat. 964.
[3] 54 Stat. 929.
[4] Executive Order 9054, Feb. 7, 1942.

the War Department but was later transferred to the Department of Commerce.

Agencies providing aids to navigation have also been shifted periodically. The Bureau of Lighthouses was transferred from the Department of Commerce to the Coast Guard in 1939. Marine Inspection and Navigation was first in the Treasury Department, then the Department of Commerce and Labor, and then the Coast Guard, at first temporarily (1942) and later permanently (1946). The Coast Guard itself is in the Treasury Department in peacetime and in the Navy during war.

The principal highway activities of the federal government were for many years carried on by the Bureau of Public Roads in the Department of Agriculture. In 1939 these functions were transferred to the Public Roads Administration in the Federal Works Agency. Recently the Public Roads Administration was made part of the newly established General Services Administration (Federal Property and Administrative Services Act of 1949, Public Law 152, 81 Cong. 1 sess.). However, under Reorganization Plan No. 7 of 1949, the president has recommended transfer of Public Roads' functions to the Department of Commerce (H. Doc. 228, 81 Cong. 1 sess.).

In spite of these shifts in the location of federal transportation agencies, neither a satisfactory placement of individual transport functions nor an organization capable of an over-all view of the problems of transportation has been achieved. This failure has led to the creation during the past 15 years of the following special commissions, committees, and study groups for the purpose of finding solutions to transport problems:[5]

---

[5] For origin, purpose, and findings of each investigating group see App. C. In addition to the investigations carried on by these *ad hoc* agencies, committees of Congress have inquired into various phases of the transportation problem. For example, the House Committee on Interstate and Foreign Commerce instituted a general investigation of transportation policy in March 1946 (Special Subcommittee on Transportation of the Committee on Interstate and Foreign Commerce authorized by H. Res. 318, 79 Cong. 2 sess.). So far this committee has made no final recommendation with respect to the organizational phases of national transportation activities. And the Senate Committee on Interstate and Foreign Commerce has recently launched a broad investigation into all aspects of transportation policy (S. Res. 50, 81 Cong. 1 sess.).

1. Federal Coordinator of Transportation
2. The Committee of Three
3. The Committee of Six
4. Select Committee on Investigation of Executive Agencies of the Government
5. Board of Investigation and Research
6. National Resources Planning Board Study
7. President's Air Policy Commission
8. Congressional Aviation Policy Board
9. President's Advisory Committee on the Merchant Marine

This periodical and somewhat random search for a solution of the transportation problem produced much useful information and general agreement on one point: the need for a closer grouping of transportation functions. But otherwise, the various groups reached strikingly different conclusions with respect to the basic nature of the problem, as well as the appropriate means of correction. It is therefore not surprising that neither the legislative nor executive branch of government has discovered in these studies any logical basis for the rearrangement and improvement of government activities in the transportation field.

The most obvious explanation for the failure of these various study groups to produce constructive and consistent results is found in the narrowly restricted terms of reference under which they operated. The investigations conducted by five of the nine special groups centered on the then critical problem of a single form of transportation. In the thirties the dominant concern was with the financial distress of the railroads, and more recently the financial and operating difficulties of the airlines and merchant marine have attracted official attention. Manifestly, investigating commissions instructed to seek solutions for the immediate and pressing problems of one segment of the transportation industry are precluded from a broad and long-range view of the transportation problem. For example, the recent President's Air Policy Commission expressed the belief that "sometime within the near future" the executive transportation functions of the government should be centered in a Department of Transportation. However, presumably because of its limited terms of reference, the recommendation for immediate action was to place the government's executive functions relating to civil aviation in a "Department of Civil Aviation" located within the Department of Commerce. No explanation was offered as to how this organizational arrangement would contribute to the realization of unified executive treatment of the transportation problem.

There is a second and highly significant reason why these study groups failed to produce any generally acceptable basis for administrative reorganization. Most of the recommendations ignored the controlling fact that transport regulation, whether punitive or benevolent, is not an effective administrative vehicle for long-range transportation programing. In the first place, the supply and character of transport facilities and the recent technological trends affecting cost and service have not been determined primarily by regulatory processes but by public expenditures of billions of dollars for transport promotion. In the second place, the jurisdiction of federal regulatory agencies has of necessity been limited to only one segment of the transportation field, namely, the regulation of for-hire carriers in interstate commerce. The tremendous volumes of private transportation equipment and of intrastate and local for-hire transport services lie beyond the direct jurisdiction of federal regulation.

As matters now stand, the federal government, in attempting to determine the volume and character of transportation services, divides this responsibility between promotional and regulatory agencies in such a way that there is no possibility of effective programing. Thus in the field of air transportation, an orderly development involves both physical facilities, such as air navigation aids and airports, and the determination of routes over which public carriers shall operate. At present the CAA plans the physical facilities, but determination of the public carrier services to be provided is left to the jurisdiction of the CAB. Because of the inherent nature of regulatory functions, the actual route pattern determination in this field has been based on a case-by-case approach rather than on a study of general transportation needs.

In effect, planning of the route pattern under the regulatory agency becomes a negative function involving acceptance or rejection of individual applicants for route certificates. The absence of a planned route pattern for commercial aviation has been evident in the financial distress of the carriers; and the preoccupation of the CAB with day-to-day decisions on individual cases has removed any disposition toward devising broad plans to guide these decisions toward ultimate objectives. The President's Air Policy Commission reflected the inevitable dissatisfaction with depending on regulatory processes to achieve a satisfactory conception of long-range programing when it concluded that failure of the CAB in this area suggested the CAA as the more logical agency to determine an acceptable route pattern.

The problem has been seen to apply no less obviously in the operations of the ICC. Here again, the Commission has been so engrossed in individual cases and in details of regulation that it has been unable and unwilling to take the leadership in formulating and carrying out a railroad consolidation plan. In fact it has considered long-range programing a deterrent to sound railroad unification.

The Federal Coordinator concluded more than a decade ago that it was not possible for a regulatory agency to provide the type of initiative required to guide a desirable development of the transportation system:

Students of Government relations to transportation have often pointed out a defect in our system of regulation, and that is the absence of any sufficient provision for planning and prevention. Regulation is essentially a means of curing evils after they arise. It would be better, of course, if they could be prevented in advance. There is need for foresight—for consideration and comprehension of tendencies and trends and where they are leading, in order that those that are desirable may be encouraged and those that are undesirable discouraged.

Anyone who has served on the Commission knows that it is not well adapted to such work. Its functions are performed under quasi-judicial procedure. Its attention is occupied with specific cases which must be decided. It has little time for thought and research on broad lines. It is difficult for commissioners to confer with parties on controversial issues, without constant need of protecting their own position in the event that they are called upon to play the part of judges in actual litigation. Planning and prevention are not matters which can well be handled at off times or as side issues. They require single-minded, concentrated attention.[6]

Despite these inherent characteristics of the regulatory commission, the Coordinator sought to achieve the necessary transportation research and planning by delegating the functions to a single commissioner. The more obvious solution of removing this responsibility from the regulatory sphere altogether, and lodging it in the executive branch where it belongs, was not suggested.

Both the so-called Committee of Three and Committee of Six recommended the establishment of some governmental agency, other than the ICC, to deal with the problems of transport planning and promotion. The major reasons for the establishment of such an agency are summarized by the Legislative Committee of the ICC itself:

Summing up, the transportation situation has become so complex and is changing so rapidly that it demands, we believe, the continual attention of an agency of the Federal Government which is not preoccupied with the quasi-judicial routine of regulation. The reasons for this were fully stated in the report of the Committee of Three, and again in the last annual report of the Commission, and were at least partially recognized in the report of the Committee of Six. The need was also made clear in the report of the National Transportation Committee in 1933, and in the reports of the Federal Coordinator of Transportation. It is a need which is supplied in many countries by an executive department headed by a cabinet officer. The "railroad problem," which is in reality the "transportation problem," admits of no speedy cure, but will respond only to a prolonged and steady course of treatment.[7]

It is difficult to understand why this simple and straightforward solution of establishing an executive agency was never reached despite the findings which clearly pointed to this need.

[6] *Fourth Report of the Federal Coordinator of Transportation on Transportation Legislation*, H. Doc. 394, 74 Cong. 2 sess. (1936), p. 42.
[7] *Omnibus Transportation Bill*, Hearings before the House Committee on Interstate and Foreign Commerce on H.R. 2531 and 4862, 76 Cong. 1 sess., Pt. 4 (1939), p. 1580.

ORGANIZATION, CIVILIAN TRANSPORTATION AGENCIES, JULY 1, 1949

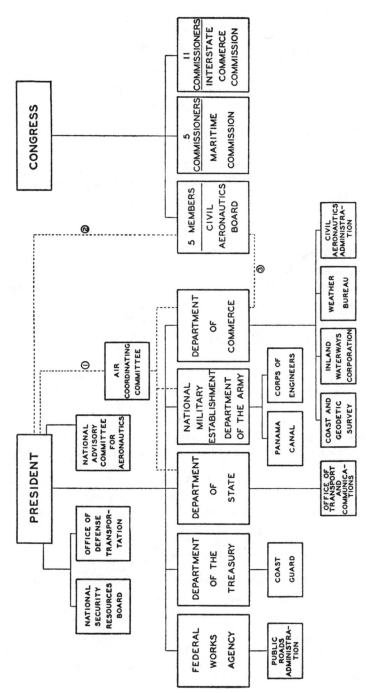

① COORDINATION BY EXECUTIVE ORDER.
② INTERNATIONAL AIR ROUTES.
③ FOR HOUSEKEEPING PURPOSES.

One reason, perhaps, has been the failure to distinguish clearly between economic regulation on the one hand and promotional and administrative activity on the other, and to confine the operation of both the promotional and regulatory agencies to their respective jurisdictions. As the Commission pointed out: "One of the weaknesses of the Transportation Board, proposed by the Committee of Six, is that it does not heed the distinction between the functions of planning and promotion and those of quasi-judicial regulation nor the objections to combining them."[8]

The analysis in this study has again indicated the necessity for recognizing the basic distinction between the administrative and programing aspects of national transportation policy on the one hand and the regulation of the rates and standards of service of individual business firms on the other. We have therefore concluded (1) that all activities of the national government designed to assure the best physical plant and the most effective operation of the transportation system should be brought together in a single executive agency, and (2) that a clarified regulatory program centering in the maintenance of fair standards of rate and service competition and applicable to all major forms of transportation should be vested in a reconstituted regulatory tribunal.

## II. A DEPARTMENT OF TRANSPORTATION

The consolidation of government programing and operating functions into a single executive agency has a fourfold purpose: (1) to facilitate the application of uniform standards in determining the justification of projects involving the several forms of transportation; (2) to provide appropriate machinery for the strictly administrative, operating, and policing functions of government in this field; (3) to provide a continuing and authoritative source of information for the legislative and executive branches of government concerning the financial and operating position of the several transport agencies and the adequacy of the total transportation plant to meet the needs

[8] The same, p. 1581.

of commerce and national security; and (4) to supply a going organization capable of assuming immediate responsibility for administering a wartime transportation program.

*In order to focus responsibility for achieving these objectives of transportation policy, a federal Department of Transportation should be established.* The new department should be headed by a secretary with cabinet status. Selection of this organizational arrangement in preference to the alternative of lodging the unified transportation functions in an existing department stems from the fact that a mere assembling of a group of related functions into a single agency for so-called "housekeeping" purposes will not assure realization of a given objective of public policy. On the contrary, efficient administration requires that the functions grouped for central supervision must be organically related, and have a reasonably well-defined bearing on the central purpose of the several programs involved. Accordingly, there would be placed in the new department only those responsibilities and functions that have an affirmative bearing on the maintenance of an adequate national transportation system.

The Commission on Organization of the Executive Branch of the Government[9] in effect rejected this view by proposing to place most of the transportation functions in a reorganized Department of Commerce. Thus the major promotional and operating activities of the national government affecting transportation would be included in an executive department having jurisdiction over such totally unrelated agencies and activities as the Bureau of Standards, Census Bureau, Patent Office, Fisheries, National Inventors' Council, and the Textile Foundation. However, the Commission gave two main reasons for opposing the creation of a new Department of Transportation. First, it pointed out that under a statute enacted in 1902 Congress gave the Department of Commerce broad responsibility in the field of transportation. This, of course, is a totally irrelevant historical fact. For the purpose of any study of governmental reorganization is to determine whether the historical

[9] Created by act of July 7, 1947, 61 Stat. 246. Herbert Hoover, Chairman.

placement of functions meets current requirements. Second, the Commission observed that: "It would be quite inadvisable for the Federal Government to set up a department which would be devoted entirely to the problems of one industry."[10] This statement raises the question first as to whether the Department of Agriculture or the Post Office Department are not subject to the same criticism. But more fundamentally, the "one industry" argument reveals a misconception of the nature of national action in the field of transportation.

The federal government is engaged on a large scale in the provision and control of transportation facilities and services. Federal action in this field involves actual participation in a wide variety of services such as the administration of the federal-aid highway program; the operation of aids to air navigation and airport construction; the administration of airline and merchant marine subsidies; the construction and sale of ocean vessels; the financing and conduct of river and harbor developments, and other promotional activities in the field of water transportation; and the conduct of general research and planning activities. Manifestly, a department responsible for administering such a wide assortment of service programs would not be "devoted entirely to the problems of one industry."

An additional objection to the proposal of the Commission on Organization of the Executive Branch of the Government to group transportation functions in the Department of Commerce lies in the fact that transportation objectives are often in conflict with the immediate interests of business in general. The federal government is in the position of supplying transportation services, whereas business is one of the principal users of the service. It is apparent that the federal objective of achieving a self-sustaining transport system would be in direct opposition to the interest of shippers in obtaining the lowest possible transportation rates.

It is interesting to note that 3 of the 12 commissioners

[10] *Department of Commerce*, A Report to the Congress by the Commission on Organization of the Executive Branch of the Government, March 1949, p. 15.

dissented from a Commission proposal to place unrelated functions in the Department of the Interior:

One factor which makes an administrator unable to control and direct his agency's activities effectively is the effect (sic) [extent] to which his agency is made up of functions forming a conglomeration of largely unrelated functional activities. The proposal for organizing on the basis of public works and natural resources seems to us to insure a "holding company" type of organization—one in which the top administrator is frustrated by trying to preside over parts of many different "major purpose" programs.[11]

Avoidance of this "conglomeration of largely unrelated functional activities" is precisely the objective sought by bringing together the important transportation functions into a single-purpose executive department. Thus the creation of a federal Department of Transportation would supply an extremely important condition for carrying out national transportation policy: an administrative setting where, in the words of the Federal Coordinator of Transportation, "single-minded and concentrated attention" can be given to over-all transportation programing and the relation of transportation problems to the total economy.

To this end it would be necessary to lodge in the Department of Transportation most of the duties and responsibilities now vested in executive transportation agencies, certain promotional and administrative functions currently exercised by regulatory agencies, and several new transportation responsibilities which should be assumed by the federal government.

A. *Powers, duties, and internal organization of the Transportation Department.* The powers and duties to be vested in the Secretary of Transportation are described below. Authority and responsibility would be delegated to four assistant secretaries in charge of offices of water transportation, civil aviation, highway transportation, and railroad transportation. Additional duties relating to general supervision and interdepartmental relations would be delegated to an undersecretary.

[11] Separate report by Vice Chairman Acheson, Commissioners Pollock and Rowe, on the Department of Natural Resources in *Reorganization of the Department of the Interior,* A Report to the Congress by the Commission on Organization of the Executive Branch of the Government, March 1949, p. 72.

PROPOSED ORGANIZATION, CIVILIAN TRANSPORTATION AGENCIES

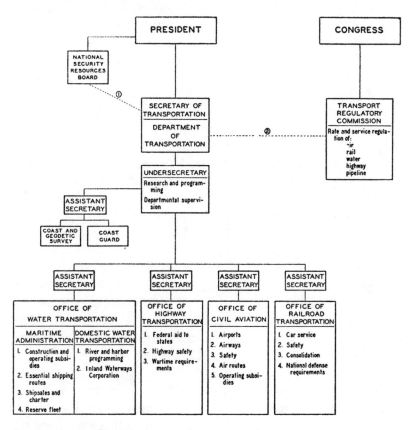

① COORDINATION—NATIONAL SECURITY.
② DEPARTMENT REPRESENTATION BEFORE COMMISSION.

1. *Office of Water Transportation.* The assistant secretary in charge of this office would have immediate responsibility for administering all federal promotional, operating, and programing activities in the field of domestic and foreign water transportation. The office would be constituted and its major duties defined by the following transfer of functions from existing agencies.[12]

[12] Amendment of the various statutory authorizations under which existing bureaus and agencies now operate would be necessary in order that the Secretary of Transportation might have substantive authority over the constituent elements of his department.

a. *Promotional, administrative, and subsidy responsibilities transferred from the Maritime Commission.* The administrative and planning aspects of the Commission's work are predominant, and the national defense significance of the shipping and shipbuilding industries requires close direction at cabinet level. It is concluded, therefore, from both the objectives and the character of the work performed, that the conduct of these operations should be placed under executive authority. The executive branch of the government would be responsible for planning the routes to be operated by American flag vessels, determining the subsidy policies, and administering the program. Aside from these promotional and administrative duties, however, certain residual functions of a semijudicial nature would have to be transferred to a regulatory agency, including the selection of carriers and control over rate conference agreements and discriminatory practices.

Under this arrangement, the assistant secretary for water transportation would have under his immediate jurisdiction the promotional features of the present Maritime Commission, including programing and contracting, and the execution of plans and contracts. In addition, he would be responsible for passing upon the need, justification, and financing of river and harbor improvements.

The fact that administration of merchant marine policy was transferred from an executive department to an independent commission by the Merchant Marine Act of 1936 raises the question of why it is now proposed that major responsibilities be returned to an executive agency. The primary explanation is that the functions which we propose to vest in an executive agency are primarily promotional and managerial in nature and should not have been placed in a regulatory tribunal in the first instance. Presumably, the legislative decision to create an independent Maritime Commission was based on two assumptions: (1) that rate and service regulation for water transportation enterprises should be organizationally combined with promotional programs involving administration of construction and operating subsidies; and (2) that the independent commission form of organization was essential, since stability, continuity of policy, and impartiality were indispensable to satisfactory regulation.

The first of these two assumptions was abandoned in 1940 with the legislative transfer of jurisdiction over coastal and intercoastal shipping from the Maritime Commission to the Interstate Commerce Commission. This left an "independent commission" in control of a promotional program that is inseparable from executive responsibilities affecting the national security and the conduct of foreign affairs. Manifestly, merchant marine policy designed primarily to maintain a fleet adequate for national emergencies must be adapted to and co-ordinated with the changing requirements of diplomacy and military plans. Similarly, there is a growing need for mutual adjustments between the policies governing international water and air transportation. Since major responsibility for international aviation is lodged in the executive branch of the government, the removal of merchant marine supervision to a status of relative independence creates a damaging division of executive responsibility.

b. *Transfer of Inland Waterways Corporation from the Department of Commerce for liquidation.* The period of experimentation with the federal barge lines has been prolonged far beyond what was initially intended by the Congress. This subsidized experiment provides no basis for demonstrating the economic feasibility of barge operations. Even with the support of public capital the corporation has been unable to achieve profitable operations or to maintain its equipment in serviceable condition. These considerations, together with the nullifying effects of subsidized water transportation on rate regulation, point to the need for abandonment of this project.

c. *Programing of waterway improvements transferred from Corps of Engineers, Department of the Army.* Programs for inland river improvement are formulated by the Corps of Engineers with no reference to general transportation problems. To carry out national transportation policy, it would be necessary for policies governing the planning of waterway improvements to be established by the Department of Transportation.

Because of the multiple operations of the Corps of Engineers in the field of water resource development, however, it is not suggested that the Corps itself be transferred to the Department of Transportation. In recent years there has been an upward trend in the emphasis placed on flood control, power development and other nonnavigation features of the water resources program. Wherever the Corps of Engineers may be located in the government structure, however, it is obvious that all navigation projects and multiple-purpose projects having navigation features should be reviewed by the Transportation Department to determine the economic desirability of such navigation proposals from the standpoint of transportation requirements.

The highly questionable economic justification of a large part of the federal government's river and harbor development program has been pointed out repeatedly in studies of transportation. The fact that several hundred million dollars are committed each year to inland waterway improvements, many of which could not conceivably be justified from a transportation viewpoint, is one of the most serious indictments of federal transportation policy.

Sound federal policy would seek to eliminate such waste of public funds, and reduce to a minimum the disruptive effects of subsidized water competition. The federal government should insist that all future waterway projects recommended in the interests of transportation be evaluated in detail by the Transportation Department. Further elimination of wasteful expenditure could be accomplished through the imposition of tolls or requirements for state matching of federal funds. The exact nature of these measures would require the study and recommendation of the Transportation Department.

2. *Office of Civil Aviation.* This office would have immediate responsibility for all federal programs involving the promotion of civil aviation, both domestic and international: the programing, financing, and operation of physical facilities, route pattern development, and the promotion of aviation safety.

The major functions, powers, and duties of the office would derive from transfers from existing agencies.

a. *Airway, airport planning, and aviation safety duties transferred from CAA.* The planning and provision of airways, the formulation of an airport plan and the administration of the federal-aid program for airport development, as well as certain research and educational activities, are obviously of a promotional character. Aviation safety activities of the CAA, including administration and enforcement functions should continue to be carried out by an executive agency.

b. *Safety activities and route pattern development transferred from CAB.* Safety responsibilities in the field of aviation are now divided between the CAA and the CAB. The conclusion has been reached that the promulgation of safety rules and standards together with their administration should be removed from the jurisdiction of a commission dealing with economic regulation and centered in an executive agency.[13] Because of the highly technical nature of this function, an administrative and engineering agency is better adapted to this work than an economic regulatory body. The CAA is staffed with engineering and technical personnel, and maintains an extensive field service. It is in day-to-day contact with the industry and its problems, and with the operations of the various aids to air navigation.

With respect to accident investigation, the CAA, which has been delegated by the CAB to perform all investigation work except that involving major airline accidents, should be given the full responsibility in this field. The importance of airline safety however, has led to the conclusion that a three-member board should be attached to the secretary's office to hold public hearings and determine the cause of all major air carrier accidents, and such other accidents as may be specified by the secretary. The members of this hearing tribunal would be named by the secretary to serve when the need arose.

The air route pattern as developed by the CAB is characterized by a lack of considered planning and has resulted instead

[13] Chap. 4.

from case-by-case decisions with respect to individual certificate applications. This agency has provided further demonstration of the inherent inability of a regulatory body to take an active role in research and planning. It seems obvious that route planning, which is one of the most important promotional tools, should be lodged in the promotional rather than the regulatory agency.

Because of the financial difficulties which have resulted from ill-advised expansion of route patterns and airline competition, it will be necessary to correct the air route pattern as promptly as possible, and to furnish a plan to guide the future development of the air transportation system. The route plan should be finally approved by a co-ordinating staff attached to the office of the secretary. It would be in the nature of an advisory plan for the guidance of the regulatory agency. The Department of Transportation would appear before the regulatory body, however, to urge the granting of operating rights to conform within reasonable limits to the over-all plan of the Department.

c. *Air-mail subsidies.* Operating subsidies for domestic carriers should be eliminated as soon as possible. It appears, however, that financial assistance for international aviation will be necessary for an extended period to maintain American flag lines in competition with subsidized foreign carriers. In any event, operating subsidies to the extent required should be divorced from the remuneration for transportation of mail. Appropriations for such subsidy payments would be made for that specific purpose, to be administered by the Department of Transportation. Subsidies would be "out in the open" rather than buried in postal payments.

One of the initial research responsibilities of the Department of Transportation would be to formulate a tangible base for determining the need for aviation subsidies and the appropriate means of payments, and to present such a program for legislative consideration.

d. *Elimination of current federal activities.* In connection with its general responsibilities, the Office of Civil Aviation should facilitate the transfer of certain activities from federal to state control. For example, it would appear wise for the federal government to retire from the development of small airports for private flying. Interest in these facilities is primarily local, and the need for developing a national system of airports serving interstate and international transportation is a problem of much more pressing federal interest.

In the field of aviation safety, the federal government is now moving in the direction of transferring certain enforcement and certification responsibilities to designated private organizations or individuals, or to state governments. Among the operating functions which should ultimately be shifted to nonfederal jurisdiction are the enforcement of safety regulations and accident investigation as they pertain to noncarrier aircraft. Ultimately it may be desirable also for the registration of noncarrier aircraft and the licensing of private pilots and other personnel to be handled by the state, provided that uniform national standards are adopted. The potential magnitude of aviation field activities indicates that considerable advantage and net savings will accrue through a shift of responsibility to the states, where organizations and personnel are in many cases available to perform these additional functions.

3. *Office of Highway Transportation.* The assistant secretary for highway transportation would be charged with responsibility for administrative and promotional work in connection with federal grants to the states for highway work; for research and planning functions; for certain federal roadbuilding operations; and for safety activities relating to interstate motor carriers.

a. *Federal-aid highway activities transferred from Federal Works Agency, Public Roads Administration.* Highway responsibilities now carried out by the Public Roads Administration are of a promotional character and would be included in the Office of Highway Transportation. However, the recent extension of federal-aid activity from a limited system of main highways to a 600,000 mile system of all classes of highways and streets raises important policy issues. The federal government has so diffused its activities in this field that the objective of assuring the provision of a national system of highways may ultimately be defeated. In view of state and local roadbuilding capabilities, there appears to be no persuasive reason for the current expansion of federal action. More important, the large-scale modernization requirements of our principal interstate highways suggest the desirability of concentrating federal activity where the federal role is clearly justifiable.

b. *Motor carrier safety functions transferred from the ICC.* The ICC is now authorized to prescribe rules and regulations governing operating safety applicable to common, contract, and private carriers engaged in interstate commerce. Aside from rule making, the Commission, through the field staff of its Bureau of Motor Carriers, works co-operatively with state enforcement agencies in the attempt to achieve uniformity between federal and state safety standards and enforcement practices.

Commission activities in this field are highly technical in nature and can be administered effectively only through continuing co-operation with state agencies. The most extensive and tested machinery for this type of governmental co-operation now exists in the Public Roads Administration. For in carrying out the federal-aid program, the Administration deals continuously with the states and conducts exhaustive studies of traffic conditions, physical and operating characteristics of motor vehicles, and the relationship of these factors to highway design.

Safety regulations and enforcement techniques must be based on such studies, for they reveal the chief elements that condition highway safety. It would therefore appear that federal responsibility for highway safety should be integrated with administration of the federal-aid program. This would provide not only a more adequate technical basis but more appropriate machinery for the prescription and enforcement of desirable standards. Eligibility for federal highway funds could be limited to the states enforcing the prescribed federal standards. The validity of such a stipulation is indicated by the fact that the bulk of all interstate commerce by motor vehicle transportation is carried by the federal-aid highway system.

The states have been required, from the outset of the federal-aid program, to establish acceptable highway organizations and administrative procedures in order to qualify for federal aid. If highway safety is considered less important to the national interest than efficient administration, it would appear wise for the federal government to leave safety matters to the states.

c. *War requirements inventory.* A further highway transportation function would be to maintain for emergency purposes an inventory of all motor vehicle equipment, its location, condition, and use, and the requirements of motor transport for tires, fuel, and repair parts.

4. *Office of Railroad Transportation.* Thus far the structure of the proposed Transportation Department has been provided primarily by transfers of existing agencies and of certain functions from existing agencies. These transfers in themselves would not provide the structure of an over-all transportation agency necessary for carrying out national transportation policy. An additional requirement is the creation in the department of an Office of Railroad Transportation which would be responsible for keeping Congress and the president informed regarding the adequacy of basic railroad facilities and equipment for the demands of normal commerce and national security. In this connection the office would assess the impact on the rail carriers of general economic conditions and federal promotional activities in other fields of transportation; and it would recommend effective measures to assure that these impacts did not jeopardize the operating condition of the railroad system. This office would also be charged with setting up the necessary machinery to assure efficient railroad transportation in time of war. In addition, certain activities relating to railroad car service and safety would be transferred from the Interstate Commerce Commission to the Department of Transportation.

a. *Formulation of a railroad consolidation plan.* Efforts of the federal government to achieve effective railroad consolidation have failed. The Interstate Commerce Commission has shown no disposition to attack forthrightly the consolidation problem which all investigations, including those of the ICC itself, have shown to be necessary. Since it is apparent that a regulatory commission is ill-equipped to carry out a planning responsibility of this nature, responsibilities in this field should be placed in the executive department. Specifically, the department should be authorized and directed by statute to prepare within a specified period of time a general plan for railroad consolidation.

One of the major purposes of systematic railroad consolidation is to adjust the corporate and operating structure of the carriers to the new competitive organization of the transportation system. It is therefore essential that the plan be formulated with the full knowledge of and provision for the impact of government promotional programs. There can be no permanent value to any plan for railroad consolidation that does not take full cognizance of the competitive implications of current and projected public expenditures that are designed to improve the range and quality of highway, air, and water services.

The technical complexities of the consolidation task are accentuated by the fact that, if the problem is to be solved at all, it must be attacked as a whole and disposed of within a relatively short fixed period. We therefore suggest that, pending completion of the consolidation plan (preferably not more than two years), a moratorium be placed on all forms of railroad unification. This would require temporary suspension of ICC powers to approve railroad consolidations, mergers, and acquisition of control.[14] At the end of this period authority would be restored to the ICC to supervise the corporate and operating rearrangement of the railroads within the framework of the general consolidation plan. The Commission would be vested with limited powers of compulsion in connection with individual consolidation proposals.

b. *Car service and safety functions transferred from ICC.*

[14] Control over joint rates and through routes, abandonments, and the use of other transport media by railroads would not be affected.

The railroad car service and safety activities now being carried on by the ICC divert the attention of the Commission from its primary responsibilities and add to its administrative burdens. There are no persuasive reasons why functions of this type should be carried out under the "independent commission" form of organization. They are primarily technical in nature and involve routine inspection and enforcement activities. Except for the discriminatory aspects of car supply, these functions do not constitute integral parts of the regulatory program. On this point the following significant observations have been made by an official who has had extensive experience both as a commissioner and in an executive agency:

. . . for some years now I have served in the dual capacity of Interstate Commerce Commissioner and Director of the O.D.T. In the Commission I am a member of Division 3 and am the Commissioner in charge of the Bureau of Service. I have, with the consent of the Commission (a creature of the Congress, the Legislative branch of the Government), operated the Bureau of Service and with the consent of the Executive I have operated O.D.T., a part of the Executive branch of the Government, and have unified their activities. I fail to see any real distinction whatever in the character of their respective activities.[15]

In final analysis, the basic purpose of government control in this field is to assure an equitable allocation of railroad cars among regions and shippers under emergency conditions. But experience has demonstrated that the regulatory mechanism is inadequate to deal with the problem of railroad car supply and allocation in periods of critical and prolonged shortage. Thus during the past war this responsibility was delegated to the Office of Defense Transportation, a temporary executive agency. Transferring this function to a Department of Transportation would give continuing jurisdiction to the type of administrative organization required for effective discharge of this responsibility when the service is of critical importance.

[15] Statement of Col. J. M. Johnson, Director of Office of Defense Transportation on S. 1812 before Subcommittee of Senate Committee on Interstate and Foreign Commerce, Mar. 9, 1948 (mimeo.), p. 11.

Jurisdiction over railroad safety matters has been vested in the Commission through a long series of special enactments which have never been incorporated into the Interstate Commerce Act.[16] It is significant that over a long period of years the Commission has of necessity relied primarily on the carriers to initiate technical improvements in safety appliances and to police their uniform application. Any other approach would have required an extensive staff of technicians and a large field force for policing purposes. Supervision of such an organization would further divert the Commission from its complex and specialized duties of regulating rates and standards of competition.

It is primarily for this reason that railroad safety responsibilities should be transferred from the ICC to the Department of Transportation. For there is a pressing need for expediting Commission action, particularly in the field of rate regulation.

B. *Office of the Secretary of Transportation.* Success in achieving national transportation objectives would be determined in large part by the conduct of transportation research and planning in the office of the secretary. It is the absence of such activity at the present time, and the absence of over-all direction stemming from it, which account in no small measure for the ill-advised and conflicting transportation activities now being sponsored by the federal government.

1. *General research and programing.* The secretary of transportation should be responsible for advising the Congress as to the following: (a) the physical needs of the transportation system, including all forms of transport; (b) the priority of these needs; and (c) the costs and desirable methods of defraying such costs. To provide such advice would necessitate continuing studies of traffic trends; desirable route patterns for rail, air, and water carriers; the financial condition of the carriers; possible further areas where federal action is needed, or areas in which federal activity might be reduced or eliminated.

The Department of Transportation here proposed would

---

[16] The Safety Appliance Act; Locomotive Inspection Act; Hours of Service Act; Signal Inspection Act; Ash Pan Act, etc.

comprise some 35,000 persons at current levels of employment. Under present policies it would be responsible for the expenditure of at least a billion and a quarter dollars annually. The size of the department and the magnitude of its responsibilities point to the importance of a top level research and programing staff. These and other transportation research, planning, and programing activities carried on by a staff reporting to the undersecretary would furnish a basis for formulating and activating national transportation policy. Among the responsibilities of this staff would be the following:

(a) Examination of all promotional programs in the light of the peacetime objective of achieving the most effective transportation system at the lowest cost, with due consideration for the development and promotion of desirable technological changes.

(b) Determination of civilian transportation requirements and capacities for presentation to the National Security Resources Board for co-ordination with the military, in order to assure specific estimates of national security requirements where these call for facilities in excess of normal peacetime needs.

(c) Development of operating plans and techniques to permit immediate effective operation of the transportation system in time of war.

(d) Determination of the feasibility of various programs for financing transportation facilities through user charges, including the development of plans for federal airways charges and a system of waterway tolls.

(e) Conduct of studies on such problems as the feasibility of government ownership of railroad rights of way as a compromise measure in the event that the coexistence of privately owned rail facilities and publicly provided air, highway, and water facilities proves infeasible.

(f) Investigation of possible consolidation of field operations and physical research activities. The federal government maintains separate engineering staffs for this work in connection with its highway and airport operations, yet many similar problems are encountered with respect to materials, design, construction methods, soil investigations, and the like.[17] Laboratory research dealing with these physical problems, as well as engineering assistance or inspection in the field, might also be consolidated to advantage. Right-of-way problems, including land acquisition, zoning, and related problems also suggest the possibility of effective handling by one staff.

2. *Service agencies.* Consideration should also be given to transferring to the department two existing agencies that supply general service and policing functions for transportation.

a. *Coast Guard.* The principal functions of the Coast Guard relate to the provision of aids to navigation and the promotion of safety. It is believed that the present location of the Coast Guard in the Treasury Department has no reasonable basis in the nature of the work the Coast Guard performs. If there are no compelling reasons for retaining this organization in the Treasury Department, its transfer to a Department of Transportation appears to be the logical alternative.

b. *Coast and Geodetic Survey.* The major part of the work of this organization relates to the provision of aids to navigation for water and air transportation, although certain other functions of a general application are also included in its program.

If these organizations are transferred to the department, it would appear desirable to preserve them as individual operating units, reporting to an assistant secretary in charge of service functions.

C. *Summary of departmental organization.* In accordance with the foregoing organizational changes, the Department of Transportation would include all of the transportation activities of the federal government with the exception of rate regulation, the issuance of operating certificates, and carrier unifications. These functions require relative freedom from political influence; stability of policy; and the benefit of judicial procedures made possible under the independent commission form of organization. Specifically, the department would include:

(1) The existing functions of the Public Roads Administra-

---

[17] The Public Roads Administration field staff now numbers 980, and the CAA airport field staff totals 575.

tion, Civil Aeronautics Administration, Coast and Geodetic Survey, Coast Guard, the Maritime Commission (except minor regulatory functions), the Corps of Engineers (policy determination only, in connection with navigation projects), and the Inland Waterways Corporation.

(2) In addition, certain functions now being carried out by regulatory agencies: Civil Aeronautics Board responsibilities for aviation safety, route pattern determination, awarding of operating subsidies; Interstate Commerce Commission responsibilities for motor carrier safety, railroad safety, car service operations.

(3) Certain new functions, including the establishment of a railroad consolidation plan and an inventory of war requirements.

### III. A TRANSPORT REGULATORY COMMISSION

There is a need for rearrangement of regulatory organization and procedure as well as revision of basic regulatory policy. With respect to organizational problems, two major defects have been emphasized:

1. *The intermingling of promotional and administrative functions with regulatory responsibilities has created problems for the commissions and the executive branch of government.* The independent commission was conceived, is constituted, and has operated as a deliberative body. The prime objective is to achieve impartiality in the settlement of controversies, stability and continuity of policy, and decisions based on a factual record. An agency organized and institutionally adjusted for this type of performance is ill-adapted to the exercise of management functions that require aggressive, flexible, and expeditious action. Experience has demonstrated that the location of such functions in a commission form of organization results either in the indifferent performance of management and promotional activities or in diverting the attention of the commission from its major regulatory duties.

In important instances the delegation of promotional and management responsibilities to commissions has removed from the chief executive some of the powers and administrative tools that are required to carry out the constitutional responsibilities of the executive branch of government. For example, one of the major objectives of merchant marine policy is to maintain in being a fleet adequate for the requirements of national security. The instrumentalities provided for this purpose consist chiefly in the administration of construction and operating subsidies and the supervision of the reserve fleet—all predominantly technical, administrative, and management activities. Yet, the major powers and duties involved in carrying out this program are vested in an independent commission. They are thus deliberately removed as far as possible from the control of the executive branch where responsibility rests for the management of the military establishment and the conduct of foreign affairs. The creation of a Department of Transportation and the transfer from the various commissions to that department of the functions outlined above would restore essential controls to the executive department. These transfers would at the same time leave the regulatory process free of functional and operating encumbrances.

2. *Without further change in the present regulatory organization, there would remain an undesirable administrative diffusion of the regulatory program.* The Maritime Commission would be left with a residual control over ocean shipping to noncontiguous territories, reparations, and supervision of rate conference agreements. The Civil Aeronautics Board would be left with control over the rates and operating rights of the airlines. And the Interstate Commerce Commission would retain control over rail, highway, domestic water, and pipeline agencies. We have discovered no organizational or technical obstacles to the consolidation into a single Transport Regulatory Commission of the basic economic controls over the rates and competitive standards of transport enterprises. On the contrary, we have found that such administrative consolidation is necessary in order to achieve declared regulatory objectives. National policy is now dedicated to the impartial treatment of all forms of transportation, nondiscriminatory rates, the main-

tenance of workable competition, and the integration of the several forms of transportation into an efficient, economical, and progressive national system.

*For these reasons, the creation of a national Transport Regulatory Commission would be required to administer a revised program of public regulation applicable to all forms of transportation.* The keystone of this regulatory system would be the regulation of competitive rates, operating rights, and structural organization of individual firms. The basic purpose of such regulation would be to prescribe the standards of rate and service competition that would assure the economic allocation of traffic among the several forms of transportation, and to guarantee impartiality in the granting and denial of operating privileges to individual firms. The Commission would, of course, retain the accounting, reporting, cost finding, and other ancillary functions essential to the effective discharge of its major regulatory duties.

The rearrangements proposed here would be accomplished in the main through the following amendments to current regulatory statutes:

1. Consolidate with Part III of the Interstate Commerce Act the controls now exercised by the Maritime Commission over shipping to noncontiguous territories, reparations, supervision of rate conferences, and the selection of individual firms to be made eligible for subsidized operation over the foreign shipping routes declared essential by the Department of Transportation.

2. Add a new Part V to the Interstate Commerce Act, incorporating the present provisions of the Civil Aeronautics Act dealing with rates, operating rights, consolidation, security issues, reports and investigations, but deleting from the latter the present Declaration of Policy and the provision for using airmail payments as a subsidy device.

3. Amend the rule of rate making with a view to restoring to private management essential controls over the general level of transportation rates.

4. Provide statutory recognition of the right and duty of the

secretary of transportation to appear before the Commission to present the views of the executive branch of the government with respect to the rates, service, and operating adjustments required to maintain the transportation system in a condition adequate to serve the needs of commerce and the national security.

The present declaration of regulatory policy added to the Interstate Commerce Act by the Transportation Act of 1940 would require no substantial alteration. And it would appear wise to vest in the Transport Regulatory Commission broad discretion with respect to its internal organization and operating procedure.

In the past, considerable controversy has arisen with respect to the place of the so-called "independent commission" in the general structure of government. Suggestions have been made for the consolidation of all transportation functions into a single executive department; however, with the strictly regulatory activities retained in a so-called independent board or commission included within the department only for "housekeeping" purposes. In other words, the regulatory commission under these circumstances would bear the same general relationship to the department that now exists between the Civil Aeronautics Board and the Department of Commerce. There appear to be no persuasive reasons for or advantage in this particular type of arrangement. The economies expected from unified administrative supervision have not materialized, and the need for retaining the independence of action of the regulatory body has never been seriously questioned. It has therefore been concluded that the Transport Regulatory Commission should be constituted on a bipartisan basis with the commissioners appointed by the president for overlapping terms and removable only for nonperformance of statutory duties.

*If executive and managerial functions are restored to the executive branch, there would appear to be no justification for direct control by the executive branch over the regulatory phases of national transportation policy.* The regulation of rates and the selection of carriers entitled to operate for-hire transportation services are aspects of federal transportation activity which require a high degree of impartiality and the provision of all possible safeguards against the pressures of private interests or the intrusion of political considerations. Determination of these matters, involving the distribution of privileges and the financial position of private business, requires fair hearings and reasonable continuity of policy in the decisions rendered. The independent commission form of organization provides the best opportunity for maintaining these administrative standards.

Public regulation of transport enterprises has been rooted from the outset in the ethical and moral concepts of fairness, justness, and reasonableness. The legislature has not succeeded in reducing these general values to quantitative formulas or even to very tangible standards of measurement. Although the statutory prohibitions against discrimination in matters of rates and service have been refined somewhat over the years, the determination of what particular rate, or rate relationship, or competitive practice constitutes actual discrimination remains largely a matter of administrative interpretation.

Nor do the regulatory statutes provide tangible standards to guide the Commission in deciding when the public needs a new or different kind of service, or which individual among a number of applicants should be granted the privilege of supplying that service. Thus the regulatory agencies are ordinarily authorized to grant or deny operating rights in accordance with their interpretation of "the public necessity and convenience."

Under these circumstances, it has been generally agreed that equity as among individual applicants and a desirable degree of continuity and stability in the control of rate relationships can best be achieved through the deliberations of a continuing, full-time, and expertly staffed agency removed from the immediate control of Congress or the president.

It is particularly important that reasonable stability and continuity of competitive rate relationships be preserved. Radical and frequent alteration in the nation's transportation rate structure would throw the industrial and commercial processes of the country into chaos. In an economy organized around national markets, highly competitive in character, the location of industry and channels of trade would be subject to paralyzing uncertainties and dislocations by preferential rate making or by the threat of a volatile rate structure.

Transport regulation administered by an independent commission is specifically designed to avoid the rapid and unpredictable alterations of policy and procedure. Commission form of control does not preclude orderly adjustment where investigation and study indicate the need for change, but the process is time consuming, complex, and at times ponderous. Experience indicates, however, that the wastes inherent in this regulatory process can more readily be supported by the economic system than could the uncertainty and disruption that would be possible and likely under direct legislative regulation or executive control.

# APPENDIXES

# APPENDIX A

# STATISTICAL DATA

## 1. UNITED STATES TRANSPORTATION FACILITIES[a]

### I. BASIC TRANSPORT FACILITIES

| Type of Facility | Miles |
|---|---|
| Highways (surfaced) | 1,757,000 |
| Railways (first track) | 226,438 |
| Airways (domestic) | 39,368 |
| Pipelines (petroleum) | 141,887 |
| Improved inland waterways | 27,300 |
| Airports | 6,210[b] |

### II. UNITS OF TRANSPORTATION EQUIPMENT

| Type of Equipment | Number |
|---|---|
| Railway locomotives | 45,511 |
| Railway passenger train cars | 45,978 |
| Electric surface and rapid transit cars | 33,962 |
| Railway freight cars | 1,793,344 |
| Passenger automobiles | 30,545,000 |
| Trucks | 6,492,000 |
| Buses—transit, school, intercity | 161,000 |
| Private planes and non-scheduled carriers | 96,722 |
| Scheduled air carriers | 1,023 |
| Commercial vessels on inland waterways | 18,995[c] |
| Merchant fleet vessels | 4,861 |

[a] Data for: highways from Public Roads Administration; railways, locomotives, passenger train cars, and freight cars, ICC *Statistics of Railways in the United States, 1946*, Tables 14 and 21; airways, CAA Program Engineering Section; pipelines, American Petroleum Institute, *Petroleum Facts and Figures* (1947), p. 138; inland waterways, The American Waterways Operators, Inc., *Inland Waterway Transportation in America*, February 1948, pp. 2, 3; airports, CAA Release 281, Aug. 1, 1948; transit cars, American Transit Association, *Transit Fact Book, 1947*, p. 2; automobiles and trucks, estimates by Automobile Manufacturers Association, *Automobile News—Annual Almanac Issue for 1948*, p. 40; buses, *Motor Truck Facts* (1947 ed.), p. 55; air carriers, CAA Release 286, Aug. 1, 1948; inland waterway vessels, Statistical Division, Corps of Engineers, Department of the Army; merchant fleet vessels, *Report of the President's Advisory Committee on the Merchant Marine*, November 1947, Table 2, p. 26.

[b] Number.

[c] As of Dec. 31, 1945.

## 2. Distribution of Intercity Transportation in the United States, 1947[a]

|  | Millions of Ton-Miles | Per Cent of Total | Millions of Passenger-Miles | Per Cent of Total |
|---|---|---|---|---|
| Coach ........... |  |  | 27,660 | 7.88 |
| Pullman .......... |  |  | 12,261 | 3.49 |
| Commutation ...... |  |  | 6,011 | 1.71 |
| Total railway ....664,467 | | 66.78 | 45,932 | 13.08 |
| Bus .............. |  |  | 23,404 | 6.66 |
| Automobile ....... |  |  | 274,008 | 78.01 |
| Truck ........... 77,919 | | 7.83 |  |  |
| Total highway ... 77,919 | | 7.83 | 297,412 | 84.67 |
| Inland waterways (including Great Lakes) ........148,358 | | 14.91 | 1,845 | .53 |
| Pipelines (oil) ......104,153 | | 10.47 |  |  |
| Airways (domestic) . 104 | | .01 | 6,057 | 1.72 |
| Total ...........995,001 | | 100.00 | 351,246 | 100.00 |

[a] Data, except railway passenger-miles, from *62d Annual Report of the Interstate Commerce Commission 1948*, p. 15. Railway passenger-miles from ICC *Statistics of Railways in the United States, 1947*, Tables 44 and 52.

## 3. Passenger Transportation by Intercity Public Carriers, 1937-48[a]

(In billions of passenger miles)

| Year | Railroad (Excluding commutation) | | | Domestic Airline | Intercity Bus |
|---|---|---|---|---|---|
|  | Coach | Pullman | Total |  |  |
| 1937 ........12.4 | | 8.1 | 20.5 | 0.4 | 12.7 |
| 1938 ........10.2 | | 7.4 | 17.6 | 0.5 | 15.6 |
| 1939 ........11.1 | | 7.5 | 18.6 | 0.7 |  |
| 1940 ........12.5 | | 7.3 | 19.8 | 1.0 |  |
| 1941 ........16.1 | | 9.2 | 25.3 | 1.4 |  |
| 1942 ........31.0 | | 17.9 | 48.9 | 1.4 | 21.5 |
| 1943 ........57.9 | | 24.7 | 82.6 | 1.6 | 27.4 |
| 1944 ........63.3 | | 26.9 | 90.2 | 2.3 | 26.5 |
| 1945 ........59.4 | | 26.9 | 86.3 | 3.4 | 26.9 |
| 1946 ........39.0 | | 19.8 | 58.8 | 5.9 | 25.6 |
| 1947 ........27.7 | | 12.2 | 39.9 | 6.1 | 23.4 |
| 1948 ........24.3 | | 11.0 | 35.3 | 5.8 | 26.0 (est.) |

[a] 1937-47 data for railroad passenger-miles from ICC, *Statistics of Railways in the United States*, Tables 44 and 52; for airlines and intercity bus miles from ICC annual reports; 1948 data for railroads from ICC Statement M-250, December 1948; for airlines from CAB release 45-20, Mar. 21, 1949; for buses from National Association of Motor Bus Operators.

## 4. Transportation Expenditures by Shippers and Travelers, 1947[a]

| Transportation Medium | Millions of Dollars | Per Cent of Total |
|---|---|---|
| Automobile[b] | 17,387 | 45.8 |
| Steam railway | 8,973 | 23.7 |
| Private truck[c] | 5,867 | 15.5 |
| Truck (interstate common carrier) | 2,126 | 5.6 |
| Local transit | 1,391 | 3.7 |
| Bus (interstate common carrier) | 536 | 1.4 |
| Railway express | 313 | .8 |
| Domestic air carriers | 365 | 1.0 |
| Pipeline[d] | 325 | .9 |
| Domestic water | 241 | .6 |
| Pullman | 115 | .3 |
| International air carrier | 209 | .5 |
| Electric railway | 80 | .2 |
| Total | 37,928 | 100.0 |

[a] Data represent operating revenues for public carriers and estimates of cost for private carriers. An additional sum of approximately 2.5 billion dollars was spent for transportation facilities and services by federal, state, and local governments, without recovery through user taxes. (Steam railway, railway express, pullman, electric railway, domestic water, pipeline, bus and truck data from *62nd Annual Report of the Interstate Commerce Commission, 1948*, p. 14; domestic air carriers from CAA *Statistical Handbook of Civil Aviation* (1948), p. 74; international air carriers from Air Transport Association of America; local transit from *Transit Fact Book*, American Transit Association (1948); p. 21.

[b] Derived from consumption expenditure data of the Department of Commerce.

[c] Based on current truck registrations related to expenditure data contained in *Immediate Relief for the Railroads*, H. Doc. 585, 75 Cong. 3 sess., Apr. 11, 1938, Table p. 9.

[d] Oil pipelines under jurisdiction of the ICC.

## 5. CURRENT APPROPRIATIONS AND PERSONNEL, FEDERAL TRANSPORTATION AGENCIES[a]

| Agency | Appropriations for Fiscal Year Ending June 30, 1949 | Personnel | |
|---|---|---|---|
| | | Actual Employment July 1, 1948 | Budget Bureau Ceiling Oct.-Dec., 1948 |
| Department of Agriculture Forest Roads and Trails .$ | 15,050,000 | 2,290 | 2,370 |
| Department of Commerce Coast and Geodetic Survey .............. | 10,255,000 | 2,628 | 2,663 |
| Inland Waterways Corporation .......... | 498,800 | 1,551 | 1,700 |
| Civil Aeronautics Administration .......... | 100,370,000[b] | 17,056 | 17,670 |
| Civil Aeronautics Board .. | 3,450,000 | 621 | 683 |
| Office of Defense Transportation ............. | 340,000[c] | 44 | 34 |
| Panama Canal .......... | 13,249,000 | 5,268 | 5,279 |
| Department of the Army Corps of Engineers .... | 167,489,100 | 38,990 | 46,000 |
| Department of the Treasury Coast Guard .......... | 140,138,755 | 4,125 | 5,177 |
| Federal Works Agency Public Roads Administration .............. | 435,758,854 | 3,129 | 3,400 |
| Interstate Commerce Commission ........... | 10,894,317 | 2,301 | 2,453 |
| National Advisory Committee for Aeronautics .. | 47,905,000[d] | 6,264 | 7,125 |
| U. S. Maritime Commission | 101,988,751[e] | 6,816 | 7,037 |
| Alaska Railroad ......... | 17,000,000[f] | 2,542 | — |
| Total ...............$ | 1,064,387,577 | 93,625 | — |

[a] Appropriations data from appropriation laws for 1949. Actual employment figures for majority of agencies from *Organization of Federal Executive Departments and Agencies*, Organization Chart to accompany Report No. 4, Senate Committee on Expenditures in the Executive Departments, July 1948. Actual employment figures for Forest Roads and Trails, Panama Canal, Corps of Engineers, and personnel ceiling from Bureau of the Budget.

[b] Plus 12 million dollar contract authorization for air-navigation facilities, and 37 million dollar contract authorization for federal-aid airport program until June 30, 1953.

[c] $60,000 of this amount shall be available exclusively for terminal leave payments.

[d] Plus 18.2 million dollar contract authorization for contracts entered into prior to July 1, 1950.

[e] Plus 75 million dollar contract authorization.

[f] Plus 12 million dollar contract authorization.

6. FEDERAL EXPENDITURES FOR TRANSPORTATION, 1940-50[a]

(In millions of dollars)

| Purpose of Expenditure | Actual | | | | | | | | | Estimate | |
|---|---|---|---|---|---|---|---|---|---|---|---|
| | 1940 | 1941 | 1942 | 1943 | 1944 | 1945 | 1946 | 1947 | 1948 | 1949 | 1950 |
| Merchant Marine .. | 98 | 44 | 641 | 3,032 | 3,885 | 3,183 | 375 | 281[b] | 183 | 154 | 185 |
| Navigation Aids and Facilities ........ | 166 | 162 | 138 | 126 | 79 | 65 | 93 | 246 | 231 | 329 | 382 |
| Highways ......... | 170 | 179 | 174 | 187 | 164 | 105 | 90 | 238 | 356 | 488 | 533 |
| Aviation .......... | 24 | 57 | 136 | 227 | 204 | 138 | 98 | 121 | 136 | 195 | 255 |
| Regulation ........ | 12 | 13 | 16 | 17 | 32 | 30 | 22 | 23 | 15 | 15 | 15 |
| Other services ..... | 43 | 2 | 4 | 36[b] | 30[b] | 145[b] | 26[b] | 8[b] | 34 | 40 | 53 |
| Total .......... | 513 | 457 | 1,109 | 3,553 | 4,334 | 3,376 | 652 | 339 | 955 | 1,221 | 1,423 |

[a] *The Budget of the United States Government for Fiscal Year 1950*, p. 1398.
[b] Excess of credits, deduct.

7. MAIL PAY YIELD PER MAIL TON-MILE, 1948[a]

| Carriers | Amount | Carriers | Amount |
|---|---|---|---|
| **Trunk Lines** | | Southwest ............... | 30.54 |
| American ................$ | .57 | Trans-Texas .............. | 33.72 |
| Braniff .................. | 2.19 | West Coast .............. | 46.34 |
| Chicago & Southern ....... | 3.93 | Wisconsin Central[d] ........ | 50.56 |
| Colonial ................ | 12.90 | | |
| Continental ............. | 7.56 | **International Carriers** | |
| Delta .................. | 3.51 | American Airlines ........$ | .68 |
| Eastern ................. | .68 | American Overseas ....... | 2.37 |
| Inland ................. | 6.09 | Braniff[e] ................. | 88.56 |
| Mid-Continent ........... | 4.05 | Chicago & Southern ...... | 172.21 |
| National ................ | 4.44 | Colonial ............... | 35.21 |
| Northeast ............... | 16.97 | Eastern ................. | .67 |
| Northwest .............. | 1.56 | National ............... | 8.51 |
| Capital ................. | 5.55 | Northwest .............. | 2.84 |
| T.W.A. ................. | .88 | Panagra ................ | f |
| United ................. | .91 | | |
| Western ................ | 3.18 | **Pan American** | |
| | | Alaska ................. | 4.47 |
| **Feeder Lines** | | Atlantic ............... | 4.53 |
| All American ............$23.46 | | Latin American .......... | 3.14 |
| Challenger .............. | 24.78 | Pacific ................. | 2.66 |
| Empire ................. | 50.71 | **T.W.A.** ................... | 3.38 |
| Florida ................. | 83.88 | | |
| Los Angeles ............. | 13.09 | United ................. | .76 |
| Monarch ................ | 39.23 | | |
| Piedmont[b] .............. | 48.44 | **Territorial Carriers** | |
| Pioneer ................. | 20.98 | Caribbean .............. | 24.43 |
| Robinson[c] .............. | 25.43 | Hawaiian .............. | .60 |

[a] CAB *Recurrent Report of Financial Data*, 4th quarter, 1948.
[b] Inaugurated Feb. 20, 1948.
[c] Inaugurated Feb. 24, 1948.
[d] Inaugurated Sept. 19, 1948.
[e] Inaugurated June 4, 1948.
[f] Not available, May 5, 1949.

## 8. FEDERAL EXPENDITURES FOR RIVERS AND HARBORS, 1922-48[a]

(In thousands of dollars)

| Year Ending June 30 | New Work | Maintenance | Total |
|---|---|---|---|
| Expenditures | | | |
| 1922 .............. | 18,601 | 19,051 | 37,652 |
| 1923 .............. | 22,855 | 20,197 | 43,052 |
| 1924 .............. | 37,313 | 22,182 | 59,495 |
| 1925 .............. | 40,086 | 23,435 | 63,521 |
| 1926 .............. | 32,110 | 24,958 | 57,068 |
| 1927 .............. | 27,621 | 25,207 | 52,828 |
| 1928 .............. | 32,605 | 27,490 | 60,095 |
| 1929 .............. | 40,932 | 26,615 | 67,547 |
| 1930 .............. | 50,647 | 29,258 | 79,905 |
| 1931 .............. | 56,776 | 32,783 | 89,559 |
| 1932 .............. | 57,832 | 32,673 | 90,505 |
| 1933 .............. | 56,052 | 29,529 | 85,581 |
| 1934 .............. | 87,902 | 28,154 | 116,056 |
| 1935 .............. | 135,460 | 33,383 | 168,843 |
| 1936 .............. | 73,245 | 34,104 | 107,349 |
| 1937 .............. | 102,658 | 38,535 | 141,193 |
| 1938 .............. | 101,238 | 38,516 | 139,754 |
| 1939 .............. | 90,080 | 39,547 | 129,627 |
| 1940 .............. | 83,405 | 42,695 | 126,100 |
| 1941 .............. | 52,608 | 41,578 | 94,186 |
| 1942 .............. | 49,201 | 46,008 | 95,209 |
| 1943 .............. | 40,449 | 50,163 | 90,612 |
| 1944 .............. | 30,213 | 40,780 | 70,993 |
| 1945 .............. | 12,636 | 52,599 | 65,235 |
| 1946 .............. | 25,584 | 61,299 | 86,883 |
| 1947 .............. | 35,664 | 64,571 | 100,235 |
| 1948 .............. | 47,725 | 68,002 | 115,727 |
| Total .......... | 1,441,498 | 993,312 | 2,434,810 |

[a] Data for 1922-40 from Board of Investigation and Research, *Public Aids to Domestic Transportation*, H. Doc. 159, 79 Cong. 1 sess., Sept. 19, 1944, p. 335. Includes an allocation of certain flood control projects assumed to be partly for the aid of navigation. Data for 1941-46 based on *Annual Report of the Chief of Engineers U. S. Army*, 1941 to 1946. 1947 and 1948 data from Bureau of the Budget. Figures include 25 per cent of multiple purpose projects on lower Mississippi River.

## 9. FEDERAL FUNDS AUTHORIZED FOR HIGHWAYS, 1917-48[a]

(In thousands of dollars)

| Fiscal Year | Primary System | Federal-Aid Highway System | | | | | All Other[b] | Total |
|---|---|---|---|---|---|---|---|---|
| | | Secondary, Feeder, and Farm-to-Market Roads | Grade Crossing Elimination | Urban Areas | Total | | | |
| 1917 .......... | 5,000' | | | | 5,000 | 1,000 | 6,000 |
| 1918 .......... | 10,000 | | | | 10,000 | 1,000 | 11,000 |
| 1919 .......... | 65,000 | | | | 65,000 | 4,000 | 69,000 |
| 1920 .......... | 95,000 | | | | 95,000 | 4,000 | 99,000 |
| 1921 .......... | 100,000 | | | | 100,000 | 4,000 | 104,000 |
| 1922 .......... | 75,000 | | | | 75,000 | 3,500 | 78,500 |
| 1923 .......... | 50,000 | | | | 50,000 | 8,000 | 58,000 |
| 1924 .......... | 65,000 | | | | 65,000 | 4,500 | 69,500 |
| 1925 .......... | 75,000 | | | | 75,000 | 5,500 | 80,500 |
| 1926 .......... | 75,000 | | | | 75,000 | 7,000 | 82,000 |
| 1927 .......... | 75,000 | | | | 75,000 | 8,000 | 83.000 |
| 1928 .......... | 75,000 | | | | 75,000 | 7,500 | 82,500 |
| 1929 .......... | 75,000 | | | | 75,000 | 9,500 | 84,500 |
| 1930 .......... | 75,000 | | | | 75,000 | 88,000 | 163,000 |
| 1931 .......... | 125,000 | | | | 125,000 | 22,579 | 147,579 |
| 1932 .......... | 125,000 | | | | 125,000 | 137,000 | 262,000 |
| 1933 .......... | 125,000 | | | | 125,000 | 423,936 | 548,936 |
| 1934 .......... | | | | | | 245,285 | 245,285 |
| 1935 .......... | | | | | | 415,472 | 415,472 |
| 1936 .......... | 125,000 | | | | 125,000 | 18,287 | 143,287 |
| 1937 .......... | 125,000 | | | | 125,000 | 13,500 | 138,500 |
| 1938 .......... | 125,000 | 25,000 | 50,000 | | 200,000 | 22,333 | 222,333 |
| 1939 .......... | 125,000 | 25,000 | 50,000 | | 200,000 | 25,118 | 225,118 |
| 1940 .......... | 100,000 | 15,000 | 20,000 | | 135,000 | 15,667 | 150,667 |
| 1941 .......... | 115,000 | 15,000 | 30,000 | | 160,000 | 23,792 | 183,792 |
| 1942 .......... | 100,000 | 17,500 | 20,000 | | 137,500 | 226,650 | 364,150 |
| 1943 .......... | 100,000 | 17,500 | 20,000 | | 137,500 | 118,949 | 256,449 |
| 1944 .......... | | | | | | 30,000 | 30,000 |
| 1945 .......... | | | | | | | |
| 1946 .......... | 225,000 | 150,000 | | 125,000 | 500,000 | 33,850 | 533,850 |
| 1947 .......... | 225,000 | 150,000 | | 125,000 | 500,000 | 25,000 | 525,000 |
| 1948 .......... | 225,000 | 150,000 | | 125,000 | 500,000 | 25,000 | 525,000 |
| Total .......... | 2,880,000 | 565,000 | 190,000 | 375,000 | 4,010,000 | 1,977,917 | 5,987,917 |

[a] Public Roads Administration, *The Public Roads Administration and its Work*, November 1946.
[b] Includes special authorizations, and authorizations for forest highways, national parks and parkways, and public lands.

## 10. FEDERAL SUPPORT FOR HIGHWAYS, 1921-48[a]

(Dollar figures in millions)

| Year | Total Revenues for Highways | Federal Funds | Per Cent Federal to Total Funds |
|------|------|------|------|
| 1921 | 1,014 | 81 | 8.0 |
| 1922 | 1,065 | 82 | 7.7 |
| 1923 | 1,153 | 84 | 7.3 |
| 1924 | 1,273 | 100 | 7.9 |
| 1925 | 1,574 | 102 | 6.5 |
| 1926 | 1,732 | 95 | 5.5 |
| 1927 | 1,955 | 93 | 4.8 |
| 1928 | 2,030 | 96 | 4.7 |
| 1929 | 2,172 | 93 | 4.3 |
| 1930 | 2,331 | 146 | 6.3 |
| 1931 | 2,229 | 202 | 9.1 |
| 1932 | 1,858 | 198 | 10.6 |
| 1933 | 1,714 | 307 | 17.9 |
| 1934 | 2,021 | 669 | 33.1 |
| 1935 | 1,927 | 554 | 28.7 |
| 1936 | 2,517 | 1,038 | 41.2 |
| 1937 | 2,400 | 790 | 32.9 |
| 1938 | 2,711 | 1,079 | 39.8 |
| 1939 | 2,609 | 929 | 35.6 |
| 1940 | 2,483 | 751 | 30.2 |
| 1941 | 2,320 | 537 | 23.1 |
| 1942 | 1,960 | 330 | 16.8 |
| 1943 | 1,625 | 186 | 11.4 |
| 1944 | 1,586 | 119 | 7.5 |
| 1945 | 1,758 | 74 | 4.2 |
| 1946 | 2,393 | 168 | 7.0 |
| 1947 | 2,632 | 324 | 12.3 |
| 1948 | 2,969 | 398 | 14.8 |

[a] Public Roads Administration, Table HF-1, March 1947 and February 1949. Amounts are approximate.

11. Apportionment of Federal Highway Authorizations Among the States, Fiscal Year Ending June 30, 1948[a]

(In millions of dollars)

| State | Amount | State | Amount |
|---|---|---|---|
| New York | 33.0 | Arkansas | 7.4 |
| Texas | 28.1 | Louisiana | 7.3 |
| Pennsylvania | 24.3 | Washington | 7.2 |
| Illinois | 22.5 | Oregon | 6.9 |
| California | 21.7 | Florida | 6.8 |
| Ohio | 19.5 | New Mexico | 6.2 |
| Michigan | 16.2 | South Dakota | 6.1 |
| Missouri | 14.0 | South Carolina | 6.1 |
| Minnesota | 12.1 | North Dakota | 5.8 |
| Indiana | 11.8 | Arizona | 5.6 |
| Wisconsin | 11.5 | West Virgina | 5.2 |
| Georgia | 11.3 | Idaho | 4.8 |
| North Carolina | 11.1 | Nevada | 4.7 |
| Iowa | 10.8 | Wyoming | 4.7 |
| Kansas | 10.4 | Maryland | 4.7 |
| Massachusetts | 10.1 | Connecticut | 4.6 |
| Oklahoma | 9.9 | Utah | 4.5 |
| Tennessee | 9.8 | Maine | 3.8 |
| Alabama | 9.5 | Puerto Rico | 3.0 |
| New Jersey | 9.2 | District of Columbia | 2.9 |
| Kentucky | 8.7 | Rhode Island | 2.9 |
| Virginia | 8.6 | Hawaii | 2.2 |
| Nebraska | 8.2 | New Hampshire | 2.2 |
| Mississippi | 7.8 | Vermont | 2.0 |
| Montana | 7.7 | Delaware | 2.0 |
| Colorado | 7.5 | | |

[a] *Work of the Public Roads Administration, 1947*, Table 4, p. 64.

## 12. Traffic, Mileage, and Financial Data for Domestic Trunk Line Carriers, 1938-48[a]

(All data except air route miles are in millions)

| Year | Net Profit or Loss[b] | Air Route Miles[b] | Revenue Plane Miles | Available Seat Miles | Revenue Passenger Miles | Mail Ton-Miles | Operating Profit or Loss | Total Operating Revenue | Total Operating Expenses |
|---|---|---|---|---|---|---|---|---|---|
| **Fiscal Year** | | | | | | | | | |
| 1938 | | 39,267 | 67 | 905 | 444 | 7.1 | $ 1.5 def. | $ 40.1 | $ 41.6 |
| 1939 | | 39,782 | 74 | 1,036 | 549 | 7.9 | 1.6 | 47.7 | 46.1 |
| 1940 | | 44,643 | 95 | 1,470 | 861 | 9.3 | 7.1 | 66.3 | 59.3 |
| 1941 | | 46,453 | 123 | 2,102 | 1,187 | 11.2 | 3.9 | 84.9 | 81.0 |
| 1942 | | 49,297 | 133 | 2,349 | 1,510 | 15.7 | 14.0 | 105.9 | 91.9 |
| 1943 | $13.3[c] | 54,502 | 96 | 1,717 | 1,411 | 28.3 | 29.9 | 110.7 | 80.8 |
| 1944 | | | 115 | 2,033 | 1,819 | 42.3 | 26.5 | 131.7 | 105.3 |
| **Calendar year** | | | | | | | | | |
| 1944 | 18.8[c] | 62,937 | 139 | 2,437 | 2,178 | 51.1 | 36.4 | 160.9 | 124.5 |
| 1945 | 16.9 | 67,149 | 206 | 3,785 | 3,336 | 65.0 | 34.0 | 214.6 | 180.6 |
| 1946 | 6.0 def. | 79,485 | 305 | 7,490 | 5,903 | 32.9 | 5.6 def. | 311.5 | 317.1 |
| 1947 | 20.2 def. | 111,786 | 312 | 9,152 | 6,011 | 32.9 | 20.9 def. | 352.5 | 373.4 |
| 1948 | 5.0 def. | 115,484 | 316 | 9,980 | 5,823 | 37.5 | 2.1 def. | 413.0 | 411.0 |
| **Percentage change 1945-48** | | 72.0 | 53.4 | 163.7 | 74.5 | -42.3 | -94.1 | 92.5 | 127.6 |

[a] Data from worksheets of Tariffs and Service Division, Civil Aeronautics Board; *Annual Report of the Civil Aeronautics Board* (1943) and (1947); CAB Economic Bureau, *Annual Airline Statistics* (calendar year 1945); CAB *Recurrent Report of Financial Data and Recurrent Report of Mileage and Traffic Data*, 4th quarter, 1947; CAB Accounting and Rates Division.

[b] Net profit and air route miles data are for calendar year. Data for net profit not available prior to 1943.

[c] Includes about $200,000 for 1943 and $300,000 for 1944 and All American Aviation, Inc., Caribbean Atlantic Airlines, and Hawaiian Airlines.

## 13. Chronology of Increased Railway Rates, Fares, and Charges, 1946

*(Ex Parte No. 162 and Reopened Ex Parte No. 148)*

Date on which petition was filed by carriers
with the Interstate Commerce Commission . . April 15, 1946
Interim relief, pending hearing and final disposition of petition, sought by carriers;
emergency hearings ordered by ICC . . . . . . April 26, 1946
Emergency hearings held . . . . . . . . . . . . . . . . . May 6-13, 1946
Date of interim decision . . . . . . . . . . . . . . . . . June 20, 1946 (264 I.C.C. 695)
(Permitting restoration of increases author-
ized Mar. 2, 1942, in *Ex Parte No. 148*
under suspension since May 15, 1943,
with certain modifications.)
Date on which findings became effective . . . . July 1, 1946
Further hearings held:
Sessions for receiving testimony conducted
in various cities . . . . . . . . . . . . . . . . . . . . . July 22-Sept. 20, 1946
Oral argument at Washington . . . . . . . . . . . Sept. 23-28, 1946
Date submitted . . . . . . . . . . . . . . . . . . . . . . . . . Oct. 25, 1946
Date decided . . . . . . . . . . . . . . . . . . . . . . . . . . . Dec. 5, 1946 (266 I.C.C. 537)
(Increase in passenger fares authorized
Jan. 21, 1942, continued in effect with-
out expiration date.)
Date on which findings became effective . . . . . Jan. 1, 1947
Findings in decision of Dec. 5, 1946, modi-
fied with respect to increases authorized on
sulphur, in carloads, from Texas mines to
Galveston, Texas, for movement beyond by
water . . . . . . . . . . . . . . . . . . . . . . . . . . . . . . . . Mar. 3, 1947 (268 I.C.C. 169)

14. RATE OF RETURN, EXPENDITURES FOR ADDITIONS AND BETTERMENTS, NATIONAL INCOME, TRAFFIC UNITS, CLASS I RAILROADS 1920-48[a]

| Year | Rate of Return[b] | | Expenditures for Additions and Betterments | | National Income | | Traffic Units[c] | |
|---|---|---|---|---|---|---|---|---|
| | Per Cent | Index 1929 =100 | Millions of Dollars | Index 1929 =100 | Millions of Dollars | Index 1929 =100 | Millions | Index 1929 =100 |
| 1920 | .... | | | | | | 532,582 | 100.6 |
| 1921 | ....2.99 | 57.1 | 557.0 | 65.3 | | | 404,600 | 76.4 |
| 1922 | ....3.75 | 71.6 | 429.3 | 50.3 | | | 432,216 | 81.6 |
| 1923 | ....4.57 | 87.2 | 1,059.1 | 124.1 | | | 512,174 | 96.8 |
| 1924 | ....4.49 | 85.7 | 874.7 | 102.5 | | | 482,973 | 91.2 |
| 1925 | ....5.07 | 96.8 | 748.2 | 87.6 | | | 508,003 | 96.0 |
| 1926 | ....5.35 | 102.1 | 885.1 | 103.7 | | | 537,408 | 101.5 |
| 1927 | ....4.64 | 88.5 | 771.6 | 90.4 | | | 517,573 | 97.8 |
| 1928 | ....5.01 | 95.6 | 676.7 | 79.3 | | | 516,342 | 97.5 |
| 1929 | ....5.24 | 100.0 | 853.7 | 100.0 | 87,355 | 100.00 | 529,357 | 100.0 |
| 1930 | ....3.59 | 68.5 | 872.6 | 102.2 | 75,003 | 85.9 | 454,242 | 85.8 |
| 1931 | ....2.20 | 42.0 | 361.9 | 37.1 | 58,873 | 67.4 | 355,421 | 67.1 |
| 1932 | ....1.38 | 26.3 | 167.2 | 19.6 | 41,690 | 47.7 | 269,786 | 51.0 |
| 1933 | ....2.03 | 38.7 | 103.9 | 12.2 | 39,584 | 45.3 | 283,703 | 53.6 |
| 1934 | ....1.99 | 38.0 | 212.7 | 24.9 | 48,613 | 55.7 | 306,761 | 58.0 |
| 1935 | ....2.16 | 41.2 | 188.3 | 22.1 | 56,789 | 65.0 | 321,021 | 60.6 |
| 1936 | ....2.88 | 55.0 | 299.0 | 35.0 | 66,941 | 76.6 | 381,622 | 72.1 |
| 1937 | ....2.56 | 48.9 | 509.8 | 59.7 | 73,627 | 84.3 | 407,218 | 76.9 |
| 1938 | ....1.62 | 30.9 | 226.9 | 26.6 | 67,375 | 77.1 | 330,963 | 62.5 |
| 1939 | ....2.56 | 48.9 | 262.0 | 30.7 | 72,532 | 83.0 | 376,248 | 71.1 |
| 1940 | ....2.94 | 56.1 | 429.1 | 50.3 | 81,347 | 93.1 | 418,163 | 79.0 |
| 1941 | ....4.28 | 81.7 | 543.0 | 63.6 | 103,834 | 118.9 | 533,478 | 100.8 |
| 1942 | ....6.34 | 121.0 | 534.9 | 62.7 | 136,486 | 156.2 | 744,765 | 140.7 |
| 1943 | ....5.75 | 109.7 | 454.3 | 53.2 | 168,262 | 192.6 | 902,008 | 170.4 |
| 1944 | ....4.73 | 90.3 | 560.1 | 65.6 | 182,260 | 208.6 | 927,389 | 175.2 |
| 1945 | ....3.77 | 71.9 | 563.0 | 65.9 | 182,808 | 209.3 | 863,518 | 163.1 |
| 1946 | ....2.75 | 52.5 | 562.0 | 65.8 | 178,204 | 204.0 | 720,703 | 136.2 |
| 1947 | ....3.41 | 65.1 | 864.7 | 101.3 | 202,500 | 231.9 | 744,243 | 140.6 |
| 1948 | ....4.38[d] | 83.6 | 1,269.0 | 148.6 | 224,400 | 256.9 | 715,542 | 135.2 |

[a] Sources of basic data: Rate of return, Sheet 2, Carriers' Exhibit 34 (J. H. Parmalee) *Ex parte* 168; Expenditures for additions and betterments, Sheet 31, Exhibit 96, *Ex parte 162, Increased Railway Rates, Fares and Charges, 1946,* for years 1920-22, Sheet 35, Exhibit 34, *Ex parte 168, Increased Freight Rates, 1948* for 1923-48; National income from *National Income Supplement to Survey of Current Business,* July 1947, p. 19, Table 1 for 1929-46; 1947 and 1948 data from *Survey of Current Business,* February 1949, p. 10. Source of traffic unit data shown in note c.

[b] Represents rate of return of net railway operating income on net investment in railway property used in transportation service (investment in road and equipment, materials and supplies and cash) after accrued depreciation.

[c] Traffic units represent the sum of revenue ton-miles and revenue passenger miles, with the passenger miles weighted according to the ratio between revenue per passenger mile and revenue per ton-mile. Mileage figures from ICC *Statistics of Railways in the United States,* Statement 33 for years 1920-28. Statement 37 for years 1929-37. Table 158 for years 1938-47, and ICC Statement M-220(OS-D), December 1948 for 1948. Revenue data from Sheet 22. Carriers' Exhibit 34 (J. H. Parmalee) *Ex parte* 168.

[d] Computed on investment at beginning of year.

15. CHRONOLOGY OF INCREASED RAILROAD FREIGHT RATES, 1947

(*Ex Parte No. 166*)

| Action Taken | Approximate Amount Per Cent |
|---|---|

Date on which petition was filed by carriers with the
Interstate Commerce Commission .............. July 3, 1947
Petition amended ........................... July 23, 1947
Petition supplemented and further amended ....... Sept. 5, 1947
Motion of petitioners for temporary interim increase
of 10 per cent ............................. Sept. 9, 1947
Hearings held ............................... Sept. 9-19, 1947
   (Hearings directed chiefly to motion of petitioners
   for interim increase, and major and larger ques-
   tions deferred for further hearing at times and
   places hereafter to be announced.)
Date of interim decision ....................... Oct. 6, 1947
Date on which interim findings became effective .... Oct. 13, 1947    8.9
Further hearings held ......................... Nov. 3-Dec. 8, 1947
Report on further hearings
  Date decided (interim report) ................ Dec. 29, 1947
  Effective date ............................. Jan. 5, 1948 with   10.0
                        number of ex-
                        ceptions to ex-
                        pire June 30, 1948.
Report on further hearings
  Date decided ............................. April 13, 1948
  Effective date ............................. May 6, 1948
    Superseding interim increases—Eastern territory ............... 30.0
                                Southern territory .............. 25.0
                                Zone 1 of Western territory ....... 25.0
                                Interterritorially ............... 25.0
                                Western territory, except Zone 1 ... 20.0
Report on further consideration
  Date decided ................................ July 27, 1948
  Effective date ............................. Aug. 21, 1948
  (Only change in percentage increases allowed in Apr. 13, 1948 report
  is reduction from 25 per cent to 22.5 per cent in permitted increase
  in rates between Western territory, other than Zone I of Western
  Trunk Line territory, and Zone I of Western Trunk Line territory.
  Protective service rates increased from 10 to 15 per cent. Many
  maxima increased.)

## 16. Chronology of Nonoperating Organizations' 1948 Wage and Hour Demand

Date on which request of 16 nonoperating organizations was filed ................................Apr. 8, 1948
    Organizations requested: (1) 48 hours' pay for 40-hour week; (2) Overtime pay for work in excess of 8 hours per day, time and a half for Saturdays, and double time for Sundays and holidays; (3) General wage increase of 25 cents per hour

Carriers filed counter proposals ....................Apr. 19, 1948
    For (1) changes in working rules and practices which the carriers consider necessary and desirable for more efficient railroad operation if the employees' requests are granted, or (2) a general wage increase of 10 cents an hour in settlement of all matters in dispute in present case

Bargaining conferences held ......................May-Oct. 1948

Emergency Board of 3 members created to investigate dispute ......................................Oct. 18, 1948

Public hearings held ...........................Oct. 26-Nov. 27, 1948

Hearings before Emergency Board extended "not to exceed 30 days from Nov. 17, 1948" ..............Nov. 17, 1948

Report to president by Emergency Board recommended. .Dec. 17, 1948
    (1) 48-hour pay for 40-hour work week
    (2) No punitive pay for Sat., Sun., holidays as such
    (3) Some rules should be changed to conform to 40-hour week, others need not be
    (4) General pay increase of 7 cents an hour

Negotiations renewed ............................Jan. 5, 1949

Emergency Board reconvened at request of both railroads and unions to dispose of issues involving monthly-rated employees and yardmasters. These issues were not originally submitted to the Board ....Feb. 2, 1949

Emergency Board returned decisions on above issues and on method of applying five-day week to working conditions ......................................Mar. 13, 1949

Railroads and nonoperating organizations reached agreement embodying recommendations of Emergency Board ......................................Mar. 20, 1949

## 17. CHRONOLOGY OF 1948 INCREASED RAILWAY RATES AND CHARGES

### (Ex Parte 168)

Date on which petition was filed by carriers for increase in coal, coke and iron ore rate (ICC No. 30052) .......................................Aug. 26, 1948

Date on which notice for discontinuance of this petition (ICC 30052) was filed and new petition requesting general increase of 8 per cent was substituted ......................................Oct. 1, 1948

Hearing set for Nov. 30, 1948, in Washington, D.C. .....Oct. 1, 1948

An amended rate increase petition was filed by carriers asking 13 per cent long-term increase with 8 per cent immediate interim boost ....................Oct. 12, 1948

Hearing on amended petition set for Nov. 30 by the Commission ......................................Nov. 2, 1948

Hearings held in which discussion was mainly on 8 per cent portion asked for interim relief ..............Nov. 30-Dec. 4, 1948

Further hearings held in Washington, D.C. ...........Dec. 8-10, 1948

Commission issued decision granting interim increase varying from 4 to 6 per cent within territories ......Dec. 29, 1948

Commission announced hearings on permanent 13 per cent increase (including interim 8 per cent) for various places and dates. General hearings in Washington Mar. 1, 1949. Oral argument in Washington on May 16 .....................................Feb. 1, 1949

Commission issued notice of revised regional hearings schedule ......................................Feb. 4, 1949

Hearings in Washington, D.C. .....................Mar. 1-9, 1949

Regional hearings began ..........................Mar. 14, 1949

18. AVERAGE RATE ON DIVIDEND YIELDING STOCK, PERCENTAGE OF
STOCK NOT YIELDING DIVIDENDS AND NET INCOME AS
PERCENTAGE OF STOCKHOLDERS' EQUITY, CLASS I
RAILROADS, 1920-47[a]

| Year | Amount of Stock Outstanding (In millions of dollars) | Per Cent of Stock not Yielding Dividends | Average Rate on Dividend Yielding Stock (Per Cent) | Stockholders' Equity[b] (In millions of dollars) | Net Income (In millions of dollars) | Net Income as Per Cent of Stockholders' Equity |
|------|------|------|------|------|------|------|
| 1920 |       |      |     | 10,228 | 431 | 4.2 |
| 1921 | 7,303 | 41.2 | 7.0 | 10,341 | 314 | 3.0 |
| 1922 | 7,242 | 38.9 | 6.2 | 10,371 | 370 | 3.6 |
| 1923 | 7,357 | 36.3 | 6.3 | 10,716 | 555 | 5.2 |
| 1924 | 7,548 | 33.4 | 6.4 | 11,140 | 558 | 5.0 |
| 1925 | 7,633 | 31.6 | 6.6 | 11,503 | 701 | 6.1 |
| 1926 | 7,685 | 29.1 | 7.3 | 11,920 | 809 | 6.8 |
| 1927 | 7,831 | 28.0 | 7.3 | 12,142 | 673 | 5.5 |
| 1928 | 8,080 | 24.6 | 7.1 | 12,763 | 787 | 6.2 |
| 1929 | 8,185 | 22.2 | 7.7 | 13,267 | 897 | 6.8 |
| 1930 | 8,267 | 21.5 | 7.6 | 12,998 | 524 | 4.0 |
| 1931 | 8,272 | 25.3 | 5.3 | 12,721 | 135 | 1.1 |
| 1932 | 8,245 | 66.7 | 3.4 | 12,394 | 139 def. | 1.1 def. |
| 1933 | 8,233 | 68.5 | 3.7 | 12,188 | 6 def. | .04 def. |
| 1934 | 8,226 | 65.3 | 4.7 | 11,988 | 17 def. | .1 def. |
| 1935 | 8,219 | 65.2 | 4.4 | 11,774 | 8 | .06 |
| 1936 | 8,030 | 63.6 | 5.3 | 11,427 | 165 | 1.4 |
| 1937 | 8,123 | 60.0 | 5.2 | 11,298 | 98 | .9 |
| 1938 | 8,149 | 67.5 | 3.1 | 10,936 | 123 def. | 1.1 def. |
| 1939 | 8,149 | 67.0 | 4.7 | 10,761 | 93 | .9 |
| 1940 | 8,160 | 61.4 | 5.0 | 10,676 | 189 | 1.8 |
| 1941 | 7,933 | 58.9 | 5.7 | 10,722 | 500 | 4.7 |
| 1942 | 7,947 | 43.0 | 4.5 | 11,165 | 902 | 8.1 |
| 1943 | 7,918 | 41.3 | 4.6 | 11,723 | 873 | 7.5 |
| 1944 | 7,961 | 40.9 | 5.3 | 12,338 | 667 | 5.4 |
| 1945 | 8,009 | 42.2 | 5.5 | 12,666 | 450 | 3.6 |
| 1946 | 8,036 | 43.8 | 5.4 | 12,716 | 287 | 2.2 |
| 1947 | 7,892 | 43.1 | 5.4 | 13,066 | 480 | 3.7 |

[a] Basic data for amount and rate of stock for 1921-46 from p. 37, Carriers'
exhibit 92 (J. H. Parmelee), *Ex parte 166, Increased Freight Rates, 1947.* Data
for net income and stockholders' equity for 1920-46 from ICC, *Statistics of
Railways in the United States.* 1947 data from Association of American Railroads.

[b] Represents total stock plus corporate surplus.

**19. Operating Results of 131 Class I Railroads, 1939-41 Average[a]**

| | All Class I Railroads | | 66 Class I Carriers in 19 Systems | |
|---|---|---|---|---|
| | Millions of Dollars | Per Cent of Total | Millions of Dollars | Per Cent of Total |
| **Rate-of-return 6 per cent or higher** | | | | |
| Total net investment | 1,656 | 7.1 | | |
| Total operating revenues | 402 | 8.8 | | |
| Net railway operating income | 128 | 16.9 | | |
| Net income | 103 | 39.7 | | |
| Dividends paid | 87 | 52.4 | | |
| **Rate-of-return 4.00-5.99 per cent** | | | | |
| Total net investment | 2,413 | 10.4 | 2,010 | 13.6 |
| Total operating revenues | 519 | 11.4 | 429 | 14.3 |
| Net railway operating income | 111 | 14.7 | 104 | 21.5 |
| Net income | 61 | 23.5 | 62 | 40.9 |
| Dividends paid | 22 | 13.1 | 30 | 42.4 |
| **Rate-of-return 2.00-3.99 per cent** | | | | |
| Total net investment | 16,850 | 72.5 | 12,116 | 82.0 |
| Total operating revenues | 3,292 | 72.3 | 2,483 | 82.6 |
| Net railway operating income | 494 | 65.3 | 368 | 76.1 |
| Net income | 129 | 49.5 | 101 | 66.7 |
| Dividends paid | 57 | 34.4 | 41 | 57.6 |
| **Rate-of-return 1.99 or lower** | | | | |
| Total net investment | 2,322 | 10.0 | 647 | 4.4 |
| Total operating revenues | 341 | 7.5 | 92 | 3.1 |
| Net railway operating income | 23 | 3.1 | 12 | 2.4 |
| Net income | 33 def. | 12.7 def. | 11 def. | 7.6 def. |
| Dividends paid | 0.2 | 0.1 | — | — |
| **Total** | | | | |
| Total net investment | 23,241 | | 14,773 | |
| Total operating revenues | 4,554 | | 3,004 | |
| Net railway operating income | 756 | | 483 | |
| Net income | 261 | | 151 | |
| Dividends paid | 167 | | 71 | |

[a] Total net investment from Form A reports of the carriers to the Association of American Railroads, other data from ICC, *Statistics of Railways in the United States, 1939* and *1941*, Table 58.

## 20. Operating Results of Missouri Pacific System and Atlantic Coast Line System, 1939-41 Average[a]

| | Rate-of-Return | Total Net Investment | Railway Operating Revenue | Net Railway Operating Income | Net Income | Dividends Declared |
|---|---|---|---|---|---|---|
| | | | (In thousands of dollars) | | | |
| Missouri Pacific System | | | | | | |
| Beaumont, Sour Lake and Western | 9.33 | 6,972 | 3,099 | 651 | 478 | — |
| Missouri-Illinois | 7.72 | 7,344 | 2,386 | 567 | 473 | — |
| St. Louis, Brownsville and Mexico | 6.64 | 26,107 | 7,357 | 1,734 | 1,012 | — |
| New Orleans, Texas and Mexico | 5.24 | 17,417 | 2,653 | 914 | 862 def. | — |
| Texas and Pacific | 3.08 | 175,062 | 28,597 | 5,393 | 2,023 | 593 |
| Missouri Pacific | 2.52 | 531,990 | 94,028 | 13,438 | 6,144 def. | — |
| International-Great Northern | .67 | 54,444 | 12,281 | 365 | 2,375 def. | — |
| San Antonio, Uvalde and Gulf | — | 6,226 | 1,319 | 317 def. | 552 def. | — |
| Atlantic Coast Line System | | | | | | |
| Georgia R. R. Lessee Organization | 7.24 | 13,259 | 4,482 | 961 | 59 | — |
| Clinchfield | 6.03 | 68,225 | 8,962 | 4,116 | — | — |
| Charleston and Western Carolina | 4.99 | 11,334 | 2,827 | 566 | 283 | 156 |
| Louisville and Nashville | 4.83 | 404,276 | 101,973 | 19,529 | 12,136 | 7,020 |
| Western Ry. of Alabama | 3.04 | 6,735 | 2,020 | 205 | 167 | 321 |
| Nashville, Chattanooga and St. Louis | 2.73 | 89,646 | 16,710 | 2,454 | 1,070 | 256 |
| Atlantic Coast Line | 2.35 | 263,408 | 54,864 | 6,207 | 4,587 | 283 |
| Atlanta and West Point | 1.48 | 4,366 | 2,079 | 65 | 82 | 37 |
| Atlanta, Birmingham and Coast | — | 6,057 | 3,855 | 46 def. | 32 def. | — |

[a] Total net investment from Form A reports of the carriers to the Association of American Railroads, other data from ICC, *Statistics of Railways in the United States, 1939* and *1941*.

## 21. OPERATING RESULTS OF 127 CLASS I RAILROADS (REPRESENTING 131 CARRIERS), 1947[a]

| | All Class I Railroads | | 60 Class I Carriers in 19 Systems | |
|---|---|---|---|---|
| | Millions of Dollars | Per Cent of Total | Millions of Dollars | Per Cent of Total |
| Rate-of-return 6 per cent or higher | | | | |
| Total net investment | 2,226 | 9.7 | 9 | .1 |
| Total operating revenues | 936 | 10.8 | 3 | .1 |
| Net railway operating income | 176 | 22.6 | 0.7 | .2 |
| Net income | 139 | 29.0 | 0.5 | .3 |
| Dividends paid | 83 | 35.0 | — | — |
| Rate-of-return 4.00-5.99 per cent | | | | |
| Total net investment | 6,670 | 29.2 | 3,939 | 27.5 |
| Total operating revenues | 2,634 | 30.3 | 1,575 | 28.1 |
| Net railway operating income | 311 | 39.8 | 191 | 44.1 |
| Net income | 256 | 53.5 | 130 | 58.6 |
| Dividends paid | 90 | 38.0 | 56 | 50.2 |
| Rate-of-return 2.00-3.99 per cent | | | | |
| Total net investment | 7,350 | 32.1 | 4,455 | 31.1 |
| Total operating revenues | 2,663 | 30.7 | 1,724 | 30.8 |
| Net railway operating income | 224 | 28.7 | 147 | 34.0 |
| Net income | 95 | 19.8 | 71 | 32.1 |
| Dividends paid | 48 | 20.4 | 35 | 31.8 |
| Rate-of-return 1.99 and lower | | | | |
| Total net investment | 6,640 | 29.0 | 5,910 | 41.3 |
| Total operating revenues | 2,452 | 28.2 | 2,300 | 41.0 |
| Net railway operating income | 70 | 8.9 | 94 | 21.7 |
| Net income | 11 def. | 2.3 def. | 20 | 9.0 |
| Dividends paid | 16 | 6.6 | 20 | 18.0 |
| Total | | | | |
| Total net investment | 22,886 | | 14,313 | |
| Total operating revenues | 8,685 | | 5,602 | |
| Net railway operating income | 781 | | 434 | |
| Net income | 479 | | 222 | |
| Dividends paid | 236 | | 111 | |

[a] Total net investment from Form B reports of the carriers to the Association of American Railroads, other data from financial reports of the carriers to the Interstate Commerce Commission.

# FEDERAL AGENCIES PERFORMING ANCILLARY SERVICES FOR AIR AND WATER TRANSPORTATION

## THE WEATHER BUREAU

The rapid postwar expansion of civil aviation resulted in a corresponding increase in the requirements for aviation weather service. Expenditures in 1948 for weather service in direct aid to air commerce amounted to 5.7 million dollars, or 27 per cent of total Weather Bureau expenditures.[1]

Ninety airway weather reporting stations are operated by the Bureau to provide the reports required for scheduled air carrier operation. Regional airway forecasts, prepared in airway forecast centers, cover the entire area of continental United States, as well as the Alaskan area. Terminal forecast centers provide specific information concerning expected weather conditions at the major terminals throughout the country and in Alaska and the Hawaiian Islands. Flight advisory weather service units, located in the CAA airway traffic control centers throughout the United States, provide controllers with a specialized type of weather service for the protection of aircraft in flight.

The Weather Bureau is responsible for matters before the International Civil Aviation Organization pertaining to meteorology, and it aids in the establishment of meteorological facilities and services to meet the needs of international aviation operations. In accordance with an agreement completed between the military and the Weather Bureau, the latter has assumed responsibility for staffing approximately 60 foreign stations throughout the world.

## NATIONAL ADVISORY COMMITTEE FOR AERONAUTICS

The role of the National Advisory Committee for Aeronautics is to "supervise and direct the scientific study of the problems of flight with a view to their practical solution."[2] As the government agency charged with responsibility for scientific aeronautical research, the NACA co-ordinates the basic research programs of the government; conducts fundamental scientific investigation; and encourages and supports research in scientific and educational in-

[1] The Budget of the United States Government for Fiscal Year 1950, p. 463.
[2] 38 Stat. 930, approved Mar. 3, 1915.

stitutions. The results of the Committee's research are made available to the military services and other government establishments, to industry, to air transport operators, to scientific and educational institutions and libraries, and to others concerned.

The Committee has established standing technical subcommittees which prepare and recommend research programs. Most of the problems recommended for investigation are assigned to the Committee's laboratories, but some are assigned to the National Bureau of Standards, to the Forest Products Laboratory, or by contract to scientific and educational institutions. The present primary concern of the NACA is in the field of high-speed flight.[3]

NACA maintains three laboratories, in Virginia, Ohio, and California. Its expenditures totaled 37.5 million dollars in 1948, or four times the 1941 budget. In the eight years 1941-48, total outlays approximated 212 million dollars.

EXPENDITURES OF THE NATIONAL ADVISORY COMMITTEE
FOR AERONAUTICS, 1941-48[a]

| Fiscal Year | Amount |
| --- | --- |
| 1941 | $ 8,136 |
| 1942 | 11,786 |
| 1943 | 23,948 |
| 1944 | 29,799 |
| 1945 | 33,192 |
| 1946 | 32,051 |
| 1947 | 35,190 |
| 1948 | 37,543 |

[a] *The Budget of the United States Government for Fiscal Year, 1950,* p. 1388.

## THE COAST GUARD, DEPARTMENT OF THE TREASURY

Aids to air and water transportation are provided through the Coast Guard, which constitutes a branch of the land and naval forces of the United States operating under the Treasury Department in time of peace and as part of the Navy in time of war, or whenever the president directs.[4] The Coast Guard represents an amalgamation into one service of the activities of the old Revenue Cutter Service, the Life-Saving Service, the Lighthouse Service,[5] and the Bureau of Marine Inspection and Navigation.[6]

[3] *Annual Report of the NACA, 1946,* pp. 1-2.
[4] Act of Jan. 28, 1915, 38 Stat. 800, as amended.
[5] Transferred from Department of Commerce pursuant to sec. 2 (a), Pt 1. of Reorganization Plan II effective July 1, 1939, 53 Stat. 1432.
[6] Transferred from Department of Commerce by Executive Order 9083, dated Feb. 28, 1942. Transfer made permanent and Bureau of Marine Inspec-

As the federal maritime police, the Coast Guard is responsible for maritime law enforcement; saving and protecting of life and property; provision of navigation aids to maritime commerce and to air commerce over the oceans; promotion of the efficiency and safety of the American merchant marine; and preparedness for military operations.

The Coast Guard establishes and maintains some 36,000 navigation aids, such as lights, lighthouses, lightships, radio beacons, radio direction finder stations, buoys, and unlighted beacons on the sea, lake coasts, rivers, and all territories under United States jurisdiction.[7] It maintains stations along the coasts and on the Great Lakes which engage in search and rescue work, aerial reconnaissance, and co-operation with other federal agencies in law enforcement, mapping, and other duties.[8]

As a further aid to shipping, the Coast Guard operates to protect life and property on the high seas and navigable waters of the United States by rendering assistance to vessels (as well as aircraft) in distress, caring for shipwrecked persons, removing dangers to navigation, and protecting shipping from the danger of icebergs. In co-operation with the Weather Bureau, cutters are stationed at sea on transoceanic air routes to provide ocean weather service, and the International Ice Patrol is maintained by the Coast Guard in the North Atlantic.

Other functions related to the safety and efficiency of the merchant marine include the investigation of marine disasters, approval of plans for the construction, repair, and alteration of facilities; approval of materials, equipment, and appliances; the issuance of certificates of inspection; the administration of load-line requirements; the control of log books; the numbering of undocumented vessels; the licensing and certificating of personnel; and the promulgation and enforcement of rules for lights, signals, speed, steering, sailing, passing, anchorage, and movement of vessels.[9]

Inspections during the fiscal year 1948 were completed on 7,513 vessels pursuant to the responsibility of the Coast Guard for the certification of the worthiness of merchant vessels. A large number of construction and repair projects were undertaken in support of more than 20,000 Coast Guard shore structures, and considerable

---

tion and Navigation abolished by Reorganization Plan III of 1946, effective July 16, 1946, 60 Stat. 1097.

[7] Exception: Panama Canal Zone.

[8] The Coast Guard furnishes transportation to government agents in the performance of their duties and on occasion transports United States mail over certain water routes. It also publishes information on aids to navigation.

[9] *United States Government Manual, 1947*, pp. 170-73.

development work was carried on in methods of navigational aid and in the adaptation of helicopters to the special requirements of the Coast Guard service.

UNITED STATES COAST GUARD APPROPRIATIONS, 1938-49[a]
(In millions of dollars)

| Year | Operating Expense | | Total Operating Expenses[b] | Capital Plant Replacements, Improvements, and Additions | Retire-ment Benefits | Grand Total |
| | Military Pay and Allowances | Civilian Salaries | | | | |
| --- | --- | --- | --- | --- | --- | --- |
| 1938 | 16.3 | .6 | 22.5 | 1.2 | 1.8 | 25.5 |
| 1939 | 16.1 | .6 | 24.2 | 4.0 | 2.0 | 30.2 |
| 1940 | 18.9 | 5.9 | 37.2 | 2.4 | 3.0 | 42.6[c] |
| 1941 | 24.5 | 5.6 | 53.9 | 21.8 | 3.2 | 78.9 |
| 1942 | 55.4 | 4.9 | 99.6 | 181.8 | 3.3 | 284.7 |
| 1943 | 296.5 | 9.3 | 390.6 | 112.0 | 3.6 | 506.2[d] |
| 1944 | 390.6 | 7.7 | 463.1 | 1.0 | 3.7 | 467.8 |
| 1945 | 366.8 | 7.2 | 434.2 | – | 4.2 | 438.4 |
| 1946 | 299.2 | 6.8 | 347.1 | 3.5 | 5.0 | 355.6[e] |
| 1947 | 70.9 | 6.8 | 110.5 | 4.8 | 8.9 | 124.2 |
| 1948 | 65.9 | 5.6 | 94.8 | .4 | 10.8 | 106.0 |
| 1949 | 71.3 | 4.2 | 117.0 | 11.1 | 12.0 | 140.1 |

[a] Ebasco Services, Inc., *Study of the United States Coast Guard,* January 1948, Exhibit B-1, p. 258. Data for 1949 from Public Law 727, 80 Cong. 2 sess.
[b] This total includes "Other Operating Expenses," in addition to personnel.
[c] As of July 1, 1939, the Bureau of Lighthouses was transferred from the Department of Commerce to the Coast Guard.
[d] As of March 1, 1942, the Bureau of Marine Inspection and Navigation was transferred from the Department of Commerce to the Coast Guard.
[e] Balance of appropriation after rescissions.

The licensing and certificating of merchant marine personnel resulted in the issuance of 137,017 documents. During the year 10,184 investigations of cases involving negligence, incompetence, and misconduct were made.[10] In addition to its responsibility to enforce navigation laws, the Coast Guard is empowered by Congress to enforce any law of the United States on navigable waters and the high seas.

In 1938 annual appropriations for the Coast Guard totaled 25.5 million dollars. Transfer of the Bureau of Lighthouses to the Coast Guard in 1939, however, occasioned the absorption of over 5,000 civilians, while transfer of the Bureau of Marine Inspection and Navigation in 1942 involved transfer of approximately 1,000 civilians. These transfers considerably increased the financial requirements

[10] *Annual Report of the Secretary of the Treasury, 1948,* pp. 153-54.

of the Coast Guard; but the expanded functions of the organization as part of the Navy during the war precipitated the heaviest increase in spending. In 1941 the Coast Guard appropriations increased to three times the 1938 figure, or 79 million dollars; and by 1943 appropriations reached a peak of more than half a billion dollars. The 1949 appropriations totaled 140 million dollars, a level several times greater than prewar.[11]

### UNITED STATES COAST AND GEODETIC SURVEY, DEPARTMENT OF COMMERCE

The Coast and Geodetic Survey in the Department of Commerce is responsible for aeronautical charts and for surveying and charting the coasts of the United States and its possessions to ensure safe navigation.[12] Its functions also include the determination of geographical positions and elevations along the coasts and in the interior of the country, to co-ordinate the coastal surveys and provide a framework for mapping and other engineering work. It furnishes tide and current tables to mariners. Observations are made of the earth's magnetism in all parts of the country, to furnish magnetic information useful to the mariner, aviator, and radio engineer.

### OFFICE OF TRANSPORT AND COMMUNICATIONS, DEPARTMENT OF STATE

Among the responsibilities of this office are the formulation and co-ordination of State Department policy as it relates to aviation, ocean shipping, and inland water transport. Activities in water transport include analysis of international aspects of shipping; observation and review of developments in the maritime services and laws of other countries; and the formulation of recommendations regarding foreign policy aspects of government assistance to shipping and discriminatory laws or practices against American shipping. The Office aids in the conduct of negotiations between foreign governments and the Maritime Commission and formulates policy on matters involving the effect of ocean-freight and marine-insurance rates on foreign trade. It interprets international conventions concerning seamen; and analyzes regulatory measures and standards that affect shipping and trade.

The Aviation Division of the Office of Transport and Communi-

---

[11] Ebasco Services, Inc. *Study of the United States Coast Guard,* Exhibit B-1, p. 258.

[12] The Coast and Geodetic Survey had its origin in 1807 when a survey of the coasts of the United States was authorized by act of Congress. (2 Stat. 413.) Later legislation extended the work of the Geodetic Survey across the country and to additional types of work.

cations participates in the promotion of air transport abroad by negotiating international agreements covering landing rights and air navigation, and by handling problems relating to international airports and airways. The Division participates in international aviation conferences and represents the Department in various international bodies dealing with aeronautical affairs.

## AIR COORDINATING COMMITTEE

The Air Coordinating Committee was established by the president in 1946 for the purpose of achieving full development and integration of United States aviation policies and activities.[13] It is composed of federal agencies having a primary interest in aviation, and its members include:

Under Secretary of State
Under Secretary of the Treasury
Second Assistant Postmaster General
Under Secretary of Defense
Chairman of the Civil Aeronautics Board
Assistant Director of the Bureau of the Budget (nonvoting)

The function of the ACC is to examine matters affecting more than one participating agency, to develop and recommend government policy, and to co-ordinate the aviation activities of the agencies to the extent permitted by law, except activities relating to the exercise of quasijudicial functions. The ACC acts upon unanimous decisions of its members, with provision for submission to the president of unresolved questions. On matters affecting the interests of nonmember agencies, provision is made for representatives from such agencies to be consulted and given full voting participation.

The activities of the ACC are divided among three divisions, covering technical, economic, and industrial problems. The work of each division is performed by personnel representing the federal agencies having an interest in the problems involved. It also maintains a panel to prepare materials relating to the United States' position on matters before the International Civil Aviation Organization.

## INTERNATIONAL CIVIL AVIATION ORGANIZATION

The United States is a member of the International Civil Aviation Organization which is an association of nations established for the purpose of promoting international aviation. ICAO had its origin in the Chicago Conference in 1944, when plans for such an organization were initiated to prepare for the peacetime preservation and

[13] Executive Order 9781, Sept. 19, 1946.

development of international aviation standards established by the allied military air services during the war.

ICAO comprises an assembly of all its members, which meets annually. It has also a council of 21 member countries which is in practically continuous session. In addition, a secretariat is maintained in Montreal. The work of ICAO consists of the development of uniform standards for air navigation and other technical matters; the maintenance and extension of operating agreements among nations operating in air commerce; maintenance of international aviation statistics and information concerning international agreements; and the arrangement of financial support for international air navigation facilities and services.

The 1949 budget of ICAO amounts to 2.6 million dollars, and the quota allotted to the United States amounts to approximately 20 per cent of the total. The Air Coordinating Committee is the medium through which the government maintains contact with ICAO and through which United States representatives are instructed as to the United States' position on various matters before the international organization.[14]

### THE PANAMA CANAL

The Panama Canal is operated by a government corporation as a public service enterprise. The primary function of the corporation is to provide and maintain a waterway to permit vessels to pass from one ocean to the other, and to handle such traffic as presents itself for transit with a maximum of safety and a minimum of delay. This involves maintenance of the waterway, operation of the locks, and the control of traffic through the Canal, which in turn involves the provision of emergency repairs, fuel, supplies, and the various supplementary services incidental to shipping.

A second function of the Panama Canal is that of supplying necessary services to shipping and the Canal operating force, which services are provided under centralized control by the various business units of the Panama Canal and Panama Railroad Company. These include oil and coal bunkering plants; storehouses for food and other essential supplies; marine repair shops; harbor terminal facilities; a railroad line across the Isthmus; and water and electric power systems. During the fiscal year 1947, a total of 6,372 vessels passed through the Canal, of which 5,017 were toll-paying and 1,265 were toll-free transits.[15] The amount collected in tolls from 1915 to

---

[14] *International Civil Aviation 1945-1948*, Department of State publication No. 3131, May 1948, pp. 32, 34.

[15] Naval and other vessels owned and operated in the government service of the United States and Republic of Panama, war vessels of the Republic of

1947 (the Canal was opened to traffic August 15, 1914) was 555 million dollars.

The Panama Railroad Company was incorporated in 1849 under the laws of the State of New York for the purpose of constructing and operating a railroad across the Isthmus. When the concession rights and property of the New French Canal Company were purchased in 1904, ownership of the stock of the Panama Railroad Company was transferred to the United States Government. The railroad company is an adjunct to the Panama Canal, and its operations are supervised by a board of directors functioning under the direction of the secretary of war. As the operations of the railroad complement those of the Canal, the governor of the Canal is generally elected president of the railroad company. The Panama Railroad Company operates a steamship line from the Canal Zone to New York as a common carrier.

---

Columbia, and vessels transiting solely for the purpose of having repairs made at the Canal shops are exempt from the payment of tolls. The percentage of free transits was 20 per cent in 1947. *Annual Report of the Governor of the Panama Canal, 1947,* p. 3.

# APPENDIX C

# PROPOSALS FOR REORGANIZING NATIONAL TRANSPORTATION ACTIVITIES

## FEDERAL COORDINATOR OF TRANSPORTATION

Under the Emergency Railroad Transportation Act of 1933, the office of the Federal Coordinator of Transportation was established.[1] Among the studies issued by the Coordinator, the "Report of the Federal Coordinator of Transportation on Transportation Legislation" pointed out that:

The ultimate objective is, of course, a system of transportation for the Nation which will supply the most efficient means of transport and furnish service as cheaply as is consistent with fair treatment of labor and with earnings which will support adequate credit and the ability to expand as need develops and to take advantage of all improvements in the art. . . .[2]

To attain this objective, the Coordinator cited the need for "some centralized control which will concern itself with planning and prevention as well as with the cure of evils after they arise."[3]

. . . It must deal with the future provision of new facilities, with the proper coordination of those which exist, and with the development of sound general policies affecting both service and rates; prevent unnecessary duplication and waste; promote the use of each agency of transportation, in cooperation with the others, primarily in the service to which it is economically best adapted; check the forms of endless chain rate cutting or service promotion which have come to be known as destructive competition; and protect the public against unreasonable charges and unjust discriminations.

As a further part of this work of planning, prevention, and coordination, attention must be given to public as well as private expenditures, and to the extent to which various forms of transportation are, through such public expenditures or otherwise, in effect subsidized by Government. It is conceivable that such subsidies may in some situations be justified, and also that where they have been granted in the past it may be

---

[1] 48 Stat. 211. Sec. 2 of that act read: "In order to foster and protect interstate commerce in relation to railroad transportation by preventing and relieving obstructions and burdens thereon resulting from the present acute economic emergency, and in order to safeguard and maintain an adequate national system of transportation there is hereby created the office of Federal Coordinator of Transportation. . . ."

[2] H. Doc. 89, 74 Cong. 1 sess. (1934), p. 8.

[3] The same, p. 9.

impracticable to rectify the situation now; but certainly we should know what has been and is being done in this respect, correct all conditions which are unjust and capable of correction, and understand the consequences of what may be done for the future.[4]

In order to provide for such functions in the federal government, it was recommended that the task be placed under the jurisdiction of a single member of the Interstate Commerce Commission, who would be designated by the president and given the title of Coordinator of Transportation. His duties would be as follows:

1. To keep informed as to the management, operation, and development of all agencies of public transportation . . . and the promotion of a national system of transportation which will meet public needs.

2. To report each year on the state of transportation in the Nation and recommend any legislation that the public welfare may seem to him to demand. . . .

3. To consult and advise with the President and with all executive departments having to do with transportation, and to appear before committees of Congress. . . .

4. To promote joint conferences between groups of carriers or others having a direct interest in transportation, with a view to reconciling differences of opinion, composing controversies, discouraging destructive competition, and encouraging cooperation.

5. To bring to the attention of the carriers situations in which they appear to be incurring unnecessary expense or suffering loss of revenue because of undue competition or lack of proper coordination; and, in the event that they prove unable or unwilling to correct such situations, to enter appropriate orders, subject to review by the Commission. . . .

6. To conduct such inquiries as the public welfare in transportation may in his opinion demand. . . .

7. To administer in behalf of the President, any codes of fair competition for transportation agencies which the law may permit, as not in conflict with regulation by the Commission.[5]

## THE COMMITTEE OF THREE

With the railroads in serious financial difficulty in 1938, the president called upon three members of the Interstate Commerce Commission to consider what action might be taken by the federal government for the relief and improvement of the situation. The fact that the president had no agency in the executive branch which was concerned with the problems of the railroads required that an *ad hoc* committee be established to consider these questions. Membership on the committee was drawn from the federal agency familiar with the railroad problem, but an agency which in its day-

[4] The same.
[5] The same, p. 30.

to-day operations had no need for keeping abreast of the physical and financial conditions of the railroads, and no responsibility for seeking solutions.

In his letter to the Congress the President asked for:

. . . special consideration of the fact that matters relating to transportation in its wider sense are now dealt with by the following departments or agencies of the Government:

1. The Bureau of Public Roads of the Department of Agriculture.
2. The Bureau of Air Commerce of the Department of Commerce.
3. The United States Maritime Commission.
4. The Division of Transportation of the Bureau of Foreign and Domestic Commerce of the Department of Commerce.
5. The Interstate Commerce Commission.
6. The Lighthouse Service of the Department of Commerce.
7. The Bureau of Navigation and Marine Inspection of the Department of Commerce.

These agencies deal with special phases of transportation rather than the transportation problem in its broader national aspect. Some of the functions are executive, some are legislative, and some are judicial.

From the point of view of business efficiency, such as a private corporation would seek, it would seem to be the part of common sense to place all executive functions relating to all transportation in one Federal department—such as the Department of Commerce, the Department of the Interior, or some other old or new department. At the same time all quasi-judicial and quasi-legislative matters relating to all transportation could properly be placed under an independent commission—a reorganized Interstate Commerce Commission. And such action would be highly constitutional.[6]

The Committee recommended a number of financial measures for the relief of current financial difficulties; but for a long-term program it suggested that a Federal Transportation Authority be created for two years to plan and promote action by railroad companies to eliminate waste and consolidation.

### THE COMMITTEE OF SIX

Later in 1938 the President again appointed a committee to consider the transportation problem and recommend legislation. On this occasion the so-called Committee of Six recommended creation of a new agency to study the transportation problem, and ultimately to carry on all federal promotional and regulatory activity. The Committee's recommendation was specifically as follows:

[6] *Immediate Relief for Railroads,* H. Doc. 583, 75 Cong. 3 sess. (1938), pp. 2-3.

*Transportation Board.* A new and independent agency to be created, charged with the duty of investigating and reporting to the Congress concerning the relative economy and fitness of the several modes of transportation and the extent to which any of them is now being subsidized, with its recommendations for futher legislation. Thereafter to be charged with responsibility for administering as to all modes of transportation regulatory provisions relating to certificates of convenience and necessity covering new construction or operations and abandonments of facilities or operations, and the approval of the issuance of securities, consolidations, mergers, leases, acquisitions of control, interlocking directorates, etc., and to exercise all functions of a research or promotional nature relating primarily to any mode of transportation now vested in other agencies or bureaus.[7]

#### SELECT COMMITTEE TO INVESTIGATE THE EXECUTIVE AGENCIES OF THE GOVERNMENT

The Select Committee to Investigate the Executive Agencies of the Government, created in 1936, was called upon to recommend such changes in organization as might be in the interest of simplification, efficiency, and economy.[8] In the transportation section of this study, prepared by the Brookings Institution, consideration was given to the possibilities of administrative reorganization under the then existing transportation policies. It was considered first that:

. . . an articulated national policy relative to Federal promotional activity must be substituted for the present collection of divergent policies. Second, administrative machinery adapted to the application of this policy should be created, and certain adjustments should be made in the distribution of regulatory functions.[9]

Two proposals were made to achieve these objectives: (1) Consolidation in a single agency (a Department of Transportation or a Division of Transportation in the Department of Commerce) of all promotional work of the federal government carried on in the primary interests of transportation. (2) Reallocation of regulatory functions, calling in most cases for concentration of regulatory activity in the Interstate Commerce Commission.

#### BOARD OF INVESTIGATION AND RESEARCH

The Transportation Act of 1940 provided for the appointment by the president of a three-man Board of Investigation and Research

[7] *Report of Committee Appointed September 20, 1938, by the President of the United States to Submit Recommendations upon the General Transportation Situation*, Dec. 23, 1938, p. 4.

[8] 74 Cong. 2 sess., S. Res. 217, Feb. 24, 1936.

[9] *Investigation of Executive Agencies of the Government*, S. Rept. 1275, 75 Cong. 1 sess. (1937), p. 451.

to consider the transportation problem once again.[10] The statute provided that the Board should investigate the relative economy and fitness of the several types of carriers; the methods by which each type can and should be developed so that there may be provided a rational transportation system adequate to meet the needs of the commerce of the United States, of the Postal service, and of the national defense; the extent to which right-of-way or other transportation facilities and special services have been or are provided from public funds without adequate compensation; and the extent to which taxes are imposed on the several carriers by various agencies of government.

Among the Board's recommendations was the suggestion that three new permanent federal agencies should be created in the field of transportation:

. . . A promotional and research agency, which may be entitled the Federal Transportation Authority; an advisory board, to be constituted as a National Transportation Advisory Council; and an office of Public Transportation Counsel in the Department of Justice.

The Federal Transportation Authority might be established as an independent organization, or set up as an activity of the Department of Commerce. It would have the primary task of developing means of effectuating the national transportation policy. It would give consideration to the development of sound and consistent policies for the expenditure of public funds in the promotion of transportation, and in the performance of this duty it would investigate all proposals for substantial Federal expenditures for the construction or improvement of transportation facilities. It would be authorized to appear before regulatory bodies in proceedings relating to matters committed to its jurisdiction. It would have facilities for research, and would make studies of the relative economy and fitness of carriers and on other questions relating to its duties. It would not supersede existing agencies but would coordinate the policies which they would execute, subject to congressional direction, and it would report on its work directly to the President and to Congress.

In planning and conducting its work the Authority should have the benefit of the advice of people with extensive practical experience in transportation affairs and related fields. To fill this need the National Transportation Advisory Council would be constituted, composed of individuals specially qualified by knowledge of transportation, labor, finance, agriculture, and industry, drawn for the most part from private life but including some representatives of Federal agencies and departments. The Advisory Council would confer periodically with the Authority and make suggestions as to program, reporting to the President and Congress independently.

The Office of Public Transportation Counsel would be established in the Department of Justice, and it would represent, in administrative and

[10] 54 Stat. 953.

court proceedings relating to transportation, the various interests of the Government and the interests of those not otherwise adequately represented. . . .[11]

## NATIONAL RESOURCES PLANNING BOARD STUDY

In accordance with the request of the President dated January 20, 1940, the National Resources Planning Board prepared a report on "Transportation and National Policy," with the advice of the heads of the various federal transportation agencies, who made up the Advisory Committee for the transportation study. The conclusion with respect to federal organization was as follows:

A National Transportation Agency should be established to coordinate all Federal development activity in transportation along the lines of a general and progressive plan under appropriate legislative directives. Existing development agencies would be absorbed as divisions of the new Agency. Apart from the normal development functions of these agencies, it would be the special responsibility of the Agency to undertake leadership in programs for transport consolidation, terminal unification and reconstruction, coordination of the various transport media, and encouragement of the development of new forms of transport within their respective economic spheres. Active cooperation with the regulatory agencies would be required, but the National Transportation Agency would be responsible for the unification of the Federal Government's planning, development, and administrative functions in the field of transportation.[12]

## PRESIDENT'S AIR POLICY COMMISSION

Among the more recent special studies in the transportation field has been the report of the Air Policy Commission which was appointed by the president in 1947 to consider problems of national aviation policy.[13]

The Commission recommended that the government's executive functions relating to civil aviation remain under the direction of the Secretary of Commerce, who shall have immediately under him a Secretary of Civil Aviation in charge of a Department of Civil Aviation. This department would have all the functions of the present CAA, the responsibility for safety regulations now in the CAB, as well as certain duties in connection with an Aircraft Development Corporation. In addition, it would perform administrative

[11] *Practices and Procedures of Governmental Control*, H. Doc. 678, 78 Cong. 2 sess. (1944), pp. 175-76.
[12] National Resources Planning Board, *Transportation and National Policy*, H. Doc. 883, 77 Cong. 2 sess., May 1942, p. 14.
[13] *Survival in the Air Age*, A Report by the President's Air Policy Commission, Jan. 1, 1948.

housekeeping functions for the CAB and an independent Air Safety Board.

The Commission expressed the belief, however, that "sometime within the near future" the executive transportation functions of the government should be centered in a Department of Transportation, in order effectively to co-ordinate the development of all forms of transportation.

The Department of Commerce presently contains a nucleus of transportation agencies, namely, the Civil Aeronautics Administration, the Inland Waterways Corporation, and the transportation activities of the Bureau of Foreign and Domestic Commerce. The Weather Bureau and the Coast and Geodetic Survey, both of which provide services for transportation, are also a part of the Department of Commerce. And it should be noted that the President's Advisory Committee on the Merchant Marine has just recommended that all functions of the Maritime Commission, other than quasi-legislative and quasi-judicial, be transferred to the Department of Commerce. Although the Weather Bureau and the Coast and Geodetic Survey would not be included in the Department of Civil Aviation, these two organizations could be included in the Department of Transpartation.[14]

The independent, semijudicial bodies in the transportation field should be brought into the Department of Transportation, but for housekeeping purposes only.

### CONGRESSIONAL AVIATION POLICY BOARD

This Joint Board of the Congress was established in 1947.[15] In its report, the recommendation was made that the CAA be abolished and in its place an "Office of Civil Aviation" established in the Department of Commerce, which would be concerned with the airways and airport programs as well as other promotional and educational functions. The Office of Civil Aviation would be handled by two bureaus—the Federal Airways Service and the Bureau of Aeronautical Development, which would administer the Federal Airport Act and other promotional activities of the present CAA. It was believed that these functions should be kept apart from the functions of making and administering rules and regulations and retained in an organization that could readily be transferred to the military in a national emergency. The CAB should be made responsible for promulgation, administration, and enforcement of regulations relating to competency of airmen and certification involving equipment. The Federal Airways Service would promulgate and ad-

---

[14] The same, p. 141.
[15] 61 Stat. 676.

minister regulations relating to the movement of aircraft in flight and at airports. The CAB would hear and determine appeals from the Federal Airways Service in cases involving violations of regulations. Also recommended was an independent Director of Air Safety Investigation to be appointed by the president, responsible for investigation and analysis of accidents.[16]

### PRESIDENT'S ADVISORY COMMITTEE ON THE MERCHANT MARINE

When the President appointed this Advisory Committee in 1947, he stated as his reason the fact that:

. . . the United States faces critical problems in connection with the construction, modernization, and maintenance of an adequate fleet of passenger and freight vessels......................................

Although our present need is primarily for passenger ships, our ship construction program as a whole merits careful consideration ..........

I feel that the whole problem should be carefully studied in all its phases by a group of citizens equipped by background and training to counsel the Government and assist it in formulating a program to strengthen our merchant marine. . . .[17]

The Committee concluded that the organizational structure of the Maritime Commission set up in the Merchant Marine Act of 1936 is wholly inadequate to permit effective execution of the many diverse activities involved in merchant shipping problems.

. . . These activities at present range from the preparation of economic studies and research through the technical questions of detailed design. They embrace the construction, ownership, operation, and disposal of ships and of maritime shore facilities. They involve financial or banking relations with the industry, the determination of fitness of the various shipping companies, the training of licensed and unlicensed operating personnel, the establishment of minimum manning and wage scales and of minimum working conditions on subsidized vessels, the issuance of insurance, the setting and regulation of certain freight rates, the determination of fair and of reasonable compensation, the distribution of shipbuilding work, and the maintenance of a field organization for the inspection of government-owned vessels building and in operation, and for the preservation of laid-up reserve fleets and shore facilities.[18]

The Committee found that there is no assurance of a vigorous flexible administration of policy under the present structure of the

[16] *National Aviation Policy,* Report of the Congressional Aviation Policy Board, 80 Cong. 2 sess., March 1948.

[17] *Report of the President's Advisory Committee on the Merchant Marine,* November 1947, p. vi.

[18] The same, p. 67.

Commission. It was "strongly recommended," therefore, that the Maritime Commission be reorganized: (1) A Maritime Administration should be created under a single administrator who, in time of peace, would report to the Secretary of Commerce and who should be charged with the executive and operative functions assigned to the Maritime Commission; and (2) A Maritime Board should be appointed, composed of five commissioners as set up in the 1936 act, in whom would be vested the quasilegislative and quasijudicial functions for which the Maritime Commission is now responsible.

# INDEX

# INDEX

Abandonment
control over, 352
railroad, 2, 187, 225
resistance against, 351
waterway, 88, 127
Acquisition of control
air carriers, 307
motor carriers, 306
railroads, 306, 331
*See also* Consolidation *and* Co-ordination.
Act to Regulate Commerce, 1887, 185, 230, 316
Agriculture, Department of, 105, 108, 389
Air cargo, 145, 150, 266
Air Commerce Act of 1926, 65
Air Commerce, Bureau of, 379
Air Coordinating Committee, 18, 70, 437
Air Mail Act of 1925, 47
Air-mail payments
feeder-lines, 49, 220
history of, 46
international carriers, 45, 396
methods, 44, 396
per cent of airline revenue, 49
Post Office Department position, 18, 46, 51, 269, 379, 389
service rate, 217, 269
*See also* Subsidy.
Air Navigation Development Board, 25n
Air Safety Board, 62, 65, 71, 74, 380
Air Transport Command, 143
Aircraft
accident investigation, 62, 395
accidents, 60
design, 40, 124
manufacturing, 149
registration, 17, 76
Airline Pilots Association, 65
Airlines
accidents, 60, 79

competition, 200
defense role, 144
feeder-lines, 218
financial position of, 221
issues raised, 223
mileage of, 203, 219
limitations on management, 212
noncertificated carriers, 266
operating certificates, 196
trunk-lines, 200
financial position of, 22, 203
mileage of, 203, 422
route pattern, 197, 383, 396
use of airports, 36
use of airways, 27
*See also* Acquisition of control, Co-ordination, Rates, Regulation.
Airports
current program, 35
federal aid, 32, 42
Federal Airport Act, 33
financing trend, 30, 37
government ownership, 36
military use, 40
municipal, 29
National Airport Plan, 33
number and type, 29
relief expenditures, 30, 34
state action, 41
user payments, 35
Airways
all-weather system, 23
cost responsibility, 27
expenditures, 21
future costs, 24
future requirements, 22
mileage and facilities, 19
planning, 395
use of, 28
Aitchison, Commissioner Clyde B., 183n, 279n, 330n
Allocation of resources, 126, 351, 358

451

Allocation of traffic, 126, 136, 229, 246, 270, 351, 371, 407

American Waterways Operators, Inc., 91

Arbitration Boards, 279n, 282n, 284n

Armour, Merrill, 76n

Army Civil Functions Appropriation Act of 1949, 85

Army, Department of the, 85, 102n, 393

Association of American Railroads, 325, 331n

Automobile, 3, 4, 39, 127, 139, 146, 155

Aviation safety
  accident investigation, 62, 80
  aircraft design, 40, 124
  enforcement, 77, 395
  federal activity, 62, 397, 405
  number of accidents, 60
  state role, 75, 80


Barge lines. See Inland Waterways Corporation and Rates.

Barriger, John W., 324n

Behncke, David L., 65

Board of Engineers for Rivers and Harbors, 84

Board of Investigation and Research, 25, 36, 46n, 52, 87, 89, 190n, 193n, 443

Bollinger, L. L., 31n, 37n, 38n

Branch, Harlee, 221n, 223n

Budget, Bureau of the, 85, 133

Burchmore, John S., 235n

Bus transportation, 3, 111, 115, 127, 155


Canals, 11, 87

Capital requirements
  airports, 36
  airways, 27
  barge lines, 91
  highway, 115
  See also Railroad.

Car service, 399, 401

Cargo aircraft. See Air Cargo.

Certificates of public necessity and convenience, 186, 197, 310

Civil Aeronautics Act of 1938, 44, 58, 62, 140, 169, 178, 209, 218

Civil Aeronautics Administration
  airport and airway activities, 19, 33
  functions of, 17, 135
  reorganization proposal, 395
  safety responsibility, 63, 69
  statutory basis for, 17, 178

Civil Aeronautics Authority, 31, 62, 178, 368, 380

Civil Aeronautics Board
  air-mail payments, 47
  air-mail subsidy, 51
  evaluation of, 207
  integration policy, 309
  operating permits, 196
  reorganization proposal, 395
  route pattern determination, 197, 201
  safety responsibility, 64
  statutory basis for, 17, 179
  unification policy, 307

Civil Works Administration, 34

Coast Guard, 18, 74, 381, 404, 433

Coast and Geodetic Survey, 18, 404, 436

Coastal and intercoastal shipping
  ICC control of, 182, 393
  rail competition, 259
  relation to national security, 103, 157
  subsidy, 264

Commerce, Department of, 381, 383, 389, 393

Commission on Organization of the Executive Branch of the Government, 388

Committee of Six, 325, 340n, 382, 385

Committee of Three, 382, 385

Competition
air, 200, 265
air cargo, 270
merchant shipping, 95, 122, 158
objectives of regulating, 246, 362
rail-highway, 256
rail-water, 250, 259
railroad, 298, 325
Congestion
airport, 23
airway, 28
highway, 110
Consolidation of railroads
defects of plan, 318, 339
general plan of, 339, 344, 376
history of, 318, 376
ICC administration of, 318, 339, 344, 384
mandatory aspect, 321, 342, 376
pooling of revenue, 317, 327
present status of, 321
recapture of excess earnings, 318
recommended changes, 324, 331, 339, 376, 399
voluntary aspect, 339, 376
weak and strong railroad problem, 318, 325
Co-ordination and integration, 305
air-rail, 311
air-water, 309
airlines, 309
CAB administration of, 309, 369
ICC administration of, 308, 369
motor carriers, 305n, 306
rail-motor, 308
statutory basis for, 180n, 305
water carriers, 305n
See also Consolidation.
Corps of Engineers, 84, 135, 393
Cost allocation
air-mail, 56
airport, 38
airway, 27
waterway, 89
Cost finding
CAB cargo experiment, 267
CAB feeder-line experiment, 220

problems of, 248, 363
user charges, 248
value-of-service concept, 249n, 250
Cost of transportation, 3, 4, 87
Council of State Governments, 41n
Craven, Leslie, 343n

Denison Act of 1928, 238
Department of Transportation, 387
Dewey, Ralph L., 323n
Discrimination. See Rate discrimination.

Eastman, Joseph B., 213, 213n, 247n, 248n, 250n, 277, 327n, 328
Economic justification
CAB feeder-line experiment, 219
precedence of national security, 138
vague standards, 355, 357
waterways, 86, 92, 394
Edwards, Ford K., 249n
Emergency Railroad Transportation Act of 1933, 173, 257n, 272, 320n, 440
Employment in federal transport agencies, 5, 403, 416
Expenditures for transportation
by federal government, 9, 122
by users, 3

Federal aid
airports, 32
basis of federal participation, 123
divergence of policy, 132
expenditures, 9
future programs, 121
highways, 11, 105, 365, 419, 420
lack of uniform procedure, 356
matching requirements, 33, 106
objectives of, 13
railroads, 11
scope and results, 11

Federal Aid Airport Act of 1946, 33
Federal Aid Highway Act of 1944, 110
Federal Aid Road Act of 1916, 106
Federal Barge Lines. *See* Inland Waterways Corporation.
Federal Coordinator of Transportation, 52, 87, 88n, 173, 320, 321, 331, 341, 342, 382, 384, 390, 440
Federal transportation agencies appropriations and personnel, 416
  existing organization, 386
  proposed reorganization of, 391
  providing ancillary services, 432
Federal Works Agency. *See* Public Roads Administration.
Feeder-lines. *See* Airlines.
Feeder roads. *See* Secondary road program.
Financing transportation facilities principles of, 125
  revision of policy, 357
  user charges, 129
Foreign trade, 157, 159
Forest highways, 112
Forest Service, 113, 150
Foster, William C., 73n
Fourth Section Relief, 231, 259
Franklin, Walter S., 298n, 299n

Harvard Business School, 37
Helicopter, 18
Hepburn Act of 1906, 272n
Highways
  expenditures, federal, 106, 110
  expenditures from state user taxes, 109
  federal role, 105, 114, 224
  financial trends, 108
  for national defense, 119, 156
  foreign, 114
  forest, 112
  modernization of, 116, 355
  property taxes for, 108

research, 108
strategic, 141

Independent commissions concept of, 368, 408
  usurpation of executive functions, 136, 393
Ingersoll, A. C., 90n, 91
Inherent advantage, 241, 256, 362
Inland waterways. *See* Rivers and harbors.
Inland Waterways Corporation, 89, 237n, 240, 243
  barge-rail competition, 250
  Federal Barge Lines, 89, 237
  financial condition of, 90
  reorganization proposal, 393
  subsidy issue, 239, 250
Intercoastal shipping. *See* Coastal and intercoastal shipping.
Intercoastal Shipping Act of 1933, 97
Interior, Department of, 105, 108, 390
International aviation
  air-mail payments, 45, 396
  air-sea co-ordination, 309
  and ocean shipping, 148, 181, 393
  CAB control of, 18, 135, 197
  national defense aspects, 148
  presidential approval of permits, 135, 197
  rate regulation, 229n
  route pattern, 135
International Civil Aviation Organization, 18, 58, 437
International relations, 1, 148
Interstate Commerce Act
  history of, 176n
  objectives of, 175
  proposed amendments to, 374, 407
Interstate Commerce Commission functions of, 182, 186, 273, 367, 393

policy re rail-barge differentials, 241
position re Federal Barge Lines, 93
procedural delays in administration, 278, 373
statutory basis for, 175
*See also* Regulation, Consolidation, Co-ordination, *and* Rates.
Interstate Highway System, 111, 118, 120, 156

Johnson, Colonel J. M., 401
Joint Congressional Aviation Policy Board, 59, 68, 446
Joint rates. *See* Rate discrimination.
Joint Research and Development Board, 23
Joint use of facilities
advantages of, 127
airports, 40
airways, 19, 28
waterways, 88

Koch, A. S., 75n

Labor
effect of consolidation on, 323
and railroad costs, 281
*See also* Arbitration boards.
Land, E. S., 200n, 204n
Landing fees, 36
Landis, James M., 66n, 67n
Lee, Frederick B., 26n
Leonard, William N., 319, 320n, 340n
Lighthouses, Bureau of, 381, 435
Lightplanes. *See* Private flying.
Loans, ship construction, 97
Local government
airport development, 30, 41
highway work, 106
Locklin, D. Philip, 330n
Long and short haul clause, 231, 259

MacDonald, Thomas H., 111n, 115n, 119n
Mail payments
merchant marine, 95
*See also* Air-mail payments.
Maintenance
airway, 22
highway, 115
waterway, 82, 89
Mann-Elkin Act, 272n
Marine Inspection and Navigation, Bureau of, 381, 435
Maritime Commission
functions of, 98, 135, 181
history of, 94, 380
petition re rail-water competitive rates, 260
reorganization proposal, 392
McElfresh, R. E., 37n, 38n
Merchant Fleet Corporation, 380
Merchant marine
federal expenditures for, 9, 95
long-range construction program, 99
national defense issue, 100
promotion of, 94, 181
reserve fleet, 99, 101, 159
scope of federal activity, 95
ship disposal, 99
subsidy program, 94
Merchant Marine Act of 1936, 94, 140, 392
Merchant Ship Sales Act of 1946, 380
Military Air Transport Service, 144
Miller, Commissioner, 187n, 346n
Mills, Frederick C., 288
Minimum rate regulation. *See* Rates.
Mississippi Valley Association, 238, 243
Mitchell, Commissioner R. F., 295n
Motor Carrier Act of 1935, 169, 176n, 187, 231, 305n
Motor carriers
and rail competition, 256

inventory of equipment, 399
number of regulated carriers, 192
operating certificates, 187
regulation of, 187
Motor Carriers, Bureau of, 398
Motor vehicle traffic trends, 115, 355

National Industrial Traffic League, 295
National Security
airlines, 142
highway, 119, 155
issues of, 138
merchant marine, 157
rail-coastal water competition, 259
railroad, 159, 286, 290
National Security Resources Board, 156, 160
National Transportation Inquiry, 171n
Nelson, James C., 191n, 193n, 195n

Ocean shipping. See Merchant marine.
Office of Defense Transportation, 401

Palmer, Howard S., 283n
Panama Canal, 97, 114, 438
Panama Canal Act, 1912, 185
Panama Railroad, 439
Parmelee, J. H., 285n, 292n
Passen, Alan, 37n, 38n
Passenger transportation statistics, 3, 414
Pay-as-you-go finance, 127
Permits, operating
air carrier, 197
international air carriers, 197
motor carrier, 188
pipeline, 188
water carrier, 193
Pierson, Warren Lee, 206

Pipelines, 2, 14, 141, 188, 357
Planning
airport, 40, 135, 395
airway, 135, 395
federal promotion of, 123
highway, 106, 108
lack of, 351, 356
national defense, 140
relation to executive branch, 134, 383
waterway, 85
Pooling of revenue
ICC experiments with, 327
See also Consolidation of railroads.
Post Office Department, 18, 46, 51, 269, 379, 389
President's Advisory Committee on the Merchant Marine, 100, 382, 447
President's Air Policy Commission, 59, 68, 144, 201, 210, 215, 382, 384, 445
President's Special Board of Inquiry on Air Safety, 59, 71
Private flying, 28, 38, 43, 124, 397
Private ownership
defects of airline management, 212
dilution of railroad management functions, 273, 371
government policy, 182
Programing of public expenditures
assessing relative importance of projects, 355
economic standards, 371
major defects, 353
national defense, 356
Promotion, federal activity in
basis for, 123
conflicts with regulation, 134, 362
defects in, 134
extent of, 9
Prototype Bill, 150
Public works programs, 128

Public Roads Administration, 105, 107, 381, 397

Radio Technical Commission for Aeronautics, 23n, 24n
Rail-barge rates. *See* Rate discrimination.
Railroads
  abandonments, 2, 187, 225
  acquisition of control, 306, 331
  additions and betterments, 152, 290
  competition, 250, 298
  construction, 187, 317
  corporate organization, 332, 346, 375
  credit position, 286, 289
  federal land grants, 11
  federal neglect of, 137, 360
  financial position of, 151, 278, 332, 373
  government ownership of, 130, 151, 182, 342, 361
  investment in, 289, 364
  limitations on management, 273, 371
  national defense aspect, 150
  reorganizations, 290, 332
  right of way, 130, 403
  *See also* Consolidation, Co-ordination, Rates, *and* Safety.
Rate cases
  *Air Freight Rate Investigation,* 267n
  *All-Rail Commodity Rates Between Calif., Oreg., and Wash.,* 262n
  *Class Rate Investigation, 1939,* 233n, 250n
  *Fifteen Percent Case, 1931,* 213n, 275n, 327
  *General Commodity Rate Increase, 1937,* 328, 346n
  *Grain Proportionals, Ex-Barge to Official Territory,* 251n
  *Grain To, From and Within Southern Territory,* 255n

  *Lake Cargo Coal Case,* 256n
  *New Automobiles in Interstate Commerce,* 257n
  *1946 Increased Freight Rates (Ex Parte 162),* 279
  *1947 Increased Freight Rates (Ex Parte 166),* 281, 286n, 296n, 298n
  *1948 Increased Freight Rates (Ex Parte 168),* 285n
  *Pacific Coast Fourth Section Applications,* 260n
  *Petroleum and Petroleum Products, Calif. to Ariz.,* 247n, 257n
  *Rail and Barge Joint Rates,* 237n
Rate discrimination, 229, 365
  interterritorial freight differentials, 233
  long and short haul clause, 231
  rail-water differentials, 237, 366
Rate of return
  airline, 216
  railroad, 272, 332
Rates
  air-mail service, 269
  ICC regulation of general level of, 272, 374
  minimum, CAB control of, 265; ICC control of, 246, 267, 374
  rule of rate making, 257, 267, 272, 374, 407
  subsidy issue, 363
  water-competitive, 259
  *See also* Cost finding, Rate cases, Rate discrimination.
Regulation
  certificate control, 185
  conflicts with promotion, 134, 362
  contrast between CAB and ICC, 265
  declaration of policy, 176
  objectives of, 173, 371
  rate. *See* Rates.

Relative efficiency and economy, 171, 246, 272, 353
Rivers and harbors
authorization of projects, 84
Board of Engineers for Rivers and Harbors, 84
Corps of Engineers, 84
current program, 85
economic justification, 84, 86, 89, 92, 394
expenditures, 81
facilities and traffic, 83
financing, 86
planning, 393
tolls, 88

Safety
aviation, 59, 395. See also Aviation safety.
motor carrier, 398
railroad, 400
state enforcement, 398
Secondary road program, 110, 115, 118
Select Committee on Investigation of Executive Agencies of the Government, 443
Sharfman, I. L., 344, 345n
Sherman Antitrust Act of 1890, 317
Ship disposal, 99
Shipbuilding
foreign, 102
maintenance in peacetime, 100
war programs, 94, 157
Shipping Act of 1916, 96, 169n, 232
Shipping, Bureau of, 94n, 380
Smith, Harold D., 66n
State action
airports, 35, 41
aviation safety, 75, 80
highway development, 106, 117
State aeronautics authorities, 41
State, Department of, 18, 197, 436
Stern, Ben, 75n
Stockpiling of materials, 155

Subsidy
airline, 27, 51, 209, 212, 396
airport, 36
airway, 26
competitive effect of, 148, 181, 366
effect on rate regulation, 237, 244
highway, 11
merchant marine, 11, 95, 264
waterway, 11, 86, 237, 251, 366
Supreme Court decisions
on discrimination, 233n, 234
on fair competition, 177n, 195n, 251, 253
on railroad rate agreements, 317

Tankers, 101, 146
Terminals
inland water, 90
need for modernization of, 355
rail, 130
See also Airports.
Thompson, Chester C., 92n
Tipton, Stuart G., 313n
Tolls, 87, 127, 359
Traffic
by carrier, 3, 414
highway, 115
potentials, 128
trends, 2, 414
wartime, 102
Transport Regulatory Commission, 407
Transportation Act of 1940, 98, 131, 140, 169, 176n, 181, 188, 235, 240, 241, 257, 305n, 331, 408, 443
Transportation expenditures, 3, 415
Transportation system, description of, 1, 413
Treasury, Department of the, 381, 404, 433
Truck, 115, 127, 155, 158, 360
Tully, Arthur H., 31n

Uniform standards
  air safety regulations, 76
  airports, 40
  federal promotion of, 123, 126,
    357, 387
U. S. Shipping Board, 96, 380
U. S. Shipping Board Emergency
  Fleet Corp., 96
User charges, 359
  advantages of, 125, 129
  airports, 35
  airways, 25
  highway, 109
  issues created, 15, 248
  recommended policy, 371
  research, 403

War, Department of, 31, 119, 381
War Shipping Administration, 98,

    380, 260
Water carriers
  air-water co-ordination, 309
  congressional policy re, 90, 237
  number of regulated carriers,
    193
  operating certificates, 193
  regulation of, 193
  route pattern, 96, 392
  *See also* Competition, Co-ordina-
    tion, Rates.
Waterways. *See* Rivers and Har-
  bors.
Weather Bureau, 18, 432
Welliver, Edward M., 192n
Westwood, Howard C., 200n
Wheeler, Lt. Gen. R. A., 85n
Works Project Administration, 107
Wright, T. P., 67n